Y0-EKS-344

Student Guide for Learning Economics

to accompany

Byrns/Stone

ECONOMICS

Sixth Edition

Student Guide for Learning Economics

to accompany

Byrns/Stone
ECONOMICS
Sixth Edition

Ralph T. Byrns
University of Colorado-Boulder

Gerald W. Stone
Metropolitan State College of Denver

HarperCollins*CollegePublishers*

Student Guide for Learning Economics to accompany Byrns/Stone, ECONOMICS, Sixth Edition

Copyright © 1995 HarperCollins College Publishers

All rights reserved. Printed in the United States of America. No part of this book may be used or reproduced in any manner whatsoever without written permission with the following exceptions: testing material may be copied for classroom use. For information, address HarperCollins College Publishers, 10 East 53rd Street, New York, NY 10022.

ISBN: 0-673-99347-7

4 5 6 7 8 9 10-ML-01 99 98

Contents in Brief

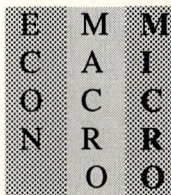

How to Study Economics

No doubt about it. Economics is among the most challenging topics that many of you will encounter during your college educations. This *Student Guide for Learning Economics* will help focus your study so that the time you devote to this fascinating subject is as productive as possible. Before you work on any chapter in this study guide, you should thoroughly read (and perhaps, reread) the corresponding material in our texts, *Economics, Macroeconomics*, or *Microeconomics*. The "Contents in Brief" for this study guide provides cross-references so that you can discern which chapter here corresponds to a particular chapter from the text you are using.

Conscientious use of this study guide is the single factor that seems to differentiate students who do well in our courses from those who do poorly. This guide, instead of introducing new material, will aid you in learning and retaining the material in your text. You will find that time spent working through this study guide will pay huge dividends when you take examinations that test your mastery of economic concepts. More importantly, we hope that five years from now you remember and are able to apply economic reasoning to everyday problems. If you have any suggestions that you believe would make this guide more useful for other students, please send your comments to us, c/o HarperCollinsPublishers, 10 East 53rd Street, New York, NY 10022-5299.

A General Plan for Studying Economics

Superficial cramming is very unlikely to succeed in an economics course. Keeping up is crucial. Educational research indicates that learning is most effective when you are exposed to information and concepts in several ways over a period of time. You will learn more economics and retain it longer if you read, see, hear, communicate, and then apply economic concepts and information. This material is much more than a few facts and glib generalizations; understanding economics requires reflection. Here is one systematic study strategy that many students have found successful in economics, and have adapted for other classes.

Visual Information

Don't let the extensive graphs in economics frighten you. There is a brief review of graphical analysis at the end of Chapter 1 of your text. The introductory modules in our *MacroStudy* and *MicroStudy* programs and this *Student Guide for Learning Economics* also open with sets of helpful exercises. Avoid the agony of trying to memorize each graph by taking the time to learn how graphs work. Proceed to Chapter 2 of your text only after you quell your anxiety a bit. (Be sure that you also understand simple algebra. The algebra in the text is elementary, and should prove no problem if you have learned the material from a basic course.) As you become familiar with graphs, you may be surprised to find yourself mentally graphing many noneconomic relationships, and even more amazed to find this process enjoyable.

Reading

Schedule ample time to read your assignments, and try to use the same quiet and cool (but not cold) room every day. Avoid drowsiness by sitting in a hard chair in front of a desk or table. Think about the material as you read. Many students spend hours highlighting important points for later study, for which they somehow never find time. Too frequently, busy work substitutes for thinking about economics. Try to skim a chapter; then go back and really focus on five or six pages. Don't touch a pen or pencil except to make margin notes cross-referencing related materials you already know.

Writing

After a healthy dose of serious reading, close your text and outline the important points with a half-page of notes. If you cannot briefly summarize what you just read, put your pen down and re-read the material. You have not yet digested the central ideas. Don't be surprised if some concepts require several readings. Be alert for graphs and tables that recapitulate important areas. When you finish each chapter, read its Chapter Review, work through all Problems, and outline good, but brief, answers to all Questions for Thought and Discussion.

Listening

Most lectures blend your instructor's insights and examples with materials from the text, but few students conscientiously do assignments before lectures. You will have a major advantage over most of your classmates if you do, and will be able to take notes selectively. Focus on topics that your instructor stresses but which are not covered in depth in the text. Notes from lectures should supplement, not duplicate, your text.

Teaching

Your instructors know that they learn their subject in greater depth every time they teach it. Teaching exposes you to previously unfamiliar aspects of a topic because you must conceptualize and verbalize ideas so that other people can understand them. Take turns with a classmate in reading the text's Key Points (in the Chapter Review) to each other. After one person reads a Key Point aloud, the other should explain it in his or her own words. Study groups work well in this way, but you may learn economics even more thoroughly if you simply explain economic concepts to a friend who has never studied it.

Applications

Working through the material from this *Student Guide* that parallels each chapter of the text will make it easier to comprehend the economic events regularly featured in the news. When this happens, you will be among the minority who truly understand economic and financial news. Use economic reasoning to interpret your day-to-day behavior, and that of your friends and relatives. This will provide unique insights into how people function and how the world works.

Examinations

Following the preceding suggestions should prepare you for minor tests and quizzes. To prepare for major exams and finals:

1. Read the Chapter Reviews for all chapters that will be covered on the examination. Keep a record of each Key Point that you could not explain to an intelligent friend who had never taken an economics course.

2. Return to each Key Point that you have not grasped adequately. Read the text material that covers it and rework the parallel parts of the accompanying chapter from your *Student Guide*.

3. Discuss any Key Point is not clear to you with a friend.

4. Skim the Glossary included in your package for a last minute refresher before your final exam.

See if this technique works for you. We know that this is a tall order, but if you conscientiously follow these study tips, we guarantee you an enjoyable and enlightening course.

Acknowledgments

We would like to thank Professor Stephen Stageberg of *Mary Washington College* and Professor John P. David of *West Virginia Institute of Technology* for their diligent error-checking. Their work proved to be very helpful. We also want to thank two students who brought past errors to our attention: Stuart Garden, *University of Maine*, and Carol Treeful, *Babson College*. Thanks to their hard work, we hope this edition is error-free.

Chapter 1
Economics: The Study of Scarcity

Chapter Objectives

The economic concepts presented in this chapter provide a general framework for understanding the remainder of this book. After you have read and studied this introductory chapter you should be able to explain why scarcity is the basic economic problem; describe various kinds of productive resources and the payments to the owners of these resources; discuss a number of fundamental economic concepts, including the nature of economic prices, opportunity costs, and efficiency; discuss the nature of scientific theory, including its evolution into common sense, and the use of Occam's Razor; and distinguish normative from positive economics, and macroeconomics from microeconomics.

Chapter Review: Key Points

1. *Economics* is concerned with choices and their consequences, and focuses on ways that individuals and societies allocate their limited resources to try to satisfy relatively unlimited wants.

2. *Scarcity* occurs because our relatively unlimited wants cannot be completely met from the limited resources available. A good is scarce if people cannot freely get all they want, so that the good commands a positive price. Scarcity forces all levels of decision makers from individuals to society at large to resolve three basic economic questions:
   a. *What* will be produced?
   b. *How* will production occur?
   c. *Who* will use the goods produced?

3. *Goods* include anything that adds to human happiness, while *bads* are things that detract from it. *Economic goods* are costly; *free goods* are not.

4. *Production* occurs when knowledge or technology is used to apply energy to materials to make them more valuable.

5. The *opportunity costs* of choices are measured by the subjective values of the best alternative you sacrifice. *Absolute prices* are monetary, and are useful primarily as indicators of *relative prices*, which are the prices of goods or resources in terms of each other, and which provide information and incentives to guide our decisions.

6. *Resources* (factors of production) include:
    a. *Labor*. Productive efforts made available by human beings. Payments for labor services are called *wages*.
    b. *Land*. All natural resources. Payments for land are called *rents*.
    c. *Capital*. Improvements that increase the productive potential of other resources. Payments for the use of capital are called *interest*. When economists refer to capital, they mean physical capital rather than financial capital, which consists of paper claims to goods or resources.
    d. *Entrepreneurship*. The organizing, innovating, and risk-taking function that combines other factors to produce. Entrepreneurs are rewarded with *profits*.

7. *Economic efficiency* occurs when a given amount of resources produces the most valuable combination of outputs possible. In an efficient economy, no transactions are possible from which anyone can gain without someone else losing.
    a. *Allocative efficiency* requires production of the things people want.
    b. *Distributive efficiency* requires consumers to adjust their purchasing patterns to maximize their satisfactions from given budgets.
    c. *Productive (technical) efficiency* is obtained when a given output is produced at the lowest possible cost. Another way of looking at efficiency is that it occurs when the opportunity cost of obtaining some specific amount of a good is at its lowest.

8. *Common sense* is theory that has been tested over a long period and found useful. In general, good theory accurately predicts how the real world operates. *Occam's Razor* suggests that the simplest workable theories are the most useful or "best."

9. *Positive economics* is scientifically testable and involves value-free descriptions of economic relationships, dealing with "what is." *Normative economics* involves value judgments about economic relationships and addresses "what should be." Normative theory can be neither scientifically verified nor proven false.

10. *Macroeconomics* is concerned with aggregate (the total levels of) economic phenomena, including such items as Gross National Product, unemployment, and inflation. *Microeconomics* concentrates on individual decision making, resource allocation, and how prices and output are determined.

Matching Key Terms And Concepts

SET I

____ 1. microeconomics

____ 2. Occam's razor

____ 3. positive economics

____ 4   land

____ 5. model

____ 6. normative economics

____ 7. macroeconomics

____ 8. entrepreneurship

____ 9. financial capital

____ 10. production

a. The simplest workable theory is the best theory.

b. Economic theory that is, at least theoretically, scientifically testable and free of value judgments.

c. Securities and other paper claims to goods or resources.

d. The organizing, risk-taking, and innovating resource.

e. Contestable theories rife with value judgments.

f. Using technology to apply energy to make materials more valuable.

g. Nonhuman resources other than capital.

h. The study of individual decisions made by consumers and firms.

i. Focuses on aggregate, or economy-wide, variables.

j. A representation of a theory.

SET II

____ 1. technology

____ 2. capital

____ 3. *Homo economicus*

____ 4. labor

____ 5. rent

____ 6. scarce good

____ 7. profits

____ 8. investment

____ 9. depreciation

____ 10. wages

a. Desired amounts of a good exceed those freely available.

b. Improvements to natural resources that make them more productive.

c. The view that humans maximize their satisfaction or wealth.

d. The hours of human effort available for production.

e. Payments for labor services.

f. Physical capital accumulation.

g. Decreases in capital because of wear-and-tear.

h. Entrepreneur's reward.

i. Payment for the use of land.

j. The "recipes" used to combine resources for production.

SET III

___ 1. interest

___ 2. free good

___ 3. opportunity cost

___ 4. scarcity

___ 5. relative prices

___ 6. economic efficiency

___ 7. absolute prices

___ 8. production efficiency

___ 9. equity

___ 10. consumption efficiency

a. The value foregone whenever people make choices.

b. Adds to human happiness, but is not scarce.

c. Payments to capital owners.

d. When this is reached, further gains in happiness to anyone require losses to someone else.

e. Achieving maximum satisfaction from given budgets.

f. The basic economic problem.

g. Prices of goods or resources in terms of each other.

h. Prices of goods or services in terms of some monetary unit.

i. Fairness.

j. Getting maximum output from given resources.

True/False

___ 1. Economics resembles accounting or finance in being more relevant for business firms than individuals.

___ 2. Complexity is desirable in a scientific theory.

___ 3. Unlike theory, common sense emphasizes practicality.

___ 4. Normative economics is concerned with what should be, rather than what is.

___ 5. Macroeconomics focuses on aggregate variables such as national income, employment, and inflation.

___ 6. Occam's Razor is more relevant for other sciences than it is for economics.

___ 7. Economic reasoning is involved anytime people choose one thing instead of another.

___ 8. Models are less complicated and formal than theories.

___ 9. Positive economic analysis can help in determining how to reach politically-set economic goals.

___ 10. Positive economics specifies the value judgments used to draw inferences in economic analysis.

___ 11. Successful entrepreneurs combine resources productively.

___ 12. Financial capital refers to all improvements made to land, machinery, and equipment.

___13. Payments for the use of capital services are called profit.

___14. Deciding to take a nap is an economic decision.

___15. Self sufficiency is an efficient goal for everyone.

___16. A good is scarce if the amounts people desire exceed the amounts freely available.

___17. Prices are a meaningless concept in economies that do not use money.

___18. Economic considerations shape even such decisions as selecting a spouse or determining how many children to have.

___19. Opportunity costs are incurred while you study economics.

___20. Most of the best things in life are free.

Standard Multiple Choice

There Is One Best Answer For Each Question.

___ 1. Economics involves broadly studying how:
  a. political power is used unethically to make money.
  b. resources are allocated to satisfy human wants.
  c. proper nutrition and budgeting benefit your family.
  d. to get away with cheating the Internal Revenue Service.
  e. different species are environmentally interdependent.

___ 2. Scientific attempts to describe economic relationships are:
  a. factual and can never be wrong.
  b. accurate ways to predict political viewpoints.
  c. known as positive economics.
  d. directed at the fairness of social programs.
  e. intended to boost the egos of entrepreneurs.

___ 3. Disagreements between economists arise most commonly in:
  a. microeconomic reasoning.
  b. normative economics.
  c. positive economics.
  d. applications of common sense.
  e. macroeconomic theories.

___ 4. Economists:
  a. hardly ever agree on anything.
  b. agree on much of economic theory.
  c. never make value judgments.
  d. accurately predict the effects of all economic policies.
  e. disagree most about positive economics.

___ 5. Unnecessary complexity in a theory is a violation of:
  a. common sense.
  b. the principle of nonsatiety.
  c. the law of supply and demand.
  d. Occam's razor.
  e. the anti-parsimony corollary.

6. Which of the following LEAST explains the widespread but erroneous view that economists seldom agree?
   a. The media focus on controversy, not agreement.
   b. Politics shapes policymaking more than does economic logic.
   c. Economists who are political appointees often feel obligated to support the president even if they disagree privately.
   d. Economic policies embody controversial value judgments.
   e. Economic policy is more scientific than economic theory.

7. Macroeconomics is primarily concerned with aggregates. Which of the following is not a macroeconomic aggregate?
   a. Decisionmaking by a household.
   b. The unemployment rate, and inflation levels.
   c. National income.
   d. The supply of money.
   e. Fiscal policies of the federal government.

8. Decisions made in households, firms, and government are the focus of:
   a. positive economics.
   b. environmental economics.
   c. microeconomics.
   d. normative economics.
   e. macroeconomics.

9. When less of a good than people want is freely available, the good is:
   a. in short supply.
   b. a free good.
   c. a luxury good.
   d. scarce.
   e. a necessity.

10. Which of the following comes closest to being a free good?
   a. A wino's lunch, dug from the trash behind a restaurant.
   b. Hot lunches provided to needy students at school.
   c. Bacon and eggs bought with food stamps.
   d. A record you bought from money earned by picking up aluminum cans in your spare time.
   e. Free public education.

11. TINSTAAFL is an acronym suggesting that:
   a. tax inspectors never see the awful affects from levies.
   b. tenants in need should take all assets from landlords.
   c. there is no such thing as a free lunch.
   d. temperance in non-satiety together are adequate for life.
   e. tyrants in Nirvana seldom try avoiding acceptably full lunches.

12. Opportunity costs will always exist as long as:
   a. an economy has money
   b. relative prices are variable
   c. the opportunity to make money exists
   d. something has to be given up to get something else
   e. production is unregulated

13. Labor, land, capital, and entrepreneurship are all:
   a. examples of technology.
   b. allocative mechanisms.
   c. resources, or factors of production.
   d. tools of capitalistic exploitation.
   e. natural resources.

___14. An economy suffers from production inefficiency if:
   a. water runs off lawns and down big city streets when it is greatly needed by remote drought-stricken farmers.
   b. it operates in a region of diminishing returns.
   c. costs increase when production is expanded.
   d. a consumer could gain by buying different goods.
   e. costs could be reduced by using resources differently.

___15. Opportunity costs are the values of the:
   a. monetary costs of goods and services.
   b. best alternatives sacrificed when choices are made.
   c. minimal budgets of families on welfare.
   d. profits gained by successful entrepreneurs.
   e. freedom people enjoy in a socialist economy.

___16. Economic equity refers to the:
   a. financial settlements in civil court cases.
   b. balance of national trade.
   c. fairness of some economic arrangement.
   d. hidden costs passed on to consumers.
   e. gross value of any stocks or bonds you own.

___17. Economic efficiency for the entire economy requires that:
   a. potential gains to anyone necessitate losses to another.
   b. all goods be produced at their lowest possible opportunity costs.
   c. maximum-valued output is obtained from given resources.
   d. all benefits are obtained at the lowest possible cost.
   e. All of the above.

___18. Which of the following statements is normative?
   a. Higher oil prices will increase the inflation rate.
   b. A tariff on textiles would tend to increase the wages of domestic textile workers.
   c. Tax rates on the working poor should be reduced.
   d. Other things equal, if the price of an item is reduced, consumers will to buy more of it.
   e. If interest rates remain high this quarter, business investment will continue to be weak.

___19. Knowledge used to combine resources productively is called:
   a. entrepreneurship.
   b. capitalism.
   c. investment.
   d. technology.
   e. comparative advantage.

___20. The process by which capital becomes worn out or obsolete is known as:
   a. capital attenuation.
   b. disinvestment.
   c. bankruptcy.
   d. disinflation.
   e. depreciation.

Chapter Review (Fill-In Questions)

1. Scarcity is a result of _____ resources confronted by _____ wants.

2. Three basic economic questions are posed by scarcity and must be resolved by all economic systems: _____ economic goods will be produced, _____ will resources be utilized in production? _____ will get to consume the economic goods produced?

3. _____ is the process of using knowledge to apply energy to materials so that they are more valuable. The knowledge used to combine resources for production is referred to as _____.

4. _____ is the residual after all economic costs are paid out of a firm's revenues, and is received by _____, who organize the firm's activities, innovate new products and technologies, and take business risks.

5. People act rationally and purposefully to _____ their _____.

6. When economists say price or cost, they typically mean the value of the best _____ forgone when choices are made, rather than monetary prices. This is known as _____, or alternative cost. These costs are implicit in all choices, even when it is not obvious that conventional "economics" is involved.

7. Theory is judged by how well it _____ how the world works. _____ expresses a common preference among scientists for simple, rather than complex, workable theories.

8. _____ is the study of employment, inflation, money, the level of taxation, the relative prices of two or more countries' currencies, unemployment, national income, economic growth, and similarly aggregated variables. _____ is a more localized study of the consequences of interactive decisionmaking by individual consumers and firms.

9. _____ occurs when the opportunity cost of producing a given amount of goods is _____.

10. There is _____ efficiency if a consumer experiences maximum satisfaction from a given _____.

Unlimited Multiple Choice

Warning: Each Question Has From Zero To Four Correct Answers.

___ 1. Economics is a(n):
   a. study of decisionmaking and its consequences.
   b. mathematical and physical science, like chemistry.
   c. concern only for people who are miserly.
   d. "apparatus of the mind."

___ 2. A positive economic statement can be scientifically tested to see if it is false. Which of the following are positive economic statements?
   a. The economy will grow faster if tax rates are cut.
   b. A high tax on tobacco will severely cut cigarette smoking.
   c. People would have fewer children if their tax deductions for having them were increased.
   d. The federal budget should be balanced annually.

___ 3. Theories are:
   a. much more complicated than common sense.
   b. scientific only if based on normative value judgments.
   c. proven if only a few unimportant exceptions exist.
   d. developed when we collect data, try to explain how things work, and then test for validity.

___ 4. According to the characterization of humans as *Homo economicus*, all human behavior is:
   a. assumed to be self-interested, including charitable acts.
   b. intended to generate monetary profits.
   c. aimed at maximizing pleasure and minimizing pain.
   d. guided by an instinct to perpetuate the species.

___ 5. The basic economic questions scarcity poses for every society, and which must somehow be resolved, include:
   a. *what* quantities of which goods should be produced?
   b. *how* will the chosen goods be produced?
   c. *who* will use the goods that are produced?
   d. *which* system most efficiently distributes free goods to the needy?

Problems

1. Suppose the price of entry to your local swimming pool rises from $2 to $3 per day, while movie tickets rise from $5 to $7. Which of these forms of entertainment has become relatively more costly? _____

2. Classify the following statements as positive or normative. (CAUTION: Whether a statement is true or false has little to do with whether it is positive or normative. The possibility of testing the truth or falsity of a hypothesis (at least theoretically) distinguishes positive theories from untestable normative statements.)

   a. Relatively fewer people are poor under capitalism than under socialism. _____

   b. Higher union wages cause inflation. _____

   c. Federal budget deficits make investors pessimistic and drive up interest rates. _____

   d. American workers should not have to compete with cheap foreign labor. _____

   e. Bad weather abroad benefits most American farmers. _____

   f. Grass is pink during months that are spelled with an "r" at the end. _____

   g. It is better to be rich than to be poor. _____

   h. On average, annual income is influenced positively by education. _____

3. Fill in the table below by determining the relative price of each item in terms of all the other items.

Money Price	Item	Relative price in terms of lunches	Relative price in terms of haircuts	Relative price in terms of books	Relative price in terms of stereos	Relative price in terms of surfboards
$5	lunch	1 lunch	_____	_____	_____	_____
$10	haircut	_____	1 haircut	_____	_____	_____
$20	book	_____	_____	1 book	_____	_____
$100	stereo	_____	_____	_____	1 stereo	_____
$500	surfboard	_____	_____	_____	_____	1 surfboard

ANSWERS

	Matching			True/False		Multiple Choice		Unlimited MC
Set I	**Set II**	**Set III**						
1. h	1. j	1. c	1. F	11. T	1. b	11. c	1. ad
2. a	2. b	2. b	2. F	12. F	2. c	12. d	2. abc
3. b	3. c	3. a	3. F	13. F	3. b	13. c	3. d
4. g	4. d	4. f	4. T	14. T	4. b	14. e	4. ac
5. j	5. i	5. g	5. T	15. F	5. d	15. b	5. abc
6. e	6. a	6. d	6. F	16. T	6. e	16. c	
7. i	7. h	7. h	7. T	17. F	7. a	17. e	
8. d	8. f	8. j	8. F	18. T	8. c	18. c	
9. c	9. g	9. i	9. T	19. T	9. d	19. d	
10. f	10. e	10. e	10. F	20. F	10. a	20. e	

Chapter Review (Fill-in Questions)

1. scarce or limited; unlimited
2. What; How; Who
3. Production; technology
4. Profit; entrepreneurs
5. maximize; satisfaction or happiness
6. alternative; opportunity cost
7. predicts; Occam's Razor
8. Macroeconomics; Microeconomics
9. Productive efficiency; minimized
10. distributive (consumption); income or budget

Problems

1. The price of entry to your local swimming pool rises by 50% (($3 - $2)/$2)), while the price of movie tickets rises only 40% (($7 - $5)/$5)). Therefore , the price of a swim at your local pool has become relatively more costly.

2. a. Positive b. Positive c. Positive d. Normative e. Positive f. Positive g. Normative h. Positive

3. See the table below.

Money Price	Item	Relative Price in terms of lunches	Relative price in terms of haircuts	Relative price in terms of books	Relative price in terms of stereos	Relative price in terms of surfboards
$5	lunch	1 lunch	.5 haircuts	.25 books	.05 stereos	.01 surfboards
$10	haircut	2 lunches	1 haircut	.5 books	.10 stereos	.02 surfboards
$20	book	4 lunches	2 haircuts	1 book	.20 stereos	.04 surfboards
$100	stereo	20 lunches	10 haircuts	5 books	1 stereo	.2 surfboards
$500	surfboard	100 lunches	50 haircuts	25 books	5 stereos	1 surfboard

Optional Material: Graphical Techniques In Economics

Be sure that graphical analysis is not a mystery when you launch into economics. Take the time now to work through "Graphical Techniques in Economics" at the end of Chapter 1 of your text. That done, carefully do the following exercises, and work through the first computerized module of your copy of the Byrns & Stone *MacroStudy* or *MicroStudy* programs. The graphs that pervade economics will not appear as formidable to you as they do to the many students who suffer from "graphobia." After you have studied this material on Graphical Techniques you should be able to: (1) Plot data using the Cartesian Coordinate system. (2) Use descriptive graphs to answer questions, and (3) Measure and interpret the slopes and intercepts of lines.

Cartesian Coordinates

Problem 1

Plot the following pairs of coordinates on the figure below.

a. (1,1)
b. (-5,8)
c. (-8,-8)
d. (5,-7)
e. (3,8)
f. (9,-2)
g. (-9,2)
h. (-5,5)
i. (8,4)
j. (2,-2)
k. (-3,-4)
l. (-4,-9)

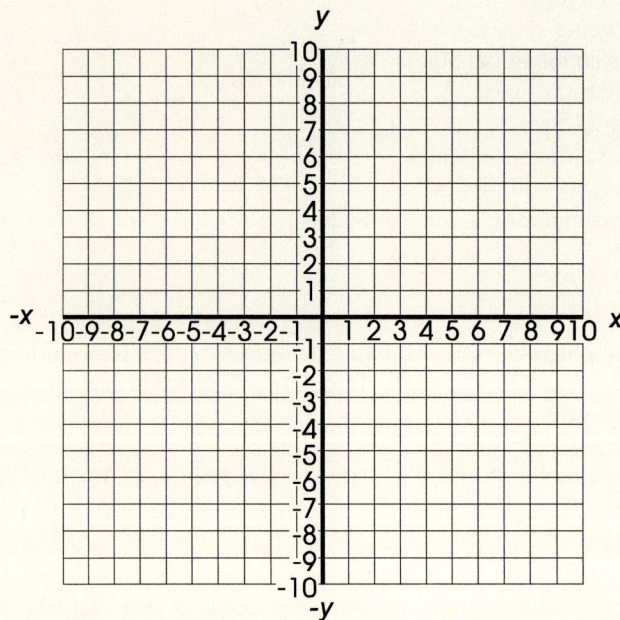

Problem 2

New "How-to-Get-Rich-Quick" books appear regularly, while old ones go out of print. Another employee at your firm (a publisher) used the letters a through l to plot monthly data for 1993 in Figure 2, showing changes in the number of "get rich" books in print and the percentage changes in worldwide sales per book.

a. You want to see if these data are related, but first you need to match the letters from the figure below with their corresponding months in the table below.

Letter	Month	Δ in # of Books	% Δ in Sales per Book
___	Jan.	-3	+2
___	Feb.	-5	+8
___	Mar.	+4	-3
___	Apr.	0	+1
___	May.	-2	0
___	Jun.	+4	-2
___	Jul.	-3	+1
___	Aug.	+7	-4
___	Sep.	+9	-3
___	Oct.	+8	-2
___	Nov.	+3	0
___	Dec.	-4	+8

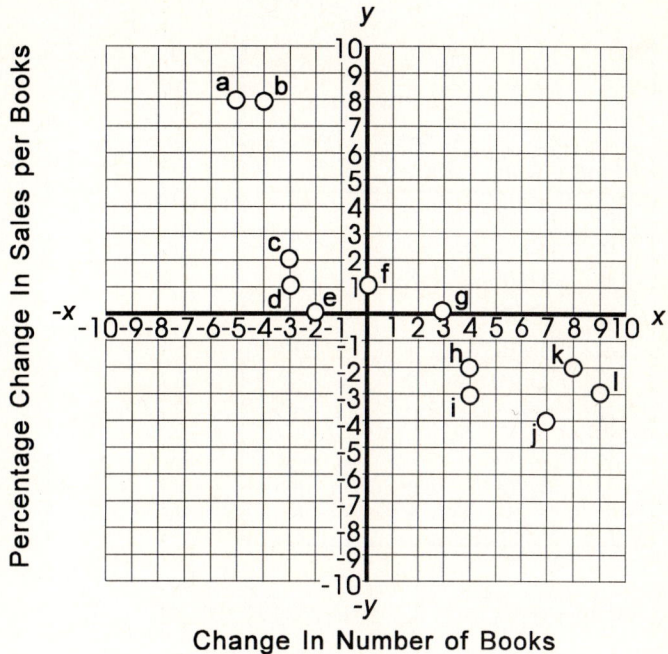

Change In Number of Books

b. After you match the graphed points with their corresponding months, the company president wants to know if there is a relationship. Your opinion is that there is a _____ (positive/negative/no) relationship. This means that as more "get rich" books are in print, sales per book (14) _____ (rise/fall/are unaffected).

Problem 3

Wall Street gurus constantly search for variables that predict stock market movements. A stockbroker develops a theory that percentage increases in sales of new yellow cars indicate consumer optimism and, hence, suggest that the Dow Jones stock market index (DJI) will rise by some percentage the next year.

a. Plot the data from the table below into the figure below for the broker, using a, b, c, and so on.

Point	Year	% Δ in Yellow Cars Sold	% Δ in next year's DJI
a	1976	1	10
b	1977	-5	10
c	1978	-8	-8
d	1979	6	-8
e	1980	4	4
f	1981	-5	-5
g	1982	9	-3
h	1983	5	-3
i	1984	0	5
j	1985	-7	-2

Percentage Change In Next Year's DJI

Percentage Change In Yellow Cars Sold

b. Looking at the data you just plotted, do you think the broker's theory is good or bad?_____ Why?_____

Problem 4

Graph the relationships between x and y (based on the formula $y = mx + b$) if the intercept b and the slope m have the following values. You need to set x equal to some arbitrarily selected values, and then calculate corresponding values for y. Label each line with the corresponding letter, from a through f. Identify negative relationships with an asterisk.

a. $b = 100$ $m = 1$
b. $b = -100$ $m = 1$
c. $b = 100$ $m = -1$
d. $b = -100$ $m = -1$
e. $b = 200$ $m = -2$
f. $b = -200$ $m = 1/2$

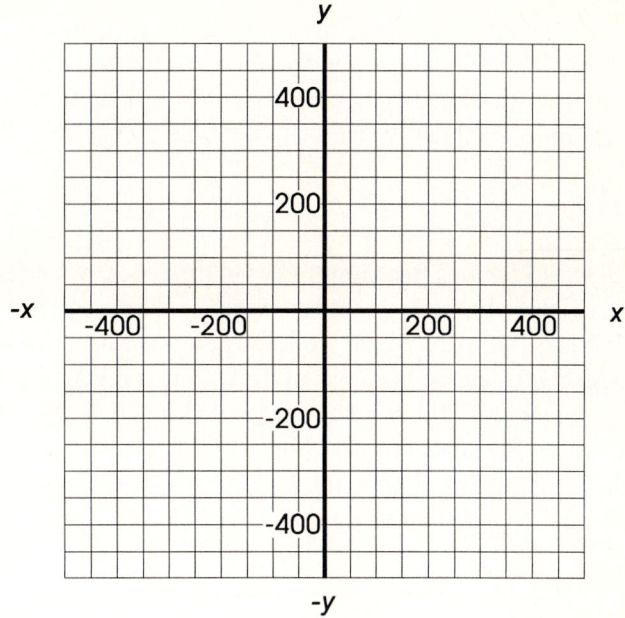

Descriptive Graphics

Problem 5

Age/earnings profiles show how people's incomes vary with their ages. Use the typical profile in the figure to answer the following questions.

a. On average, the peak earning age is _____ ?

b. The slope of the line between age 20 and 50 is _____ ? How is that slope interpreted? _____ _____

c. The slope of the line between age 50 and 65 is_____? Between age 65 and 70, the slope is? _____

Graphical Analysis Of Areas

While in grade school you learned such formulas as: the area of a rectangle (A) equals the base (b) times the height (h), or A = bh. The following problems show how such calculations are useful in graphically analyzing individual expenditures or the costs of firms.

Problem 6

A world famous restaurant, Les Gourmandes, often features Quiche Lorraine as its luncheon special. Over the years, it has discovered how prices affect daily sales, as graphed in the figure below. If you draw lines from the points we have identified to the vertical and horizontal axes, you can calculate the areas of the resultant rectangles to fill in the table and find out how quiche revenues are influenced by the price charged. (Why? Because base times height (bh) is the same as price (P) times quantity (Q), and PQ equals total revenue.) Does the negative relationship between price and quantity seem reasonable? Why? (Answer this question for yourself at this point. We explore the reasons why such relationships are negative in Chapter 3.)

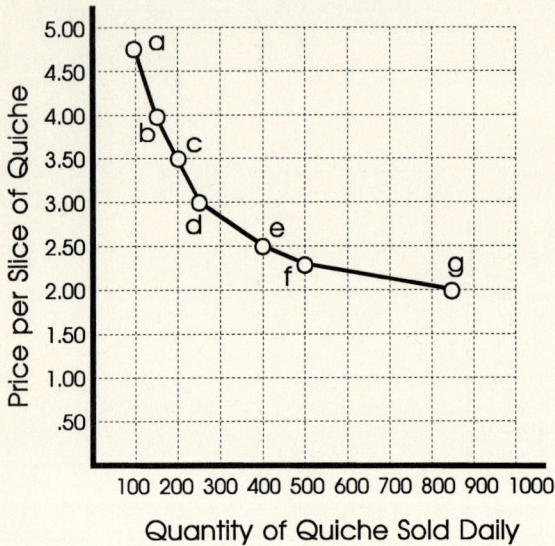

Point	Price (P)	Quantity (Q)	Total Revenue (P × Q)
a	_____	_____	_____
b	_____	_____	_____
c	_____	_____	_____
d	_____	_____	_____
e	_____	_____	_____
f	_____	_____	_____
g	_____	_____	_____

Problem 7

Suppose that a U.S. Department of Agriculture study suggests the relationship shown in the figure below between the price (P) of kumquats and the quantities (Q) that farmers are willing to produce. Fill in the table to indicate how the total dollar revenues of kumquat farmers vary with the changes in market conditions that cause prices to vary. (Hint: You must compute the areas of rectangles much as you did in the preceding problem.) Shade the area representing farmers' total income (P x Q) when kumquats are 50 cents a pound. Use a different shading technique to show how much extra revenue they receive if they sell as much as they want to when the price is 60 cents per pound. Does the positive relationship we have shown between price and farmers' willingness to produce seem reasonable? Why? (Answer this question for yourself at this point. We explore reasons for such positive relationships in Chapter 3.)

Point	Price (P)	Quantity (Q)	Total Revenue (P × Q)
a	_____	_____	_____
b	_____	_____	_____
c	_____	_____	_____
d	_____	_____	_____
e	_____	_____	_____
f	_____	_____	_____
g	_____	_____	_____

Problem 8

a.   Plot the data from the table below into the figure, and connect all the data points with a smooth curve.

Y	X
6	1
8	2
10	3
8	4
6	5
4	6
3	7
4	8
6	9
7	10

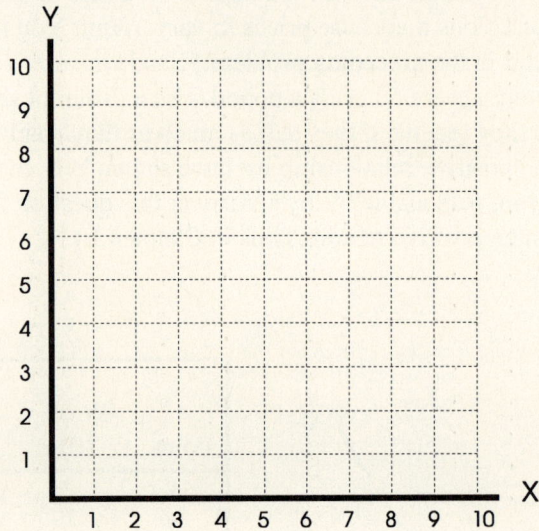

b.   Based on your graph, this curve reaches a maximum when x takes on a value of _____ and the slope of the curve at this point is equal to _____.

c.   This curve reaches a minimum when x takes on a value of _____ and the slope of the curve is equal to _____.

d.   If one wished to find the slope of the curve at any particular point, it would be necessary to draw a _____ to the curve at that point.

ANSWERS

Problem 1

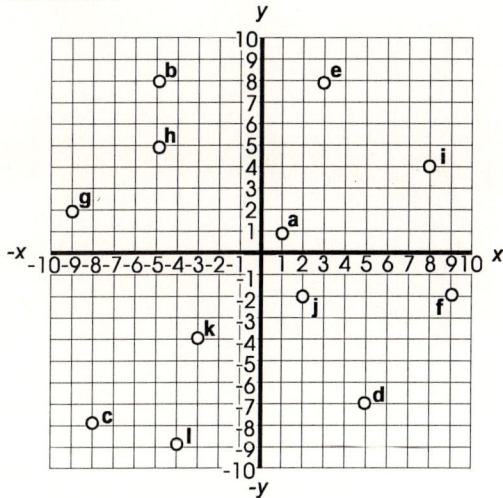

Problem 2

a. See table below
b. negative; fall

Letter	Month	Δ in # of Books	% Δ in Sales per Book
c	Jan.	-3	+2
a	Feb.	-5	+8
i	Mar.	+4	-3
f	Apr.	0	+1
e	May.	-2	0
h	Jun.	+4	-2
d	Jul.	-3	+1
j	Aug.	+7	-4
l	Sep.	+9	-3
k	Oct.	+8	-2
g	Nov.	+3	0
b	Dec.	-4	+8

Problem 3

a. See figure below.
b. This theory does not appear to work very well because the data points are randomly scattered without any apparent correlation.

Percentage Change in Yellow Cars Sold

Problem 4

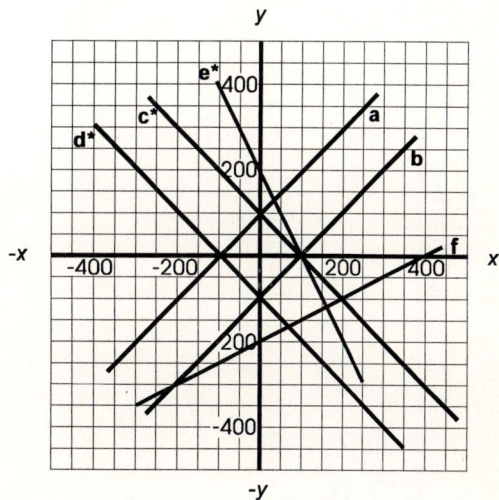

Problem 5

a. 50
b. 1000; for each extra year in age, the typical individual in this age range earns $1000 more annually.
c. -7500/15 = -500; -17,500/5 = -3,500.

Problem 6

POINT	PRICE (P)	QUANTITY (Q)	TOTAL REVENUES (P x Q)
a	4.75	100	475
b	4.00	150	600
c	3.50	200	700
d	3.00	250	750
e	2.50	400	1000
f	2.25	500	1125
g	2.00	850	1700

Problem 7

POINT	PRICE (P)	QUANTITY (Q)	TOTAL REVENUES (P x Q)
a	.40	2	.8 million
b	.50	6	3.0 million
c	.60	9	5.4 million
d	.70	12	8.4 million
e	.90	14	12.6 million
f	1.20	16	19.2 million
g	1.50	18	27.0 million

Problem 8

a. See the figure below
b. 3, 0
c. 7, 0
d. tangent

Chapter 2
Scarcity in a World in Transition

Chapter Objectives

After you have read and studied this chapter, you should be able to show how goods, resources, and incomes move among households through firms and government. You should be able to explain how comparative advantage, specialization, and trade can increase production and consumption. You should be able to use production possibilities curves to describe scarcity, increasing opportunity costs, and choice. You should be able to explain how alternative allocative mechanisms work, and understand some basic differences between capitalism and socialism.

Chapter Review: Key Points

1. *Households* ultimately own all wealth and provide all resources to business firms or government in exchange for income with which to buy goods. Interactions between households, firms, and government are shown in *circular flow* models.

2. *Comparative advantage* is a guide to efficient specialization: You gain by specializing in production where your opportunity costs are lowest and trading your output for things other people can produce at lower opportunity cost.

3. A *production-possibilities frontier (PPF)* shows the maximum combinations of goods a society can produce. *PPF* curves assume (**a**) fixed resources ; (**b**) constant technology; and (**c**) full and efficient employment of all scarce resources.

4. Opportunity costs are the values of outputs if resources were deployed in their next best alternatives. Opportunity costs are not constant because resources are not equally suited for all types of production. Increasing a particular form of production invariably leads to *diminishing returns* and *increasing opportunity costs*, so *PPF* curves are concave (bowed away) from the origin.

5. The idea that "a point of diminishing returns" has been reached is sometimes cited as a reason for ceasing an activity. This is usually a misuse of this phrase-- people intend to say that a point of negative returns has been reached. An activity is often worth doing even though diminishing returns are encountered.

6. *Economic growth* occurs when technology advances or the amounts of resources available for production increase. Economic growth is reflected in outward shifts of the production-possibilities curve; more of all goods can be produced.

7. The choices a society makes between consumption and investment goods affects its future production-possibilities curve. Lower saving and investment restricts economic growth and *PPF* expansion.

8. *PPF*'s shapes illustrate different countries' comparative advantages. Trade allows a nation's people to consume far more goods than they could produce in isolation.

9. Alternative *allocative mechanisms* include: (**a**) the *market system*, (**b**) *brute force*, (**c**) *queuing*, (**d**) *random selection*, (**e**) *tradition*, and (**f**) *government*.

10. Many different economic systems are used in attempts to resolve the problem of scarcity. They can be classified by who makes the decisions (*centralized* or *decentralized*) and who owns the resources (*public* versus *private*).

11. Property is privately owned under pure *capitalism* and government follows *laissez-faire* (hands-off) policies. Thus, decisions are decentralized and rely on individual choices in a market system. Under *socialism*, government acts as a trustee over the nonhuman resources jointly owned by all citizens, with many socialist economies also relying heavily on centralized production and distribution decisions.

Matching Key Terms And Concepts

SET I

___ 1.	centralized decision making	**a.**	Capitalism's answer to "who owns?".
___ 2.	random selection	**b.**	When more goods can be produced with fewer resources.
___ 3.	laissez-faire	**c.**	"We do it this way because we always have."
___ 4.	tradition	**d.**	Equal shares.
___ 5.	economic growth	**e.**	Might makes right, and right makes mine.
___ 6.	queuing	**f.**	First-come/first-served.
___ 7.	technological advance	**g.**	A draft for military service is an example.
___ 8.	brute force	**h.**	Minimal government.
___ 9.	private property	**i.**	One path to this is to increase investment.
___ 10.	egalitarianism	**j.**	System of economic planning that was used in the former Soviet Union.

SET II

_____ 1. socialism

_____ 2. increasing costs

_____ 3. mixed economy

_____ 4. law of diminishing returns

_____ 5. production possibilities frontier

_____ 6. markets

_____ 7. capitalism

_____ 8. command economy

_____ 9. "fee simple"

_____ 10. comparative advantage

a. The least restrictive form of property rights.

b. A society in which most major economic decisions are centralized.

c. Any activity eventually becomes more difficult the further it is extended.

d. When your opportunity cost of producing some good is lowest, so that you gain by trading for something else for which your opportunity cost is relatively high.

e. Government acts as "trustee" over most nonhuman resources.

f. Depicts limits to the amounts that given resources can produce.

g. Enables buyers and sellers to transact.

h. Emphasizes private property rights and laissez-faire policies.

i. A logical extension of the law of diminishing returns.

j. Some property and decisions are private, others are governmental.

True/False Questions

_____ 1. Queuing allocates on a first-come, first-served basis and may be used to discourage the consumption of particular goods.

_____ 2. In the United States most economic decisions are made in markets in which prices and productivity are major factors determining what is produced and who gets what.

_____ 3. Economic planners try to encourage high unemployment rates so that the economy will have the reserves needed for growth.

_____ 4. The means of production are individually owned by citizens in socialist economies.

_____ 5. High rates of investment tend to raise labor productivity and stimulate the creation of new products and technologies.

_____ 6. Most people view random selection as inequitable, but it is an extremely efficient mechanism for distribution choices.

_____ 7. Brute force inefficiently diverts productive resources into protecting what we have or taking from others.

___ 8. Laissez-faire policies mean that government play a minimal role.

___ 9. The broadest of property rights are called fee simple property rights.

___10. Tradition as a mechanism for resolving economic issues is used more today than at any previous time in history.

___11. Resolutions to intertribal and international disputes have historically often relied on brute force.

___12. Decreasing opportunity costs cause production possibilities frontiers to be concave from the origin.

___13. If an economy operates inside its production possibilities frontier, additional output can be produced without costs.

___14. Production possibilities curves can illustrate scarcity, opportunity costs, efficiency, and competitive choices.

___15. A society can move along its production possibility frontier without incurring any opportunity costs.

Standard Multiple Choice

There Is One Best Answer For Each Question.

___ 1. When you specialize in that which you can do at relatively low cost and buy from others that which they can produce at relatively low cost, all parties mutually gain by exploiting:
  a. subdivisions of labor.
  b. comparative advantage.
  c. centralized coordination.
  d. diversified investment.
  e. diseconomies of scale.

___ 2. People have a comparative advantage in a good if their:
  a. satisfaction from it exceeds that from other goods.
  b. production costs are relatively low.
  c. production of all goods is faster than their neighbors.
  d. purchases of imports are cheaper than domestic goods.
  e. psychic enjoyment exceeds the market price.

___ 3. Production possibilities curves can be used to illustrate:
  a. scarcity.
  b. full employment and efficiency.
  c. opportunity costs, and choice.
  d. diminishing returns and increasing costs.
  e. All of the above.

___ 4. Production possibilities frontiers depend on the assumption that:
  a. resources are variable in supply.
  b. there are unlimited goods.
  c. the economy is expanding.
  d. all resources are efficiently employed.
  e. technology advances quickly.

___ 5. Operating inside society's PPF is a:
   a. way to stimulate economic growth.
   b. result whenever the capital stock depreciates rapidly.
   c. drawback of capitalism relative to socialism.
   d. sign that population is outstripping the food supply.
   e. symptom of inefficiency.

___ 6. Production possibilities frontiers shift outward when the economy's:
   a. full employment level is reached.
   b. state of technology advances.
   c. demand for output increases.
   d. productive resources are efficiently utilized.
   e. capital stock depreciates rapidly.

___ 7. If more goods can be produced from given resources than was previously possible, there has been a/an:
   a. technological advance.
   b. expansion of the resource base.
   c. change in the convexity of the PPF.
   d. increased investment and growth of the capital stock.
   e. enhanced financial investment.

___ 8. If an economy is operating efficiently, economic growth will tend to be greater if:
   a. capital depreciates and becomes obsolete rapidly.
   b. threats of war divert resources to national defense.
   c. people's saving rises to allow greater investment.
   d. funds for research and development are reduced.
   e. the law of diminishing returns is fully operative.

___ 9. One important reason why production possibilities frontiers are concave from the origin is that:
   a. production costs fall because of diminishing returns.
   b. capitalistic economies tend to operate inefficiently.
   c. technology advances faster than it can be utilized.
   d. prosperity reduces people's work incentives.
   e. resources vary in suitability among types of production.

___ 10. A society in which your occupation is determined primarily by your parents' jobs bases many allocative decisions on:
   a. queuing.
   b. tradition.
   c. brute force.
   d. the market place.
   e. random selection.

___ 11. Allocation by queuing entails waste because some people:
   a. are forced to work at the same profession their parents did.
   b. are randomly selected to perform jobs that do not maximize their potential productivity .
   c. must inefficiently protect themselves from other people's "bullying".
   d. are incapable of having their needs met in this fashion.
   e. spend long unproductive periods waiting in line.

___12. Rights to drill for oil on government property are often assigned by lottery. You submit your name and, if you are lucky, you win drilling rights. This is an example of:
a. brute force.
b. queuing.
c. random selection.
d. tradition.
e. egalitarianism.

___13. Trying to distribute goods according to needs is:
a. achieved in command economies.
b. an equitable answer to the basic "What" and "How" questions.
c. in practice, often a way for those who judge needs to be classed as needy.
d. an explanation of why many poor people prefer pure capitalism.

___14. Consumer tastes tend to be efficiently met when decisions are made:
a. individually.
b. by democratic voting.
c. in a command economy.
d. by queuing and random selection.

___15. John Locke thought that property rights derived from:
a. a person's inheritance.
b. the usefulness of goods.
c. saving and investing.
d. human labor.

___16. Most economists agree that property rights are determined primarily by:
a. laws and regulations.
b. the labor theory of value.
c. brute force.
d. supply and demand.

___17. The U.S. economy is most accurately characterized by relatively:
a. decentralized decisionmaking.
b. public ownership of productive resources.
c. egalitarian distributions of goods.
d. persistent full employment.
e. strict reliance on tradition to determine occupations.

___18. A government that follows laissez-faire policies:
a. specifies production plans in detail.
b. invariably aids the rich at the expense of the poor.
c. keeps "hands off" of most economic decisions.
d. stimulates investment through supply-side tax policies.
e. monitors trends to keep pace with what consumers want.

___19. A command economy:
a. uses laissez-faire government policies.
b. bases decisions on kolkhoz roundtables.
c. meets consumer wants most efficiently.
d. encourages a private property system.
e. requires detailed centralized decision making.

___20. Government acts as a trustee of nonhuman resources under:
a. laissez-faire capitalism.
b. traditional feudalism.
c. fee simple property rights systems.
d. socialism.
e. mercantilist monarchies.

Chapter Review (Fill-In Questions)

1. Interactions between households, business firms, and government are shown in _____ models.

2. Output and consumption rise when _____ advantage guides us into areas of _____ in which our opportunity costs of production are relatively low.

3. If the current output combination is inside the production possibilities frontier, some resources are _____; points outside the PPF are _____.

4. A typical production possibilities curve is concave (bowed away) from its origin because of _____ opportunity costs. The costs of producing any good eventually rise as output is expanded because _____ returns are encountered.

5. Diminishing returns are encountered along a PPF because resources are _____, and tend to be relatively _____ for different forms of production.

6. Several allocative mechanisms are available to any society to make choices between competing demands. They include _____, _____, _____, _____, _____, and _____.

7. The United States largely relies on a _____ form of decision making. The opposite of this form, used in China and elsewhere, is _____ decision making.

8. Government is minimal and follows _____ policies under pure capitalism. No society is either purely capitalistic or socialistic, so we all live in _____ economies.

Unlimited Multiple Choice

Warning: Each Question Has From Zero To Four Correct Answers.

___ 1. Production possibilities frontiers are concave from their origins because:
   a. all forms of production use identical mixes of all resources.
   b. costs fall consistently as resources are increased for any single output.
   c. capital, land, and labor are used in different intensities to efficiently produce various goods.
   d. resources are not equally suited to all forms of production.

___ 2. Economic growth can result from:
   a. an increased resource base.
   b. advances in production technology.
   c. consumer saving that facilitates investment.
   d. job-training programs for the unskilled.

3. In a command economy,
   a. the central government makes major economic decisions.
   b. most nonhuman factors of production are held by government as "trustee" for the populace.
   c. matching production choices to people's wants is a very difficult task.
   d. there is relatively little private property.

4. The foundations of pure capitalism include:
   a. private rights to property.
   b. inheritance as the major pathway to a high income.
   c. laissez-faire government policies.
   d. exploitation of labor, the real source of all wealth.

5. A comparative advantage in some good requires that you:
   a. are able to produce it at relatively low opportunity cost.
   b. can make it better and faster than any other producers.
   c. encounter minimal marketing costs in finding buyers for it.
   d. be self-sufficient in all goods.

Problems

Problem 1

Some health care professionals use the slogan "the best care for the most people" to defend the American medical system against critics. Suppose current levels of medical resources (15% in 1994) yield this PPF curve going through points a and b.

a. Point _____ must be attained to make the above slogan true.

b. Attaining this point would require either more _____ or an advance in _____.

c. This PPF is concave from below because medical resources _____ in their _____ for different types of medical care.

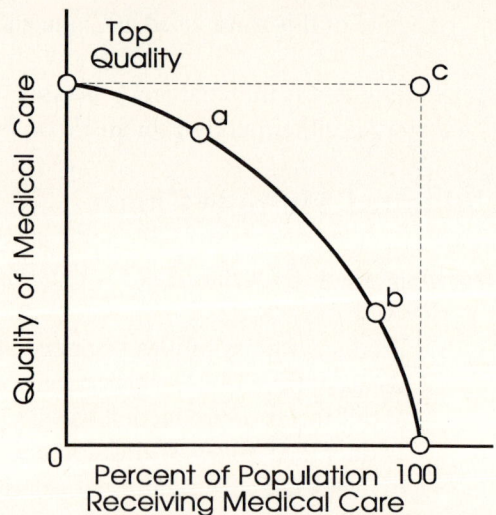

d. A PPF that conformed to the above slogan would look unusual because it would _____
_____.

Problem 2

These five identical production possibilities frontiers (PPF's) show the tradeoffs between agricultural goods and consumer durables (goods that provide services over a number of years; e.g., cars, appliances, bicycles, etc) for the country of Lilliput.

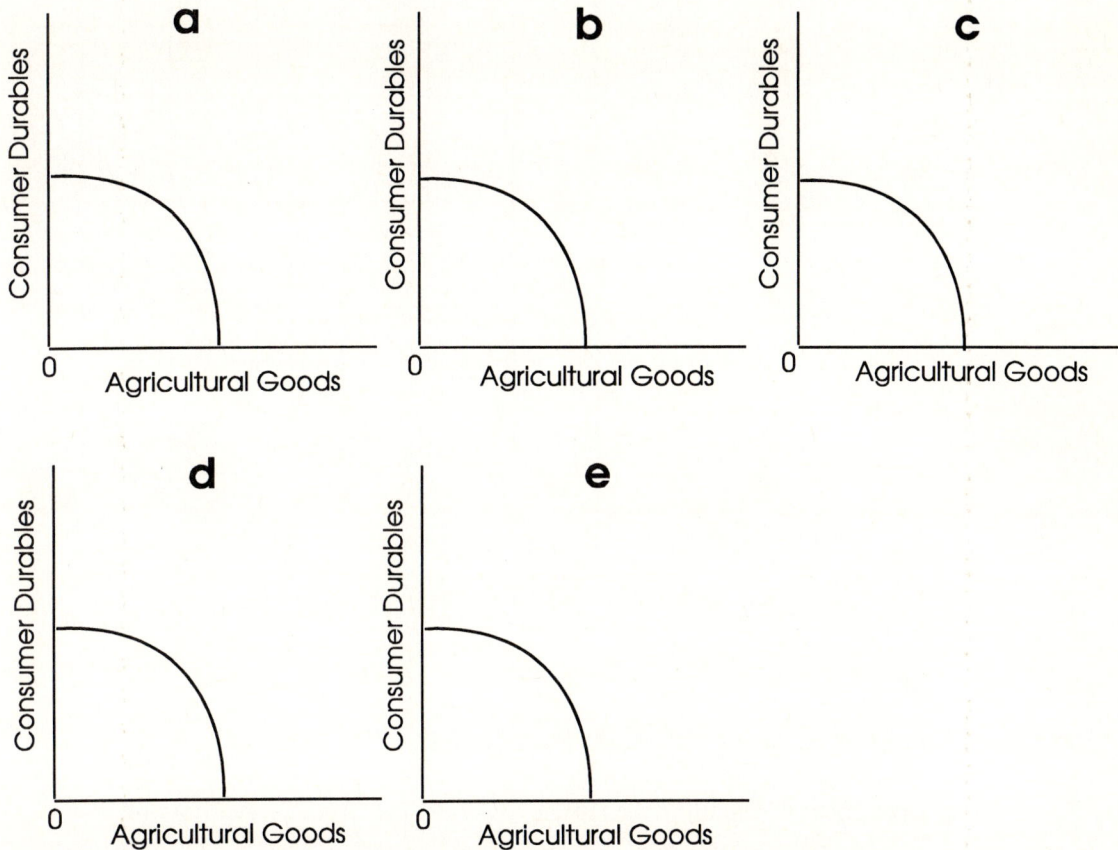

Graph Lilliput's new PPF in the appropriate figure (a through e) when:

a. Technological advances are achieved in agriculture.

b. Technological advances are achieved in the production of consumer durables.

c. The median education level of all workers increases by three years.

d. Investment in capital goods steadily declines over the ensuing decade.

e. Millions of acres of arable land are claimed from the ocean.

Problem 3

This table shows the menu of production possibilities confronting Atlantis, a newly rediscovered "lost" continent.

Combi-nation	Roller Blades (Pairs)	Hand Grenades	Opportunity Costs (Hand Grenades in terms of Roller Blades)
A	7	0	_____
B	6	10	_____
C	5	19	_____
D	4	27	_____
E	3	34	_____
F	2	40	_____
G	1	45	_____
H	0	49	_____

a. Plot the eight bundles of goods and smoothly connect the points in the figure.

b. How is this production possibilities frontier shaped? _____

c. What conditions must be met for Atlantis to produce on its PPF? _____

d. Fill in the opportunity cost column in the table.

e. Roller blades are transformed into hand grenades at (constant, diminishing, increasing) opportunity costs.

Problem 4

Use this figure to answer the following True/False questions.

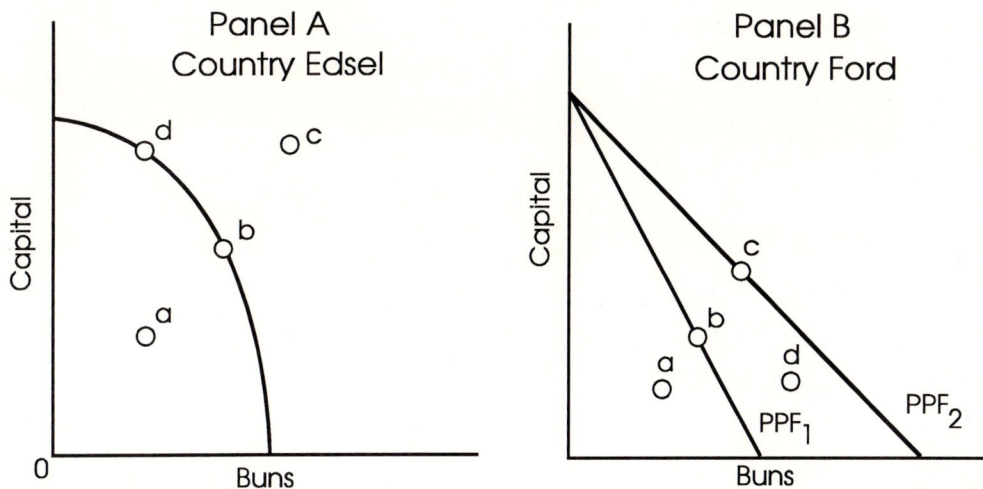

Panel A
Country Edsel

Panel B
Country Ford

_____ a. The Edselian economy can move from point d to point b without incurring any opportunity costs.

_____ b. Fordic capital can be transformed into buns at constant opportunity costs along both production possibilities frontiers.

_____ c. Ever greater costs are incurred in producing buns as capital production is expanded in Edsel.

_____ d. Edselian capital is transformable into buns only at increasing opportunity costs.

_____ e. Increased demand could move Edsel from point b to point c.

_____ f. Edsel could move from point a to point b rather than point d costlessly.

_____ g. Edsel's production possibilities frontier suggests increasing opportunity costs.

_____ h. Land, labor, and capital probably are used in a fixed ratio in producing both capital and buns in Ford.

_____ i. Opportunity costs are incurred when Ford moves from point b to point d instead of point c.

_____ j. Point a is easily attained in both countries.

Problem 5

The countries of Vinlandia and Crude both produce wine and oil. More specifically, if all resources are used to produce a single good, Vinlandia could produce four times as much wine as Crude, which could produce four times as much oil as Vinlandia. Also, the maximum output of wine that Crude can produce is equal to the maximum output of oil that Vinlandia can produce; and the maximum output of oil that Crude can produce is equal to the maximum output of wine that Vinlandia can produce.

a. Vinlandia has a comparative advantage in the production of _____, while Crude has a comparative advantage in the production of _____.

b. Graph Vinlandia's and Crude's PPF in the figure and label both curves PPF_V and PPF_C respectively.

c. Graph the consumption possibilities frontier that Vinlandia and Crude can obtain if both countries specialize and trade, and label this curve as CPF.

d. With the onset of specialization and trade, Vinlandia will trade _____ gallon(s) of _____ for _____ gallon(s) of _____ produced in Crude.

e. As a result of specialization and trade, Vinlandians will be able to consume more _____ and Crudeians will be able to consume more _____.

Wine (millions of gallons)

0   Oil (millions of gallons)

Problem 6

Use this figure to answer the following True/False questions.

Panel A
Ruritania

Panel B
Urbana

(Both panels: vertical axis labeled "Investment Goods", horizontal axis labeled "Present Goods", origin at 0, curves labeled PPF with points a, b, c, d, e.)

___ a. If these countries have equal resources, Urbana is more technologically advanced than Ruritania.

___ b. Both countries confront diminishing returns in producing both products.

___ c. Ruritania invests more at point d than at point c.

___ d. If Ruritania were at point a, it could move to point d.

___ e. In both countries, point a implies underemployment of resources and inefficiency.

___ f. Opportunity costs are constant along Urbana's production possibilities frontier.

___ g. Ruritanian consumption exceeds investment at point d.

___ h. Each country can grow faster by moving along its PPF frontier towards the investment goods axis.

___ i. Urbana can move from point e to point c costlessly.

___ j. If they share the same technologies, Ruritania possesses more resources than Urbana.

Problem 7

A map of Apabana, a Central American country divided into seven 1,000,000-acre sectors, is shown in the figure. The potential harvests of bushels of apples (A) or bananas (B) per acre are shown for each sector. Growing apples in a sector means that you lose bananas proportionally, and vice versa. For example, growing 60 million bushels of apples in sector X requires three-quarters of the land in X, leaving room for growth of only 25 million bushels of bananas.

Sector	R	S	T	W	X	Y	Z
Costs: Apples in terms of Bananas							
Costs: Bananas in terms of Apples							

R — 120 A 60 B
S — 110 A 70 B
T — 100 A 80 B
W — 90 A 90 B
X — 80 A 100 B
Y — 70 A 110 B
Z — 60 A 120 B

N

a. Fill in the table by computing the costs of apples in terms of bananas, and vice versa, for each sector.

b. Apple production costs the fewest bananas in sector _____.
c. Banana production costs the fewest apples in sector _____.

d. Suppose that only bananas were grown in all sectors except Z, which was reserved for apple production. Harvests, in millions of bushels, would be _____ bananas and _____ apples.

e. If only apples were grown in sector R, with all other sectors being used for bananas, output (in millions of bushels) would be _____ bananas and _____ apples.

f. Together, the results of answers d and e suggest that it would be _____ to grow _____ north of sector _____.

g. If you had to pay five apples for four bananas, where would only apples be produced? Only bananas? In which sector might both be produced?

h. Construct a production possibilities frontier for Apabana in the left-hand figure below.

i. Construct a curve in the right-hand figure below relating the cost of apples (in terms of bananas) to each possible output of apples. Put apple production on the horizontal axis, and the cost of extra apples on the vertical axis. (As you will soon learn, this is a supply curve.)

(Left graph: vertical axis "Bananas" with gridlines at 100, 200, 300, 400, 500, 600, 700; horizontal axis "Apples" with gridlines at 100, 200, 300, 400, 500, 600, 700.)

(Right graph: vertical axis "Banana's Sacrificed per Apple" with gridlines at 0.5, 1.0, 1.5, 2.0; horizontal axis "Apples" with gridlines at 100, 200, 300, 400, 500, 600, 700.)

Problem 8

Two dimensional graphs limit the tradeoffs we normally illustrate with a PPF. However, with a little ingenuity we can accommodate a third output. We do this by drawing a family of PPF curves rather than a single curve, with each curve reflecting a different assumed level of production for the third good. Consider three commodities apples (a), bananas (b), and coconuts (c). The family of curves in this figure shows the tradeoff between apples and bananas, holding coconut production constant along each curve. We portray changes in coconut output possibilities by shifting among these curves.

a. How does the figure represent the law of increasing cost (diminishing returns) for apples?

    _____

    _____

    _____

    _____

b. How does the figure represent the law of diminishing returns for coconuts?

    _____

    _____

    _____

    _____

Production Possibilities Curves for Three Outputs

(Figure: axes "b" (Bananas) vertical, "a" (Apples) horizontal, with curves labeled PPF (c=400), PPF (c=300), PPF (c=200), PPF (c=100).)

Problem 9

When Alferd and Zachariah, two pioneers, operate independently, their average daily production and consumption over the course of a year are shown in the table.

	Daily Hours Worked	Average Daily Production and Consumption
Alferd	6	2 pounds of buffalo meat
	2	4 pounds of pinto beans
Zachariah	2	4 pounds of buffalo meat
	6	2 pounds of pinto beans

a. Who has the comparative advantage in hunting? _____

b. Who has the comparative advantage in farming? _____

c. Fill in the table below on the assumption that Alferd and Zachariah begin to specialize and trade, and that their tastes are sufficiently similar so that they end up eating identical diets.

	Daily Hours Worked	Average Daily Production	Average Daily Consumption
Hunter name: _____	8	___ pounds of _____	___ pounds of _____ ___ pounds of _____
Farmer name: _____	8	___ pounds of _____	___ pounds of _____ ___ pounds of _____

Problem 10

Suppose Bruno can brew 50 barrels of beer or bake 800 pizzas per year while Gino can brew 100 barrels of beer or bake 600 pizzas.

a. How much beer is sacrificed for each pizza Bruno bakes? _____

b. How much beer is sacrificed for each pizza Gino bakes? _____

c. In the absence of trade, both Bruno and Gino will devote half their time to producing both goods, and Bruno will consume _____ barrels of beer and _____ pizzas, while Gino will consume _____ barrels of beer and _____ pizzas.

d. If Bruno and Gino begin to specialize and trade, then overall pizza consumption will increase by _____ pizzas and overall beer consumption will increase by _____ barrels.

Problem 11[*]

We suggest that you tackle this challenging production-possibilities problem only after solving all previous questions. **Hint**: Efficiency requires that **scarce** resources be fully employed. In this problem, full employment for labor in some instances may require that other (nonscarce?) resources be unemployed.

Suppose an automobile may be produced by either (a) 5 workers and 1 robot, or (b) 3 workers and 2 robots; while a refrigerator requires either (c) 3 workers and 1 robot, or (d) 2 workers and 2 robots. Now suppose that an isolated factory has 60 workers and 15 robots employed. Filling in this table requires ingenuity and some trial-and-error experimentation. Good luck!

Autos	0	1	2	3	4	5	6	7	8	9	10	11	12
Refrigerators													
Idle Robots													
Unemployed Workers													

*Adapted with permission from Paul G. Coldagelli, author of "Production Possibilities Curves for Three Outputs", and "A Challenging Production Possibilities Problem" in *Great Ideas for Teaching Economics*, 4/e, edited by Ralph T. Byrns and Gerald W. Stone, Jr., Glenview, IL: Scott, Foresman and Company, 1989.

ANSWERS

Matching		True/False		Multiple Choice		Unlimited Multiple Choice
Set I	Set II					
1. j	1. e	1. T	9. T	1. b	11. e	1. c, d
2. g	2. i	2. T	10. F	2. b	12. c	2. a, b, c, d
3. h	3. j	3. F	11. T	3. e	13. c	3. a, b, c, d
4. c	4. c	4. F	12. F	4. d	14. a	4. a, c
5. i	5. f	5. T	13. F	5. e	15. d	5. a
6. f	6. g	6. F	14. T	6. b	16. a	
7. b	7. h	7. T	15. F	7. a	17. a	
8. e	8. b	8. T		8. c	18. c	
9. a	9. a			9. e	19. e	
10. d	10. d			10. b	20. d	

Chapter Review (Fill-in Questions)

1. circular flow
2. comparative advantage; specialization
3. unemployed/underemployed; unattainable
4. increasing; diminishing
5. specialized; suited
6. brute force; random selection; queuing; tradition; government; the market system
7. decentralized; centralized
8. laissez-faire; mixed

Problem 1

a. c
b. resources; technology
c. vary; suitability
d. form a right angle

Problem 2

a-e. See figures a-e below.

Problem 3

a. See figure at right.
b. concave from the origin
c. full employment and efficient use of all scarce inputs
d. 1/10, 1/9, 1/8, 1/7, 1/6, 1/5, 1/4
e. increasing

Atlantis' Production Possibilities Frontier

Problem 4	Problem 5	Problem 6	Problem 7
a. F	a. wine; oil	a. F	a. See table below.
b. T	b. See Figure 11.	b. T	b. R
c. F	c. See Figure 11.	c. F	c. Z
d. T	d. 1; wine; 1; oil	d. T	d. 510; 60
e. F	e. wine & oil;	e. T	e. 570; 120
f. F	wine & oil	f. F	f. inefficient; bananas; W
g. T		g. T	g. Sectors R and S would produce only apples T might produce both and W, X, Y, and Z would produce only bananas.
h. T		h. T	h. See Figure 12.
i. T		i. F	i. See Figure 13.
j. T		j. T	

Figure 11

Sector	R	S	T	W	X	Y	Z
Costs: Apples in terms of Bananas	1/2	7/11	4/5	1.0	5/4	11/7	2.0
Costs: Bananas in terms of Apples	2.0	11/7	5/4	1.0	4/5	7/11	1/2

Figure 12

Figure 13

Sector	Cost	Apples
R	1/2	120
S	7/11	230
T	4/5	330
U	1.0	420
V	5/4	500
W	11/7	570
X	2.0	630

Problem 8

a. The concavity (from the origin) of all these PPFs yields increasing costs for apples: As the number of apples produced grows, the number of bananas sacrificed per extra apple rises.

b. Widening the gap between PPF curves as more coconuts are produced (shrinking the apple/banana PPF towards the origin) illustrates the increasing costs of coconuts in terms of either apples or bananas.

Problem 9

a. Zachariah
b. Alferd
c. See table.

	Daily Hours Worked	Average Daily Production	Average Daily Consumption
Hunter name: Zachariah	8	16 pounds of meat	8 pounds of meat 8 pounds of beans
Farmer name: Alferd	8	16 pounds of beans	8 pounds of meat 8 pounds of beans

Problem 10

a. 1/16 or .0625
b. 1/6 or .167
c. 25; 400; 50; 300
d. 100; 25

Problem 11

See table.

Autos	0	1	2	3	4	5	6	7	8	9	10	11	12
Refrigerators	15	14	13	12	11	10	9	8	6	5	3	2	0
Idle Robots	0	0	0	0	0	0	0	0	1	1	2	0	3
Unemployed Workers	15	13	11	9	7	5	3	1	2	0	1	1	0

Chapter 3
Demand and Supply

Chapter Objectives

After you have read and studied this chapter you should be able to explain the concept of marginalism in decisionmaking; explain the laws of demand and supply; describe the major determinants of demand and supply, and also show how they can respectively cause the demand and supply curves to shift; and show what is meant by a market equilibrium and explain how it is achieved.

Chapter Review: Key Points

1. Rational decision making is governed by evaluations of the relative benefits and costs of *incremental* or *marginal* changes.

2. The *law of demand.* People buy less of a good per period at high prices than at low prices. *Demand curves* slope downward and to the right, and show the quantities demanded at various prices for a good.

3. Changes in market prices cause changes in *quantity demanded*. There is a *change in demand* (the demand curve shifts) when there are changes in influences other than a good's own price. These determinants include:
   a. tastes and preferences;
   b. income and its distribution;
   c. prices of related goods;
   d. numbers and ages of buyers;
   e. expectations about prices, income, and availability;
   f. taxes, subsidies, and regulations.

4. Consumers buy more of a good per period only at lower prices because of:
   a. The *substitution effect*--the cheaper good will now be used more ways as it is substituted for higher priced goods;
   b. *Diminishing marginal utility*-- consuming the additional units ultimately does not yield as much satisfaction as consuming previous units, so demand prices fall as consumption rises;
   c. The *income effect*--a lower price for any good means that the purchasing power of a given monetary income rises.

5. *The law of supply.* Higher prices cause sellers to make more of a good available per period. The *supply curve* shows the positive relationship between the price of a good and the quantity supplied. Supply curves generally slope upward and to the right because:
   a. diminishing returns cause opportunity costs to increase;
   b. to expand output, firms must bid resources away from competing producers or use other methods (such as overtime) that increase cost;
   c. profit incentives are greater at higher prices.

6. In addition to the price paid to producers of a good, supply depends on:
   a. the number of sellers;
   b. technology;
   c. resource costs;
   d. prices of other producible goods;
   e. producer's expectations; and
   f. taxes, subsidies, and regulations.

7. Changes in prices cause *changes in quantities supplied,* while changes in other influences on production or sales of goods cause shifts in supply curves that are termed *changes in supply.*

8. When markets operate without government intervention, prices tend to move towards *market equilibrium* so that quantity supplied equals quantity demanded. At this point, the demand price equals the supply price.

9. When the market price of a good is below the intersection of the supply and demand curves, there will be *shortages* and pressures for increases in price. If price is above the intersection of the supply and demand curves, there will be *surpluses* and pressures for reduction in price.

10. Supply and demand are largely independent in the short run.

Matching Key Terms And Concepts

Set I

___ 1. market

___ 2. supply price

___ 3. *ceteris paribus*

___ 4. marginalism

___ 5. market price

___ 6. complementary goods

___ 7. substitute goods

___ 8. inferior goods

___ 9. demand price

___ 10. joint product

a. A consumer's subjective value from having a bit more of a good.

b. Right-hand gloves and left-hand gloves.

c. Goods for which demands increase as income decreases.

d. Coffee and tea.

e. The view that rational decision makers weigh the costs and benefits of the last extra bit of an activity.

f. Mechanism that enables buyers and sellers to transact.

g. Beef and leather.

h. The minimum payment that will induce a bit more production.

i. Must be in accord with consumers' subjective evaluations before they will purchase a good.

j. "All other influences are held constant".

Set II

___ 1. substitution effect

___ 2. law of demand

___ 3. change in quantity demanded

___ 4. income effect

___ 5. change in demand

___ 6. law of supply

___ 7. surpluses

___ 8. equilibrium

___ 9. shortages

___ 10. diminishing marginal utility

a. Relationships between quantities demanded and price are negative.

b. When neither shortages nor surpluses exist in a market.

c. Extra units of a good add declining amounts of satisfaction.

d. Adjustments people make solely because relative prices change.

e. Occurs when prices are below equilibrium.

f. Effect on a demand curve when the price of a substitute changes.

g. People's adjustments when price changes alter purchasing power.

h. Quantities supplied are positively related to price.

i. A movement along a demand curve.

j. Caused when prices are artificially held above equilibrium.

True/False Questions

_____ 1. Most decisions (business and otherwise) are made at the margin.

_____ 2. The term "demand" can mean that people desire a good, but are still unable to afford it.

_____ 3. Supply must equal demand for equilibrium to occur.

_____ 4. Other things constant, an increase in the wages of labor used in the production of a particular good will cause the supply curve of that good to shift to the right.

_____ 5. For an entire demand curve to shift to the right, all determinants of demand except price must be stable.

_____ 6. If a firm produces durable goods and expects the price of the good to fall in the future, it would not be unreasonable for the firm to deplete or sell down its inventory.

_____ 7. Purchases by individuals can be considered "dollar votes" which signal and direct business decisions.

_____ 8. Increases in income decrease supplies of inferior goods.

_____ 9. The demand curve for a good shows the relationship between its price and the quantity demanded, assuming that all other determinants are constant.

_____ 10. When a market is in equilibrium, a change in supply or demand always results in a shortage or surplus.

_____ 11. Most markets maintain stable equilibria for long periods.

_____ 12. Equilibrium supply prices exceed demand prices by the same ratio that quantity demanded exceeds quantity supplied.

_____ 13. If quantity demanded exceeds quantity supplied, then a shortage exists.

_____ 14. In equilibrium, a change in quantity demanded results if there is a change in supply.

_____ 15. In equilibrium, a change in quantity supplied implies that demand has shifted.

Standard Multiple Choice

There Is One Best Answer For Each Question.

___ 1. If Jill's demand price for a mountain bike exceeds the $500 price tag, then:
- a. Jill will purchase the bike.
- b. mountain bikes are an inferior good.
- c. Jill will not purchase the bike.
- d. mountain bikes are a normal good.
- e. surpluses of mountain bikes are likely.

___ 2. Which term implies that people are able and willing to pay for something?
- a. Need.
- b. Demand.
- c. Requirement.
- d. Necessity.
- e. Desire.

___ 3. The market demand for a good is least affected by the:
- a. incomes of consumers.
- b. prices of related goods.
- c. costs of resources.
- d. number of buyers.
- e. expectations about price changes.

___ 4. When demand decreases, the demand curve shifts:
- a. down and to the left.
- b. in a clockwise rotation.
- c. up and to the right.
- d. counter-clockwise.
- e. away from the origin.

___ 5. A demand curve would not shift if there were changes in the:
- a. tastes and preferences of consumers.
- b. size or distribution of national income.
- c. price of the good.
- d. number or age composition of buyers.
- e. expectations of consumers about availability.

___ 6. Demand is positively related to income for:
- a. inferior goods.
- b. normal goods.
- c. complementary goods.
- d. joint products.
- e. substitute goods.

___ 7. People's adjustments to relative price changes are termed:
- a. demonstration effects.
- b. substitution effects.
- c. wealth effects.
- d. adaptive effects.
- e. income effects.

___ 8. If price cuts in video recorders cause expanded cable TV hookups, these are:
- a. luxury goods.
- b. substitute goods.
- c. normal goods.
- d. inferior goods.
- e. complementary goods.

9. In the short run, an increase in the relative price of a good increases the:
   a. state of technology.
   b. supply of the good.
   c. quantity of the good demanded.
   d. quantity of the good supplied.
   e. profits of capital owners.

10. Improvements in technology shift:
    a. demand up and to the right.
    b. production possibilities towards the origin.
    c. demand down and to the right.
    d. supply to the right, away from the vertical axis.
    e. supply up and to the left.

11. When quantity supplied exceeds quantity demanded:
    a. a surplus will occur.
    b. equilibrium is achieved.
    c. a shortage will occur.
    d. consumers will bid up prices.
    e. suppliers' inventories will be depleted.

12. Decreases in the desire and willingness to pay for additional units of some good are best explained by the:
    a. substitution effect.
    b. principle of diminishing marginal utility.
    c. income effect.
    d. law of diminishing supply.
    e. law of demand.

13. Examples of joint goods (by-products in production) would include:
    a. shirts, ties, and socks.
    b. cameras and film.
    c. college tuitions and textbooks.
    d. vitamin pills and surgery.
    e. water skiing and electricity from a hydroelectric dam.

14. Expectations of price hikes for a durable good tend to:
    a. increase production, but only for later sale.
    b. cause firms to increase their inventories.
    c. decrease supply in the very short run.
    d. increase consumers' demands.
    e. All of the above.

15. Which of the following will NOT result in a change in the supply of camcorders?
    a. New firms enter the industry.
    b. Capital costs increase.
    c. Prices of photographic equipment increase dramatically.
    d. Production technology advances rapidly.
    e. Consumers increasingly prefer camcorders over cameras.

16. The market for a good is in equilibrium if the:
    a. supply and demand are equal.
    b. price equals costs plus a fair profit.
    c. rate of technological change is steady.
    d. quantity supplied equals the quantity demanded.
    e. government properly regulates demands and supplies.

___17. An increase in the quantity demanded of a good can be caused by an increase in:
   a. supply.
   b. inflationary expectations.
   c. consumer incomes.
   d. the price of a substitute good.
   e. federal income tax rates.

___18. Other things constant, an improvement in overall technology that allows more output to be produced with the same level of inputs causes:
   a. a movement up and along the supply curve, resulting in both a higher equilibrium price and quantity.
   b. a leftward shift of the supply curve so that less is offered for sale at every price.
   c. no movement of the supply curve but a fall in price and an increase in the quantity supplied.
   d. a rightward shift of the supply curve so that more is offered for sale at every price.
   e. None of the above are correct.

___19. Market prices that are below equilibrium tend to create:
   a. surpluses of the good.
   b. declines in resource costs.
   c. pressures for research and development.
   d. shortages of the good.
   e. buyers' markets.

___20. Given the list below, all of the following will cause the demand curve to shift to the left except:
   a. an increase in the price of a substitute good.
   b. a reduction in consumer income if the good is normal.
   c. an increase in the price of a complementary good.
   d. an increase in income if the good is inferior.
   e. consumer tastes change so that they no longer want the good.

Chapter Review (Fill-In Questions)

1. The _____ unit of a thing is the last bit of that thing; _____
   is the idea that rational decisions are based on the assessments of the costs and benefits of
   the final increments of an activity.

2. The law of demand states that consumers will purchase _____ of a good the
   lower its opportunity cost (relative price), and vice versa. The basic reason for this is the
   _____ effect, which reflects the adjustments people make solely because of
   changes in relative prices. A secondary reason for most goods is the _____
   effect, which measures the adjustments people make because price changes alter consumers'
   _____.

3. Another way to explain the negative relationship between relative prices and quantities
   demanded is the principle of _____, which suggests that a
   point is eventually reached where added consumption of any good yields ever
   _____ gains of satisfaction.

4. Factors other than the price of a good that can affect purchases include _____,
   _____, _____, _____, and _____.

5. The law of supply states that higher prices induce sellers to offer consumers
   _____ of their product, and vice versa. The supply curve depicts the
   _____ amounts of a good that firms are willing to place on the market at various
   prices.

6. Markets permit buyers and sellers to communicate their desires and complete transactions. In
   so doing, markets reach _____. When quantity demanded exceeds quantity
   supplied, the current price is too low and a _____ exists. This is known as a
   _____ market. If the current price is above the equilibrium price, there is a
   _____ of the good, which is known as a _____ market.

Unlimited Multiple Choice

Warning: Each Question Has From Zero To Four Correct Answers.

___ 1. According to the law of demand, consumers will purchase more of a good when:
   a. the relative price of the good falls.
   b. incomes increase.
   c. the market price of the good rises.
   d. the supply price increases.

___ 2. In the short run, the market demand for ice cream should:
   a. shift to the right upon the arrival of a heat wave.
   b. slope upwards to depict the inverse relationship between its price and the quantity of ice cream demanded.
   c. remain stationary when the price of ice cream falls.
   d. grow to accommodate any increase in the supply of ice cream.

___ 3. In the market for gasoline, one would expect the:
   a. supply curve to be stable in spite of OPEC's uneven history of trying to establish inordinately high oil prices.
   b. demand curve to continually shift to the right, if more and more gas-guzzling automobiles are purchased.
   c. demand for gasoline to decrease when acceptable and economical substitutes are developed and marketed.
   d. supply curve to shift to the right if the government began taxing oil companies more heavily.

___ 4. The quantity demanded of a good adjusts to changes in:
   a. the price of a substitute good.
   b. the price of a complementary good.
   c. consumers' income.
   d. tastes and preferences.

___ 5. Marginalism is a term that is generally used to describe:
   a. the idea that most decisions entail weighing the relative costs and small changes in behavior.
   b. the price of purchasing more of a normal good.
   c. the manner in which the supply curve shifts in response to an increase in the price of a good.
   d. changes in consumer tastes and preferences that occur only in the long run.

Problems

Problem 1

Use the data in this table to answer the following questions.

a. Draw demand curves for consumers X, Y, and Z, respectively, in Panels A, B, and C of the figure below, and label them as D_0.

Consumer X's Demand Schedule		Consumer Y's Demand Schedule		Consumer Z's Demand Schedule	
Price	Quantity Demanded	Price	Quantity Demanded	Price	Quantity Demanded
$10	0	$10	0	$10	0
9	0	9	3	9	1
8	0	8	5	8	5
7	1	7	7	7	8
6	2	6	9	6	11
5	4	5	12	5	12
4	6	4	15	4	15
3	10	3	18	3	18
2	15	2	21	2	20
1	21	1	24	1	23
0	25	0	25	0	25

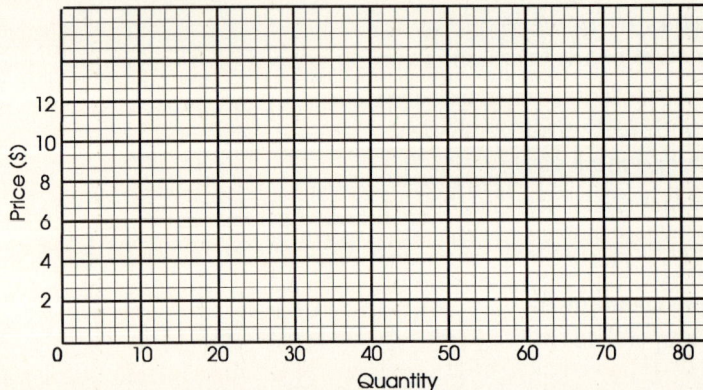

Panel A
Consumer X

Panel B
Consumer Y

Panel C
Consumer Z

Panel D
Market

b. Draw the resulting market demand curve in Panel D and label it as D_M. Explain how you derived the demand curve for the entire market. _____

c. Assume that demands for this good by individuals X and Y double, but fall by half for individual Z. Revise their demand curves (labeling them as D_1 in the figure above), and then redraw the market demand curve and label it as D_{M1}.

Problem 2

Use the market demand curves D_0, D_1, and D_2, in this figure to answer the following questions.

a. A movement from point a to point b represents what?_____
Why? _____
What might account for this movement? _____
_____

b. A movement from point a to point c represents what?_____
Why? _____
What might account for this movement? _____
_____

c. A movement from point a to point d represents what?_____
Why? _____
What might account for this movement? _____

d. A movement from point a to point e represents what?_____
Why? _____ What might account for this movement? _____
_____

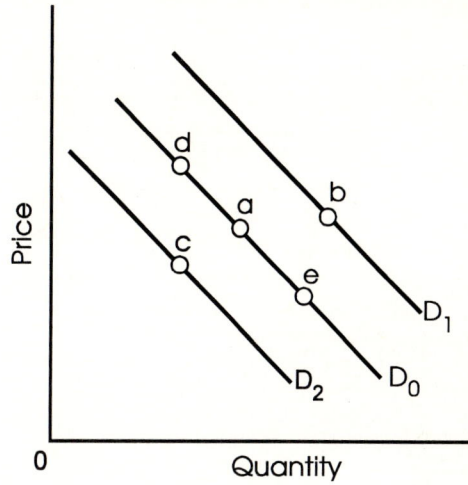

Problem 3

Use the market supply curves S_0, S_1, and S_2 in this figure to answer the following questions .

a. A movement from point a to point b represents
    what?_____
    Why? _____
    What might account for this movement? _____
    _____

b. A movement from point a to point c represents
    what?_____
    Why? _____
    What might account for this movement? _____
    _____

c. A movement from point c to point d represents
    what?_____
    Why? _____
    What might account for this movement? _____

d. A movement from point b to point e represents what?_____
    Why? _____ What might account for this movement? _____
    _____

Problem 4

Use these market supply and demand schedules for electric drills to answer the following questions.

Price	Quantity Demande d (1,000s)	Quantity Supplied (1,000s)
$10	32	4
$20	28	7
$30	24	10
$40	20	13
$50	16	16
$60	12	19
$70	8	22

a. Draw the market supply and demand
    curves for electric drills in the figure.

b.   The equilibrium price in this market is _____.

c.   The equilibrium quantity of drills is _____ thousand monthly.

d.   If the price were $30, there would be a _____ of _____ thousand drills monthly.

e.   If the price were $60, there would be a _____ of _____ thousand drills monthly.

Problem 5

The demand curve for Xebs is represented by D_X. The demand curves for Yoozs , (a substitute good for Xebs) and Zorks (a complement to Xebs) are given by D_Y and D_Z respectively.

Suppose the price of Xebs increases. Indicate the effect(s) of this price change on the graphs in the figure.

Problem 6

The concepts of average and marginal occur in many areas other than economics.

a. What happens to your average for this class if your score on the next (marginal) test is above your current average? _____ Suppose that you do not do quite as well on the final exam as on your next test. How is it possible for your average to rise even though the marginal test (final exam) score is falling? _____

b. Shaquille O'Neal, a 7' center for the Orlando Magic basketball team, walks into your class. What happens to the average height of people in your classroom? _____ To the average income? _____

c. How could an increase in the rate of inflation this year reduce the average rate of inflation over a decade? _____

d. How are marginal and average values related? _____
    _____

Problem 7

Identify the following pairs of goods as substitutes (S), complements (C) or joint products (JP).

a. VCRs and rental video cassettes. _____

b. Salt and pepper. _____

c. Yogurt and ice cream. _____

d. Ball-point pens and paper. _____

e. Beer and wine. _____

f. Wool and cotton. _____

g. Tea and honey. _____

h. Lumber and paper. _____

i. Eggs and hash browns. _____

j. Footballs and ham. _____

Problem 8

If oil prices suddenly fell after rising rapidly for years, what would you expect to happen to the:

a. demand for small cars? _____

b. demand for luxury sedans? _____

c. demand for air travel? _____

d. supply of synthetic fabrics? (Most are made from petroleum products) _____

e. demand for wool and cotton? _____

Problem 9

Around the middle of January, the annual crop of mink furs is put on the auction block. How will the supplies and demands for mink pelts be affected when:

a. wearing fur in public increasingly elicits jeers and harassment from strangers? _____
    _____

b. other fur-bearing animals become increasingly classified as endangered species. _____
    _____

c. the price of mink food rises. _____

d. a sharp, worldwide (1929-type) depression occurs. _____

e. higher income tax rates and a new wealth tax are imposed while the revenues are used to raise welfare payments. _____

ANSWERS

Matching		True/False		Multiple Choice		Unlimited Multiple Choice
Set I	**Set II**					
1. f	1. d	1. T	9. T	1. a	11. a	1. a
2. h	2. a	2. F	10. F	2. b	12. b	2. a, c
3. j	3. i	3. F	11. F	3. c	13. e	3. b, c
4. e	4. g	4. F	12. F	4. a	14. e	4. None
5. i	5. f	5. F	13. T	5. c	15. e	5. a
6. b	6. h	6. T	14. T	6. b	16. d	
7. d	7. j	7. T	15. T	7. b	17. a	
8. c	8. b	8. F		8. e	18. d	
9. a	9. e			9. d	19. d	
10. g	10. c			10. d	20. a	

Chapter Review (Fill-in Questions)

1. marginal; marginalism
2. more; substitution; income; purchasing power
3. diminishing marginal utility; smaller
4. tastes and preferences; income; number of buyers; price of related goods; and expectations
5. more; maximum
6. equilibrium; shortage; sellers; surplus; buyers

Problem 1

a. See panels A-D on next page.
b. Horizontal summation of individual demand curves.
c. See panels A-D on next page.

Problem 2

a. increase in demand; curve shifted rightwards; increase in income, more favorable consumer preferences, or some other parallel change in a determinant besides the good's own price.
b. decrease in demand; curve shifted leftward; decrease in income, increase in the price of a complement, or some other parallel change in a determinant besides the good's own price.
c. decrease in quantity demanded; movement along the curve; increase in the price of the good.
d. increase in quantity demanded; movement along the curve; decrease in the price of the good.

Panel A
Consumer X

Panel B
Consumer Y

Panel C
Consumer Z

Panel D
Market

Problem 3

a. increase in supply; curve shifted to the right; decrease in resource price, technological advances, or some other change in determinant besides the good's price.
b. decrease in supply; curve shifted to the left; increasing resource prices, reduction in the number of sellers, or some other change in a determinant besides the good's price.
c. increase in quantity supplied; movement along a curve; increase in price.
d. decrease in quantity supplied; movement along a supply curve; decrease in price.

Problem 4

a. See figure at right.
b. $50
c. 16
d. shortage, 14
e. surplus, 7

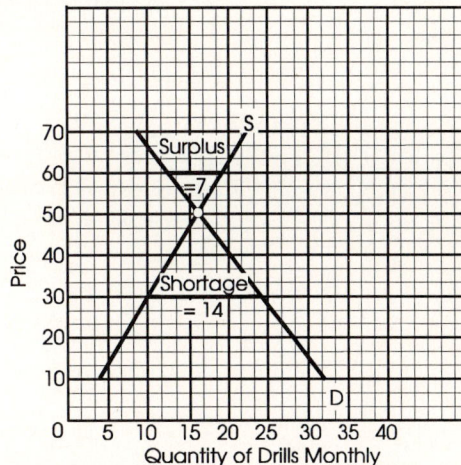

Problem 5

Demand for substitute good (Yoozs) increases, demand for complement (Zorks) decreases.

Problem 6

a. Your average increases; as long as your marginal grade is above your average grade, it will pull up your average grade.
b. Average height increase; average income increases.
c. As long as this year's (marginal) increase is less than the decade's average, the average rate of inflation for the decade will decline.
d. Whenever a marginal value is greater than the average value, the average will be pulled up; whenever a marginal value is below the average, the average will be pulled down.

Problem 7

a. C
b. C
c. S
d. C
e. S
f. S
g. C
h. JP
i. C
j. JP

Problem 8

a. Demand will decrease.
b. Demand will increase.
c. Demand will most likely increase.
d. Supply will increase.
e. Demand will decrease (price of synthetics will fall).

Problem 9

a. Demand will decrease.
b. Demand will rise as substitutes become scarce.
c. Supply will decrease.
d. Demand will decrease because mink pelts are a luxury.
e. Demand will decrease, and higher taxes might reduce supply.

Chapter 4
Markets and Equilibrium

Chapter Objectives

After you have read and studied this chapter you should be able to explain how prices and quantities change to reflect movements in supplies and demands; describe the effects of government price controls (price ceilings and price floors) on the market's ability to efficiently allocate society's scarce resources and also show how price controls prohibit a market from achieving an equilibrium price and quantity; list some of the activities performed by speculators, arbitrageurs, and intermediaries in the market place; offer suggestions about how supply and demand interact to shape the activities in markets that you might encounter in the future; state how the market system answers the **"what"**, **"how"**, and **"for whom"** questions; and list the five economic goals for government in a market economy.

Chapter Review: Key Points

1. Increases in supplies or decreases in demands tend to reduce prices. Decreases in supplies or increases in demands tend to raise prices. Increases in either supplies or demands tend to increase quantities. Decreases in either supplies or demands tend to shrink quantities. If both supply and demand shift, the effects on price and quantity may be either reinforcing or at least partially offsetting. (You need to review this important material if these points make little sense to you.)

2. *Transaction costs* arise because information and mobility are costly. This allows the price of a good to vary between markets, and to approach its equilibrium erratically.

3. *Intermediaries* prosper by reducing transaction costs incurred in getting goods from ultimate producers to ultimate consumers. *Speculators* facilitate movements towards equilibrium because they increase demand by trying to buy when prices are below equilibrium, and increase supply by selling when prices exceed equilibrium. This dampens price swings and cuts the costs and risks to others of doing business.

4. *Arbitrage* involves buying where prices are low and selling where prices are higher. If price spreads exceed transaction costs, arbitrage is risklessly profitable. Competition for opportunities to arbitrage dampens profit opportunities and facilitates efficiency by ensuring that price spreads between markets are minimal.

5. Government can set monetary prices at values other than equilibrium price, but *price ceilings* or *price floors* do not "freeze" opportunity costs; instead, these *price controls* create economic inefficiency and either shortages or surpluses, respectively.

6. The market system tailors production according with consumers' demands in answering the basic economic question of "*What?*" will be produced. Competition tends to compel efficient forms of production in answering "*How?*" production will occur. Markets answer the "*Who?*" question by producing for those who own valuable resources .

7. Where the price system is incapable of providing certain goods or fails to supply the socially optimal levels, government steps in to supplement the private sector in five major ways. It attempts to:
    a. provide a legal, social and business environment for stable growth;
    b. promote and maintain competitive markets;
    c. redistribute income and wealth equitably;
    d. alter resource allocations in an efficient manner where public goods or externalities are present; and
    e. stabilize income, employment, and prices.

8. If *negative externalities* (costs) exist, the private market will provide too much of the product and the market price will be too low because full production costs are not being charged to consumers. If *positive externalities* (benefits) exist, too little of the product will be produced by the private market and market price will be too high, requiring government subsidy or government production or provision of the commodity.

9. Once *public goods* are produced, it is costly to exclude people from their use (the *nonexclusion* problem), and everybody can consume the goods simultaneously with everyone else (the *nonrivalry* problem). The free market fails to provide public goods efficiently because of the "free-rider" problem.

10. Total spending on goods and services by all three levels of government exceeds 20 percent of U.S. GDP. State and local governments spend the bulk of their revenues on services that primarily benefit people in their community and rely heavily on the property and sales taxes as a source of revenue. Federal spending is generally aimed at activities that are national in scope. Over 90 percent of federal revenue comes from individual and corporate income taxes plus Social Security and other employment taxes. Transfer payments through government account for an additional 10% of U.S. national income.

Matching Key Terms And Concepts

Set I

____ 1. arbitrage

____ 2. price controls

____ 3. externalities

____ 4. speculator

____ 5. public goods

____ 6. price floor

____ 7. price ceiling

____ 8. intermediaries

____ 9. invisible hand

____10. minimum wage laws

____11. transaction costs

a. Government imposed price ceilings or price floors that hinder the market's ability to ration goods efficiently.

b. Adam Smith's name for automatic market adjustments.

c. Their incomes depend on cutting transaction costs for others.

d. Emerge because information and mobility are costly.

e. Risklessly buying at a low price in one market and then selling at a higher price in another market.

f. Can be enjoyed by many people simultaneously, but restricting access is prohibitively expensive.

g. Floors that may cause the unskilled to be unemployed.

h. A legal limitation that causes a surplus.

i. A legal limitation that causes a shortage.

j. Examples include ticket scalpers.

k. Benefits or costs of an activity spill over to third parties.

Set II: An answer may be used more than once.

What happens to equilibrium price and quantity when:

____ 1. both supply and demand increase?

____ 2. both supply and demand decrease?

____ 3. supply increases and demand decreases?

____ 4. supply decreases and demand increases?

____ 5. supply grows and demand is constant?

____ 6. demand grows; supply remains the same?

____ 7. supply falls and demand is constant?

____ 8. demand declines and supply is constant?

____ 9. corn prices rise--what happens to wheat?

____10. How will an oil discovery affect the price of gasoline?

a. Price and quantity will increase.

b. Price and quantity will fall.

c. Equilibrium price will fall and quantity will rise.

d. Equilibrium price will rise and quantity will fall.

e. Equilibrium price rises, but quantity changes are indeterminate.

f. Equilibrium price falls, but quantity changes are indeterminate.

g. Equilibrium quantity rises, but price changes are indeterminate.

h. Equilibrium quantity falls but price changes are indeterminate.

True/False Questions

_____ 1. Prices depend on demand alone, while quantities depend primarily on supply.

_____ 2. Long-term shortages or surpluses are, with very few exceptions, the results of government price controls.

_____ 3. Federal minimum wage laws are examples of price ceilings, and most utility rates are examples of price floors.

_____ 4. Increases in supplies put upward pressure on market prices and tend to increase the quantities of a good sold.

_____ 5. Price controls are legal restrictions that often prevent monetary prices from reaching equilibrium levels.

_____ 6. Speculation tends to hinder movements of prices and quantities towards market equilibrium.

_____ 7. Allocative efficiency is aided if decision makers consider all costs of their actions.

_____ 8. According to Adam Smith, the behavior of both business firms and individual consumers is governed by altruism.

_____ 9. If the equilibrium price is below a price ceiling, a market tends to generate surpluses.

_____10. The opportunity costs of consumption tend to increase if price ceilings below equilibrium price are imposed.

_____11. Transaction costs arise because consumers do not have complete information about the price and availability of goods in all markets.

_____12. Arbitrage generates riskless profits from buying low in one market and then selling at a higher price in another.

_____13. Intermediaries will not be successful unless they reduce the transaction costs of getting goods from ultimate producers to consumers.

_____14. Price supports for agricultural products generate surpluses that consumers value less than their costs to society.

_____15. Black markets and consumer queues are signs that price ceilings restrict monetary prices below equilibrium.

_____16. A tax is progressive if higher incomes are taxed proportionately less than lower incomes.

_____17. Externalities occur when parties other than those directly making decisions are affected by an activity.

_____18. At present, well over half of all goods produced in our economy are directly controlled or allocated by government.

_____19. Efficiency requires government to produce public goods.

_____20. National defense is the classic example of a negative externality.

Standard Multiple Choice

There Is One Best Answer For Each Question.

___ 1. The first comprehensive work on economics was written by Adam Smith in 1776 and entitled An Inquiry into the Nature and Causes of the:
   a. Laws of Supply and Demand.
   b. Wealth of Nations.
   c. Sovereignty of the Marketplace.
   d. Distribution of Income Among the Social Classes.
   e. Efficiency Gained from Competition.

___ 2. When the price of a good is below the intersection of its supply and demand curves, there will be:
   a. surpluses.
   b. shortages.
   c. "frozen" opportunity costs.
   d. excessive unemployment.
   e. None of the above.

___ 3. If the supply and demand for a product both increase, the:
   a. price will rise.
   b. quantity will increase.
   c. price will remain stable.
   d. profits of competitors will increase.
   e. welfare of society rises.

___ 4. The market price of video recorders will rise if:
   a. reading becomes more popular.
   b. supply increases.
   c. technology advances.
   d. imports are prohibited.
   e. consumers substitute towards cable TV.

___ 5. Buying at a low price in one market and selling at a higher price elsewhere is not:
   a. a risk-free way to make profits.
   b. called arbitrage.
   c. a cause of price spreads between markets.
   d. a mechanism that increases demand in the low-price market.
   e. a mechanism that increases supply in the high-price market.

___ 6. The transaction costs of conveying goods from producers to consumers are reduced by agents known as:
   a. arbitrageurs.
   b. efficiency consultants.
   c. commission houses.
   d. intermediaries.
   e. consortiums.

___ 7. Speculators tend to:
   a. increase the risks to other firms.
   b. reduce the volatility of prices.
   c. cause economic booms and busts.
   d. eliminate transaction costs.
   e. always make profits.

___ 8. Providing a stable business environment, promoting growth, and maintaining competitive markets are examples of the:
   a. social allocation of resources.
   b. economic functions of government.
   c. externalities of government.
   d. economic incidence on consumers.
   e. duties of trade unions.

9. All transaction costs would be zero if:
    a. a law was passed that required prices to be cut in half.
    b. information and transportation were costless.
    c. prices could not legally exceed production costs.
    d. rapidly rising input and output prices were eliminated.
    e. the operation by intermediaries was efficient.

10. Government price controls may reduce the supply of a good to the extent that they:
    a. artificially stimulate demand.
    b. prevent pollution and industrial blight.
    c. raise the costs of production.
    d. are based on laissez faire government policies.
    e. generate cyclical shortages and then surpluses.

11. Laws used to keep market prices from rising are called:
    a. wage and/or price ceilings.
    b. rationing and subsidies.
    c. allocations and redemptions.
    d. arbitrage and arbitration.
    e. None of the above.

12. Long term price ceilings are likely to cause:
    a. shortages.
    b. queues.
    c. black markets and corruption.
    d. economic inefficiency.
    e. All of the above.

13. Minimum wage laws are examples of:
    a. government assistance that aid people on welfare.
    b. direct benefits from union membership.
    c. price floors, and create surplus labor and unemployment.
    d. arbitrage exercised by government bureaucrats.
    e. price ceilings that create labor shortages.

14. Ignoring economic factors when designing social policies is:
    a. appropriate because morality does not depend on money.
    b. likely to cause results that are incompatible with intentions.
    c. recommended by advocates of laissez faire policies.
    d. a major reason why income is equitably distributed.
    e. mandated by the 27th amendment to the U.S. Constitution.

15. Harsher punishments for drug pushers than addicts cannot be blamed for higher:
    a. prices for illegal drugs than free market prices.
    b. rates of street crime by addicts.
    c. profits reaped by successful pushers who are uncaught.
    d. rates of addiction than would exist in a free market.
    e. police corruption because pushers can offer big bribes.

___16. Government's macroeconomic role is most closely related to the goal of providing or promoting:
a. a common defense.
b. a stable legal system and business environment.
c. purchasing power, employment, and economic growth.
d. equity in the distribution of income.
e. positive externalities in public goods.

___17. Negative (cost) spillovers:
a. result in too much of a product at too low a price.
b. are exemplified by air pollution and education.
c. are exemplified by transportation an immunization.
d. result in too little of a product at too high a price.
e. are caused by wastes of taxpayers' dollars.

___18. Government provision of a public good does not require the good to be:
a. scarce so that opportunity costs exist.
b. nonrival.
c. nonexclusive.
d. produced by government.
e. exclusive.

___19. Which of the following activities is least likely to generate negative externalities?
a. Driving while intoxicated.
b. Smoking a cigar in a restaurant.
c. Parking on your front lawn for months while repairing your car.
d. Failing to bathe during the hot summer months.
e. Getting an inoculation against a contagious disease.

___20. If a good is nonexclusive, people will:
a. all vote for maximum possible government provision
b. buy the good according to their tastes and preferences.
c. not care if the good generates negative externalities.
d. try to be "free riders".
e. have a high benefit/cost ratio from its purchase.

Chapter Review (Fill-In Questions)

1. Market _____ occurs at the price where quantity demanded equals quantity _____.

2. A shortage occurs when the market price is _____ the equilibrium price because a greater quantity of the good is _____ than supplied. If the market price exceeds the equilibrium price, there is a _____ because greater quantities of the good are _____ than are demanded by consumers.

3. If demands increase while supplies decline, prices _____ but quantity changes are _____. When there are increases in both demands and supplies, _____ will increase but the change in _____ is indeterminate.

4. When a maximum legal price is set, it is called a price _____, whereas if the government sets a minimum legal price, it is called a price _____.
Price ceilings do not hold economic prices down; opportunity costs rise because of increases in _____ costs, and price ceilings typically cause _____.
Price floors on the other hand often cause _____; and the production costs of these surpluses are _____ their values to consumers.

5. Successful speculators tend to reduce the volatility of _____ and absorb the _____ to others of doing business. Intermediaries are successful only to the extent that they are able to reduce the _____ incurred in transmitting goods from producers to consumers. The process of _____ entails buying at a low price in one market and selling at a higher price elsewhere.

6. When a consumer enters the market for a particular good, he might "shop" in order to gather information. This "shopping", however, generates _____ as the consumer accumulates information about product prices and availability.
_____ costs are also associated with the mobility of goods, resources, and people between markets.

7. If market (price) signals from consumers to business are incorrect, too little or too much of a good will be provided. These problems usually exist when _____ are involved or when the commodity or service in question is a _____ good.

8. A tax is said to be progressive if the percentage tax rate _____ as income rises. Regressive taxes are those where the tax rate _____ as income rises.

Unlimited Multiple Choice

The following questions have from zero to four correct answers.

___ 1. Market equilibrium is said to occur when the:
   a. government strictly controls price-gouging businesses.
   b. market experiences neither surpluses nor shortages.
   c. market price equates the quantities demanded and supplied.
   d. quantity demanded equals a governmentally imposed quota.

___ 2. The economic functions of government include:
   a. providing a reasonably certain legal, social, and business environment for stable growth.
   b. promoting and maintaining competitive markets.
   c. providing public goods and adjusting for externalities.
   d. stabilizing income, employment, and the price level.

___ 3. Price ceilings that are below market-clearing prices keep:
   a. monetary prices from rising except in black markets.
   b. a lid on opportunity costs.
   c. consumers from being "ripped off."
   d. incentives strong for the Invisible Hand to work its magic.

___ 4. Examples of "intermediary" operations include:
   a. speculators.
   b. retail outlets.
   c. arbitrating.
   d. ticket scalpers.

___ 5. Competitive markets:
   a. translate consumer wants into production by firms.
   b. are stationary by nature.
   c. aid buyers and sellers in communicating their wants, and facilitate beneficial exchanges of goods and resources.
   d. are all very similar.

Problems

Problem 1

Use the information in this table to answer the following questions about the market for battery-powered thermal socks. (Quantities are in millions of pairs of socks annually.)

Quantity Demanded	Price ($)	Quantity Supplied
0	10.00	20
2	9.50	18
4	9.00	16
6	8.50	14
8	8.00	12
10	7.50	10
12	7.00	8
14	6.50	6
16	6.00	4
18	5.50	2
20	5.00	0

a. Plot the supply and demand curves in the figure, being sure to label both axes; label the curves S_0 and D_0 respectively.

b. What is the equilibrium price? _____ Quantity? _____

c. Does the demand schedule illustrate the law of demand? _____ Why?
_____

d. Does the supply schedule illustrate the law of supply? _____ Why? _____

e. Draw in a price ceiling of $6.00. What would occur? _____

f. Draw a price floor of $9.50. What would occur? _____

g. Assume that the quantities demanded and supplied double at each price. Plot the new supply and demand curves and label them S_1 and D_1 respectively.

h. What is the new equilibrium price? _____ Quantity? _____

i. List factors that could have increased demand: _____

j. List factors that could have increased supply _____

Problem 2

Consider the (hypothetical) market for rental apartments in Paris as illustrated in this figure. Assume that the model represents a typical two-bedroom, single bath apartment.

a. Suppose that the rental market for single family apartments in Paris is initially competitive. The equilibrium rent for a typical apartment is _____, and at this rate, _____ apartments will be rented.

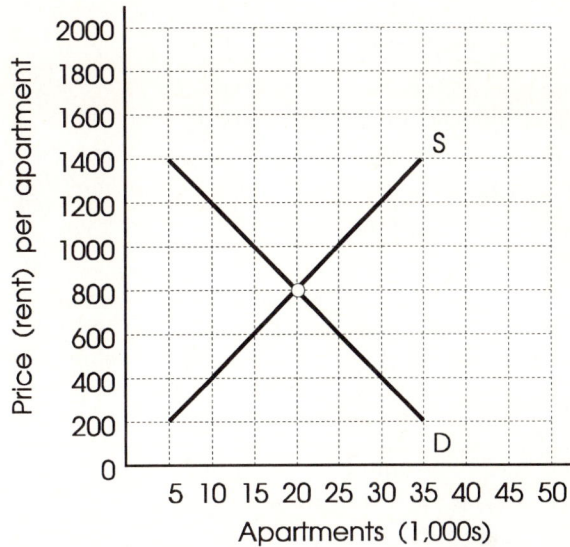

b. Now let the government impose rent controls or a _____ of $400 per apartment. This controlled price is _____ (above/below) the market equilibrium price by an amount equal to _____ per apartment. The government's motive for imposing the rent control is most likely to be that of making the typical apartment more _____ for the average family.

c. As a result of the controls, there is a _____ (surplus/shortage) of apartments in Paris equal to _____ rental units. At the controlled rent, _____ apartments could be rented; however, landlords will be willing and able to supply only _____ units.

d. At the controlled rent, apartment hunters would be willing and able to pay _____ per unit when only _____ apartment units are available rather than go without housing.

e. Even though rent controls ideally would help maintain affordable housing, they introduce several distortions in the rental housing market. One likely distortion is that it will take the average family _____ (more/less) time to find an apartment in Paris. Another likely distortion is that landlords will be _____ (more/less) willing to pay for maintenance, and so the quality of apartments will most likely _____. A third problem that rent controls may cause in Paris is that the return on the landlord's investment in apartments will likely _____ (increase/decrease), and as a result, the stock of available rental apartments will _____ (rise/decline) over time.

Problem 3

Supply and demand curves S_0 and D_0 represent the original situation in the market for top quality Brahma bulls. Use information from the figure to answer these questions about this market.

a. What is the original equilibrium price? _____
   Quantity? _____

b. If demand moves to D_1 because dietitians recommend that all people over 40 become vegetarians, what is the new equilibrium price? _____ Quantity? _____

c. Beginning with the original curves, if supply shifts to S_1 with the introduction of beef-up antibiotics, what is the new market-clearing price? _____ Quantity? _____

d. Assuming simultaneous shifts to D_1 and S_1, what is the new equilibrium price? _____ Quantity? _____

The Brahma Bull Market

e. The movement from point a to point c represents what on the demand side? _____
   What on the supply side? _____

f. The movement from point a to point b represents what on the demand side? _____
   What on the supply side? _____

g. The movement from point b to point d represents what on the demand side? _____
   What on the supply side? _____

h. The movement from point c to point d represents what on the demand side? _____
   What on the supply side? _____

i. Looking only at the original set of demand and supply curves (D_0, S_0), what would occur if the price were set at P_2? _____ Why? _____

j. Looking only at the new set of demand and supply curves (D_1, S_1) what would occur if the price were set at P_1? _____ Why? _____

Problem 4

Demand curve D_L in this figure represents the demand for unskilled labor services by business firms, and S_L represents the supply of unskilled labor services offered by households. Money wage rate W_e is the market-clearing wage rate, but W_m denotes the minimum money wage rate imposed on this labor market by federal law. Use this information to answer the following true/false questions.

___a. The minimum money wage rate is an example of a price floor.

___b. At wage rate W_e, the quantity of labor demanded equals the quantity supplied.

___c. Employment is greater at W_m than at W_e.

___d. The federal government has created a buyers' market in the labor market.

___e. At wage rate W_m, unemployment equals L_2 minus L_1.

___f. Unemployment would fall if the government discontinued its legal minimum for the money wage rate.

___g. The minimum wage reduces employers' costs of discriminating.

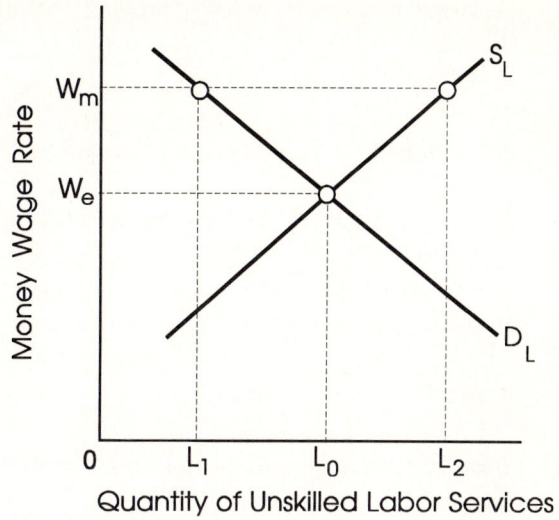

Problem 5

Draw supply and demand diagrams on scratch paper to help you answer the following questions.

a. There is a major technological breakthrough in producing natural gas from coal. What happens in the market for natural gas? _____
    The market for coal? _____

b. Gasoline prices soar. What happens in the markets for big cars? _____
    Bicycles? _____ Tune-up shops? _____
    Rapid -transit systems? _____

c. What happens to quantity, if a price ceiling of $10 a pair is imposed on denim jeans? _____ To quality? _____
    Is the government doing jeans wearers a favor? _____

d. In 1994, the government announces a major renewal of space exploration. In 2001, this program is discontinued. What will happen in the market for aeronautical engineers in 1994-1995? _____ Between 1995 and 2001? _____
    Between 2001 and 2002? _____ After 2002? _____

e. There is a radical overhaul and simplification of the income tax system. What happens in the market for accountants? _____ Lawyers? _____ Erasers? _____

Problem 6

Use the tax and income information listed in this table to answer the following questions.

a. Fill in the average tax rate column in the table.

b. What is the marginal rate of taxation (ΔTax /ΔIncome) when income increases from $10,000 to $15,000?

    _____

c. What kind of tax is depicted in the table? _____

Income($)	Total Taxes ($)	Average Tax Rate
10,000	5,000	_____
15,000	6,750	_____
20,000	8,000	_____
25,000	8,750	_____
35,000	9,000	_____
50,000	10,000	_____

d. Can you think of any taxes that fit this pattern?_____

ANSWERS

Matching		True/False		Multiple Choice		Unlimited Multiple Choice
Set I	Set II					
1. e	1. g	1. F	11. T	1. b	11. a	1. bc
2. a	2. h	2. T	12. T	2. b	12. e	2. abcd
3. k	3. f	3. F	13. T	3. b	13. c	3. a
4. j	4. e	4. F	14. T	4. d	14. b	4. abcd
5. f	5. c	5. T	15. T	5. c	15. d	5. ac
6. h	6. a	6. F	16. F	6. d	16. c	
7. i	7. d	7. T	17. T	7. b	17. a	
8. c	8. b	8. F	18. F	8. b	18. d	
9. b	9. d	9. F	19. F	9. b	19. e	
10. g	10. c	10. T	20. F	10. c	20. d	
11. d						

Chapter Review (Fill-in Questions)

1. equilibrium; supplied
2. lower than; demanded; surplus; supplied
3. rise; indeterminate; quantity; price
4. ceiling; floor; transaction; shortages; surpluses; above
5. prices; risks; transaction costs; arbitrage
6. costs; transaction
7. externalities; public
8. rises; falls

Problem 1

a. See figure.
b. $7.50; 10 million.
c. Yes; The relationship between price and quantity demanded is inverse (negative).
d. Yes; The relationship between price and quantity supplied is direct (positive).
e. See figure; a shortage, since 16 units would be demanded but only 4 units would be supplied.
f. See figure; a surplus, since 18 units would be supplied but only 2 units would be demanded.
g. See figure.
h. $7.50; 20 million pairs.
i. favorable change in tastes and preferences; rise in income or the number of buyers; drop in price of a complementary good or rise in the price of a substitute good; increase in price expectations.
j. decline in resource costs; increase in technology; decreases in the prices of substitutes in production; an increase in the numbers of suppliers, expectations that durables' prices will fall.

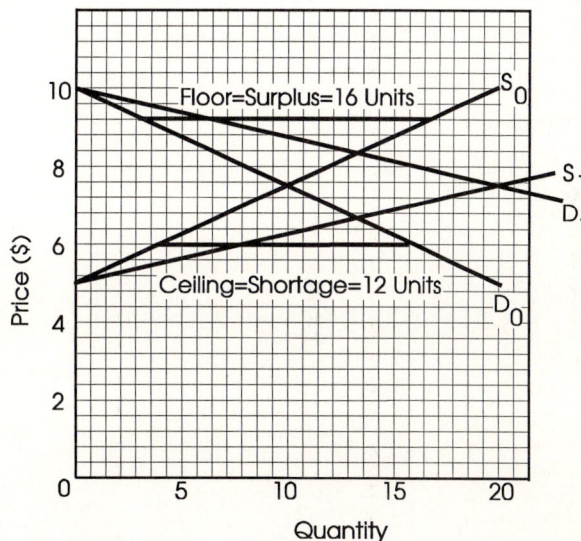

Problem 2

a. $800; 20 thousand
b. price ceiling; below; $400; affordable
c. shortage; 20 thousand; 30 thousand; 10 thousand
d. $1,200; 10 thousand
e. more; less; decline; decrease; decline

Problem 3

a. P_3, Q_1
b. P_2, Q_0
c. P_1, Q_3
d. P_0, Q_2
e. increase in quantity demanded; increase in supply
f. increase in demand; increase in quantity supplied
g. increase in quantity demanded; increase in supply
h. increase in demand; increase in quantity supplied
i. shortage; quantity demanded at P_2 exceeds quantity supplied
j. surplus; quantity supplied at P_1 exceeds quantity demanded

Problem 4

a. T
b. T
c. F
d. T
e. T
f. T
g. T

Problem 5

a. supply increases; demand increases
b. demand decreases; demand increases; demand increases; demand increases
c. quantity supplied decreases while quantity demanded increases; quality decreases; no
d. demand increases; supply increases; demand decreases; supply decreases
e. demand decreases; demand decreases; demand decreases

Problem 6

a. See table.
b. 35% (($6,750 - $5,000)/($15,000 - $10,000))
c. regressive
d. some sales taxes, tobacco and alcohol taxes

Income($)	Total Taxes ($)	Average Tax Rate
10,000	5,000	50%
15,000	6,750	45%
20,000	8,000	40%
25,000	8,750	35%
35,000	9,000	25.7%
50,000	10,000	20%

Chapter 5
Foundations of Macroeconomics

Chapter Objectives

After you have read and studied this chapter you should be able to describe different phases of business cycles and explain early business cycle theories; identify the major determinants of Aggregate Supply and Aggregate Demand; use Aggregate Demand and Aggregate Supply curves to (crudely) illustrate movements of economy wide levels of prices, output, and employment; and describe the historical record of American business fluctuations.

Chapter Review: Key Points

1. *Business cycles* are alternating periods of expansion and contraction, which break down into four phases: (**a**) *peak* (boom), (**b**) *contraction* (recession or downturn), (**c**) *trough* (depression), and (**d**) *expansion* (recovery or upturn). As measured from peak to peak by the National Bureau of Economic Research, cycles average about 4 years, with some as short as 18 months, while others have lasted a decade. Reference dates are established after detailed scrutiny of data from past cycles.

2. Marriages and divorces alike tend to be positively related to the business cycle. Mental disorders, some physical diseases, suicides, crimes, and illegitimate births are inversely related to business conditions. That is, they all rise when the economy turns down. Declines in income and the negative social effects of slumps have prompted policy-makers to look for ways to keep the economy on a steady path.

3. Many early business cycle theories were *external shock* theories, focusing on sources of instability outside the economic system such as war or weather conditions.

4. *Joseph Schumpeter* developed a business cycle theory around major innovations that may partially explain major long-term business fluctuations. He cited the developments of railroads, automobiles, and similar innovations as generating significant investment leading to tremendous spurts of economic growth.

5. *Psychological theories* of business cycles use people's herd instincts to explain extended optimism or pessimism. These theories may partially account for the cumulative nature of business cycle downturns or recoveries, but provide little insight into the reasons for turning points.

6. *Classical macroeconomics* focuses on the supply side. It relies on market forces to automatically ensure full employment, and views recessions as self-extinguishing without a role for government.

7. The prolonged Great Depression seemed to refute classical theory. The demand-oriented theories of John Maynard Keynes dominated economic thought from 1936 through the 1960s. *Keynesian macroeconomics* concludes that government can adjust Aggregate Demand through its tax and spending policies.

8. *Aggregate Demand* is based on spending by (**a**) consumers, (**b**) investors, (**c**) government, and (**d**) foreigners (i.e., net exports). The *Aggregate Demand curve* is negatively sloped because a higher price level causes reduced spending on our domestic output because of (**a**) the *wealth effect*, (**b**) the *foreign sector substitution effect*, and (**c**) the *interest rate effect*.

9. The single most important determinant of *consumer spending* is disposable income. Other major determinants of consumption and saving include: (**a**) wealth and expectations of future income, (**b**) the average size and age composition of typical households, (**c**) household balance sheets and stocks of consumer goods, and (**d**) consumer expectations regarding prices and availability of products.

10. *Investment* in capital refers to purchases of new output that can be used in the future to produce other goods and services. There are three major components of investment: (**a**) new business and residential structures, (**b**) machinery and equipment, and (**c**) inventory accumulation.

11. The quantity of investment is determined primarily by expected returns from investment which, in turn, depend on (**a**) expectations about the business environment, (**b**) rates of technological change and innovation, (**c**) existing stocks of capital relative to total production, and (**d**) investment costs, which depend most on the interest rate.

12. *Exports* (*X*) add to Aggregate Demand, but reduce Aggregate Supply. (Goods sold to foreigners are not available to Americans.) *Imports* (*M*) boost Aggregate Supply but may reduce Aggregate Demand. (Buyers of imports spend less on American goods.) Exports and imports are reasonably balanced, so *net exports* (*X* - *M*) affect Aggregate Demand relatively little. The foreign sector is, however, vital, because it provides (**a**) markets for our production and (**b**) imported goods that would be more costly if produced only domestically.

13. The *Aggregate Supply curve* is positively sloped because, when business conditions change, firm can adjust prices more rapidly than production costs. Prosperity increases profit per unit, so firms hire more resources and produce more output.

14. Aggregate Supply curves shift in response to changes in (**a**) supplies of resources, (**b**) technology, (**c**) government policies that affect costs, or (**d**) net imports.

15. Increases in Aggregate Demand raise national income and output, the price level, and employment. Expansion of Aggregate Supply pushes prices downwards and facilitates growth of employment and national income and output.

Matching Key Terms And Concepts

Set I

_____ 1. Aggregate Demand curve

_____ 2. business cycles

_____ 3. wealth effect

_____ 4. Joseph Schumpeter

_____ 5. external shock theories

_____ 6. classical economics

_____ 7. Aggregate Supply curve

_____ 8. Keynesian economics

_____ 9. stagflation

_____ 10. increase in Aggregate Supply

a. Cycles are caused by outside disturbances.

b. Can be caused by technological advances.

c. Believes government can counter business cycles by adjusting Aggregate Demand.

d. One reason why the Aggregate Demand curve is negatively sloped.

e. Declines in output precipitate rising prices.

f. Major innovations partly explain long cycles.

g. A positive relationship between goods available economy-wide and the price level.

h. Alternating expansion and contraction.

i. A negative relationship between economy-wide domestic production and the price level.

j. Market forces ensure long-run full employment.

Set II

_____ 1. Aggregate Supply shifts leftward

_____ 2. Aggregate Supply shifts rightward

_____ 3. Aggregate Demand shifts leftward

_____ 4. Aggregate Demand shifts rightward

_____ 5. contraction

_____ 6. foreign sector substitution effect

_____ 7. recovery

_____ 8. trough

_____ 9. "capitalistic crisis"

_____ 10. the Great Depression

a. May be caused by interest rate hikes.

b. Increased preference for leisure by labor.

c. Reductions in monopoly power.

d. May be caused by an increase in planned government purchases.

e. Marxian view that business cycles would become more severe.

f. The low point of a cyclical downturn.

g. Typically follows a peak.

h. Typically follows a trough.

i. Lasted from 1929 until World War II.

j. A reason why Aggregate Demand is negatively sloped.

True/False Questions

_____ 1. During the Great Depression, the U.S. unemployment rate approached 25 percent.

_____ 2. In the U.S. the unemployment rate plummeted from 25 percent in 1929 to only 3.2 percent in 1933.

___ 3. The long wave theory of business cycles gained wide acceptance after several studies proved their existence.

___ 4. Between 1830 and 1894, Karl Marx expounded a long-wave theory of business cycles by suggesting that economic growth and development in capitalistic systems are fueled by innovations.

___ 5. During the Great Depression, the burden of economic assistance fell largely on private charities.

___ 6. The decade of the 1950s in the US was a period of rapidly accelerating economic growth, with double-digit inflation becoming slightly more serious as the years progressed.

___ 7. In the U.S., the middle 1970s witnessed our first serious brush with supply induced double-digit inflation.

___ 8. Classical economics relies heavily on the self-correcting power of automatic market adjustments to cure macroeconomic instability.

___ 9. The Great Depression was responsible for many of the governmental institutions that exist today.

___ 10. Other things constant, if the labor force became better trained and educated, the Aggregate Supply curve would shift to the left.

___ 11. All else equal, if the government were to increase its spending on national defense, the Aggregate Demand curve would shift to the right.

___ 12. Major discoveries of new deposits of raw materials would immediately expand the Aggregate Demand curve.

___ 13. Aggregate Demand curves shift when planned spending changes for consumption, investment, government, or net exports to foreigners.

___ 14. The Aggregate Supply curve reflects a positive relationship between the price level and real national output.

___ 15. Growth of Aggregate Supply is the major cause of unemployment.

Standard Multiple Choice

There Is One Best Answer For Each Question

___ 1. Which of the following is **not** one of the four phases of a business cycle?
   a. peak
   b. inflation
   c. recession
   d. trough
   e. recovery

___ 2. "Sunspot" theories of business cycles:
   a. say that booms commence when business becomes optimistic.
   b. correlate sunspot activity with innovations that spark growth.
   c. are intrinsically psychological.
   d. may be resurrected if solar energy becomes relatively inexpensive.
   e. conform to modern astrology.

___ 3. Joseph Schumpeter's theory of business cycles was:
   a. sunspot theory: that sunspots affect agricultural production.
   b. psychological: herd instincts propel waves of optimism and pessimism.
   c. long-wave innovation theory: the economy expands with significant innovation, reaches saturation, and then moves into a recession until another great innovation.
   d. "long-waves" theory: economic sine waves last 50 to 60 years.
   e. that population adjusts to the resources available, creating swings in supplies and demands.

___ 4. Psychological theories of business cycles can be used to help explain:
   a. the timing of cyclic turning points.
   b. the cumulative nature of economic recoveries or downturns.
   c. why people do not behave as if they possess a "herd instinct."
   d. why pessimism or optimism won't affect economic cycles in any way.
   e. psychoeconomic problems.

___ 5. Prosperous periods tend to engender:
   a. fewer suicides.
   b. more marriages and divorces.
   c. less crime.
   d. fewer illegitimate births.
   e. All of the above.

___ 6. Keynesian theory developed as a response to:
   a. the stagflation of the 1970s.
   b. external business cycle theories.
   c. Say's Law.
   d. extensive and prolonged unemployment in the 1930s.
   e. inflation after World War I.

___ 7. Humans are destined to live at a subsistence level according to:
   a. new classical macroeconomics.
   b. Thomas Malthus.
   c. Keynesian theory.
   d. Marxism.
   e. innovation theory.

___ 8. Which of the following could shift the Aggregate Demand curve rightward?
   a. New resources are discovered.
   b. The supply of labor increases.
   c. Tax rates are reduced.
   d. Household wealth is reduced.
   e. Investors become more pessimistic.

___ 9. Stagflation occurs when Aggregate:
   a. Technology shifts vertically.
   b. Demand shifts right.
   c. Demand shifts left.
   d. Supply shifts right.
   e. Supply shifts left.

___10. The Aggregate Demand curve is negatively sloped because of the:
   a. wealth effect.
   b. interest rate effect.
   c. foreign sector substitution effect.
   d. all of the above.
   e. none of the above.

___11. The foreign sector substitution effect suggests that a drop in the U.S. price level relative tends to increase U.S.:
   a. exports and decrease U.S. imports.
   b. imports and decrease U.S. exports.
   c. Aggregate Supply.
   d. production possibilities.
   e. None of the above.

___12. Increased Aggregate Demand tends to increase all of the following EXCEPT:
   a. national income.
   b. the price level.
   c. unemployment.
   d. national output.
   e. employment.

___13. Which of the following statements about the Great Depression is FALSE:
   a. The unemployment rate rose to a high of nearly 25 percent.
   b. Real disposable income fell sharply.
   c. Average prices fell--the economy actually experienced deflation.
   d. Most economic relief came from public welfare programs.
   e. The depression was global.

___14. Which of the following could increase both real output and the price level?
   a. An external shock that drives up resource costs.
   b. An increase in government purchases of goods and services.
   c. An increase in taxes.
   d. An external shock that reduces resource costs.
   e. Consumer expectations of price deflation.

___15. Pressure for stagflation would be most likely to emerge from increases in:
   a. average income tax refunds.
   b. the money supply.
   c. labor force education and training.
   d. the length of annual vacation leave.
   e. consumer indebtedness.

Chapter Review (Fill-In Questions)

1. Most early theories of business cycles focused on forces that were _____ to the economic system. Sunspot theories and other early theory stressed wars and shocks to _____. Psychological theories of the cycle concentrate on the herd instinct coupled with prolonged periods (or waves) of _____ and _____.

2. According to _____, variations in the magnitudes and timing of _____ and then the process of adjusting to them were the driving forces behind long cycles.

3. _____ predicted the decline and eventual overthrow of capitalism as it moved through extended business expansions and contractions because of ever greater _____ of wealth in the hands of capitalists.

4. The business cycle exhibits a strong relationship with many _____ institutions and maladies. Suicides, crime, and illegitimate births tend to be _____ related to economic activity.

5. Classical economics relies heavily on market forces to _____ move the economy to _____.

6. Persistent high rates of unemployment during the _____ of the 1930's led many to reject classical theory and, instead, accept the macroeconomic theories of _____.

7. Keynesian macroeconomics concludes that government can counter business cycles by adjusting _____ through changes in _____.

8. The idea that a lower price level encourages greater purchasing is shown in a(n) _____ curve, with a(n) _____ curve reflecting the idea that a higher average price level prompts greater production.

9. Depressions and declining prices may emerge if the _____ curve shifts leftward, while a rightward shift of this curve will result in a(n) _____ in both the price level and aggregate output. A leftward shift of the _____ curve causes _____, a recently developed term that refers to periods when the price level climbs but output falls.

Unlimited Multiple Choice

The following questions have from zero to four correct answers.

___ 1. According to Joseph Schumpeter, innovation included the:
   a. introduction of a new good.
   b. introduction of a new technology.
   c. opening of a new market.
   d. reorganization of a major industry.

___ 2. Classical economic theory:
   a. easily explained the persistence of the Great Depression.
   b. viewed full employment in the economy as unattainable.
   c. was not a business cycle theory per se; it was a systematic study of the functioning of a market economy.
   d. relies heavily on unhindered supply and demand to work.

___ 3. External force theories of business cycles:
   a. were psychological in nature.
   b. include the "sunspot" theory.
   c. consider agriculture and war as major sources of instability.
   d. view humans as herd animals.

___ 4. Aggregate Supply will increase if:
   a. technological advances increase productivity.
   b. strong union pressures increase average wage rates.
   c. the labor force increases in size.
   d. consumer spending increases.

___ 5. During the prosperous 1960s:
   a. tax cuts were effective in stimulating the U.S. economy.
   b. a trade-off between unemployment and inflation seemed to exist.
   c. the country suffered double-digit inflation rates.
   d. the expansionary effects of the Vietnam War helped push the U.S. economy to full employment.

Problem 1

This figure depicts the original Aggregate Supply (AS_0) and Demand (AD_0) curves, with output Q_e representing full employment. Answer the following True/False questions.

____ a. The original equilibrium would be at a real output level equal to Q_e with a price level of P_e (point a).

____ b. All else equal, if federal spending increased, Aggregate Demand could increase from AD_0 to AD_1.

____ c. All else equal, if business mergers reduced competition then Aggregate Supply could shift from AS_0 to AS_1.

____ d. Stagflation occurs when the economy moves from point a to point b.

____ e. The shift of Aggregate Demand from AD_0 to AD_1 could be caused by an increase in planned investment.

____ f. If Aggregate Demand were to decrease from AD_1 to AD_0 while Aggregate Supply remained constant at AS_0, a recession would occur bringing deflation and less real output.

____ g. A shift in Aggregate Supply from AS_1 to AS_0 could be caused by an increase in the capital gains tax.

____ h. Policies to reduce monopolistic practices could shift Aggregate Demand from AD_0 to AD_1.

____ i. A movement from a to b could represent a situation where external supply shocks induce an inflationary recession.

Problem 2

In the following scenarios use up arrows ($\uparrow$), down arrows ($\downarrow$), zeros (0), or question marks (?) to indicate how Aggregate Demand (AD), Aggregate Supply (AS), national income and output (NI), total employment (TE), employment rates (ER), and the price level (PL) will be affected. (Note: Both Aggregate Demand and Aggregate Supply may be affected in some instances, and long run consequences may differ from short run effects.)

a.   Twenty years after a new baby boom, millions of young workers begin to establish families and enter the work force.

AD _____ AS _____ NI _____ TE _____ ER _____ PL _____

b. A nuclear power meltdown kills hundreds of thousands, and all nuclear plants are shut down while the accident is investigated.

AD _____ AS _____ NI _____ TE _____ ER _____ PL _____

c. Investors pessimistically begin to expect lower rates of return because their consultants predict a recession.

AD _____ AS _____ NI _____ TE _____ ER _____ PL _____

d. People become increasingly conscientious about recycling glass, paper, plastic, aluminum, and other scrap metals.

AD _____ AS _____ NI _____ TE _____ ER _____ PL _____

e. Italian investors establish American plants to build Fiats, jewelry, and fine furniture.

AD _____ AS _____ NI _____ TE _____ ER _____ PL _____

f. Record harvests worldwide reduce international demands for U.S. agricultural products.

AD _____ AS _____ NI _____ TE _____ ER _____ PL _____

g. Widespread deregulation eliminates 7,000 pages of inefficient federal regulations.

AD _____ AS _____ NI _____ TE _____ ER _____ PL _____

h. A constitutional amendment is adopted requiring the federal budget to balance; income tax rates are increased, and government spending falls by $200 billion.

AD _____ AS _____ NI _____ TE _____ ER _____ PL _____

Problem 3

In the following scenarios use up arrows ($\uparrow$) or down arrows ($\downarrow$) to determine what will happen to the rates of return (RR) expected by investors, levels of investment (I), and Aggregate Demand (AD).

a. Interest rates for loanable funds fall to their lowest level in 30 years.

RR _____ I _____ AD _____

b. A proposal to slash tax rates on "capital gains" from investments is finally enacted.

RR _____ I _____ AD _____

c. Stock markets crash in Tokyo, Hong Kong, London, Australia, and New York when a Martian fleet of starships signals its intention to invade Earth.

RR _____ I _____ AD _____

ANSWERS

<table>
<tr><td colspan="2">Matching</td><td colspan="2">True/False</td><td colspan="2">Multiple Choice</td><td colspan="2">Unlimited Multiple Choice</td></tr>
<tr><td>Set I</td><td>Set II</td><td></td><td></td><td></td><td></td><td></td><td></td></tr>
<tr><td>1. i</td><td>1. b</td><td>1. T</td><td>9. T</td><td>1. b</td><td>9. e</td><td>1. abcd</td><td></td></tr>
<tr><td>2. h</td><td>2. c</td><td>2. F</td><td>10. F</td><td>2. d</td><td>10. d</td><td>2. cd</td><td></td></tr>
<tr><td>3. d</td><td>3. a</td><td>3. F</td><td>11. T</td><td>3. c</td><td>11. a</td><td>3. bc</td><td></td></tr>
<tr><td>4. f</td><td>4. d</td><td>4. F</td><td>12. F</td><td>4. b</td><td>12. c</td><td>4. ac</td><td></td></tr>
<tr><td>5. a</td><td>5. g</td><td>5. T</td><td>13. T</td><td>5. e</td><td>13. d</td><td>5. abd</td><td></td></tr>
<tr><td>6. j</td><td>6. j</td><td>6. F</td><td>14. T</td><td>6. d</td><td>14. b</td><td></td><td></td></tr>
<tr><td>7. g</td><td>7. h</td><td>7. T</td><td>15. F</td><td>7. b</td><td>15. d</td><td></td><td></td></tr>
<tr><td>8. c</td><td>8. f</td><td>8. T</td><td></td><td>8. c</td><td></td><td></td><td></td></tr>
<tr><td>9. e</td><td>9. e</td><td></td><td></td><td></td><td></td><td></td><td></td></tr>
<tr><td>10. b</td><td>10. i</td><td></td><td></td><td></td><td></td><td></td><td></td></tr>
</table>

Chapter Review (Fill-In Questions)

1. external; agriculture; optimism; pessimism
2. Schumpeter; innovations
3. Karl Marx; concentration
4. social; inversely or negatively
5. automatically; full employment
6. Great Depression; John Maynard Keynes
7. Aggregate Demand; government purchases
8. Aggregate Demand; Aggregate Supply
9. Aggregate Demand, rise; Aggregate Supply; stagflation

Problem 1

a. T
b. T
c. T
d. T
e. T
f. T
g. F
h. F
i. T

Problem 2

a. AD ↑, AS ↑, NI ↑, TE ↑, ER ?, PL ?
b. AD ↓, AS ↓, NI ↓, TE ↓, ER ?, PL ?
c. AD ↓, AS ↓, NI ↓, TE ↓, ER ↓, PL ?
d. AD 0, AS ↑, NI ↑, TE ↑, ER ↑, PL ↓
e. AD ↑, AS ↑, NI ↑, TE ↑, ER ↑, PL ?
f. AD ↓, AS 0, NI ↓, TE ↓, ER ↓, PL ↓
g. AD 0, AS ↑, NI ↑, TE ↑, ER ↑, PL ↓
h. AD ↓, AS ↓, NI ↓, TE ↓, ER ↓, PL ?

Problem 3

a. RR ↑, I ↑, AD ↑
b. RR ↑, I ↑, AD ↑
c. RR ↓, I ↓, AD ↓

Chapter 6
Employment and Unemployment

Chapter Objectives

After you have studied this chapter you should be able to explain how unemployment is measured, identify and give reasons for the differing types of unemployment, and enumerate the costs and benefits of unemployment.

Chapter Review: Key Points

1. *Voluntary unemployment* occurs when people could find work quickly, but choose to look for what they view as better jobs in terms of pay or working conditions. *Involuntary unemployment* occurs when people lack jobs, but are willing and able to work at wages commensurate with their skills.

2. *Wage stickiness* describes needed downward adjustments of wages that occur only slowly, and tends to prolong periods of unemployment. Wages tend to be "sticky" because of minimum wage laws, union contracts, and the personnel policies firms use in attempts to reduce turnover in jobs regarded as career positions by employers.

3. The *labor force* consists of all employed or unemployed civilians plus military personnel. A *labor force participation rate* is the proportion in the labor force from a specific group.

4. Part-time workers who would like to work full time are officially categorized as employed, but they also experience *part-time unemployment*. Unemployed people who are so discouraged about job prospects that they do not look for work are not counted in unemployment statistics. Some people who are not truly out of work indicate that they are to collect unemployment compensation. Thus, data for unemployment may either understate the true unemployment rate because of *discouraged workers* or overstate it because of *dishonest nonworkers*.

5. *Frictional unemployment* arises because of transaction costs associated with normal entry and exit from labor markets, layoffs or firings, or voluntary job changes. Both workers and firms "invest in information" by *searching* for jobs or screening applicants until their expected marginal benefits no longer exceed their expected marginal costs.

6. *Seasonal unemployment* arises from the annually recurring influences of weather, vacations, and the like on labor markets.

7. *Structural unemployment* results from mismatches between workers and jobs because of changes in the skill requirements of job openings or individuals lack marketable skills.

8. *Cyclicol unemployment* results from recessions.

9. Government policies that reduce work incentives or that prevent workers from securing employment (e.g., minimum wage laws) cause *induced unemployment*.

10. Unemployment causes both *economic* and *social costs.* Society as a whole suffers because of lost income and output that unemployed individuals could have produced. Individuals and their families suffer socially and psychologically when they are unemployed for long periods. Personal losses are, however, partially cushioned by such programs as unemployment compensation.

11 Unemployment is not distributed equally across all groups. Workers in manufacturing and construction are hit harder by cyclical unemployment during recessions than employees in most other lines of work, but this tendency seems to be weakening, with cyclically rising rates of unemployment among service workers and professional and technical personnel and mid level managers.

Matching Key Terms And Concepts

____ 1. cyclical unemployment

____ 2. contingency work force

____ 3. structural unemployment

____ 4. lost income costs of unemployment

____ 5. seasonal unemployment

____ 6. discouraged workers

____ 7. wage stickiness

____ 8. involuntary unemployment

____ 9. frictional unemployment

____10. induced unemployment

a. Caused by transaction costs in labor markets.
b. Typesetter replaced by computer programs.
c. Persons who want to work but have given up.
d. Annual experience of many life guards and golf pros.
e. Caused by slumps in the economy.
f. Wages are slow to adjust downward.
g. Include the opportunity costs of the output and income unemployed individuals could have produced.
h. Mostly brought about by government policies.
i. Consists of part-timers, temps, and the self-employed.
j. Persons willing to work at wages commensurate with their skills, but unable to find jobs.

True/False

____ 1. Seasonal unemployment is that unemployment associated with the business cycle.

____ 2. Globalization, the decline of manufacturing, and government policies have all contributed to the dramatic change in the demand for labor over the past few decades

____ 3. Reducing frictional unemployment is a major goal of government policymakers.

____ 4. Discouraged workers tend to overstate the unemployment rate.

____ 5. Unemployment is costly, individually and socially, and yields no benefits.

____ 6. Structural unemployment can occur if individuals have very little education.

____ 7. Cyclical unemployment tends to result in longer periods of unemployment.

____ 8 Government retraining programs are primarily targeted at people whose job losses have been induced.

____ 9. Reduced transactions costs in the labor market would also reduce frictional unemployment.

____10. Total labor force participation rates have grown over time primarily because women increasingly choose to pursue careers.

Standard Multiple Choice

There Is One Best Answer For Each Question.

___ 1. Unemployment statistics will be understated because of:
  a. welfare cheaters.
  b. unemployed college dropouts.
  c. discouraged workers.
  d. housewives.
  e. cyclical layoffs.

___ 2. Official unemployment data are based on surveys of:
  a. all firms in the country.
  b. all households in the country.
  c. all workers in the country.
  d. a sample of all U.S. households.

___ 3. People who do not work for pay because of physical disability are defined by the BLS as:
  a. in the labor force.
  b. unemployed.
  c. discouraged.
  d. not in the labor force.

___ 4. Macroeconomic policy makers are most concerned with reducing:
  a. frictional unemployment.
  b. cyclical unemployment.
  c. structural unemployment.
  d. voluntary unemployment.
  e. union strikes in key industries,

___ 5. Allocative benefits of unemployment do NOT include improvements in:
  a. the economy's overall efficiency.
  b. matches between workers and jobs.
  c. total returns from investment in labor market information.
  d. job satisfaction among workers who don't look for better jobs.

___ 6. The social and psychic costs of unemployment include the:
  a. declines in the self esteem of unemployed breadwinners.
  b. value of loot from more frequent bank robberies.
  c. transaction costs incurred by job seekers.
  d. output not produced because of inefficiency.
  e. menu and distortion costs.

___ 7. Periods of high U.S. unemployment since the 1930s have been usually been characterized by substantial:
  a. voluntary poverty for virtually all seasonally unemployed workers.
  b. induced unemployment--welfare now pays them more income than most jobless workers could earn.
  c. cyclical unemployment.
  d. structural unemployment caused by wartime dislocations
  e. seasonal unemployment.

___ 8. Defining full employment as occurring when the numbers of job vacancies and the numbers of unemployed are equal implies that, at full employment, people who want work but who lack jobs would be experiencing:
  a. cyclical unemployment.
  b. structural and frictional unemployment.
  c. involuntary unemployment.
  d. motivational underemployment.
  e. induced unemployment.

9. Induced unemployment as a concept is least relevant for a:
   a. machinist laid off by automation.
   b. person drawing unemployment compensation to help pay the costs of looking for a perfect job.
   c. teenager who could provide work worth $3.00 per hour, but not enough to cover the minimum wage of $3.35 per hour.
   d. welfare recipient who would lose all benefits by accepting a minimum wage job.

10. Discouraged workers are those who are:
    a. disenchanted with their jobs.
    b. employed in jobs that underutilize their skills.
    c. unhappy because search hasn't generated an acceptable job.
    d. so pessimistic about job prospects that they quit looking for work.

11. An ex-convict who landed a job as a college president by fraudulently claiming a Ph.D. in Marketing is officially classified by the BLS as:
    a. employed.
    b. unemployed.
    c. unreliable.
    d. overemployed.

12. Structural unemployment would apply LEAST to an individual who was a:
    a. convicted murderer with a life sentence and no chance of parole.
    b. thin department store Santa Claus in February.
    c. deposed dictator willing to retake his old job at his old income.
    d. former all-Pro guard banned from the NFL because of drug addiction.

13. Unemployed slide rule mechanics, typesetters displaced by automation, or ex-convicts whose only legal skills are making license plates, exemplify:
    a. structural unemployment.
    b. seasonal unemployment.
    c. cyclical unemployment.
    d. frictional unemployment.
    e. institutional unemployment.

14. On average, the duration of unemployment tends to be longer:
    a. during cyclical downturns.
    b. for white collar workers than in earlier eras, especially since the advent of corporate down-sizing.
    c. for people deemed over-qualified.
    d. as more generous unemployment compensation is offered.
    e. All of the above.

15. The best example of induced unemployment is given by:
    a. migrant workers in the winter time.
    b. workers who lose their jobs during a recession.
    c. laws that prohibit teenagers under 16 from working full time.
    d. workers who quit their jobs.
    e. companies that demand workers have a college education.

16. Jennifer is looking for full time work, but ignores the help wanted sign in a fast food restaurant, because she will not do this type of work. Jennifer would be considered as:
    a. involuntarily unemployed.
    b. cyclically unemployed.
    c. structurally unemployed.
    d. voluntarily unemployed.
    e. seasonally unemployed.

____17. Employees may quickly adjust to wage hikes, but are loath to take pay cuts, leading to a concept known as:
   a. voluntary unemployment.
   b. wage stickiness.
   c. cyclical unemployment.
   d. involuntary unemployment.
   e. induced unemployment.

____18. Allocative benefits from unemployment occur primarily because:
   a. slackers are easily shed.
   b. wages fall relative to capital costs.
   c. of worker retraining programs.
   d. of unemployment insurance.
   e. transaction costs are reduced for workers and firms.

____19. A split minimum wage, in which teenage trainees could be paid less than the prevailing minimum wage, would most likely:
   a. reduce induced unemployment.
   b. fuel cyclical unemployment.
   c. decrease structural unemployment.
   d. increase seasonal unemployment.
   e. reduce frictional unemployment.

____20. As long as transaction costs are positive:
   a. cyclical employment will persist.
   b. structural employment will rise.
   c. seasonal unemployment declines.
   d. frictional unemployment will exist.
   e. induced employment will be zero.

Chapter Review (Fill-In Questions)

1. The _____ consists of all employed and unemployed civilians over age 16 plus member of the military. The _____ is the percentage of the population that is in the labor force.

2. People who could find work quickly, but who choose to search for better jobs, are considered _____ unemployed. However, people are considered _____ unemployed if they are unable to find work at wages commensurate with their skills.

3. _____ unemployment occurs because matching workers with jobs absorbs time and is costly. _____ unemployment results from downturns in the business cycle.

4. Unemployment statistics as reported may understate true unemployment due to the failure to include _____, and may overstate the true level because of _____.

5. When skill requirements for a given occupation change or people have no marketable skills, _____ unemployment results. _____ unemployment occurs because some types of work are dependent upon weather or the time of the year.

6. Unemployment results in _____ as well as _____ costs such as foregone education, increased family debt, and higher crime and suicide rates.

Unlimited Multiple Choice

There Are From Zero To Four Correct Answers For Each Question.

___ 1. Frictional unemployment:
   a. could be eliminated by appropriate government programs.
   b. is a result of normal economic activity.
   c. usually results from serious structural change in the economy.
   d. arises due to transaction costs in labor markets.

___ 2. Cyclical unemployment:
   a. tends to increase the duration of unemployment.
   b. moves in tandem with business cycle.
   c. could be reduced if minimum wage legislation was repealed.
   d. historically affected construction workers more than professionals.

___ 3. Persons are classified as:
   a. unemployed if they are not employed but are available for work and made recent attempts to find jobs.
   b. unemployed if during the survey week they were waiting to report to a new job in three months.
   c. unemployed if during the survey week they were waiting to be recalled to a job from which they were laid off.
   d. part of the labor force if they were employed during the survey week.

___ 4. Structural unemployment:
   a. is of little concern to government policymakers.
   b. affects persons with antiquated skills.
   c. can be combated with job training programs.
   d. affects primarily overeducated people.

___ 5. Federal laws to punish firms that hire illegal immigrants might help reduce:
   a. induced unemployment.
   b. cyclical unemployment.
   c. seasonal unemployment.
   d. frictional unemployment.

Problems

Problem 1

In 1993, the U.S. population was 256,394,000, of whom 192,690,000 were age 16 or over. The labor force including the Armed Forces was 132,724,000, the civilian labor force was 131,387,000, and civilian employment was 123,414,000.

a. The employment/population ratio is? _____

b. The labor force participation rate for ages 16 and over is? _____

c. The total unemployment rate (including the military) is? _____

d. The civilian unemployment rate is? _____

e. Why is the total unemployment rate lower than that for civilians? _____

Problem 2

In the following scenarios, determine if the individual would be considered employed, unemployed, or not part of the labor force by the Bureau of Labor Statistics.

a. A Ph.D. in anthropology who works full-time as a cab driver while devoting three hours daily to searching for a job as a researcher or an assistant professor. _____

b. After quitting work as a cab driver, the anthropologist remodels her home six days a week, devoting only Monday mornings to looking for work as an anthropologist. _____

c. An eighth-grader who temporarily loses her job delivering papers when the printer's union at the local newspaper goes on strike.

d. A chef who chops off two fingers the day before his restaurant closes forever, draws disability pay while vacationing before looking for another job.

e. A novelist who has not written a page in months because he is unable to think of a good plot.

f. A construction worker who has free time for three weeks until the next big job starts.

Problem 3

This table illustrates population and employment data for the hypothetical country of Paradisio.

	July 1994	December 1994
Non-institutional Population	2,000,000	2,100,000
Labor Force	1,000,000	
Employed	920,000	900,000
Unemployed		50,000
Employment Rate		
Unemployment Rate		
Labor Force Participation Rate		

a.   For simplicity, assume that Paradisio has no military personnel. Complete the table.

b.   What are likely causes of the population increase? _____

c.   What has happened to the number employed? _____; and the employment
     rate?_____ Does this result seem perverse? _____ Why or why not?
     _____

d.   Why do you think the labor force declined over this period? _____ This
     type of "unemployment" is usually called _____

e.   Are discouraged workers counted in any of these statistics? _____ Which one(s)?
     _____

Answers

Matching	True/False	Multiple Choice		Unlimited	Chapter Review (Fill-in Questions)
1. e	1. F	1. c	11. a	1. bd	1. labor force;
2. i	2. T	2. d	12. a	2. abd	labor force participation rate
3. b	3. F	3. d	13. a	3. abcd	2. voluntary; involuntary
4. g	4. F	4. b	14. e	4. bc	3. Frictional; Cyclical
5. d	5. F	5. d	15. c	5. none	4. discouraged workers;
6. c	6. T	6. a	16. d		dishonest nonworkers
7. f	7. T	7. c	17. b		5. structural; seasonal
8. j	8. F	8. b	18. e		6. lost income; social
9. a	9. T	9. a	19. a		
10. h	10. T	10. d	20. d		

Problem 1

a. Total employment civilian plus armed forces (=124,751) divided by population (256,394,000) = 48.7%.

b. 68.9% (132,924,000/192,690)

c. Employment rate equals 94.0% (124,751,000/132,724,00), so the unemployment rate equals 6.0% (100% - 94.0%)

d. 6.1% (100% - 123,414,000/131,387,000)

e. 100% of military personnel are considered employed, so their inclusion must decrease the total unemployment rate.

Problem 2

a. employed

b. unemployed

c. not in labor force

d. not in labor force

e. employed

f. unemployed

Problem 3

a. See table.

b. Immigration, and the birth rate exceeds the mortality rate.

c. Employment has fallen. The employment rate has risen. No, because the labor force has declined substantially over this period.

	JULY 1994	DECEMBER 1994
Non-institutional Population	2,000,000	2,100,000
Labor Force	1,000,000	950,000
Employed	920,000	900,000
Unemployed	80,000	50,000
Employment Rate	92%	94.7%
Unemployment Rate	8%	5.3%
Labor Force Participation Rate	.50	.45

d. The July figures include high school students no longer in the labor force in December. The term seasonal unemployment is usually used to describe such situations.

e. Discouraged workers are included in population and, therefore, the labor force participation rate.

Chapter 7
Inflation

Chapter Objectives

After you have studied this chapter you should be able to explain how inflation is measured and how index numbers are constructed and used; be able to distinguish between different types of inflation as well as their causes, and enumerate the benefits and costs associated with inflation.

Chapter Review: Key Points

1. *Index numbers* are used to compare particular variables over time. The *Consumer Price Index (CPI)* measures average price changes for a given bundle of consumer goods over time. The *CPI* is based on typical consumer patterns for most of the urban population.

2. The *CPI* is used to convert nominal values to real values. It is also used extensively as an escalator clause (cost-of-living adjustment) in many contracts.

3. *Deflating* nominal variables means dividing their monetary values by (1 percent of) a price index.

4. Major difficulties in computing the *CPI* include problems inherent in adjusting the index for: (*a*) new products; (*b*) changes in the qualities of existing products; (*c*) changes in the composition of consumer expenditures; and, (*d*) already owned consumer durables such as housing.

5. The *Producer Price Index (PPI)* measures changes in the prices of goods in other than retail markets. The *GDP Deflator* adjusts GDP for changes in prices. It is composed of relevant portions of the *CPI* and the *PPI,* plus some additional prices covered by neither.

6. *Creeping inflation* occurs relatively slowly; *galloping inflation* occurs when average prices move at double-digit rates. *Hyperinflation* entails average price hikes exceeding 50 percent monthly. Inflation is generally less harmful if it is anticipated than if it is a surprise to people.

7. Inflation increases *transaction costs* by making price information obsolete faster, and it causes resources that could be used productively elsewhere to be used for repricing. These are the *menu costs* of inflation.

8. Inflation also distorts relative prices and economic decision making, and depresses incentives to save. Capital accumulation may or may not be hampered by inflation, depending on business expectations and the availability of funds for investment. These are the *distortion costs* of inflation.

9. The *discomfort (misery) index* is the sum of the inflation rate and the unemployment rate. It averaged 6-7 percent during the 1950s and 1960s. During the late 1970s and early 1980s, the index ranged from 13 to more than 20 percent. By 1990, economic growth had pushed the index below 10 percent.

10. There are *social costs of inflation* because people feel greater uncertainty during inflationary periods. People living on fixed incomes are hurt by inflation, but many transfer payments and wage contracts now have escalator clauses that adjust payments for price level changes. Borrowers tend to gain from unexpected inflation, while the ultimate lenders (e.g., savers with bank deposits) lose. When inflation boosts income, meeting a fixed mortgage payment becomes easier, so heavily mortgaged homeowners tend to gain.

Matching Key Terms And Concepts

Set I

____ 1. "deflating" nominal values

____ 2. demand-pull inflation

____ 3. discomfort (misery) index

____ 4. inflation

____ 5. real values

____ 6. cost-push inflation.

____ 7. hyperinflation

____ 8. menu costs of inflation.

____ 9. composition-shift inflation

____10. creeping inflation

a. Cost of upward revisions of price schedules.

b. Rising demand in one sector causes price hikes; falling demand in another causes layoffs.

c. An upward movement in general prices.

d. Adjusting for price level changes by dividing monetary variables by (1% of) a price index.

e. Occurs, e.g., if costly resources are increasingly wasted and misused by incompetent managers.

f. Low levels of persistent price hikes.

g. The sum of the rates of inflation and unemployment.

h. Variables measured by money but adjusted for price level changes.

i. Arises, e.g., if the money supply grows too rapidly.

j. Experienced in Germany after World War I.

Set II

___ 1.	deflation	**a.**	Measures changes in wholesale prices.
___ 2.	supply side inflation	**b.**	Wage hikes are used as an excuse to raise prices by huge firms.
___ 3.	administered price inflation	**c.**	It is common for people to hedge when guarding against this type of inflation.
___ 4.	expectational inflation	**d.**	Double-digit annual rates of inflation.
___ 5.	galloping inflation	**e.**	A decline in the general price level.
___ 6.	anticipated inflation	**f.**	Measures average prices by comparing the costs of consumer market baskets over time.
___ 7.	Consumer Price Index (CPI)	**g.**	Speeded by peoples' concerns and beliefs about future inflation.
___ 8.	distortion costs of inflation	**h.**	Current dollar values of economic variables.
___ 9.	Producers Price Index (PPI)	**i.**	Caused by a leftward shift of the Aggregate Supply curve.
___ 10.	nominal values	**j.**	Arise, in part, because inflated prices rise at different rates.

True/False

___ 1. The value of an index for the base period is normally 100.

___ 2. Consumer buying patterns seldom if ever change.

___ 3. Incomes or other money payments received by over 80 percent of our population are directly tied to the CPI.

___ 4. Direct measurement of the value that consumers ascribe to quality changes in consumer goods is relatively easy.

___ 5. The CPI undoubtedly understates hikes in the level of industrial prices.

___ 6. Inflation roughly represents a zero sum game in terms of distribution.

___ 7. The income redistribution effects of inflation invariably reduce the real level of national production.

___ 8. In the short run, the Consumer Price Index (CPI) assumes fixed consumption patterns.

___ 9. When prices are rising consistently, but at relatively low rates, we must be suffering "demand-pull" inflation.

___ 10. Uncontrolled growth of Aggregate Supply is a major cause of stagflation.

___ 11. The only country to suffer any significant hyperinflation in the twentieth century was Germany during World War II.

___12. Powerful unions that are able to increase the wages of their members are undoubtedly the principal reason for the inflation we face today.

___13. Widespread expectations of inflation generate inflationary pressures.

___14. When items on the shelf must be repriced due to inflation, the economy actually gains since workers are needed to accomplish these changes.

___15. Aggregate Supply and Demand curves operate quite differently from market demand and supply for individual goods.

Standard Multiple Choice

There Is One Best Answer For Each Question.

___ 1. In the short run, rapid growth of Aggregate Demand relative to Aggregate Supply is LEAST likely to yield:
   a. deflationary growth.
   b. growth of aggregate output.
   c. inflation of the price level.
   d. declines in unemployment rates.
   e. widespread shortages if there are economy-wide price ceilings.

___ 2. If Aggregate Supply shrinks relative to Aggregate Demand, a likely result is:
   a. stagflation, with simultaneous inflation and rising unemployment.
   b. a deep depression, like that suffered during the 1930s.
   c. deflationary growth, with income rising and the price level falling.
   d. accelerating inflation of the sort suffered in post-WWI Germany.
   e. creeping inflation accompanied by moderate real growth, like the U.S. experience of the 1950s and 1960s.

___ 3. Real income:
   a. always increases along with inflation.
   b. is the same as nominal income.
   c. is current monetary income divided by CPI/100.
   d. remains the same regardless of inflation.
   e. always rises when deflation occurs.

___ 4. The real costs of inflation do NOT include:
   a. lost income when a recession raises unemployment.
   b. the values of resources used in repricing goods.
   c. declines in capital accumulation caused by inflation.
   d. distortions due to uneven price increases.
   e. lost production because of mistakes emerging from inflation-caused confusion about what prices mean.

___ 5. The producer price index (PPI):
a. currently includes over 50,000 retail products.
b. is a general purpose index, measuring changes in prices in markets other than retail.
c. does not distinguish list from transaction prices.
d. will be less than 100 because markups are ignored.
e. is synonymous with the GDP deflator.

___ 6. Business firms may mark up their prices to compensate for increased risks they perceive from inflation. This is primarily an example of:
a. menu costs.
b. escalator costs.
c. frictional costs.
d. distortions costs.
e. capitalist exploitation of misfortune.

___ 7. When the supply of money expands too rapidly relative to the growth of the supplies of goods, or when we are close to full employment and the government spends far more than its tax revenues, the likely result is:
a. cost-push inflation.
b. administered-price inflation.
c. composition-shift inflation.
d. expectational inflation.
e. demand pull inflation.

___ 8. Which country experienced the most rapid hyperinflation?
a. China (1940-1950).
b. Brazil (1950-1970).
c. Germany (1919-1923).
d. United States (1929-1933).
e. Hungary (1945-1946).

___ 9. The Consumer Price Index (CPI) is used:
a. to convert real values to long-term nominal values.
b. as an escalator in many contracts calling for future payments.
c. to indicate the strength of policies to dampen seasonal unemployment.
d. to directly measure of real growth.
e. to ascertain consumer savings from using coupons at discount stores.

___10. The most persistent period of rapid inflation in the United States occurred:
a. in the Great Depression (1929-39).
b. after the Civil War (1865-1895).
c. during World War II (1940-1946).
d. during the Korean and Vietnam War eras (1950-1968).
e. from the late 1960s into the early 1980s.

___11. The Consumer Price Index (CPI) is most likely to overstate the inflation most consumers experience if the:
a. quality of goods changes little.
b. real values are used instead of nominal values.
c. market basket used to determine the CPI is seldom updated.
d. economy is at full employment.
e. money supply grows at a fixed rate.

___12. The major reason why comparing nominal incomes at different time periods can be meaningless is:
a. varying unemployment rates.
b. price level changes.
c. population growth.
d. technological stagnation.
e. hyperactivity.

Chapter Review (Fill-In Questions)

1. Inflation is defined as an increase in the _____ level of money prices. The average level of prices is measured using a(n) _____.

2. The _____ (CPI) measures the changes in purchasing power by comparing the cost of a sample _____ today with its cost at an earlier date.

3. If inflation is at a relatively low rate, the economy is said to be suffering from _____ inflation. However, when inflation exceeds roughly 50 percent monthly, inflation is defined as _____.

4. The discomfort index is a combination of the rates of _____ and _____.

5. When Aggregate Demand grows relatively faster than Aggregate Supply, the economy experiences _____ inflation, while if Aggregate Supply shrinks, the economy experiences _____ inflation.

6. Powerful unions that ask for excessive wage hikes are the culprit of inflation according to the _____ theory of inflation. Diametrically opposed to this theory is the notion that huge firms are the true instigators of what is known as _____ inflation.

Unlimited Multiple Choice

There Are From Zero To Four Correct Answers For Each Question.

___ 1. The major conceptual and statistical problems with the CPI occur because:
  a. the CPI is constructed primarily to adjust Social Security payments and fails to measure changes in the cost of living for other groups.
  b. such things as alcohol consumption and rock concerts are routinely excluded from all price indexes.
  c. the value and prices for personal services cannot be estimated.
  d. criminal activity is missing from the market basket of goods and services.

___ 2. Society may gain from inflation if:
  a. firms invest more today, viewing rising prices as a signal that more profits can be made and that future capital acquisitions will cost more.
  b. needed changes in relative prices occur more easily during inflation.
  c. needed expansion of government is easier because tax revenues rise at a faster rate because the personal income tax are progressive.
  d. the discomfort index for the economy grows as the inflation rate increases.

___ 3. Moderate rates of inflation:
   a. impose no real costs on society.
   b. are irrelevant to policymakers.
   c. can distort relative prices.
   d. imply that average prices rise.

___ 4. Aggregate Demand and Aggregate
   Supply are both major influences on:
   a. cost-push inflation.
   b. compositional-shift inflation.
   c. expectational inflation.
   d. administered-price inflation.

___ 5. When an economy is experiencing
   hyperinflation:
   a. people have an incentive to spend
      their money as quickly as possible.
   b. uncertainty stymies investment.
   c. barter for goods and services
      becomes more common.
   d. people have more incentive to save

Problems

Problem 1

Use the numbers in this table for nominal GDP and the GDP implicit price deflator to answer the
following questions.

a. Compute real GDP in 1982 prices and
   complete the table above.

b. What was the percentage increase in real
   GDP from 1929 to 1989? _____.

c. What has been the percentage increase in
   nominal GDP from 1929 to 1989? _____

d. What accounts for the difference between
   (b) and (c)? _____

e. Compute the percentage increase in real
   GDP for the following decades:

Year	Nominal GDP (Billions)	GDP Implicit Price Deflator (1982=100)	Real GDP
1929	103.9	14.6	_____
1933	56.0	11.2	_____
1939	91.3	12.7	_____
1949	260.4	23.5	_____
1959	495.8	30.4	_____
1969	963.9	39.8	_____
1979	2,508.2	78.6	_____
1989	5,200.8	126.3	_____

1940s _____   1950s _____   1960s _____

1970s _____   1980s _____

Problem 2

These current-dollar data cover the same bundle of consumer goods over a ten year period.

a. Compute the price index for each year, assuming that year 6 represents the base year.

b. Assume that during year 8 the industry producing one of the commodities in the market basket experienced a technological revolution, greatly enhancing product quality. If the price index was adjusted for this change in quality, what would happen to the values in the table? _____

_____

Year	Dollar Value Of Bundle	Price Index
1	20	_____
2	22	_____
3	25	_____
4	30	_____
5	40	_____
6	50	_____
7	70	_____
8	80	_____
9	90	_____
10	110	_____

Problem 3

Complete this table of hypothetical data for a specific wage earner over the period 1967-1990.

Year	CPI (1983=100)	Nominal Income (current dollars)	Real Income (1983 dollars)
1967	30	20,000	_____
1974	50	_____	56,000
1980	___	40,000	60,606
1983	100	42,000	_____
1990	130	45,000	_____

Problem 4 Use these shifts of AD and AS curves to answer the following true/false questions.

___ a. A shift from AD_1 to AD_0 would cause recession and deflationary pressure on prices.

___ b. "Supply-siders" would recommend policies that shift Aggregate Supply from AS_1 to AS_0.

___ c. Unemployment is likely to increase if Aggregate Demand moves from AD_0 to AD_1.

___ d. Stagflation is consistent with a movement from AS_1 to AS_0.

___ e. Deflationary growth is likely if the economy's equilibrium moves from w to z.

Graph with "Price Level" on the vertical axis and "National Output and Income" on the horizontal axis, showing curves AS_0, AS_1, AD_0, AD_1 and points x, y, w, z.

___ f. Employment and inflation will both increase if the economy moves from point z to x.

___ g. Real output is likely to be comparatively unaffected, but prices will soar if Aggregate Supply moves from AS_0 to AS_1 while Aggregate Demand goes from AD_0 to AD_1.

___ h. Substantial economic growth will occur with little inflation or deflation if Aggregate Demand moves from AD_0 to AD_1 while Aggregate Supply moves from AS_0 to AS_1.

___ i. A growing production possibilities frontier is paralleled by an upward movement of Aggregate Supply from AS_1 to AS_0.

___ j. The Great Depression followed a path like y→ x→ w.

Problem 5

Draw an Aggregate Demand curve and an Aggregate Supply curve, and label them, respectively, AD_0 and AS_0. Now show how demand pull inflation can occur by labeling a new Aggregate Demand curve AD_1. Label the new intersection I. Finally, using the new Aggregate Demand curve AD_1, illustrate stagflation. Label the new Aggregate Supply curve AS_1, and the new intersection S.

Price Level

0   National Output and Income

Problem 6

This table lists aggregate personal income in billions of current (nominal) dollars for selected years since 1929 and the CPI for the same years.

a. Convert the CPI to a base year of 1990 = 100 and fill in the table.

b. By what percentage did prices fall between 1929 and 1933? _____

c. If between 1990 and 1991, nominal personal income grew 6 percent and the inflation rate was 4 percent, what was the percentage growth of real personal income? _____ By how much did real personal income grow? _____

Year	Personal Income $B (Current Dollars)	CPI 1982-84 = 100	CPI 1990 = 100
1929	84.3	15.5	_____
1933	46.3	11.6	_____
1960	409.4	29.6	_____
1970	831.8	38.8	_____
1980	2258.5	82.4	_____
1983	3290.0	100.0	_____
1990	4645.6	130.7	_____

Problem 7

Spending patterns for Jennifer and Melissa are shown in this table.

	Price Year 1	Price Year 2	Price Year 3	Units Purchased Jennifer	Melissa	Average
candy bars	$0.50	$0.75	$1.00	10	30	xxx
gasoline	$1.00	$1.50	$1.80	10	8	xxx
computer disks	$1.50	$1.00	$0.80	10	2	xxx
Price Index Year 1	xxx	xxx	xxx	____	____	____
Price Index Year 2	xxx	xxx	xxx	____	____	____
Price Index Year 3	xxx	xxx	xxx	____	____	____

a. The CPI uses spending on particular goods in the base year as a proportion of total spending that year to "weight" price changes of particular goods over time. Using year 1 as the base year, compute personal price indices and fill in the price index blanks for Jennifer and Melissa. The easy way to do this is to compute how much each would have to spend in years 2 and 3 to buy their "market basket" from year 1. Then divide this amount by what each spent in year 1.)

b. Determine the average price index for Jennifer and Melissa for each year, then fill in the average column in the table.

c. Who is harmed relatively more by these changes in average prices? _____ Why?
   _____

ANSWERS

Chapter Review (Fill-In Questions)

1. average, index
2. Consumer Price Index; market basket
3. creeping; galloping or hyperinflation
4. unemployment; inflation
5. demand-side; supply-side
6. cost-push; administered price

Problem 1

a. See table.
b. (4,117.8 - 711.6)/711.6 = 478.7%
c. (5,200.8 - 103.9)/103.9 = 4,905.6%
d. inflation
e. 1940s = (1,108.1 - 718.9)/718.9 = 54.1%
   1950s = (1,630.9 - 1,108.1)/1,108.1 = 47.2%
   1960s = (2,421.9 - 1,630.9)/1,630.9 = 48.5%
   1970s = (3,191.1 - 2,421.9)/2,421.9 = 31.8%
   1980s = (4,117.8 - 3,191.1)/3,191.1 = 29.0%

Year	Nominal GDP (Billions)	GDP Implicit Price Deflator (1982=100)	Real GDP
1929	103.9	14.6	711.6
1933	56.0	11.2	500.0
1939	91.3	12.7	718.9
1949	260.4	23.5	1,108.1
1959	495.8	30.4	1,630.9
1969	963.9	39.8	2,421.9
1979	2,508.2	78.6	3,191.1
1989	5,200.8	126.3	4,117.8

Problem 2

a. See table at right.
b. The price index numbers should be lower after year 8.

Year	Current Dollar Value Of Bundle	Price Index
1	20	40
2	22	44
3	25	50
4	30	60
5	40	80
6	50	100
7	70	140
8	80	160
9	90	180
10	110	220

Problem 3

Year	CPI (1983=100)	Nominal Income (current dollars)	Real Income (1983 dollars)
1967	30	20,000	66,667
1974	50	28,000	56,000
1980	66	40,000	60,606
1983	100	42,000	42,000
1990	130	45,000	34,615

Problem 4

a. T
b. F
c. F
d. T
e. T
f. F
g. F
h. T
i. F
j. F

Problem 5

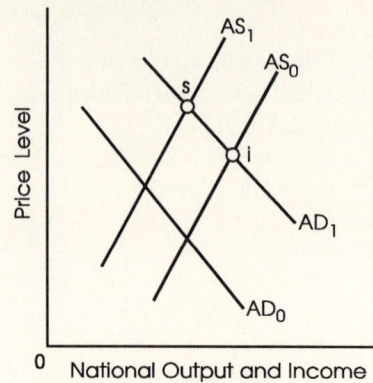

Problem 6

a. See table.
b. $(11.9 - 8.9)/11.9 = 25.2\%$.
c. $(6\% - 4\%) = 2\%$; $(\$4,645.6 \times .02) = \$92.91$ billion

Year	Personal Income \$B (Current Dollars)	CPI 1982-84 = 100	CPI 1990 = 100
1929	84.3	15.5	11.9
1933	46.3	11.6	8.9
1960	409.4	29.6	22.6
1970	831.8	38.8	29.7
1980	2258.5	82.4	63.0
1983	3290.0	100.0	76.5
1990	4645.6	130.7	100.0

Problem 7

a. See table.
b. See table.
c. Melissa is harmed relatively more because she purchases larger quantities of the item (candy bars) whose price has increased by the largest percent.

	Price Year 1	Price Year 2	Price Year 3	Units Purchased in Year 1		
				Jennifer	Melissa	Average
candy bars	\$0.50	\$0.75	\$1.00	10	30	xxx
gasoline	\$1.00	\$1.50	\$1.80	10	8	xxx
computer disks	\$1.50	\$1.00	\$0.80	10	2	xxx
Price Index Year 1	xxx	xxx	xxx	100.0	100.0	100.0
Price Index Year 2	xxx	xxx	xxx	108.3	140.4	124.4
Price Index Year 3	xxx	xxx	xxx	120.0	176.9	148.5

Chapter 8
Measuring Economic Performance and Growth

Chapter Objectives

After you have studied this chapter you should be able to: explain the concept and uses of Gross Domestic Product (GDP); explain how income and expenditure approaches estimate GDP; explain the concept of value-added; explain how disposable personal income, personal income, national income and net national product are derived from GDP accounts; explain some limitations of GDP accounting, and evaluate GDP as a measure of social well-being.

Chapter Review: Key Points

1. *GDP* is the total market value of a nation's annual production. GDP measures estimate the economic performance of an economy and are important for government policy and business decisions.

2. The *expenditures* approach to GDP sums *consumption* spending (*C*), business *investment* spending (*I*), *government purchases* (*G*), and *net exports* (*X-M*): **GDP = C + I + G + (X - M).**

3. *Gross Private Domestic Investment (GPDI)* is the economic term for business spending. To arrive at net investment, we need to subtract depreciation from GPDI.

4. Government purchases (**G**) do not include *transfer* (welfare) *payments*, which are treated as flows of income from some households to others.

5. The *income* approach to GDP sums wages, interest, rent, and profits. We use the figures available, which are (**a**) wages and salaries, (**b**) proprietors' income, (**c**) corporate profits, (**d**) rental income, and (**e**) interest. The sum of these figures is *National Income* (*NI*). Addition of *indirect business taxes*, which is not anyone's income, yields *Net National Product* (*NNP*). The *capital consumption allowance* (*depreciation*) is the difference between GDP and NNP.

6. The *value-added* approach to GDP sums the sales of all firms and subtracts their purchases of intermediate products, which are goods bought by one firm from another for further processing. Failure to exclude purchases of intermediate goods from GDP figures would result in substantial *double counting* of production.

7. GDP figures should be used cautiously. One problem is that they may be systematically biased and are often presented in an artificially precise fashion. Another is that most nonmarket production is ignored (e.g., homemakers' services, do-it-yourself projects, and the like). GDP accounts include as production many disproducts (for instance, pollution abatement equipment is added to GDP, but environmental decay is not subtracted).

8. Currencies from different countries are traded in international financial markets at *exchange rates* (relative prices) set primarily by market forces, although governments affect exchange rates directly (by buying and selling currencies), and indirectly (by imposing quotas and tariffs on goods traded internationally).

9. *Purchasing power parity* reflects cost-of-living differentials between countries.

10. According to the *law of one price*, if transactions costs are zero, relative prices for given goods or resources will be identical everywhere in the world.

11. International comparisons of GDP are especially problematic because countries differ in relative importance of do-it-yourself production, and the extent of barter and the underground economy. Ideally, per capita incomes should be adjusted for the relative purchasing power parity of currencies in different countries, but most comparisons are based on exchange rates between currencies because such data are much more readily available.

Matching Key Terms And Concepts

Set I

____ 1. exports

____ 2. Gross Domestic Product

____ 3. Measure of Economic Welfare (MEW)

____ 4. imports

____ 5. indirect business taxes

____ 6. Net National Product

____ 7. Purchasing power parity approach

____ 8. Law of one price

____ 9. transfer payments

____ 10. Exchange rate approach

a. GDP adjusted to better estimate economic welfare.

b. A way to account for cost-of-living differences between countries when comparing their GDPs.

c. National Income + Indirect business taxes + depreciation.

d. GDP minus depreciation of capital stock.

e. Uses relative nominal values of countries' currencies to make international comparisons of GDP.

f. Homogenous goods should have same price everywhere if transactions costs are zero.

g. Domestic production that is sold to foreigners.

h. Income taxed from one set of households and given to another set.

i. Sales, excise, and property taxes.

j. Goods produced abroad and purchased by consumers in this country.

Set II

___ 1. net private domestic investment

___ 2. value-added

___ 3. personal income

___ 4. capital consumption allowance

___ 5. retained earnings

___ 6. government purchases

___ 7. net exports

___ 8. personal taxes

___ 9. income approach

___10. expenditure approach

a. NI + transfer payments - corporate taxes - retained earnings.

b. C + I + G + (X - M)

c. Corporate income after taxes and dividends.

d. A way to avoid the double-counting problem.

e. X - M

f. Capital accumulation after adjusting for depreciation.

g. w + i + r + Π

h. Plus transfer payments equals government outlays.

i. Subtracted from Personal Income to calculate Disposable PI.

j. Known by accountants as depreciation.

True/False Questions

___ 1. For national income accounting purposes, sales of stocks and bonds are considered real investments.

___ 2. Final economic goods are those goods used in the production of other economic goods.

___ 3. Included in farm income is an estimate of the value of home-consumed food grown on farms but not marketed.

___ 4. Indirect business taxes are treated as a part of NI because they are payments to the factors of production.

___ 5. One way to avoid overstatement of GDP is to total the sales of firms after subtracting the values of intermediate goods purchased by each firm.

___ 6. National Income accounts consider only productive activity is transacted through the marketplace.

___ 7. For GDP accounting, the costs of the inputs government uses are treated as the value of government services.

___ 8. GDP includes adjustments for the changing value of leisure time.

___ 9. Individual income and spending are related positively to the level of economic activity.

___ 10. Changes in inventories are considered consumption.

___11. The expenditure approach adds up all income received by U.S. citizens to arrive at GDP.

___12. International GDP comparisons are most accurate when exchange rates are used to convert currencies to a common denominator.

___13. The purchasing power parity approach yields results which suggest that many countries are not as poor as the exchange rate approach indicates.

___14. Consumption expenditures equal income derived from wages and salaries since the expenditure approach and income approach yield identical GDP figures.

___15. The law of one price will not be valid for homogenous goods and services if transactions costs are positive.

Standard Multiple Choice

There Is One Best Answer For Each Question.

___ 1. Gross Domestic Product is the total market value of all:
   a. commodities sold in a year.
   b. services produced in a year.
   c. production during a year.
   d. consumer goods sold during a year.
   e. None of the above.

___ 2. National Income is the sum of ALL of the following EXCEPT:
   a. wages.
   b. savings.
   c. interest.
   d. rent.
   e. profits.

___ 3. GDP computations include only rough adjustments for changes in:
   a. the amounts of leisure time.
   b. such `disproducts' as pollution or crowding.
   c. the quality of the goods we buy.
   d. how equitably wealth is distributed.
   e. values of homemakers' services.

___ 4. Purchases of foreign-made goods should NOT be:
   a. included with other expenditures to compute our GDP.
   b. included in the GDP of the exporting country.
   c. included in the personal expenditures category of GDP, which is then adjusted by subtracting imports.
   d. value-added for the exporting country.

___ 5. The problem of "double counting" is partially cured by:
   a. summations of sales by all firms.
   b. the expenditures approach.
   c. the income approach.
   d. summations of only the values added by each firm.
   e. capital consumption allowances.

___ 6. The "father of GDP accounting" was:
   a. Oskar Morgenstern.
   b. Franscois Quesnay.
   c. John Stuart Mill.
   d. James Buchanan.
   e. Simon Kuznets.

___ 7. Transfer payments include:
   a. consumption expenditures.
   b. Social Security taxes.
   c. corporate managers' incomes.
   d. funds paid to foreign investors.
   e. Social Security benefits.

___ 8. Legalization of marijuana would cause the growth of GDP to:
   a. more accurately reflect well-being.
   b. be overstated in the very short run.
   c. be understated in the long run.
   d. decline precipitously.
   e. become stagnant.

___ 9. GDP measures do not include the:
   a. market prices of harmful goods.
   b. costs incurred to reduce pollution.
   c. government's military spending.
   d. increases in inventories during business downturns.
   e. values of "do-it-yourself" projects.

___10. Net National Product (NNP) equals:
   a. C + GPDI + G + X - M.
   b. C + S + T + M.
   c. GDP - indirect business taxes.
   d. GDP - depreciation.
   e. DPI + S.

___11. The value-added approach estimates GDP as the sum of all:
   a. sales of all firms.
   b. intermediate goods all firms use.
   c. sales of all firms minus purchases of all intermediate products.
   d. final goods minus production costs.
   e. sales minus labor costs.

___12. Corporations use their profits to pay
   a. salaries to employees.
   b. salaries and taxes or invest in capital goods.
   c. taxes to the government, dividends to stockholders, and to finance the firm's operations or expansion.
   d. buy insurance.
   e. graft to politicians, contribute to charities, and distribute foreign aid.

___13. The most accurate international measures of GDP per capita use the:
   a. expenditure approach.
   b. income approach.
   c. exchange rate approach.
   d. purchasing power parity approach.
   e. law of one price.

___14. Limitations to GDP accounting would not include problems associated with
   a. ambiguity.
   b. conceptualization.
   c. incompleteness.
   d. inaccuracy.
   e. misclassification.

___15. GDP accounting overstates a country's economic welfare if:
   a. it includes homemade production.
   b. based on purchasing power parity.
   c. negative aspects of production are not taken into account.
   d. real prices and figures are used.
   e. estimates of underground activities are included in GDP accounts.

Chapter Review (Fill-In Questions)

1. Gross Domestic Product (GDP) is the total _____ of all production during one year. One of the major reasons for measuring GDP is to provide policymakers a regular, continuing and comparable _____ of total economic activity.

2. The two main conceptual approaches to measuring GDP are the _____ approach and the _____ approach.

3. The expenditure approach looks at the expenditures of the _____ users of goods and services, which include _____, _____, _____, and _____. By adding these four expenditure categories _____ is obtained.

4. Alternatively, national income can be obtained by adding together all payments to the _____. The biggest component of national income is _____. To reconcile national income and GDP, _____ and _____ must be added to NI to obtain GDP.

5. While GDP does a pretty fair job of measuring economic performance, some notable limitations exist. Some national economic data is provided to the exact _____ where rounding would make more sense. Many forms of _____ production, such as the value of homemaker's services, are excluded.

6. Since many _____ services are not sold, valuing the output is difficult, so GDP statisticians use the next best estimate, the value of the _____.

7. One way to make international comparisons of per capita GDP is to use _____ to convert currencies to a common denominator. This approach, however, is not as accurate as the _____ approach which attempts to take into account cost of living differences between countries.

8. As a measure of well-being, GDP has many limitations. The value of _____ activities is ignored while expenditures for removing litter and pollution are included. To overcome these problems, two economists developed a(n) _____.

Unlimited Multiple Choice

There Are From Zero To Four Correct Answers For Each Question.

___ 1. Economic investment includes all:
   a. purchases of new capital equipment.
   b. changes in inventories.
   c. construction.
   d. purchases of stocks and bonds.

___ 2. Profits are used by corporations to:
   a. pay corporate profit taxes.
   b. finance investment projects.
   c. pay dividends to households.
   d. reward managers who own stock.

___ 3. Interest income:
   a. includes payments made for the use of borrowed capital (usually financial capital).
   b. has been the most rapidly growing proportion of National Income since 1990.
   c. is usually associated with the renting of real property.
   d. represents profits received by entrepreneurs

___ 4. National income:
   a. is the sum of incomes paid to owners of the various factors of production, plus retained earnings and corporate profit taxes.
   b. is normally broken down into wages, interest, rent, corporate income, and proprietor's income.
   c. equals Consumption + GPDI + Government purchases.
   d. equals GDP - (depreciation + indirect business taxes).

___ 5. Gross Domestic Product (GDP) is:
   a. an important measure of total economic activity.
   b. a crude yardstick with which to measure national well-being.
   c. based on various accounting methods, depending on the specific output or income being measured.
   d. a valuable guide when policy-makers try to determine the needs of the economy.

Problems

Problem 1

Listed below are various categories of expenditures and income used in GDP accounting. Using the numbers for these categories, specify formulas (e.g., 5 + 10 + 15) that answer questions a-f.

1. Wages and salaries
2. Rental income
3. Interest
4. Indirect business taxes
5. Capital consumption allowance
6. Personal consumption expenditures
7. Gross Private Domestic Investment
8. Corporate profits
9. Proprietors' income
10. Government expenditures on goods
11. Personal income tax
12. Government transfer payments
13. Social security taxes
14. Corporate profits tax
15. Exports
16. Imports
17. Retained earnings
18. Personal savings
19. Consumer interest payments plus personal transfers to foreigners

a. Compute GDP using the expenditure approach. _____

b. Compute GDP using the income approach. _____

c. Compute National Income. _____

d. Compute Personal Income. _____

e. Compute Disposable Income. _____

f. Compute NNP in two different ways. _____

Problem 2

Information about a specific product is given in the table below. Stage #5 is the final stage of production.

a. Fill in the column for value added.

b. The value of this commodity to be counted in GDP is?

_____

c. The sum of all values-added equals? _____

	Dollar Value of Inputs	Dollar Value of Good in Market	Value Added
Stage 1	0	100	_____
Stage 2	100	300	_____
Stage 3	300	900	_____
Stage 4	900	1,500	_____
Stage 5	1,500	2,500	_____

Problem 3

Use these GDP accounting data to answer the following questions.

a. Gross Domestic Product equals? _____

b. Net National Product equals? _____

c. Personal Saving equals?

_____

Gross Private Domestic Investment	666.1
Exports	363.2
Personal Tax Payments	498.2
State and Local Government Purchases	467.7
Capital Consumption Allowance	441.4
Imports	451.0
Personal Consumption Expenditures	2,606.1
Federal Government Purchases	364.8
Personal Income	3,298.5

Problem 4

Suppose a car dealer sells a new car in September 1994 for $10,400, but allows a trade in of $3,800 for a car that turns out to be a clunker. After $600 worth of repairs, the clunker is sold for $2,900. The new car cost the dealer $9,000.

a. What are the values added at each step? _____

_____

b. How much will GDP increase after all transactions take place? _____

Problem 5

Use the GDP data from the table:

a. GDP equals? _____

b. National Income equals? _____

c. The Capital Consumption Allowance equals? _____

d. Net National Product equals? _____

e. Personal Income equals? _____

f. Disposable Personal Income equals? _____

Wages	800
Consumption	900
Proprietor's Income	100
Gross Investment	150
Corporate Income	100
Rental Income	75
Interest	75
Government Purchases	200
Exports	100
Imports	50
Indirect Business Taxes	75
Transfer Payments	50
Personal Income Taxes	100
Corporate Retained Earnings	50
Corporate Income Taxes	75

Problem 6

Use (T) for true to indicate that the following items would be counted in GDP if known to government accountants, and (F) for false if they would not consider an item to be part of GDP.

____ a. You consume leisure you value at $1,000 during a vacation in Hawaii.

____ b. Jocko grows marijuana in his bath-tub and sells it to Bonzo for $114,000.

____ c. I spend $40 for paint to repair an old house I just bought.

____ d. A Las Vegas casino wins $10,000 from a drunken tourist.

____ e. Tito crashes his car into Franco's limousine and his insurance company pays $13,000 to repair both vehicles.

____ f. Marie Antoinette pays $7.00 for flour because she likes homemade cake.

____ g. Mr. and Mrs. Richie Rich build a $1,000,000 mansion for their family's own occupancy, but have no out-of-pocket expenses because all materials were retrieved from the city dump and all work was done by family members during summer vacations.

____ h. A carpenter repairs a neighbor's stairs for $200, but does not report it to the Internal Revenue Service.

____ i. Elvira now gets free swimming lessons, but before she married the lifeguard she paid $10 per lesson.

____ j. Engelbert pays $8.00 for a bottle of hairgrower that fails to cure his baldness.

Problem 7

Use these U.S. data for 1990 to answer questions a through h. (Dollar values are in billions).

Personal Consumption Expenditures	3,728.1
Compensation of Employees	3,286.9
Personal Taxes	718.1
Consumer Interest Payments and Personal Transfer Payments to Foreigners	109.3
Capital Consumption Allowance:	585.2
Net Interest Income	470.2
Federal Purchases of Goods and Services	438.5
Rental Income of Persons	8.5
Gross Private Domestic Investment	714.0
Corporate Profits with Inventory Adjustment	306.6
State and Local Purchases of Goods and Services	694.2
Exports	687.7
Proprietors' Income	406.1
Imports	743.7
personal income	4,719.0
Gross Domestic Product in 1982 dollars	4,147.6
U.S. population size	252.5 million

a. GDP equals? _____

b. Net National Product equals? _____

c. National Income equals? _____

d. Indirect Business Taxes equal? _____

e. Personal Saving equals? _____

f. The GDP deflator (1982=100) equals? _____

g. GDP per capita equals? _____

h. Disposable Personal Income per capita equals? _____

Problem 8

Fill in the blanks in this table which shows the various steps in making a wooden table (the sum of all the values added is $80).

Stage	Cost of Input	Sales Receipts	Value Added
Mill	___	___	___
Lumber distributor	15	___	___
Table maker	30	___	___
Delivered table	___	___	25

Problem 9

Assume a simple economy with two people, Robinson and Friday. Robinson is the boss because Friday possesses a meek personality. Robbie pays Friday $400 a year in wages to gather food and to make clothing, and $100 a year to build new housing. Friday takes the $500 total wages and gives $100 to Robinson for rent and $400 to Robinson for clothes and food that Robbie has stored for Friday. Robbie reinvests the rental income into housing and assumes that $300 of Friday's money is for wages and $100 is entrepreneurial profit.

a. What does GDP equal? _____

b. What does NNP equal? _____

c   What does NI equal? _____

ANSWERS

Matching		True/False		Multiple Choice		Unlimited Multiple Choice
Set I	**Set II**					
1. g	1. f	1. F	9. T	1. c	9. e	1. abc
2. c	2. d	2. F	10. F	2. b	10. d	2. abc
3. a	3. a	3. T	11. F	3. c	11. c	3. a
4. j	4. j	4. F	12. F	4. a	12. c	4. abd
5. i	5. c	5. T	13. T	5. d	13. d	5. abcd
6. d	6. h	6. F	14. F	6. e	14. b	
7. b	7. e	7. T	15. T	7. a	15. c	
8. f	8. i	8. F		8. b		
9. h	9. g					
10. e	10. b					

Chapter Review (Fill-In Questions)

1. market value; estimate
2. income; expenditure
3. final or ultimate; consumers; business investors; government; foreigners; Gross Domestic Product
4. resource owners; wages; capital consumption allowance; indirect business taxes
5. dollar; nonmarket
6. government; inputs
7. exchange rates; purchasing power parity
8. leisure; Measure of Economic Welfare (MEW)

Problem 1

a. $(6) + (7) + (10) + ((15) - (16))$.
b. $(1) + (2) + (3) + (8) + (9) + (4) + (5)$.
c. $(1) + (2) + (3) + (8) + (9)$
d. $(18) + (6) + (19) + (11)$.
e. $(18) + (6) + (19$.
f. $(6) + (7) + (10) + ((15) - (16)) - (5)$ or
   $(1) + (2) + (3) + (8) + (9) + (4)$

Problem 2

a. See table.
b. $2,500
c. $2,500

	Dollar Value of Inputs	Dollar Value of Good in Market	Value Added
Stage 1	0	100	100
Stage 2	100	300	200
Stage 3	300	900	600
Stage 4	900	1,500	600
Stage 5	1,500	2,500	1,000

Problem 3

a. $4,016.9 (2,606.1 + 666.1 + 832.5 + 363.2 - 451.0)
b. $3,575.5 (4,016.9 - 441.4)
c. $194.2 (3,298.5 - 2,606.1 - 498.2)

Problem 4

a. $9,000 (to car maker); $1,400 (dealer value added); $600 (repairs); -$1,500 (trade in minus repairs and resale value)
b. $9,500

Problem 5

a. $1,300 (900 + 150 + 200 + 100 - 50)
b. $1,150 (800 + 100 + 100+ 75 + 75)
c. $75 (1,300 - 1,150 - 75)
d. $1,225 (1,150 + 75)
e. $1,075 (1,150 + 50 - 50 - 75)
f. $975 (1,075 - 100)

Problem 6

a. F
b. F
c. T
d. T
e. T
f. T
g. F
h. T
i. F
j. T

Problem 7

a. 5,518.9 (C + I + G + X - M)
b. 4,933.7 (GDP - CCA)
c. 4,478.3 (w + r + i +Π)
d. 455.4 (NNP - NI)
e. 163.5 (PI - PT - C - $109.3)
f. 133.1 (($5,518.8/$4,147.6) x 100))
g. 21,857 ($5,518.8 billion/252.5 million)
h. 15,845 (PI - PT/252.5 million)

Problem 8

Stage	Cost of Input	Sales Receipts	Value Added
Mill	0	15	15
Lumber distributor	15	30	15
Table maker	30	55	25
Delivered table	55	80	25

Problem 9

a. $1,000 (GDP = C + I + G + (X-M) = 900 + 100 + 0 + 0)
b. $1,000 (GDP = NNP since there is no depreciation.)
c. $1,000 (NNP = NI since there is no government to collect indirect business taxes.)

Chapter 9
Classical Macroeconomics and
Keynesian Aggregate Expenditures

Chapter Objectives

After you have read and studied this chapter you should be able to explain why classical economists believed the economy would tend to operate at full-employment; describe the major conceptual differences between Classical and Keynesian theory; enumerate the components of Keynesian Aggregate Demand; discuss average and marginal propensities to consume and save; describe the major determinants of consumption and saving; explain the major determinants of investment; and describe how the major components add together to form Keynesian Aggregate Demand.

Chapter Review: Key Points

1. *Classical theory* is a conglomeration of the thoughts of many economic thinkers dating back to Adam Smith.

2. Classical economists based their theory on *Say's Law: Supply creates its own demand.* Coupled with assumptions that wages, prices, and interest rates are all perfectly flexible, Say's Law quickly drives a market economy towards full employment. All unemployment is considered voluntary--simply a refusal to work at the equilibrium wage. The protracted unemployment of the early 1930s diluted acceptance of classical theory and led to the development of the radically different Keynesian theory.

3. Keynesian analysis focuses on Aggregate Demand. Much of economic capacity was idle during the Great Depression. During a slow recovery from 1933 to 1940, real output expanded by over 60 percent with only slight increases in the price level. Keynesian economics treats Aggregate Supply as flat during a depression so that the price level can be ignored; it focuses primarily on how to maintain Aggregate Demand consistent with full employment.

4. *Aggregate Expenditures (AE)* encompass total spending on domestic output during a year. Aggregate Expenditures include four components: (*a*) personal consumption expenditures, (*b*) gross private domestic investment, (*c*) government purchases, and (*d*) net exports of goods and services:
$$AE = C + I + G + (X - M)$$

5. The single most important determinant of consumer spending is disposable income through its influence on *induced consumption*. Consumer spending is related directly to disposable income and is a stable component of Aggregate Expenditures. Other important determinants of consumption and saving include (*a*) wealth and expectations of future income, (*b*) customary living standards, (*c*) the sizes and age composition of typical households, (*d*) consumer goods on hand and household balance sheets, and (*e*) consumer expectations about prices and product availability. These determine the level of *autonomous consumption* (C_a).

6. The *marginal propensity to consume* (***mpc***) is the change in planned consumption arising from a given small change in disposable income; it tells us how much of an additional dollar of income will be consumed. Similarly, the *marginal propensity to save* (***mps***) is how much of an additional dollar in income will be saved, so *mpc + mps = 1.*

7. Capital investment refers to purchases of new output that can be used in the future to produce other goods and services. The three major components of investment are (*a*) new business and residential structures, (*b*) machinery and equipment, and (*c*) inventory accumulation.

8. Investment is the least stable component of Aggregate Expenditures, fluctuating widely over the course of a business cycle. The most volatile component of investment is inventory accumulation.

9. The primary factors determining the quantity of investment are (*a*) expected returns from investment, (*b*) market interest rates, (*c*) expectations about the business environment, (*d*) rates of technological change and innovation, (*e*) the level of existing stocks of business capital relative to total production, and (*f*) the costs of capital goods. All else equal, changes in items (*c*) through (*f*) shift rate of return curves, while changes in interest rates cause movements along an expected rate of return curve. In simple Keynesian models, investment is treated as *autonomous* (I_a).

10. While government spending is probably influenced by changes in income, it is even more strongly affected by the state of international relations and domestic politics. Thus government spending as a component of Aggregate Expenditures is also treated as autonomous.

11. Exports and imports are reasonably balanced, so *net exports* (*X - M*) make a comparatively small contribution to Aggregate Expenditures. Simple Keynesian models treat net exports as autonomous.

Matching Key Terms And Concepts

___ 1.	Classical economics	**a.**	Annual percentage by which profits will grow if reinvested.
___ 2.	Say's Law	**b.**	Economy will automatically adjust to full-employment.
___ 3.	autonomous expenditures	**c.**	Borrowing or drawing down savings.
___ 4.	induced expenditures	**d.**	$C + I + G + (X-M)$.
___ 5.	marginal propensity to save	**e.**	Supply creates its own demand.
___ 6.	Keynesian Aggregate Expenditures	**f.**	The change in consumption divided by the change in income.
___ 7.	45-degree Keynesian reference line	**g.**	Related to income.
___ 8.	rate of return	**h.**	Not a function of income.
___ 9.	marginal propensity to consume	**i.**	1-MPC.
___10.	break-even level of income	**j.**	$Y = C + S$.
___11.	dissaving	**k.**	The point where S is zero.

True/False Questions

___ 1. Classical economists strongly reject the idea that a capitalistic, laissez-faire economy automatically produces a full employment level of output.

___ 2. Whenever Aggregate Demand exceeds Aggregate Supply, the level of economic activity will tend to rise, and there will be pressures for output or prices, or both, to increase.

___ 3. John Maynard Keynes was the first major economist to put forth the revolutionary notion of a positive relationship between consumption and the income level.

___ 4. It is impossible for households to have negative savings.

___ 5. The marginal propensity to consume tells us how much of an additional dollar of income will be consumed.

___ 6. When the interest rate increases, the investor's opportunity cost of investment falls.

___ 7. The marginal propensity to save indirectly indicates how much of an additional dollar of income will be consumed.

___ 8. Consumption as a percentage of income increases as income increases.

___ 9. Investment spending is unaffected by changes in business expectations about the economy.

___10. Some economists attribute much of the volatility of investment to changes in the interest rate.

___11. Keynesian Aggregate Expenditure is a vertical summation of consumption, investment, government spending, and net exports.

___12. The marginal propensity to save refers to the proportion of total income saved.

___13. The marginal propensity to save is equal to the slope of the consumption function.

___14. The purchase of 100 shares of General Motors stock is not considered an investment for aggregate economic analysis.

___15. The marginal propensity to consume and marginal propensity to save added together equal one in a simple Keynesian model.

Standard Multiple Choice

There Is One Best Answer For Each Question.

___ 1. Say's Law refers to:
a. the concept that demand creates its own supply.
b. an insignificant part of classical macroeconomic theory.
c. the idea that the act of production creates an equivalent level of demand.
d. an old law that held that workers could not sue business for on-the-job injuries because they (the workers) had assumed the risks of employment by accepting the job in the first place.
e. a tendency towards unionization of the labor force.

___ 2. Classical economists thought that:
a. flexible wages and prices were the principal causes of recessions.
b. government policies and spending were needed to keep the economy at full employment.
c. the Great Depression confirmed their view of the business cycle.
d. price, wage, and interest rate flexibility can quickly cure any tendencies for a recession.
e. communist revolutions would overthrow capitalism.

___ 3. Classical macroeconomics assumes:
a. Say's law.
b. flexible prices.
c. flexible wages.
d. flexible interest rates.
e. All of the above.

4. The marginal propensity to consume (MPC) is between zero and one according to:
   a. Keynesian consumption functions.
   b. the Law of Diminishing Returns.
   c. the Law of Demand.
   d. Say's Law.
   e. the Law of Entropy.

5. Keynesian Aggregate Demand does not include:
   a. consumption (C).
   b. government purchases (G).
   c. investment (I).
   d. saving (S).
   e. net exports (X-M).

6. I spent $8,000 of my $10,000 income last year. My salary has increased to $12,000 and my MPC is .8. What will be the growth in my consumption?
   a. $2,000.
   b. $9,600.
   c. $1,600.
   d. $11,000.
   e. $400.

7. Investment is $100 billion at 6 percent interest. If the interest rate increases to 8 percent, investment will:
   a. climb to over $100 billion.
   b. remain at $100 billion.
   c. cause the rate of return from investment to fall.
   d. drop below $100 billion.
   e. decline until interest falls substantially below 6 percent, to compensate for the short term interest rate penalty.

8. The largest component of Aggregate Demand is:
   a. government spending.
   b. consumer spending.
   c. new office construction.
   d. inventory accumulation.
   e. investment.

9. Which one of the following is NOT an example of economic investment?
   a. Inventory growth.
   b. Manufacturers replacing worn out equipment.
   c. Purchases of government bonds.
   d. Newly constructed residential housing.
   e. Newly installed telephone lines.

10. If a wave of inflationary expectations newly arose and you were a new car dealer, you might expect your sales to:
    a. drop drastically.
    b. increase rapidly.
    c. remain constant.
    d. fluctuate up and down until the rumors subside.
    e. fall initially, but ultimately rise, stabilizing at a new high.

11. Keynesian theory suggests that when Aggregate Supply exceeds Aggregate Demand, economic activity will:
    a. decline, with pressure on prices to fall.
    b. decline, with pressure on prices to rise.
    c. rise, with pressure on prices to fall.
    d. remain the same.
    e. rise, with pressure on prices to rise.

___12. Which of the following is NOT an important determinant of consumption and saving?
   a. Average size and age of the household.
   b. Consumer expectation about prices and availability of products.
   c. Stocks of consumer goods on hand.
   d. Wealth.
   e. Wages relative to rates of return on capital.

___13. If income increases from $7,000 to $12,000 and saving increases by $500, the Marginal Propensity to Save is:
   a. .2.
   b. .3.
   c. .1.
   d. .05.
   e. .5.

___14. Investors will pursue investment opportunities as long as:
   a. the expected rate of return is greater than zero.
   b. saving is available for investment.
   c. they are more optimistic than pessimistic.
   d. the expected total profits over time exceeds current monetary outlays.
   e. the expected rate of return is at least as great as the interest rate.

___15. Increases in which of the following will reduce Aggregate Demand?
   a. imports (M).
   b. investment (I).
   c. government spending (G).
   d. consumption (C).
   e. marginal propensity to consume (MPC).

Chapter Review (Fill-In Questions)

1. Classical economic theory was the result of numerous studies of how markets operate. Classical theory suggested that several automatic mechanisms operate to ensure _____. The first mechanism is Say's Law, which asserts that the very act of production creates an equivalent level of _____.

2. Classical economists suggested that full employment is assured by flexible _____ and _____ in labor and product markets.

3. The high and prolonged unemployment of the Great Depression caused many to doubt classical theory. Many economists turned away from classical theory which emphasized long-run changes in _____ toward Keynesian theory which emphasized short-run changes in _____.

4. The largest component of Keynesian Aggregate Demand is consumption and the most volatile is _____. The most important determinant of consumer spending is _____.

5. Keynes's fundamental psychological law asserted that people will _____ their consumption as income increases, but by _____ than the increase in income.

6. When consumption exceeds income, _____ occurs. Autonomous consumption is _____ income.

7. The level of investment is affected by business expectations about the business climate, new technologies and the stocks of _____ relative to total output. Production from capital, as with other factors of production, is subject to _____.

8. One crucial cost of investment is the _____, which represents the opportunity cost of using funds. _____ investment refers to investment that is unrelated to income.

9. Many _____ purchases are like investment in that the benefits are received over a long period. Government _____ are not considered a part of Keynesian Aggregate Expenditures because they do not directly affect demand until the recipient actually spends the money.

10. Graphically, Keynesian Aggregate Expenditures are the _____ sum of all types of spending; consumption, investment, and government spending. Since exports and imports are reasonably balanced, _____ are sometimes ignored because they represent such a small part of Aggregate Expenditures.

Unlimited Multiple Choice

There Are From Zero To Four Correct Answers For Each Question.

___ 1. Classical economic theory:
   a. easily explained the persistence of the Great Depression.
   b. viewed full employment in the economy as unattainable.
   c. was not a theory of the business cycle per se, but rather a systematic study of the functioning of the economy.
   d. relies heavily on unhindered supply and demand to work.

___ 2. The marginal propensity to save:
   a. is the change in income caused by a small change in saving.
   b. is the proportion of income saved.
   c. is computed as $\Delta S/\Delta Y$.
   d. plus the marginal propensity to consume balances to zero.

___ 3. Major determinants of consumption and saving include:
   a. wealth and the average size and age of the household.
   b. stocks of consumer goods on hand.
   c. household balance sheets.
   d. consumer expectations about product prices and availability.

____4. Changes in inventories:
   a. are the most volatile component of investment spending.
   b. are signals to business firms of changing economic conditions.
   c. are controlled only by the actions of business firms.
   d. are uncontrollable by most business firms on a day-to-day basis.

____5. The marginal propensity to consume (MPC) is:
   a. the proportion of total income consumed.
   b. the proportion of additional income consumed.
   c. inconsistent with the fundamental psychological law of consumption as expressed by Keynes.
   d. is equal to (1-MPS).

Problems

Problem 1

Use this illustration of a classical capital market to answer the following True/False questions.

____a. The economy is in equilibrium at point b after saving increases from S_0 to S_1.

____b. Say's Law holds at point b.

____c. Say's Law does not hold at point a.

____d. The new saving curve (S_1) indicates that people have decided to save less, and, therefore, to consume more, at each income level.

____e. The movement from point a to point b represents an increase in investment demand.

____f. The movement from point a to point b reflects an increase in the willingness to save.

____g. In moving from point a to point b, the interest rate must fall to eliminate the excess supply of commodities created by the decrease in consumption.

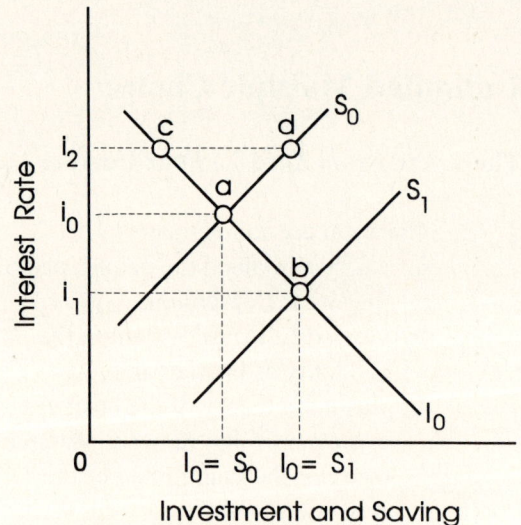

____h. Interest rate i_2 is an equilibrium rate of interest.

____i. Say's Law holds true at point c.

____j. The horizontal segment dc represents excess demand in the investment and savings market.

Problem 2

Use this figure, which illustrates the classical labor market, to answer the following questions. The original supply and demand curves are denoted S_0 and D_0 respectively. The Ps in parentheses indicate the price level.

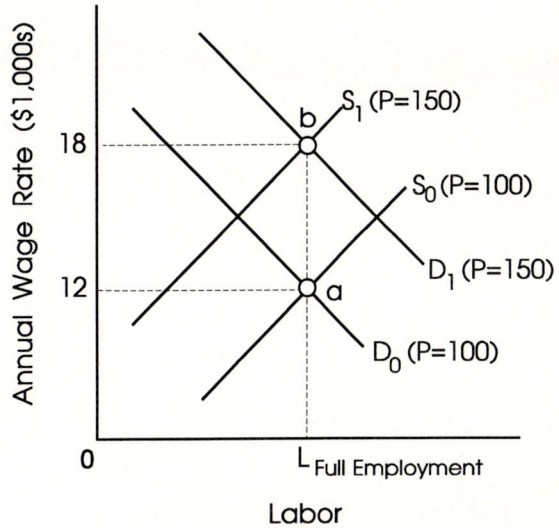

___a. Labor decisions are based on the real wage rate.

___b. The quantity of labor services demanded varies inversely with the money wage rate, assuming a constant price level.

___c. When the demand for labor shifts from D_0 to D_1, this is an indication that the general price level has declined.

___d. A 50 percent general increase in prices could cause the labor supply curve to shift from S_0 to S_1.

___e. A movement from point a to point b indicates an increase in the wage rate.

___f. A movement from point a to point b necessarily represents an increase in real wages.

___g. At point b, voluntary unemployment is zero.

___h. At point a, involuntary unemployment exists.

___i. The movement from a to b shows that, as a result of an increase in the real wage rate, business firms decide to hire fewer workers and to produce less output.

___j. A movement from point a to point b would occur if the wage rate and the general price level experience the same 50 percent increase.

___k. The average level of prices has increased 50 percent as we move from point a to point b.

Problem 3

Use responses a through g (representing line segments) to answer the following questions based on this figure:

a. -0G

b. 0G

c. df/cf

d. -ab

e. 0Y1

f. ed

g. dY2

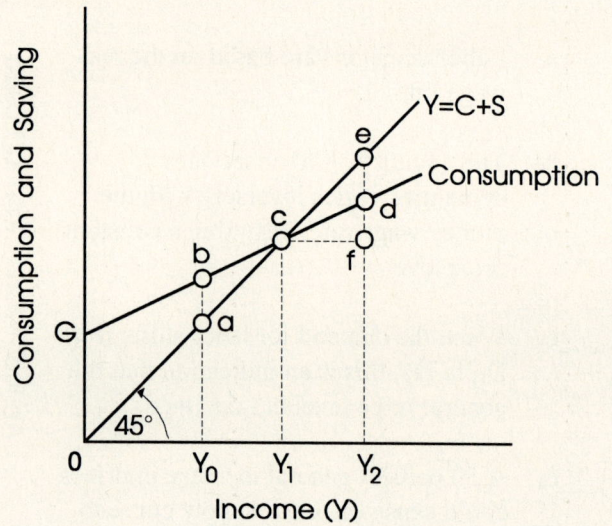

1. The break-even level of income is ____?

2. Saving at income Y_0 is equal to ____?

3. The MPC is equal to ____?

4. Autonomous consumption is equal to ____?

5. Autonomous saving is equal to ____?

6. Consumption at income Y_2 is equal to ____?

7. Saving when income is Y_2 is equal to ____?

Problem 4

Answer the following questions based on this table.

Y	C	S	MPC	MPS
$0	$100		---	---
100	175			
200	250			
300	325			
400	400			
500	475			
600	550			
700	625			
800	700			
900	775			
1,000	850			

a. Fill-in the table. Note that MPC + MPS = 1.

b. How much is the autonomous component of consumption? _____

c. Using the figure below, plot the consumption and savings schedules.

d. Draw and label the Y = C + S (45-degree) line. What is the slope of this line? _____

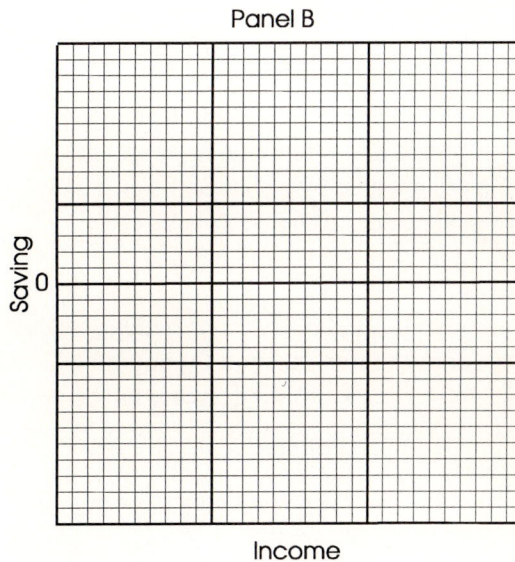

Panel A

Panel B

Consumption

Income

Saving

0

Income

0

Problem 5

Use these consumption and investment functions to answer the following true/false questions.

Panel A — Consumption vs Income, showing consumption functions C_1, C_0, C_2 with points a, b. Panel B — Investment vs Income, showing investment functions I_1, I_0, I_2 with points c, d.

___ a. The shift of the consumption function from C_0 to C_1 represents a decrease in consumption at all income levels.

___ b. The shift of the investment function from I_0 to I_2 represents an increase in investment at all income levels.

___ c. The movement from a to b along consumption function C_0 might be precipitated by a change in consumer expectations about future prices of goods.

___ d. The movement from b to a along consumption function C_0 might be brought about by a decrease in autonomous saving.

___ e. The movement from c to d along investment function I_1 represents an increase in investment at each income level.

___ f. All other factors constant, an increase in autonomous consumption implies a concomitant decrease in autonomous saving.

___ g. The movement from a to b along consumption function C0 represents an increase in induced consumption brought about by an increase in income.

___ h. The MPC increases as the economy moves upward along consumption function C_2.

___ i. All other factors constant, an upward shift in the saving function is always accompanied by a downward shift in the consumption function.

___ j. A shift in the consumption schedule from C_1 to C_2 could be caused by a decreasing desire to save.

Problem 6

Use this saving -income diagram to answer the following questions.

a. In this situation the level of autonomous
    saving equals _____; and the level of
    autonomous consumption equals

    _____.

b. The mpc equals _____; and the mps
    equals _____.

c. If the level of income is $1,800, then the
    level of induced consumption is
    _____, and the total level of
    consumption equals _____.

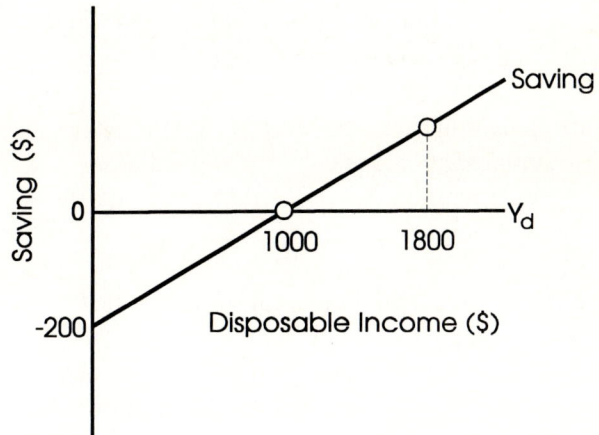

d. If the level of income were to rise to $2,200, then the amount of induced savings would
    equal _____; and the total level of savings would be _____; which naturally means that
    autonomous saving is still _____.

Problem 7

Refer to this Aggregate Expenditures diagram to answer the following questions.

a. The equilibrium level of $800 is based on a marginal propensity to consume of _____.

b. In equilibrium, the level of autonomous consumption equals_____ and induced consumption is _____; therefore, total consumption equals _____.

c. The corresponding savings function that would go with this diagram would have autonomous saving equal to _____; a mps equal to _____; and induced savings of _____ at equilibrium.

d. If the level of autonomous consumption fell to $50, then the new level of equilibrium income would equal _____, and induced consumption would equal _____. At equilibrium, total consumption equals _____; and total saving equals _____.

ANSWERS

Matching	True/False		Multiple Choice		Unlimited Multiple Choice
1. b	1. F	9. F	1. c	9. c	1. cd
2. e	2. T	10. T	2. d	10. b	2. c
3. h	3. T	11. T	3. e	11. a	3. abcd
4. g	4. F	12. F	4. a	12. e	4. abd
5. i	5. T	13. F	5. d	13. c	5. bd
6. d	6. F	14. T	6. c	14. e	
7. j	7. T	15. T	7. d	15. a	
8. a	8. F		8. b		
9. f					
10. k					
11. c					

Chapter Review (Fill-In Questions)

1. full employment; demand
2. wages; prices
3. Aggregate Supply; Aggregate Demand
4. investment; disposable income
5. increase; less
6. dissaving; unrelated to
7. capital; diminishing returns
8. interest rate; Autonomous
9. government; transfer payments
10. vertical; net exports

Problem 1		Problem 2		Problem 3	
a.	T	a.	T	1.	e
b.	T	b.	T	2.	d
c.	F	c.	F	3.	c
d.	F	d.	T	4.	b
e.	F	e.	T	5.	a
f.	T	f.	F	6.	g
g.	T	g.	F	7.	f
h.	F	h.	F		
i.	F	i.	F		
j.	F	j.	T		
		k.	T		

Problem 4

Y (Billions)	C	S	MPC	MPS
$0	$100	$-100	---	---
100	175	-75	.75	.25
200	250	-50	.75	.25
300	325	-25	.75	.25
400	400	0	.75	.25
500	475	25	.75	.25
600	550	50	.75	.25
700	625	75	.75	.25
800	700	100	.75	.25
900	775	125	.75	.25
1,000	850	150	.75	.25

a. See table at left.
b. $100
c. See figure below.
d. one

Panel A

Panel B

Problem 5

a. F
b. F
c. F
d. F
e. F
f. T
g. T
h. F
i. T
j. F

Problem 6

a. -$200; $200; (Autonomous saving and income are based on zero income.)
b. .8; .2; (As income rises from $0 to $1,000, savings increases by $200 (0-(-200)). Thus MPS = 200/1,000 = .2 and MPC = 1 - MPS = 1 - .2 = .8.)
c. $1,440; $1,640; (Induced consumption is equal to MPC x Y = .8 x $1,800 = $1,440. The total level of consumption is induced plus autonomous ($1,440 + 200 = $1,640).)
d. $440; $240; -$200; (Induced saving is equal to MPS x Y = .2 x $2,200 = $440. The total level of savings is induced plus autonomous ($440 + (-200) = $240).)

Problem 7

a. .75; (Since autonomous spending is $200 for an equilibrium income of $800, the multiplier must equal 4 and therefore the MPC is .75.)
b. $100; $600; $700; (Since autonomous spending is $200 and autonomous investment is $100, autonomous consumption must equal $100. Induced consumption is MPC x Yd = .75 x $800 = $600. Total consumption is equal to autonomous plus induced or $100 + $600 = 700.)
c. -$100; .25; $200; (Autonomous saving is the negative of autonomous consumption or -$100. The marginal propensity to save, MPS = 1 - MPC = 1 - .75 = 25. At equilibrium induced saving is equal to MPS x Y = .25 x $800 = $200.)
d. $600; $450; $500; $100 (Equilibrium income is equal to autonomous spending ($150) times the multiplier (4) or $600. At equilibrium induced consumption is MPC x Y = .75 x $600 = $450 and total consumption is autonomous plus induced ($50 + $450 = $500). Therefore, since S = Y - C, savings is $100 ($600 - $500 = $100).)

Chapter 10
Macroeconomic Equilibrium

Chapter Objectives

After you have read and studied this chapter you should be able to explain equilibrium income and employment using the Aggregate Expenditures - National Income approach, and why Keynesians differ from classical economists by emphasizing demand over supply forces; explain macroequilibrium with the savings-investment approach; explain the differences between potential and actual GDP and the concepts of recessionary and inflationary gaps; and explain the relationships between Keynesian Aggregate Supply and Demand and the average level of prices in the economy.

Chapter Review: Key Points

1. Keynesian theory suggests that erratic changes in *business investment spending* (especially inventories) play a major role in causing fluctuations in aggregate income and employment.

2. Equilibrium income and employment occur at the output level at which *Aggregate Spending equals National Output*; firms desire to produce and sell exactly the amounts consumers and investors want to purchase. Any deviation from equilibrium income sets forces in motion to drive the economy towards a new equilibrium.

3. When *planned saving equals planned investment (S = I)*, the economy will be in *equilibrium.* Actual saving and investment are equal at all times because inventory adjustments and similar mechanisms ensure this balance.

4. When *autonomous spending* in the economy increases by $1, income rises by an amount equal to the *autonomous spending multiplier* times the original $1. The multiplier exists because the original $1 in new spending becomes $1 in new income, parts of which are then spent by successive consumers and businesses. The simple autonomous spending multiplier equals: $\Delta Y/\Delta A = 1/mps = 1/(1 - mpc)$, where A represents some form of autonomous spending.

5. Investment spending fell precipitously during the 1929-33 period. The effect of this decline was to reduce equilibrium income sharply. This may have been a principal cause of the Great Depression.

6. The *paradox of thrift* appears to be an important challenge to our conventional wisdom. If more consumers decide to increase their saving, the result might be declining income, consumption, and saving.

7. *Potential GDP* is an estimate of the output the economy could produce at full employment. The *GDP gap* is the difference between potential and actual GDP.

8. The *recessionary gap* is the amount by which autonomous spending falls short of that necessary to achieve a full employment level of income; it is measured on the vertical axis. An *inflationary gap* is the amount that autonomous spending exceeds what is necessary for a full employment equilibrium and is a measure of upward pressure on the price level.

9. Aggregate Expenditure curves are constructed for a given (fixed) price level. If the price level rises, Aggregate Expenditures fall, and vice versa. This leads to a unique relationship that allows us to derive an Aggregate Demand curve from specific levels of Aggregate Spending at various price levels.

10. If the price level is constant, higher autonomous spending increases Aggregate Demand by shifting the Aggregate Demand curve to the right, and vice versa.

11. Keynes thought that raising Aggregate Demand will boost output during a depression without raising the price level. Simple Keynesian theory suggests that the Aggregate Supply curve is horizontal up to the point of full employment. Once full-employment GDP is reached, classical reasoning reigns: The Aggregate Supply curve is vertical, and increases in Aggregate Demand cannot generate extra output. In a fully-employed economy, additions to Aggregate Demand simply bid up prices and result in inflation.

Matching Key Terms And Concepts

___ 1. Keynesian equilibrium

___ 2. withdrawals

___ 3. GDP gap

___ 4. recessionary gap

___ 5. inflationary gap

___ 6. paradox of thrift

___ 7. potential GDP

___ 8. actual investment

___ 9. planned investment equals planned savings

___10. autonomous spending multiplier

a. The reciprocal of the marginal propensity to save.

b. Difference between what GDP currently is and what it would be at full employment.

c. Planned investment adjusted for unintended inventory changes.

d. Aggregate Output and Income equal planned Aggregate Expenditures.

e. Condition for a private economy macroequilibrium.

f. Deficiency in autonomous expenditures needed to reach full employment.

g. Attempts to save more actually yields less saving.

h. Occur when income is not spent on domestic output.

i. Amount that autonomous spending exceeds that needed to achieve full-employment equilibrium with price level stability.

j. National output when resources are fully employed.

True/False Questions

___ 1. Increasing government spending could eliminate an inflationary gap.

___ 2. Keynes viewed savers and investors as different groups who saved and invested for different reasons.

___ 3. In Keynesian theory, planned saving always equals planned investment.

___ 4. According to Keynesian theory, consumption expenditure is a function of the level of income.

___ 5. By definition, the recessionary gap is the amount by which Keynesian Aggregate Expenditures exceeds National Income at the full employment level of income.

___ 6. Keynes supported Say's Law in his *General Theory*.

___ 7. Firms increase employment and production in response to rising sales and unplanned declines in inventories.

___ 8. An economy will stay in equilibrium whenever actual investment equals actual saving.

___ 9. An inflationary gap occurs when Aggregate Expenditures exceed National Income at full employment.

___10. The Keynesian model suggests that autonomous injections into the economy are translated into much larger changes in incomes.

Standard Multiple Choice

There Is One Best Answer For Each Question.

___ 1. The Keynesian autonomous spending multiplier equals:
   a. government spending.
   b. 1 - MPC.
   c. 1/(1-MPS).
   d. 1/(1-MPC).
   e. unity.

___ 2. As autonomous investment rises, Keynesians expect increases in:
   a. income.
   b. employment.
   c. consumption.
   d. Aggregate Demand.
   e. All of these.

___ 3. If the MPC equals .67, then the autonomous spending multiplier equals:
   a. 3.
   b. 4.
   c. 5.
   d. 6.
   e. 7.

___ 4. The Aggregate Supply curve during a Keynesian depression:
   a. is horizontal.
   b. is vertical.
   c. tilts downward to the right.
   d. tilts upward to the right.
   e. is the negative relation between unemployment and inflation.

___ 5. A recessionary gap measures the:
   a. amount by which autonomous spending is below that needed to achieve a full employment equilibrium.
   b. amount Aggregate Spending exceeds that needed to achieve full employment.
   c. difference in real output between the classical model and the Keynesian depression model.
   d. paradox of thrift.
   e. None of the above.

___ 6. The paradox of thrift suggests that:
   a. "a penny saved is a penny earned."
   b. as consumption increases, saving decreases.
   c. as saving increases, investment declines.
   d. attempts to save more may actually reduce total saving.
   e. the less you pay, the lower your satisfaction.

___ 7. Macroequilibrium is achieved in a private economy when desired:
   a. consumption equals Aggregate Expenditures.
   b. consumption equals desired savings.
   c. investment equals desired saving.
   d. inventories equal desired saving.
   e. income equals net wealth.

___ 8. Inventories play an important role in the economic equilibrium because:
a. unintended inventory changes act as signals to producers to change their production plans.
b. they are a major component of the multiplier effect.
c. Aggregate Expenditures would be too hard to accurately measure without inventory changes.
d. savings could not be converted to investment without inventories as the means of doing so.
e. inventories are an extremely stable component of investment.

___ 9. The Keynesian point of view suggests that:
a. supply creates its own demand.
b. demand creates its own supply.
c. the market is always at equilibrium.
d. full employment is achieved as the result of natural market forces.
e. None of the above.

___ 10. Keynesians believe the depression of the 1930s was most attributable to:
a. excessive government spending.
b. reduced foreign exports.
c. reductions in investment.
d. declines in the money supply.
e. None of the above.

___ 11. If the marginal propensity to consume is .8, how much will total income rise in response to new investment of $25?
a. $5.
b. $20.
c. $25.
d. $125.
e. $200.

___ 12. An excess in autonomous spending relative to that needed for full employment is referred to as a(n):
a. inflationary surplus.
b. inflationary gap.
c. recessionary gap.
d. deflationary shortfall.
e. demand shortage.

Chapter Review (Fill-In Questions)

1. Keynesian analysis focused on _____ problems and illustrated that the economy might be stuck in a short run equilibrium in which substantial excess _____ existed.

2. In the simple Keynesian Aggregate Expenditures - National Income model, the National output schedule could be thought of as a Keynesian _____ schedule. All points along the National Income schedule represent potential equilibrium because aggregate output and income just equal aggregate spending. Whenever aggregate spending differs from aggregate income there is _____ .

3. Equilibrium occurs when Keynesian Aggregate Expenditures are just equal to _____. At this point, firms do not experience pressures to expand or contract output and they are able to maintain _____ at a level consistent with their desires.

4. Keynesian analysis assumes that only _____ adjustments will occur in situations of excess capacity. Whenever Keynesian Aggregate Expenditures exceed national output, firms typically find their _____ shrinking. To correct for this problem, business will _____ output and as a result, _____ will increase. Consequently, national income and output expands. As income expands, aggregate spending expands until both _____ and _____ are equal.

5. When an autonomous injection of spending is introduced into the economy, its effect is _____ so that equilibrium income actually increases _____ than the autonomous injection. This effect is the result of a concept referred to as the _____, and is defined by the ratio of the change in income to the change in _____. The simple spending multiplier is also defined to be equal to _____ or _____.

6. The paradox of thrift suggests that when people collectively desire to save more, they actually end up saving _____. When the economy is slipping into a recession, people generally attempt to save more, _____ the likelihood a recession will occur.

Unlimited Multiple Choice

There Are From Zero To Four Correct Answers For Each Question.

___ 1. Macroeconomic equilibrium occurs in the simple Keynesian model whenever:
   a. actual investment is equal to actual saving.
   b. unplanned changes in inventories are zero.
   c. planned investment equals planned saving.
   d. the dollar value of desired expenditures equal the dollar value of goods produced.

___ 2. Unintended inventory changes help:
   a. balance the macroeconomy.
   b. consumers balance their budgets.
   c. resolve any differences between planned saving and investment.
   d. guarantee that planned investment and planned saving will be equal at all levels of income.

___ 3. In a simple Keynesian model of the economy characterized by autonomous investment and no government, the autonomous spending multiplier is given by:
   a. 1/MPS.
   b. 1/(1-MPC).
   c. 1/MPC.
   d. 1/(MPC + MPS).

___ 4. Keynesian theory suggests that Aggregate Supply curves:
   a. fail to embody the workings of the labor market and the state of technology.
   b. are vertical when the economy reaches full employment.
   c. show the relationship between real output and the price level.
   d. show the real output that producers are willing to purchase at various income levels.

___ 5. In a simple Keynesian model, characterized by autonomous investment and no government, an autonomous spending multiplier of 5 implies that:
   a. the MPS equals .20.
   b. the MPC equals .50.
   c. new autonomous investment of $10 billion will cause income to grow by $20 billion.
   d. 1 - MPS = .80 = MPC.

Problems

Problem 1

A simple way to calculate an autonomous spending multiplier is to invert (turn upside down) the fraction representing the marginal propensity to save (mps). For example, if mps = 1/6 (roughly .167), the multiplier equals 6. Complete the following table by computing the mps and the associated multiplier (k) for each given value of the marginal propensity to consume (mpc).

MPC	MPS	k
1/2		
3/5		
2/3		
3/4		
4/5		
5/6		
6/7		
7/8		
8/9		
9/10		

Problem 2

Use this table to answer the following questions.

AE	Y	C	I	S	APC	APS	MPC	MPS
	$0	$200	$100		---	---	---	---
	500	600	100					
	1,000	1,000	100					
	1,500	1,400	100					
	2,000	1,800	100					
	2,500	2,200	100					
	3,000	2,600	100					

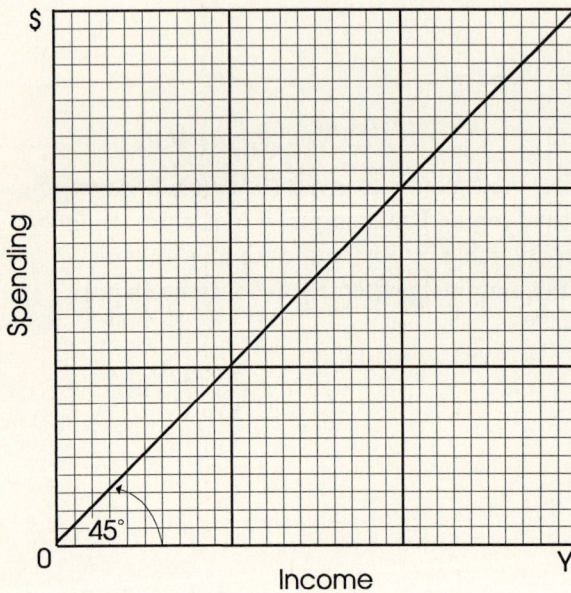

a. Complete the table and plot C, I, Y, and Aggregate Expenditures (AE) on the figure.

b. Equilibrium income is? _____

c. The multiplier is equal to? _____

d. If full employment income is equal to $2,500, the recessionary gap would be equal to _____. Show the recessionary gap on the figure. The GDP gap is equal to? _____ What causes these two to differ? _____

Problem 3

Answer the following questions based on the table below:

(1) Income (Y)	(2) Saving (S)	(3) Investment (I)	(4) S_1	(5) I_1	(6) S_2
0	-60	40		45	
100	-40	40		45	
200	-20	40		45	
300	0	40		45	
400	20	40		45	
500	40	40		45	
600	60	40		45	
700	80	40		45	
800	100	40		45	

a. Graph the saving and investment schedules on the figure.

b. Equilibrium income is? _____

c. Equilibrium saving is? _____

d. Equilibrium investment is? _____

e. Equilibrium consumption is? _____

f. The multiplier is? _____

g. Now assume that savers decide to save 25 % LESS at each income level and firms invest $45 at each income level.

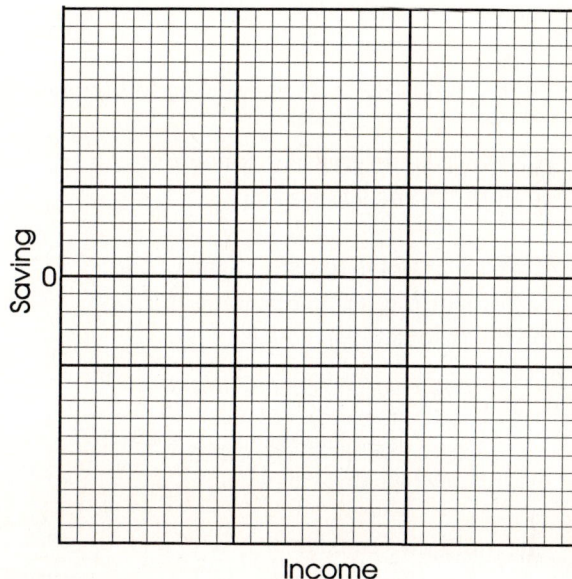

1. Fill in column 4 of the table. Then graph S_1 and I_1 on the figure.

2. The new equilibrium income level will be? _____

3. Equilibrium saving will be? _____

4. Equilibrium investment will be? _____

5. The multiplier is? _____

h. Beginning with the original saving schedule (S), assume that savers decide to save $20 more at each level of income, then fill in column 6 (S_2) of the table above.

    1. Equilibrium income will be? _____

    2. Equilibrium consumption will be? _____

    3. Equilibrium saving will be? _____

    4. The marginal propensity to consume is? _____

    5. Have consumers really saved more? _____

    6. What has happened to their standards of living? _____
       Why? _____

Problem 4

Use letters in this figure to answer the following questions:

a. If Keynesian Aggregate Spending is $C + I_1$, equilibrium income will be? _____

b. If $0Y_1$ represents full employment and Keynesian Aggregate Spending is $C + I_0$, the recessionary gap equals? _____

c. If $0Y_1$ represents full employment and Keynesian Aggregate Spending is $C + I_2$, the inflationary gap equals? _____

d. The multiplier equals? _____

Problem 5

Use the figure below to answer the following questions:

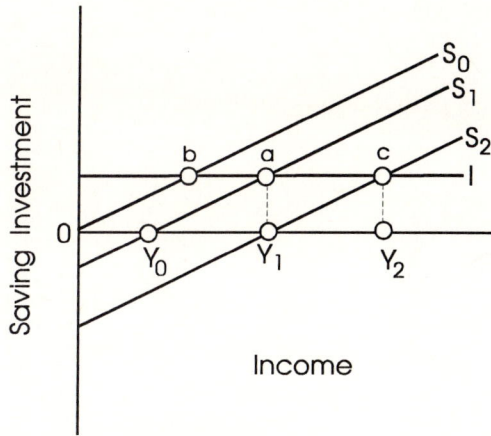

a. Using saving and investment schedules S_2 and I, answer the following (use letters):

    1. Equilibrium income is? _____

    2. The MPC is equal to? _____

    3. Saving when income is Y_1 is? _____

b. Starting with S_1, which curve shows increases in desired saving by the public? _____

c. If consumers actually desire to save less, will they end up saving less? _____

d. The multiplier is equal to? _____

Problem 6

To answer this question you may want to review the optional material included at the end of the chapter. Given below are equations for the components of Aggregate Expenditures (C + I). Use these equations to answer the following questions:

$$C = 250 + .75Y$$
$$I = 100$$

a. Graph C, I, and Aggregate Expenditures (AE) on the figure.

b. Equilibrium income is? _____

c. The autonomous spending multiplier equals? _____

d. Equilibrium consumption is? _____

e. Equilibrium saving is? _____

f. Write the equation for the saving function. _____

g. Assuming that full employment income is 1700, the recessionary gap is? _____ The GDP gap is? _____

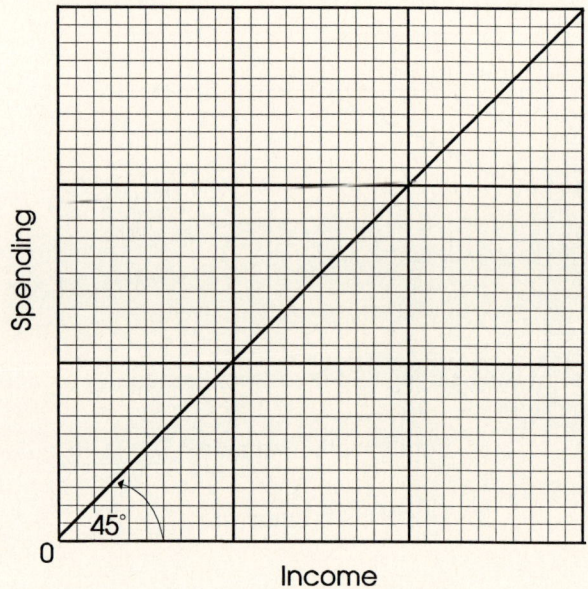

h. Assume that autonomous consumption expenditures increase from 250 to 400. What is the effect on equilibrium income? _____ On equilibrium saving? _____ Show these changes on the figure and label the new Keynesian Aggregate Expenditures curve AE_1 and the new consumption schedule C_1.

Problem 7

To answer this question you may want to review the optional material included at the end of the chapter. Given below are the equations for desired investment and saving. Use the equations to answer the following questions:

$$S = -300 + .20Y$$
$$I = 200$$

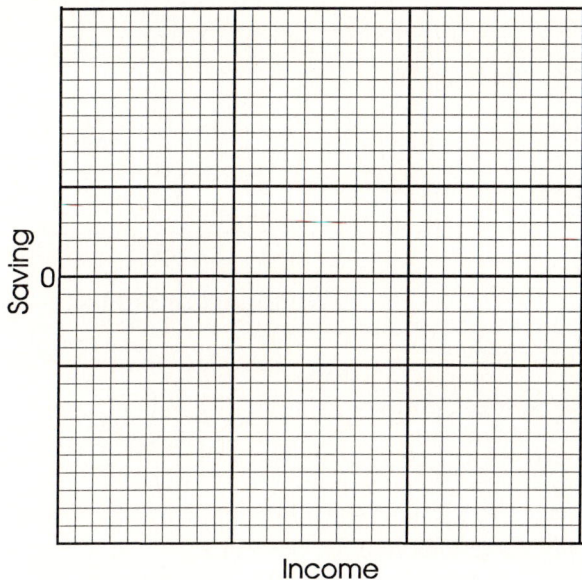

Income

a. Graph the saving and investment schedules on the figure.

b. Equilibrium income is? _____

c. The autonomous spending multiplier is?_____

d. Write the equation for the consumption function. _____

e. At an income level of 1500, planned saving is equal to? _____ Planned investment is equal to? _____ Is the economy in equilibrium? _____

Problem 8

Use this figure to answer the following questions.

a. Output level Q_1 represents _____

b. If Aggregate Demand were to fall from AD_1 to AD_0 what would be the impacts on price and quantity?_____

c. At Aggregate Demand level AD_0 the economy would most likely be in a _____

d. Using Keynesian policy tools, the move from AD_0 to AD_1 might be accomplished by

_____

e. If Aggregate Demand overshoots the AD_1 level and instead proceeds to AD_2, what would be the effect on price and quantity? _____

f. The range of the Aggregate Supply curve that corresponds to our simple Keynesian income-expenditure model is _____

g. The classical school assumed that market forces always maintained full employment. Based on that logic, what would an Aggregate Supply curve look like for a classical macroeconomic model?_____

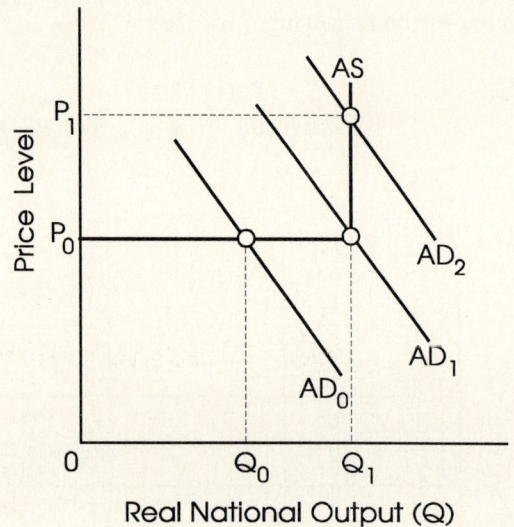

ANSWERS

Matching	True/False	Multiple Choice		Unlimited Multiple Choice
1. d	1. F	1. d	7. c	1. bcd
2. h	2. T	2. e	8. a	2. abc
3. b	3. F	3. a	9. b	3. ab
4. f	4. T	4. a	10. c	4. bc
5. i	5. F	5. a	11. d	5. ad
6. g	6. F	6. d	12. b	
7. j	7. T			
8. c	8. F			
9. e	9. T			
10. a	10. T			

Chapter Review (Fill-In Questions)

1. short run; capacity
2. Aggregate Supply; disequilibrium
3. National Income; inventories
4. quantity; inventories; increase; employment; National Income; Keynesian Aggregate Expenditures
5. multiplied; more; multiplier; autonomous spending; 1/(1 - MPC); 1/MPS
6. less, increasing

Problem 1

MPC	MPS	k
1/2	1/2	2
3/5	2/5	2.5
2/3	1/3	3
3/4	1/4	4
4/5	1/5	5
5/6	1/6	6
6/7	1/7	7
7/8	1/8	8
8/9	1/9	9
9/10	1/10	10

Problem 2

AE	Y	C	I	S	APC	APS	MPC	MPS
$300	$0	$200	$100	-$200	---	---	---	---
700	500	600	100	-100	1.20	-.20	.80	.20
1,100	1,000	1,000	100	0	1.00	0	.80	.20
1,500	1,500	1,400	100	100	.93	.07	.80	.20
1,900	2,000	1,800	100	200	.90	.10	.80	.20
2,300	2,500	2,200	100	300	.88	.12	.80	.20
2,700	3,000	2,600	100	400	.87	.13	.80	.20

a. See table and figure.
b. $1,500
c. 5
d. $200; see figure; $1000; the multiplier

Problem 3

a. See figure.
b. $500
c. $40
d. $40
e. $460
f. 5
g. (1) See figure.
   (2) $600
   (3) $45
   (4) $45
   (5) 6.7 when S is positive
h. (1) $400
   (2) $360
   (3) $40
   (4) .8
   (5) no
   (6) It has declined. Increases in desired saving reduced both equilibrium income and consumption.

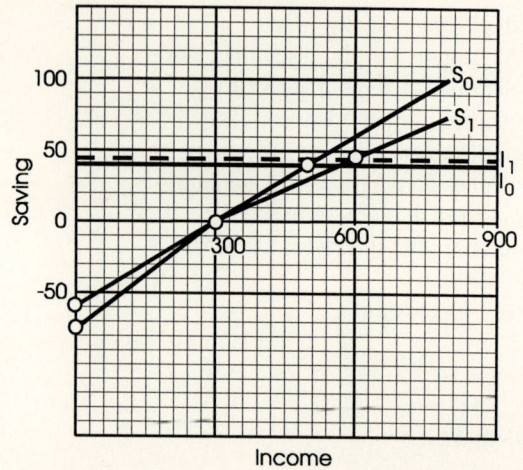

Problem 4

a. $0Y_1$
b. bf or de or A_0A_1
c. cd or A_1A_2
d. Y_0Y_1/bf or Y_2Y_1/cd or $0Y_1/0A_1$ or $0Y_0/0A_0$ or $0Y_2/0A_2$

Problem 5

a. (1) Y_2
   (2) $1 - cY_2/Y_1Y_2$
   (3) 0
b. S_0
c. no
d. Y_2Y_1/cY_2 or $Y_1Y_0/aY_1 = 1/MPS$

Problem 6

a. See figure.

b. $Y = C + I$
   $Y = 250 + .75Y + 100$
   $Y = 350 + .75Y$
   $Y - .75Y = 350$
   $.25Y = 350$
   $Y = 350/.25 = 1400$

c. $k = 1/(1-MPC)$
   $= 1/(1-.75)$
   $= 1/.25$
   $= 4$

d. $C = 250 + .75(1400)$
   $= 250 + 1050$
   $= 1300$

e. 100

f. $S = Y - C$
   $= Y - (250 + .75Y)$
   $= Y - 250 - .75Y$
   $= -250 + .25Y$

g. 75; 300

h. increases by 600; stays the same; See figure.

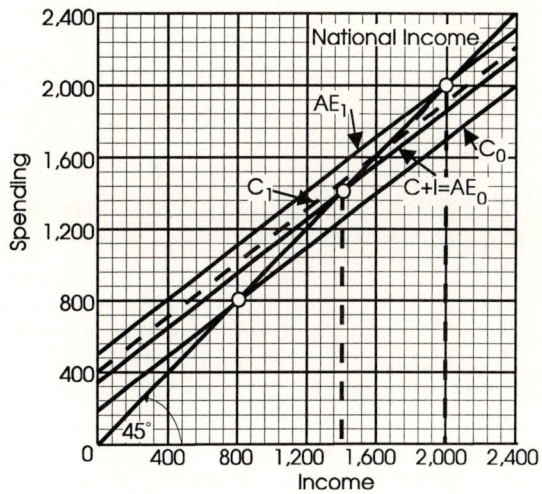

Problem 7

a. See figure.

b. Equilibrium occurs when $S = I$
   $-300 + .20Y = 200$
   $= .20Y = 500$
   $= Y = 500/.2$
   $= Y = 2500$

c. $k = 1/MPS = 1/.20 = 5$

d. $C = Y - S$
   $= Y - (-300 + .20Y)$
   $= Y + 300 - .20Y$
   $= 300 + .8Y$

e. 0; 200; no

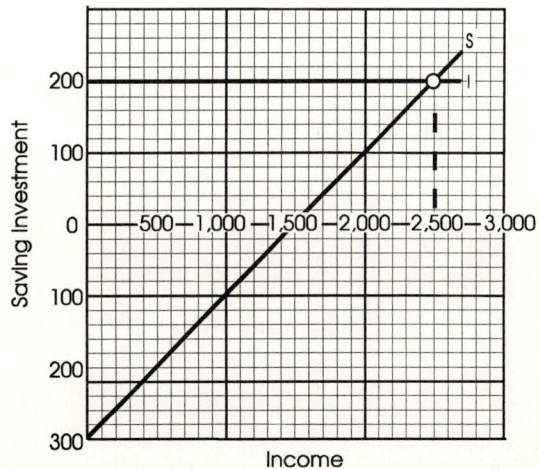

Problem 8

a. Output Q_1 represents full employment or full utilization of resources. It can also be viewed as a point on the production possibility frontier.
b. Under the assumptions of the Keynesian model as depicted here, price would not fall below P_0 but quantity would fall from Q_1 to Q_0.
c. Recession or depression.
d. New government expenditures. It could also be accomplished by increases in any of the other components of autonomous Aggregate Expenditures, such as consumption, investment or net exports.
e. Beyond AD_1 demand increases are converted into price level increases as there are no additional resources to put into the production process. Output stays at Q_1 but the price level rises from P_0 to P_1.
f. The horizontal portion where no price level changes occur.
g. Since Q_1 represents the fully employed level of economic activity, it would be reasonable to assume that a classical AS curve would be vertical at that level of output. Under these conditions, all Aggregate Demand changes are translated into price level changes.

Chapter 11
Government Taxing And Spending

Chapter Objectives

After you have read and studied this chapter you should be able to differentiate between discretionary automatic fiscal policy; explain how the autonomous spending, tax, and balanced-budget multipliers operate; distinguish between structural and cyclical deficits; and identify differences between Keynesian and new classical economic fiscal policies.

Chapter Review: Key Points

1. *Keynesian fiscal policy* is the use of federal spending and tax policies to stimulate or contract Aggregate Spending and economic activity to offset cyclical fluctuations. *Classical (supply-side) fiscal policies* rely on low tax rates and minimal government spending to allow Aggregate Supply to grow.

2. *Discretionary fiscal policy* consists of deliberate changes in federal government spending and taxation for stabilization purposes. Without congressional action *automatic stabilizers* such as corporate and personal income taxes and various transfer programs cause changes in spending and taxation as economic conditions change.

3. Increases in *government spending* increase Aggregate Expenditure and National Income through the multiplier process in the same way as changes in investment or autonomous consumer spending.

4. Changes in *net tax revenues* (tax revenues minus transfer payments) affect Aggregate Spending differently than changes in government spending. Changes in net taxes directly affect disposable income and, therefore, saving. These effects are transmitted into spending through the *autonomous tax multiplier* ($\Delta Y/\Delta T = 1 - 1/mps$), which is weaker than the spending multiplier.

5. In a Keynesian depression, the *balanced-budget multiplier* equals one, suggesting that equal increases (*decreases*) in government spending and taxes will increase (*decrease*) Aggregate Spending and equilibrium income by an equal amount. This result follows from the fact that the autonomous tax multiplier is one minus the autonomous spending multiplier.

6. *Automatic stabilizers* tend to cushion the economy. When income falls, automatic stabilizers keep the level of disposable income from falling as rapidly as income. Our progressive income tax causes tax collections to fall proportionally faster when income is falling and to increase proportionally faster when income is rising.

7. Built-in stabilizers can pose the problem of *fiscal drag*. When potential income is rising, automatic stabilizers brake the economy and slow the rate of growth.

8. The *structural deficit* is an estimate of the deficit that would be generated at full employment under existing tax and expenditure structures. This is a way to estimate the expansionary or contractionary influence of any tax and expenditure mix.

9. The *cyclical deficit* is attributable to business conditions. As unemployment grows, the cyclical deficit grows, and vice versa.

10. The *Laffer curve* indicates that high tax rates may impose such large disincentives to productive effort that Aggregate Supply and tax revenues are both restricted.

11. *Marginal tax rates* are the percentage taxes applied to small gains in additional income.

Matching Key Terms And Concepts

____ 1. fiscal policy

____ 2. fiscal drag

____ 3. automatic stabilizers

____ 4. balanced budget multiplier

____ 5. discretionary fiscal policy

____ 6. Laffer curve

____ 7. high tax rates

____ 8. government spending and transfers

____ 9. structural deficit

____10. autonomous tax multiplier

____11. cyclical deficit

a. Deliberate changes in spending and taxes for stabilization policy.

b. Retards growth in Aggregate Expenditures.

c. Examples of nondiscretionary fiscal policy.

d. Always equals one.

e. The use of government spending and tax policies to stimulate or contract economic activity to offset cyclical fluctuations.

f. Higher tax rates may either raise or lower government revenues.

g. Keynesians see as dampening spending, while new classical economists emphasize the destructive effects on production incentives.

h. -(MPC/MPS).

i. Keynesians perceive as bolstering spending, but new classical economists worry about disincentive effects on production.

j. Occurs if the economy has excessive idle capacity.

k. Tax revenues minus government outlays if the economy were producing at its capacity.

True/False Questions

_____ 1. If tax rates are increased to pay increased interest on public debt, incentives to work and invest might be diminished.

_____ 2. The biggest sources of federal tax revenues are social security, personal, and corporate income taxes.

_____ 3. Fiscal drag refers to the retarding effect that decreased government expenditures have on the economy.

_____ 4. Discretionary variations in spending and taxes are the only governmental mechanisms to control unemployment and inflation.

_____ 5. Automatic stabilizers are the mechanisms inherent in the economy to automatically dampen swings in economic activity.

_____ 6. Given the unpredictable nature of economic activity, an inflexible commitment to annually balancing the budget could prove disastrous, especially during recessionary periods.

_____ 7. In the classical model, an increase in desired Aggregate Expenditures will always induce greater production.

_____ 8. In the classical model, a decrease in desired Aggregate Expenditures is followed by a decrease in equilibrium for real production and real income.

_____ 9. Changes in government spending change Keynesian Aggregate Expenditures and National Income through the multiplier process in the same manner as changes in investment or autonomous consumer spending.

_____ 10. Because government outlays involve both spending for goods and services and transfer payments, the balanced budget multiplier is only slightly bigger than one.

_____ 11. Automatic stabilizers are also known as discretionary fiscal policy.

_____ 12. The tax increase of 1932 probably contributed to the severity of the Great Depression.

_____ 13. New classical economists and Keynesians agree that big government spending programs will boost the economy out of a slump.

_____ 14. Massive supply-side tax cuts quickly eliminated huge federal deficits in the early 1980s.

_____ 15. Cutting tax rates will tend to cure both fiscal drag and disincentives for production.

Standard Multiple Choice

There Is One Best Answer For Each Question.

___ 1. Which of the following is NOT an automatic stabilizer?
   a. Social Security payments.
   b. Unemployment compensation.
   c. An anti-inflationary tax increase.
   d. Progressive personal income tax rates.
   e. The corporate income tax.

___ 2. Using a simple Keynesian model where the mpc = .75 and government outlays and taxes are equal to $250 billion, the multiplier is equal to:
   a. 4.
   b. 1.
   c. 3.
   d. 2.
   e. 5.

___ 3. The autonomous tax multiplier equals:
   a. -MPC/MPS.
   b. 1/mps.
   c. four.
   d. three.
   e. 1/mpc.

___ 4. When built-in (automatic) stabilizers retard growth in Aggregate Spending, the problem is known as:
   a. stagflation.
   b. fiscal drag.
   c. excessive retardation.
   d. frictional inflation and unemployment.
   e. crowding-out.

___ 5. The balanced budget multiplier is:
   a. one.
   b. 1/mpc.
   c. 1/mps.
   d. 1/(1-mpc).
   e. -mpc/mps.

___ 6. Equal increases in the amount of government expenditures and taxes:
   a. have no effect on equilibrium income.
   b. cause equilibrium income to fall.
   c. cause equilibrium expenditures to increase by the same amount.
   d. cause prices to fall.
   e. cause proportional increases in the price level and unemployment.

___ 7. According to new classical economics, increases in which of the following would NOT pose disincentives for production?
   a. Marginal tax rates on wage and salary incomes.
   b. Corporate income tax rates.
   c. Tax deductions and exemptions.
   d. Government transfer programs.
   e. Government purchases of goods and services.

___ 8. The Laffer curve suggests a tradeoff between:
   a. unemployment and inflation.
   b. high tax rates and high tax revenues.
   c. consumption and investment.
   d. production and consumption.
   e. tax deductions or exemptions and a balanced budget.

9. Which of the following is smallest in absolute size?
   a. The autonomous spending multiplier.
   b. The marginal propensity to save.
   c. The balanced budget multiplier.
   d. The autonomous tax multiplier.
   e. The marginal propensity to consume.

10. Keynesians and new classical economists would be most likely to agree on which of the following as a cure for a severe recession?
    a. substantial increases in government 'public works' projects.
    b. deep cuts in government transfer programs.
    c. slashes in government purchases but hikes in transfer programs.
    d. the need to balance the federal budget.
    e. cuts in tax rates.

11. President Reagan's 1981-83 tax cuts were most in tune with ideas from:
    a. modern supply-siders.
    b. Keynesians.
    c. advocates of laws requiring annually balanced budgets.
    d. Friedrich Nietzsche.
    e. Paul Reubens.

12. Huge government budgets cause problems, according to supply-siders, for ALL of the following reasons EXCEPT:
    a. fiscal drag discourages spending.
    b. high taxes causing disincentives for work and investment.
    c. transfer payments discouraging work effort.
    d. government provisions of goods causing people who don't work to enjoy life without labor.
    e. All of these cause problems, according to supply-siders.

Chapter Review (Fill-In Questions)

1. Fiscal policy is the use of government spending and _____ policies to stimulate or contract economic activity to offset _____ fluctuations.

2. Discretionary fiscal policy is the intentional changes in government spending and taxation for the purpose of economic stabilization; whereas _____ fiscal policies are changes in spending or taxing which take place _____ (without congressional action) as economic conditions change.

3. Because all changes in injections are subject to the multiplier principle, _____ in government spending will change Aggregate Expenditures by an amount equal to the changes in autonomous injections times the multiplier. At equilibrium, injections must equal withdrawals, so when both government spending and taxation are introduced, the new equilibrium condition becomes _____. The payment of taxes will come from both consumption and _____.

4. An old idea that hikes in very high tax rates may actually lower total tax _____ is depicted by a device called the _____ curve.

5. Although Keynesians and new classical economists agree that cuts in _____ are stimulative, Keynesians view hikes in government _____ or _____ payments as stimulants for spending, while new classical economists view these outlays as retarding _____.

6. A law requiring annually balancing the budget would place policymakers in a dilemma. If declines in Aggregate Spending cause rising unemployment, balancing the budget requires that either tax revenues must be _____ or government outlays _____. Unfortunately, it is ambiguous as to whether higher tax _____ will yield more tax _____.

Unlimited Multiple Choice

There Are From Zero To Four Correct Answers For Each Question.

___ 1. New classical economists and Keynesians would probably agree that:
   a. tax rate hikes reduce equilibrium income.
   b. cuts in government spending reduce national income.
   c. cuts in government transfer payments increase real income.
   d. expanding taxes and spending equally results in equivalent growth of our national income.

___ 2. Incorporating autonomous taxes (T_a) into simple Keynesian models:
   a. shifts the withdrawal schedule upward by MPC x T_a.
   b. shifts the investment schedule downward by the same amount as tax revenue.
   c. shifts the government expenditure function upward.
   d. shifts the Aggregate Expenditures schedule downward by an amount exceeding tax revenues.

___ 3. Macroeconomic equilibrium occurs:
   a. when planned injections are greater than planned withdrawals.
   b. at the point where autonomous taxes equal autonomous government expenditures, assuming a balanced budget fiscal policy, and no induced government expenditure or induced taxation.
   c. when autonomous consumption equals autonomous saving.
   d. only at full employment income in the Keynesian model.

___ 4. An autonomous spending multiplier of 4 implies:
   a. that an increase in autonomous consumption of $10 billion will cause income to increase by $40 billion.
   b. that a decrease in autonomous investment of $40 billion will cause income to fall by $160 billion.
   c. that a simultaneous increase in both autonomous government expenditures and autonomous taxes of $20 billion will cause income to increase by $20 billion, all else equal.
   d. an MPC of .80, assuming consumption to be the only induced type of expenditure.

___ 5. A Constitutional amendment requiring annual balance of the federal budget:
   a. may be self-defeating if tax hikes and spending cuts are used in attempts to cure deficits occurring during a deep recession.
   b. would have been an excellent cure for the Great Depression.
   c. might result in inflationary policies if the economy was at full employment and the full employment budget yields a large surplus.
   d. would result in much lower tax burdens throughout the remainder of this century.

Problems

Problem 1

Complete this table by calculating the autonomous spending multiplier, tax multiplier, and balanced budget multiplier associated with each of the following values for the marginal propensity to consume (mpc).

MPC	Spending Multiplier	Tax Multiplier	Balanced Budget Multiplier
1/2			
3/5			
2/3			
3/4			
4/5			
5/6			
6/7			
7/8			
8/9			
9/10			

Problem 2

Use this table to answer the following questions:

a. On graph A plot the schedules for consumption and Keynesian Aggregate Expenditures (C + I + G). On graph B plot the saving (S), investment (I), and government (G) spending schedules.

b. Equilibrium income without government spending is _____

c. Equilibrium saving without government spending is _____

d. With government spending of $40, equilibrium income is _____

e. With government spending, equilibrium saving rises by _____

Y	S	I	G
0	-60	40	40
100	-40	40	40
200	-20	40	40
300	0	40	40
400	20	40	40
500	40	40	40
600	60	40	40
700	80	40	40
800	100	40	40
900	120	40	40
1,000	140	40	40
1,100	160	40	40
1,200	180	40	40

Graph A

Graph B

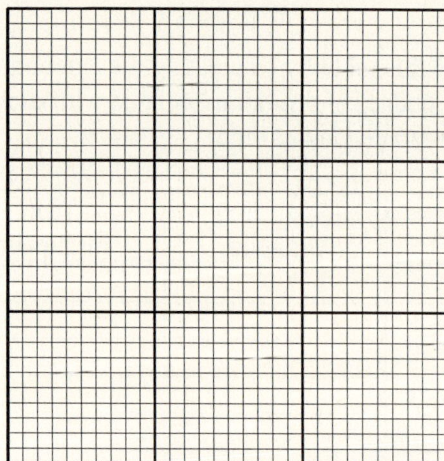

Problem 3

Use this figure to answer the following T/F questions. Assume that $1,200 billion represents full employment national income and that the autonomous spending multiplier is 4.

____ a. A recessionary gap exists when the economy produces an income of $1,400 billion.

____ b. Desired autonomous expenditures corresponding to Keynesian Aggregate Expenditure schedule AE_0 is $300 billion.

____ c. An inflationary gap exists when the economy produces an income of $1,200 billion.

____ d. As the economy moves along the nominal income line from a to b, real output increases.

____ e. As the economy moves from b to c, real output increases, and the absolute price level remains unchanged.

____ f. A recessionary gap of $50 billion exists when the economy produces an income of $1,000 billion.

____ g. An inflationary gap of $50 billion exists when the economy produces an income of $1,400 billion.

____ h. The movement from b to c ultimately yields only pure price inflation.

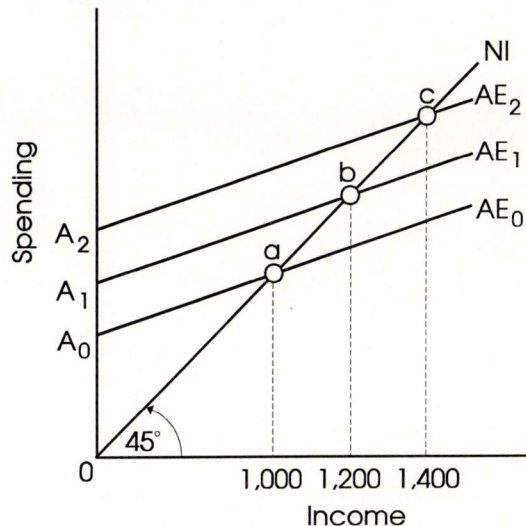

____ i. If the economy was in equilibrium at point a, the government could exactly eliminate the recessionary gap by increasing its spending by $200 billion.

____ j. If the economy was in equilibrium at point c, full employment (without inflation) could be restored by decreasing both government spending and taxes by 200.

Problem 4

Use this table to answer the following questions:

Before Government				After Government						
Y	C	S	I	G	T	Y-T	C_1	S_1	S_1+T	I+G
0	400		100	200	200					
200	500		100	200	200					
400	600		100	200	200					
600	700		100	200	200					
800	800		100	200	200					
1,000	900		100	200	200					
1,200	1,000		100	200	200					
1,400	1,100		100	200	200					
1,600	1,200		100	200	200					
1,800	1,300		100	200	200					
2,000	1,400		100	200	200					

a. Complete the column labeled "S."

b. Equilibrium income without government is _____

c. Now assume that government enters the picture and spends 200 without taxing. Equilibrium income would be _____ Equilibrium saving would become _____

d. Now assume that government continues to spend 200, but now levies taxes equal to 200 as well.
(1) Complete the "Y-T" column.
(2) Complete the adjusted consumption schedule (C_1). Remember that only a portion (the MPC) of taxes comes from consumption.
(3) Remember that only a portion (the MPS) of taxes come from savings. Complete the adjusted saving schedule "S_1" and the "S_1 + T" and "I + G" columns.

e. With the balanced budget (G = T = 200), equilibrium income is? _____

f. The increase in income accompanying the balanced budget hike was? _____

g. In the graph below, plot the S, S_1, I, G, T, I+G, and S_1+T schedules. Label the original equilibrium (without government) as "a" and the new equilibrium (budget balanced at 200) as "b."

Income

Problem 5

Answering Problems 5, 6, and 7 may require reviewing the Optional Material at the end of chapter. Use this table to answer the following questions:

a. Write an equation for the consumption function without taxes. _____

b. Write an equation for the saving function without taxes. _____

c. Write an equation for investment expenditure. _____

d. Write an equation for government expenditure. _____

e. Write an equation for the tax function. _____

Y	C	I	G	T
0	300	100	50	50
100	375	100	50	50
200	450	100	50	50
300	525	100	50	50
400	600	100	50	50
500	675	100	50	50
600	750	100	50	50
700	825	100	50	50
800	900	100	50	50
900	975	100	50	50
1,000	1,050	100	50	50

f. Write an equation for the consumption function with taxes. _____

g. Write an equation for the saving function with taxes. _____

h. What does equilibrium income (including the government's budget) equal? _____

i. What are the equilibrium values for C?_____ I?_____ G?_____ S?_____ T?_____

j. What kind of fiscal policy is the government pursuing in this example? _____

k. Write the condition for macroeconomic equilibrium when government both spends and taxes._____

l. Assume that $\Delta Ga = \Delta Ta = \$40$ billion, all other things held constant. What does equilibrium output equal? _____

m. Write an equation for the new consumption function with taxes. _____

n. Write an equation for the new saving function with taxes. _____

o. What are the equilibrium values for C?_____ I?_____ G?_____ S?_____ T?_____

p. Show that the balanced-budget multiplier is one. _____

Problem 6

If $G_a = 40$, $I_a = 30$, and $S = -100 + .20\ Y$;

a. What are equilibrium values for C?_____ I?_____ G?_____ Y?_____

b. If full employment national income is 700, is there an inflationary or recessionary gap?_____

c. What is the value of the inflationary or recessionary gap?_____

d. How could a tax change be used to close this gap? _____

e. What are the equilibrium values of C, I, G, and Y after solving question d for: C?_____ I?_____ G?_____ Y?_____

Problem 7

Given that $I_a = 100$, $G_a = 250$, and $C = 400 + .9Y$;

a. What are the equilibrium values of C?_____ I?_____ G?_____ Y?_____

b. If the GNP gap equals 200, is the situation inflationary or recessionary? _____

c. Solve for full employment equilibrium using a balanced budget approach. What are the full employment equilibrium values of C?_____ I?_____ G?_____ Y?_____

ANSWERS

Matching		True/False		Multiple Choice		Unlimited Multiple Choice
1. e	7. g	1. T	9. T	1. c	7. c	1. a
2. b	8. i	2. T	10. F	2. a	8. b	2. a
3. c	9. k	3. F	11. F	3. a	9. b	3. none
4. d	10. h	4. F	12. T	4. b	10. e	4. abc
5. a	11. j	5. T	13. F	5. a	11. a	5. ac
6. f		6. T	14. F	6. c	12. a	
		7. F	15. T			
		8. F				

Chapter Review (Fill-in Questions)

1. tax; cyclical
2. nondiscretionary; automatically
3. changes; I + G = S + T; saving
4. revenues; Laffer
5. tax rates; purchases; transfer; production or Aggregate Supply
6. increased; reduced; rates; revenues

Problem 1

MPC	Spending Multiplier	Tax Multiplier	Balanced Budget Multiplier
1/2	2	-1	1
3/5	2.5	-1.5	1
2/3	3	-2	1
3/4	4	-3	1
4/5	5	-4	1
5/6	6	-5	1
6/7	7	-6	1
7/8	8	-7	1
8/9	9	-8	1
9/10	10	-9	1

Problem 2

a. See figure.
b. 500
c. 40
d. 700
e. 40

Problem 3

a. F
b. F
c. F
d. T
e. F
f. T
g. T
h. T
i. F
j. T

Graph A

Graph B

Problem 4

Before Government				After Government						
Y	C	S	I	G	T	Y-T	C_1	S_1	S_1+T	I+G
0	400	-400	100	200	200	-200	300	-500	-300	300
200	500	-300	100	200	200	0	400	-400	-200	300
400	600	-200	100	200	200	200	500	-300	-100	300
600	700	-100	100	200	200	400	600	-200	0	300
800	800	0	100	200	200	600	700	-100	100	300
1,000	900	100	100	200	200	800	800	0	200	300
1,200	1,000	200	100	200	200	1,000	900	100	300	300
1,400	1,100	300	100	200	200	1,200	1,000	200	400	300
1,600	1,200	400	100	200	200	1,400	1,100	300	500	300
1,800	1,300	500	100	200	200	1,600	1,200	400	600	300
2,000	1,400	600	100	200	200	1,800	1,300	500	700	300

a. See table.
b. 1000; saving and investment are equal at Y = 1000 without government
c. 1400; 300; I + G = S when Y = 1,400.
d. See table.
e. 1200
f. 200
g. See figure.

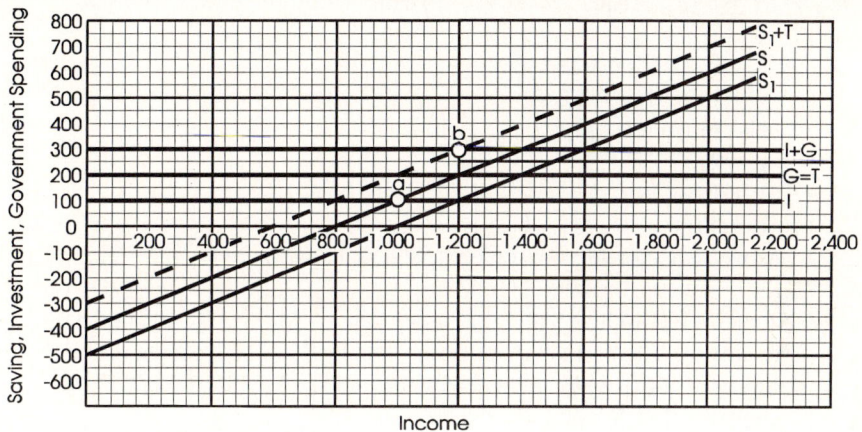

Problem 5

a. C = 300 +.75Y
b. S = -300 +.25Y
c. I = 100
d. G = 50
e. T = 50
f. C = 262.50 +.75Y; the consumption function is shifted down by the MPC x taxes or .75 X 50 = 37.50. Thus, autonomous consumption becomes 262.50 (300 - 37.50).
g. S = -312.50 +.25Y
h. Y = 1,650

$$Y = C + I + G$$
$$Y = 262.50 + .75Y + 100 + 50$$
$$Y = 412.50 + .75Y$$
$$Y - .75Y = 412.50$$
$$Y = 412.50 / .25$$
$$Y = 1,650.$$

i. C = 1,500 I = 100 G = 50 S = 100 T = 50
j. Balanced budget, since G = T

k. $I + G = S + T$
l.   1,690
m. $C = 232.50 + .75Y$
n. $S = -322.50 + .25Y$
o. $C = 1,500$ $I = 100$ $G = 90$ $S = 100$ $T = 90$
p.   Balanced budget multiplier $= \Delta Y/(\Delta Ga = \Delta Ta) = 40/(40 = 40) = 1$ or $1/.25 - .75/.25 = 1$

Problem 6

a.   (1) $S = I + G$
        $-100 + .2Y = 40 + 30$
        $-100 + .2Y = 70$
        $.2Y = 170$
        $Y = 170/.2 = 850$
     (2) $C = Y - S$
        $C = 850 - (-100 + .2(850))$
        $C = 850 + 100 - .2(850)$
        $C = 850 + 100 - 170$
        $C = 780$
     (3) $I = 30$
     (4) $G = 40$
b.   Since we have more than sufficient spending to fully employ the economy we have an inflationary gap.
c.   GNP gap $= 700 - 850 = 150$; inflationary gap $= -150/5 = -30$, where the multiplier $= 5$
d.   Our objective is to decrease national income by $150, so we must increase taxes. Since the tax multiplier is $-4 (= -.8/.2)$, taxes need to be increased by $150/4 or $37.50.
e. $C = 630$ $I = 30$ $G = 40$ $Y = 700$.

Problem 7

a. $C = 7,150$ $I = 100$ $G = 250$ $Y = 7,500$ Calculated as follows:
     $Y = C + I + G$
     $Y = 400 + .9Y + 100 + 250$
     $Y - .9Y = 750$
     $.1Y = 750$
     $Y = 7,500$
     $C = 400 + .9(7,500) = 7,150$
b.   Since the GNP gap is positive we know that there is deficient Aggregate Expenditures; therefore the situation is recessionary.
c.   Since the full employment equilibrium equals 7,700, but the economy is currently in equilibrium at 7,500, Aggregate Expenditures must be increased so that the economy will expand by $200. Since the balanced budget multiplier always equals 1, the solution is to increase government expenditures by $200 and increase taxes by $200. The new values for the variables are: $Y = 7,700$ $C = 7,150$ $I = 100$ and $G = 450$. Note that even though total consumption is equal in the before and after situations the breakdown of autonomous and induced consumption is, in fact, different.

Chapter 12
Money And Its Creation

Chapter Objectives

After you have read and studied this chapter you should be able to describe the functions money performs in a market system; differentiate between alternative forms of money and definitions of the money supply; differentiate between potential money multipliers, actual money multipliers, and the monetary base; and explain how the interactions between banks and their customers determine the amount of money in circulation.

Chapter Review: Key Points

1. *Barter* requires a *double coincidence of wants*--trade can only occur if each party has what the other wants and if divisibility poses no problems.

2. *Money* ensures this double coincidence of wants--the seller will accept money because of what it will buy, while the buyer is willing to exchange money (and thus, all else it will buy) for the good or service in question.

3. Money facilitates specialization and exchange by decreasing transaction costs. The more sophisticated the financial system, the greater the level of production and consumption and the higher the standard of living.

4. Money is a *medium of exchange*. It is used for most transactions in monetary economies.

5. Money is a *measure of value*. Used as a standard unit of account, it is the common denominator for pricing goods and services.

6. Money is a *store of value*. It is among the most nominally secure of all assets people can use to hold their wealth.

7. Money is a *standard of deferred payment*. Serving as a link between the past, present, and future, it is used as a measure of *credit* to execute contracts calling for future payments.

8. *Liquidity* is negatively related to the transaction costs incurred in exchanges of assets. *Time, certainty regarding price, and the quality of information in a market* are all dimensions of liquidity. Assets are liquid if transaction costs are low, *illiquid* if transaction costs are high.

9. *Commodity monies* (precious metals, stones, or arrowheads) have values that are independent of what they will buy. *Fiat money* (paper currency) is valuable only because it is money; its use is based on *faith.*

10. The profit governments make from printing money or stamping coins is called *seignorage.*

11. According to Gresham's Law, "Bad money drives out good."

12. The very narrowly defined money supply (*M1*) is the total of: (*a*) *currency* (coins and bills) in the hands of the nonbanking public, plus (*b*) *demand deposits* (checking accounts of private individuals, firms, and nonfederal government units in financial institutions).

13. Some highly liquid assets are viewed as near-monies and are included in broader definitions of the money supply (*M2* and *M3*) by monetary analysts who believe the spending of the public can be predicted better if these assets are included. Examples of such highly liquid assets include short-term *time deposits* (savings accounts) and *certificates of deposit (CDs).* The assets included in "money supplies" defined more broadly than *M1* are judgmental because these assets are not mediums of exchange.

14. Banks "*create*" money through loan-based expansions of demand deposits (checking account money). They make loans based on currency they hold as reserves, and these loans take the form of new demand deposit money.

15. Banks hold *reserves* that are far less than their deposit liabilities. The larger the proportion of deposits held as either excess or required reserves, the smaller are the money multiplier and resulting money supply, given some fixed total amount of reserves.

16. The *potential money multiplier* (m_p) equals 1/*rr*, where **rr** is the banking system's planned or legally required reserves as a percentage of deposits. The *actual money multiplier* is much smaller because: (*a*) households and firms hold currency that could be used as a base for the money creation process were this currency held in bank vaults as reserves against deposits; and (*b*) banks hold excess reserves to meet withdrawals of deposits.

17. The *actual money multiplier* (m_a) equals *MS/MB*, where *MS* is the money supply and *MB* is the *monetary base,* or high-powered money. Naturally, $MS = m_a MB$.

18. *Financial institutions* facilitate flows and payments of funds and provide secure places for savers' deposits. Their most important economic function is to channel funds from savers to financial investors and other borrowers through a process called *financial intermediation.* Commercial banks, savings and loan associations, mutual savings banks, credit unions, insurance companies, and stock exchanges are all financial intermediaries.

Matching Key Terms And Concepts

Set I

___ 1.   credit

___ 2.   money multiplier

___ 3.   M1

___ 4.   currency

___ 5.   Federal Reserve System

___ 6.   barter

___ 7.   seignorage

___ 8.   value of money

___ 9.   M2, M3 and L

___10.   liquidity

a.   Created in 1913 to mitigate the impact of financial crises.

b.   Extension of money; uses money as a standard of deferred payment.

c.   Always equals one in a 100 percent reserve banking system.

d.   Broader definitions of the money supply.

e.   Currency plus "checkable" deposits.

f.   Purchasing power of money.

g.   Requires double coincidence of wants.

h.   Coins and paper money.

i.   Profits made by government when it prints or coins money.

j.   Inversely related to the transactions costs incurred when an asset is bought or sold.

Set II

___ 1.   measure of value

___ 2.   potential money multiplier

___ 3.   store of value

___ 4.   reserves

___ 5.   fiat money

___ 6.   Gresham's Law

___ 7.   medium of exchange

___ 8.   actual money multiplier

___ 9.   standard of deferred payment

___10.   commodity money

a.   Money as an asset.

b.   Goods trade for money, and money trades for goods.

c.   Money that is valuable in itself.

d.   Money as a standard of credit.

e. $m_a = MS/MB$.

f.   Standard unit of account.

g.   "Bad money drives out good."

h.   Money valued only for what it buys.

i.   1/(reserve requirement ratio).

j.   Cash in bank vaults.

True/False Questions

___ 1. Currency held in bank vaults is not included in the money supply.

___ 2. The value of money and the cost of credit are both determined by supply and demand, much as the prices of other economic goods are determined.

___ 3. Commodity money is valuable only because of its purchasing power, while fiat money has substantial value independently of what it will buy.

___ 4. The most important service that money provides is that it is used to express the relative prices of goods.

___ 5. Wealth is the monetary value of all of your assets.

___ 6. Financial assets are liquid if trading them entails high transaction costs, but financial assets are illiquid if only low transaction costs would be incurred.

___ 7. The amount of funds held in the vault to meet withdrawals of deposits are called the bank's reserves.

___ 8. Money as a medium of exchange eliminates the need for a double coincidence of wants that would be required in a barter system before exchange occurred.

___ 9. Standards of living tend to be very high in money-less economies.

___10. Credit cards are a form of money.

Standard Multiple Choice

There Is One Best Answer For Each Question.

___ 1. An asset's "liquidity" refers to:
   a. the transaction costs incurred in dealing in the asset.
   b. time it takes to convert it to cash.
   c. "backing" behind a financial asset.
   d. whether it may be bought or sold.
   e. whether the asset is water soluble.

___ 2. Money is NOT a:
   a. medium of exchange.
   b. measure of value or standard unit of account.
   c. means of interpersonal utility comparison.
   d. store of value.
   e. standard of deferred payment.

___ 3. "Bad money drives out good" according to:
   a. Gresham's Law.
   b. Say's Law.
   c. Fisher's Law.
   d. Keynes' Law.
   e. Friedman's Corollary.

___ 4. An appropriate commodity money would NOT be:
   a. durable.
   b. divisible.
   c. optimally scarce.
   d. heterogeneous.
   e. portable.

___ 5. Fiat money has value because it is:
   a. backed by gold or silver.
   b. made of a precious metal.
   c. mandated by government to be accepted for payments.
   d. bereft of value as a commodity.
   e. None of the above.

___ 6. The number of relative prices in an n-good, barter economy is:
   a. n.
   b. n^2.
   c. $(n(n-1))/2$.
   d. 2^n.
   e. np.

___ 7. Relative to barter, money:
   a. facilitates specialization and exchange.
   b. increases the frequency of transactions.
   c. reduces transaction costs.
   d. finesses the "double coincidence of wants" requirement.
   e. All of these.

___ 8. A fractional reserve banking system relies most on:
   a. extensive government regulation.
   b. people keeping most of their money in banks.
   c. a stable money multiplier.
   d. a commodity base for money.
   e. None of these.

___ 9. The profits made by government when it prints/mints money are known as:
   a. exorbitant.
   b. fiat returns.
   c. legal tender.
   d. seignorage.
   e. budgetary revenue.

___ 10. If no currency exists outside bank vaults, and banks loan exactly 80 percent of total reserves, then there will be:
   a. "runs" on banks.
   b. five times as much money as reserves.
   c. excess liquidity.
   d. inflation.
   e. financial collapse.

___ 11. The potential value of the money multiplier equals:
   a. 1/mpc.
   b. 1/mps.
   c. 1/rr.
   d. 1/(rr + xr).
   e. 10rr.

___ 12. The actual money multiplier, m_a, is calculated as:
   a. -MPC/MPS.
   b. 1/rr.
   c. 1/(1-mpc).
   d. DM/Drr.
   e. MS/MB.

Chapter Review (Fill-In Questions)

1. In a(n) _____ economy, exchange occurs only when each trader has precisely what the other desires; that is, there must be a(n) _____ of wants.

2. As a _____, money provides a common denominator through which the relative prices of goods may be compared. As a _____, money is exchanged for goods, and goods are exchanged for money. As a _____, money is a relatively riskless way to hold your wealth. As a _____, money binds the past, the present, and the future, making contracts possible that call for future payments for goods delivered now.

3. _____ money has intrinsic value because it is made of something valuable, while _____ money is only valuable because of its purchasing power.

4. In a fractional reserve banking system, the ready cash in bank vaults, called _____, is far less than bank liabilities, or _____.

5. The money creation process occurs when banks receive new _____, which they then _____ to their customers.

6. The factor by which banks can expand a given amount of reserves into new demand deposits is called the _____. Its potential value is _____, where rr stands for the reserve requirement ratio. It reaches this potential value only when banks are _____ loaned-up, and when consumers and businesses hold _____.

7. When only a few banks have outflows of deposits so great that they may not be able to cover all of their liabilities instantly, they can sell _____ to other banks or borrow funds from banks having _____. The banking network facilitating these interbank borrowings is the _____ market. As a last resort, banks can borrow from the federal "bankers' bank," which is known as the _____.

Unlimited Multiple Choice

There May Be From Zero To Four Correct Answers To Each Question.

___ 1. In an economy characterized by barter:
   a. the costs of securing information about potentially profitable transactions are negligible.
   b. goods are exchanged for goods.
   c. transactions can only be carried out when there exists a double coincidence of wants.
   d. few of the advantages of specialization are ever realized.

___ 2. Money serves as a:
   a. medium of exchange.
   b. measure of value.
   c. store of value.
   d. common denominator by which relative prices are expressed.

___ 3. The potential money multiplier:
    a. is always equal to one in a fractional reserve banking system.
    b. equals 1/reserve requirement ratio.
    c. indicates the extent to which demand deposits can be expanded as the result of an initial deposit.
    d. is equal to zero in a 100 percent reserve banking system.

___ 4. Total deposits in any single bank are unlikely to be highly volatile because:
    a. flows of deposits between banks do not affect the total amounts of reserves in the banking system.
    b. the average daily amount in a given account is fairly stable on a month to month basis.
    c. most people have reasonably stable patterns of income and spending, and seldom allow their accounts to drop below some minimum value.
    d. few people use their checking accounts in purchasing goods.

___ 5. Which measures (estimates) of money are correct?
    a. M1 = currency in the hands of the nonbanking public plus funds in "checkable" accounts.
    b. L = the total market value of all assets in an economy.
    c. M2 = M1 plus small time deposits.
    d. M3 = M2 plus gold, silver, and long-term negotiable bonds.

Problems

Problem 1

This table shows the initial T-account for a monopoly bank. Assume that the reserve requirement ratio is 20 percent. Also, assume that all money is held in the bank, and that the monopoly bank is a profit maximizer, which means that it will always expand loans (IOUs) by the maximum amount permitted by law. (Thus, the bank's excess reserves are always zero.)

Assets		Liabilities	
Cash Reserves	$1,000	Demand deposits	$5,000
Loans	$4,000		
	$5,000		$5,000

a. What is the size of the money multiplier? _____

b. Write the formula for the money multiplier. _____

c. Is this a fractional reserve banking system? _____ Why? _____

d. Assume that $2,000 is deposited in the monopoly bank. Balance the bank's T-account.

Assets	Liabilities
Cash Reserves	Demand deposits
Loans	

e. By how much will demand deposits increase? _____

f. By how much have loans increased? _____

g. Explain why the monopoly bank is able to expand its loans by the maximum amount permitted by law._____

h. Why won't this be true for each bank in a multi-bank example? _____.

Problem 2

This table shows the initial T-account for another monopoly bank. Assume a reserve requirement ratio of 10 percent. Also, assume that unless otherwise indicated, all money is held in this bank, which strives to always be fully loaned up. That is, desired excess reserves are always zero.

Assets		Liabilities	
Cash Reserves	$1,000	Demand deposits	$10,000
Loans	$9,000		
	$10,000		$10,000

a. What is the size of the money multiplier? _____

b. Write the formula for the money multiplier. _____

c. Assume that an additional $2,000 is deposited in our monopoly bank. Please balance the bank's T-account. By how much will demand deposits increase? _____

Assets	Liabilities
Cash Reserves	Demand deposits
Loans	

d. By how much will loans increase? _____

e. Assume $1,000 is now withdrawn from our monopoly bank. Balance the bank's T-account.

Assets	Liabilities
Cash Reserves	Demand deposits
Loans	

f. By how much will demand deposits decrease? _____

g. By how much will loans decrease? _____

h. Assume that $500 more is withdrawn. Please balance the bank's T-account.

Assets	Liabilities
Cash Reserves	Demand deposits
Loans	

i. By how much will demand deposits decrease? _____
   Why?_____

j. By how much will loans decrease? _____

k. What are total demand deposits? _____

l. Total cash reserves? _____

m. Total loans?_____

Problem 3

Suppose there are roughly 1,000 banks in our fractional reserve banking system, that the reserve requirement ratio is 20 percent, that each bank holds an extra 5 percent as excess reserves, and that the public holds no cash. Now assume that $2,000 is deposited in the first bank.

a. Show, using the first three banks in the system, how the money supply will increase as each bank expands its loans by the full amount of any reserves greater than 25 percent of deposits.

Bank 1

Assets	Liabilities
Reserves	Demand deposits
Required Reserves	
Excess Reserves	
Loans	

Bank 2

Assets	Liabilities
Reserves	Demand deposits
Required Reserves	
Excess Reserves	
Loans	

Bank 3

Assets	Liabilities
Reserves	Demand deposits
Required Reserves	
Excess Reserves	
Loans	

b. What is the size of the money multiplier? _____

c. By how much will demand deposits increase for the system as a whole? _____

d. By how much will loans increase for the system as a whole? _____

e. Why is money creation in a multi-bank world a cumulative process? _____

f. Why should each bank limit loans to only reserves in excess of 25% of deposits? _____

Problem 4

Assume (a) a required reserve ratio is 20%, (b) each bank quickly lends out any excess reserves, and (c) the non-banking public keeps all cash in banks. Consider an initial $2,000 cash deposit by a patron of bank "A." The bank retains the required reserve and loans out the excess reserve. Complete the table below for banks "B" through "H" and then sum the columns indicated as if this transaction had passed through 1,000 or more banks in the system.

Bank	Total Reserves	Required Reserves	Excess Reserves	Loan/Money Expansion
A	2,000.00	400.00	1,600.00	1,600.00
B	1,600.00			
C				
D				
E				
F				
G				
H		xxx	xxx	xxx
Entire System	xxx		xxx	

Problem 5

This problem is designed to help you practice the various values that a money multiplier might take. In order to complete the table assume that there is a large banking system (1,000 or more banks). Additionally assume that the banks always hold enough reserves to exceed the required reserve ratio by 5%. For example, if the required reserve ratio were 25% the banks would, in reality, hold 30%. Assume that the non-banking public holds no cash reserves.

Deposit	Required Reserve Ratio	Actual Money Multiplier	Single Bank Expansion	Total Expansion By All Banks
2,000	.20			
1,000	.15			
5,000	.1166			
3,500	.05			
500	.075			

Problem 6

Required Reserve Ratio	Potential Money Multiplier	Potential Money Supply	Actual Money Multiplier	Actual Money Supply
1/10				
1/9				
1/8				
1/7				
1/6				
1/5				
1/4				

a. Fill in the potential money multiplier column.

b. Fill in the potential money supply column if there are $1 million in bank reserves (no loans have been made yet), and $1 million in currency held by the public.

c. Fill in the actual money multiplier column if banks hold ten percent (.10) in excess reserves.

d. Fill in the actual money supply column, using the information you just calculated about the actual money multiplier, and assuming that $1 million in reserves sits in banks, and that the public holds $1 million in currency.

ANSWERS

Matching		True/False	Multiple	Unlimited	Fill-In
Set I	Set II				

<table>
<tr><td colspan="2">Matching</td><td>True/False</td><td>Multiple</td><td>Unlimited</td><td>Fill-In</td></tr>
<tr><td>Set I</td><td>Set II</td><td></td><td></td><td></td><td></td></tr>
<tr><td>1. b</td><td>1. f</td><td>1. T</td><td>1. a</td><td>1. bcd</td><td>1. barter; double</td></tr>
<tr><td>2. c</td><td>2. i</td><td>2. T</td><td>2. c</td><td>2. abcd</td><td>   coincidence</td></tr>
<tr><td>3. e</td><td>3. a</td><td>3. F</td><td>3. a</td><td>3. bc</td><td>2. standard unit of account;</td></tr>
<tr><td>4. h</td><td>4. j</td><td>4. F</td><td>4. d</td><td>4. bc</td><td>   medium of exchange;</td></tr>
<tr><td>5. a</td><td>5. h</td><td>5. F</td><td>5. c</td><td>5. ac</td><td>   store of value; standard</td></tr>
<tr><td>6. g</td><td>6. g</td><td>6. F</td><td>6. c</td><td></td><td>   of deferred payment</td></tr>
<tr><td>7. i</td><td>7. b</td><td>7. T</td><td>7. e</td><td></td><td>3. commodity; fiat</td></tr>
<tr><td>8. f</td><td>8. e</td><td>8. T</td><td>8. b</td><td></td><td>4. reserves; deposits</td></tr>
<tr><td>9. d</td><td>9. d</td><td>9. F</td><td>9. d</td><td></td><td>5. deposits; loan</td></tr>
<tr><td>10. j</td><td>10. c</td><td>10. F</td><td>10. b</td><td></td><td>6. money multiplier; 1/rr;</td></tr>
<tr><td></td><td></td><td></td><td>11. c</td><td></td><td>   fully; no cash</td></tr>
<tr><td></td><td></td><td></td><td>12. e</td><td></td><td>7. loans; excess reserves;</td></tr>
<tr><td></td><td></td><td></td><td></td><td></td><td>   federal funds; FED</td></tr>
</table>

Problem 1

a. 5
b. $m_p = 1/rr = 1/.20 = 5$.
c. Yes; bank holds less than 100% against deposit liabilities.
d. See table
e. $10,000
f. $8,000
g. Monopolist doesn't have to worry about withdrawn money not returning.
h. Flows between banks in multi-bank systems prevent each from making maximum loans.

Assets		Liabilities	
Cash Reserves	$3,000	Demand deposits	$15,000
Loans	$12,000		
	$15,000		$15,000

Problem 2

a. 10
b. $m_p = 1/rr = 1/.10 = 10$
c. See table; $20,000
d. $18,000
e. See table
f. $10,000
g. $9,000
h. See table
i. $5,000; the bank rebuilds reserves by not renewing old loans or offering new ones as old ones are repaid.
j. $4,500
k. $15,000
l. $1,500
m. $13,500

Assets		Liabilities	
Cash Reserves	$3,000	Demand deposits	$30,000
Loans	$27,000		
	$30,000		$30,000

Assets		Liabilities	
Cash Reserves	$2,000	Demand deposits	$20,000
Loans	$18,000		
	$20,000		$20,000

Assets		Liabilities	
Cash Reserves	$1,500	Demand deposits	$15,000
Loans	$13,500		
	$15,000		$15,000

Problem 3

a. See table
b. 4
c. Demand deposits = $8,000
d. Loans = $6,000
e. Each bank loans a portion ((1-(rr + xr)) of its demand deposits, which in turn become demand deposits in another bank. These "new" deposits then form the basis for more lending, which continues the money creation process.
f. Each bank needs to hold on to reserves in order to meet withdrawals by customers.

Bank 1			
Assets		**Liabilities**	
Reserves	$500	Demand deposits	$2,000
Required Reserves	$400		
Excess Reserves	$100		
Loans	$1,500		

Bank 2			
Assets		**Liabilities**	
Reserves	$375	Demand deposits	$1,500
Required Reserves	$300		
Excess Reserves	$75		
Loans	$1,125		

Bank 3			
Assets		**Liabilities**	
Reserves	$281.25	Demand deposits	$1,125
Required Reserves	$225		
Excess Reserves	$56.25		
Loans	$843.75		

Problem 4

Bank	Total Reserves	Required Reserves	Excess Reserves	Loan/Money Expansion
A	2,000.00	400.00	1,600.00	1,600.00
B	1,600.00	320.00	1,280.00	1,280.00
C	1,280.00	256.00	1,024.00	1,024.00
D	1,024.00	204.80	819.20	819.20
E	819.20	163.84	655.36	655.36
F	655.36	131.07	524.29	524.29
G	524.29	104.86	419.43	419.43
H	419.43	xxx	xxx	xxx
Entire System	xxx	2,000.00	xxx	10,000.00

Problem 5

Deposit	Required Reserve Ratio	Actual Money Multiplier	Single Bank Expansion	Total Expansion By All Banks
2,000	.20	4	1,500.00	8,000
1,000	.15	5	800.00	5,000
5,000	.1166	6	4,166.66	30,000
3,500	.05	10	3,150.00	35,000
500	.075	8	437.50	4,000

Problem 6

Required Reserve Ratio	Potential Money Multiplier	Potential Money Supply	Actual Money Multiplier	Actual Money Supply
1/10	10	$11 mil.	5	$6.0 mil.
1/9	9	$10 mil.	4.7	$5.7 mil.
1/8	8	$9 mil.	4.4	$5.4 mil.
1/7	7	$8 mil.	4.1	$5.1 mil.
1/6	6	$7 mil.	3.8	$4.8 mil.
1/5	5	$6 mil.	3.3	$4.3 mil.
1/4	4	$5 mil.	2.9	$3.9 mil.

Chapter 13
The Federal Reserve System

Chapter Objectives

After you have read and studied this chapter you should be able to describe the purposes of a central bank such as the Federal Reserve System (FED); discuss the FED's primary and secondary tools and how these tools may be used; evaluate the effects of various regulations on the efficiency of the financial sector, and distinguish various types of financial intermediaries.

Chapter Review: Key Points

1. Because fractional reserve banking makes it impossible for all banks to pay all demand deposits simultaneously, government action may help resolve monetary crises. The *central bank* of a country: (a) controls the volume of money in circulation, (b) performs the government's banking functions, (c) serves as a "bankers' bank," and (d) regulates banks and other financial institutions. The central bank of the United States is the *Federal Reserve System*, or *FED*.

2. The value of the potential money multiplier (m_p) is the reciprocal of the *reserve-requirement ratio (1/rr)*. Excess reserves in the financial system and cash holdings by the public are drains on the potential multiplier. The actual multiplier (m_a) equals the *monetary base* (*MB*) -- the currency and bank reserves issued by the FED divided into the money supply (*MS*):

$$m_a = MS/MB.$$

3. The *FED's* most powerful but least used tool is its control of reserve requirements (*rr*). Raising *rr* reduces money multipliers and the money supply, and vice versa.

4. The most useful tool of the FED is *open-market operations (OMO)*. After all adjustments, open-market operations affect the monetary base, not the money multiplier. When the FED sells bonds, both bank reserves and the money supply decline. FED purchases of bonds increase bank reserves and the money supply.

5. The *discount rate (d)* is the interest rate the FED charges member banks. When the discount rate is low relative to market interest, banks hold fewer excess reserves and borrow from the FED. Consequently, the money supply grows. High discount rates relative to market interest rates cause banks to borrow less from the FED and to hold more excess reserves. The actual money multiplier and total bank reserves fall, and the money supply falls.

Matching Key Terms And Concepts

____ 1. moral suasion

____ 2. reserve requirements

____ 3. discount rate

____ 4. excess reserves

____ 5. open market operations

____ 6. margin requirements

____ 7. financial efficiency

____ 8. Federal Open Market Committee

____ 9. federal funds market

____10. central bank

a. The FED's most powerful tool.

b. Legal reserves minus required reserves.

c. Minimum differences between interest rates charged and received.

d. Interest rate banks have to pay the FED.

e. Sets policies for trading in U.S. bonds to vary the money supply.

f. The FED's most useful tool.

g. Sets "down payments" on purchases of stock.

h. Exercising persuasive powers to induce changed behavior.

i. Interbank lending of excess reserves.

j. Government's bank and "lender of last resort."

True/False Questions

____ 1. Independently of FED policies, banks influence the money supply through variations in their holdings of excess reserves.

____ 2. If the FED buys more bonds than it sells, total bank reserves are increased and the money supply grows.

____ 3. Banks will generally want to hold the same percent of excess reserves against demand deposits regardless of the reserve requirement ratio, since the percentage fluctuations of bank deposits depend on people's behavior rather than on the Federal Reserve System's reserve requirements.

____ 4. The Federal Reserve System's Open Market Committee has no influence over the total amount of currency in circulation.

____ 5. Banks and other financial intermediaries are less closely supervised than auto makers.

____ 6. The reserve requirement ratio is the FED's most powerful tool.

____ 7. If the FED decided to reduce the money supply, it could buy bonds from commercial banks.

____ 8. In the 1920's, you could purchase stock "on margin" with a down payment of as little as 10 percent.

____ 9. The Chairman of the Board of Governors is the real power in the FED.

____10. Lowering the discount rate encourages banks to borrow money from the FED.

Standard Multiple Choice

There Is One Best Answer For Each Question.

____ 1. If the FED sells bonds to banks:
    a. total bank reserves increase.
    b. the money supply decreases.
    c. the money supply increases.
    d. it offsets such policies by cutting reserve requirements.
    e. All of the above.

____ 2. The most powerful tool at the FED's disposal is:
    a. the ability to set reserve requirements.
    b. the discount rate.
    c. open market operations.
    d. moral suasion.
    e. margin requirements.

____ 3. If bankers want to retain reserves of 25 percent against all deposits, if the FED issues $100 billion in currency, and if private individuals keep all money in banks, then, once banks are "fully loaned-up" the money supply will be comprised of:
    a. $400 billion in demand deposits.
    b. $100 billion in currency + $300 billion in DDs.
    c. no additional loans could be made if the FED printed more currency.
    d. $2,500 billion in cash and DDs.
    e. None of the above.

____ 4. The most effective and efficient tool of the FED is:
    a. the reserve requirement.
    b. discount operations.
    c. margin requirements.
    d. open market operations.
    e. moral suasion.

____ 5. The FED attempts to control stock speculation through:
    a. reserve requirements.
    b. margin requirements.
    c. discount operations.
    d. moral suasion.
    e. open market operations.

____ 6. The FED's reserve requirement ratio:
    a. is its most powerful monetary tool.
    b. aids in stabilizing the money multiplier.
    c. reduces the value of the money multiplier.
    d. reduces the money supply relative to the monetary base.
    e. All of these.

____ 7. The FED's "margin requirements" refer to:
    a. down payments on stock.
    b. bank capitalization requirements.
    c. interest rate ceilings.
    d. credit controls.
    e. buying U.S. government bonds.

____ 8. A major purpose of the FED is to:
    a. print money to cover all government spending not covered by tax revenues.
    b. set interest rate ceilings as low as possible.
    c. act as a "lender of last resort."
    d. ensure the profitability of commercial banks.
    e. ensure the liquidity of social assets.

___ 9. The most powerful entity in the Federal Reserve system is the:
   a. Director of Open Market Operations.
   b. President of the New York Federal Reserve Bank.
   c. Chairman of the FED.
   d. Unified District Bank Presidents.
   e. Reserve Requirements Regulator.

___ 10. The Federal Reserve System is:
   a. privately owned and operated.
   b. extremely profitable for its investors.
   c. the tax collector for all government agencies.
   d. the central bank of the United States.
   e. the core of the International Monetary Fund (IMF).

Chapter Review (Fill-In Questions)

1. Although it is not especially useful, the FED's most powerful tool is its ability to set _____. By lowering this tool, the FED initially causes banks to have _____.

2. When the FED reduces the required reserve ratio, banks extend new loans, the _____ grows, and the _____ expands.

3. In the long run, however, changing the required reserve ratio does not affect total legal reserves, nor is the division between excess reserves and required reserves affected. Thus, changes in reserve requirements operate primarily by causing changes in the _____. Hikes in the reserve requirements ratio would cause a _____ in the money supply.

4. The FED may also change its policies about extending loans to banks, a tool known as _____. The interest rate the FED charges banks is called the _____ rate.

5. The FED's most useful tool, _____ _____ operations, is utilized when the FED, through the "open market" trading desk in New York, sells some of the U.S. Treasury bonds in its portfolio. Banks expand their holdings of bonds, but _____ in the banking system decline. Consequently, the money supply falls when banks reduce _____.

Unlimited Multiple Choice

There Are From Zero To Four Correct Answers For Each Question.

___ 1. When commercial banks:
   a. are faced with higher discount rates, they lend more money to the FED, shrinking their excess reserves and expanding the money supply.
   b. receive higher margin requirements, they increase lending.
   c. confront lower reserve requirements ratios, they create more money from a given monetary base.
   d. buy bonds from the FED, bank reserves are decreased, and the banking system will decrease loan-based demand deposits.

___ 2. Open market operations:
   a. involve the buying and selling of government bonds.
   b. are a secondary tool of the FED.
   c. enable the FED to increase or decrease the money supply.
   d. are used when other FED tools fail.

___ 3. Central banks commonly:
   a. act as "lenders of last resort."
   b. control monetary policies where they operate.
   c. collect taxes like the Internal Revenue Service under their direct control.
   d. determine tax rates and collect revenues for governments.

___ 4. The discount rate:
   a. represents the most powerful tool wielded by the FED to control the money supply.
   b. is seldom changed.
   c. is generally changed to reflect changes in market interest rates and the federal funds rate.
   d. is a secondary tool which is seldom used.

___ 5. When the required reserve ratio is lowered:
   a. the potential money multiplier decreases.
   b. the actual money multiplier decreases.
   c. banks tend to decrease loans.
   d. the monetary base increases.

Problems

Problem 1

In each box of this table indicate how the variable would change based on the events described in a through d. Write "increase," "decrease," "unchanged," or "indeterminate" as appropriate.

	Total Bank Reserves	Monetary Base	Potential Money Multiplier	Actual Money Multiplier	Money Supply
a					
b					
c					
d					

a.   The long-run effect if the FED sells bonds.

b.   The long-run effect if the FED raises the discount rate.

c.   The long-run effect if the FED raises reserve requirements.

d.   The long-run effect if the public wants more currency relative to deposits.

Problem 2

Without looking at your responses to Problem 1, fill in this table according to questions a-d. Write the word increase, decrease, unchanged, or indeterminate in the box as appropriate.

	Total Bank Reserves	Monetary Base	Potential Money Multiplier	Actual Money Multiplier	Money Supply
a					
b					
c					
d					

a.   The long-run effect if the FED buys bonds.

b.   The long-run effect if the FED lowers the discount rate.

c.   The long-run effect if the FED decreases reserve requirements.

d.   The long-run effect if the public wants less currency relative to deposits.

Problem 3

In the T-account provided, illustrate the balance sheet of the Federal Reserve Bank and a Member Bank when the Federal Reserve Bank sells $2,000 in securities to the Member Bank.

Federal Reserve Bank		Member Bank	
Assets	Liabilities	Assets	Liabilities
_____ Treasury Bonds	_____ Reserves	_____ Loanable _____ Treasury	

Problem 4

Use the knowledge you have acquired in this chapter to fill in the table.

	Monetary Base	Reserve Requirement Ratio	Potential Money Multiplier	Potential Money Supply
a	$1 billion	1/6		
b	$8 billion		5	
c		1/7		$700 billion
d			6	$100 billion

ANSWERS

Matching	True/False	Multiple Choice	Unlimited MC	Fill-In
1. h	1. T	1. b	1. cd	1. reserve requirements; excess reserves
2. a	2. T	2. a	2. ac	2. money multiplier; money supply
3. d	3. T	3. a	3. ab	3. money multiplier; reduction
4. b	4. F	4. d	4. c	4. discounting operations; discount
5. f	5. F	5. b	5. none	5. open market; reserves; loans
6. g	6. T	6. e		
7. c	7. F	7. a		
8. e	8. T	8. c		
9. i	9. T	9. c		
10. j	10. T	10. d		

Problem 1

	Total Bank Reserves	Monetary Base	Potential Money Multiplier	Actual Money Multiplier	Money Supply
a	decrease	decrease	unchanged	unchanged	decrease
b	decrease	decrease	unchanged	decrease	decrease
c	unchanged	unchanged	decrease	decrease	decrease
d	decrease	unchanged	unchanged	decrease	decrease

Problem 2

	Total Bank Reserves	Monetary Base	Potential Money Multiplier	Actual Money Multiplier	Money Supply
a	increase	increase	unchanged	unchanged	increase
b	increase	increase	unchanged	increase	increase
c	unchanged	unchanged	increase	increase	increase
d	increase	unchanged	unchanged	increase	increase

Problem 3

Federal Reserve Bank		Member Bank	
Assets	Liabilities	Assets	Liabilities
-$2,000 Treasury	-$2,000 Reserves held	-$2,000 Loanable +$2,000 Treasury bonds	

Problem 4

	Monetary Base	Reserve Requirement Ratio	Potential Money Multiplier	Potential Money Supply
a	$1 billion	1/6	6	$6 billion
b	$8 billion	1/5	5	$40 billion
c	$100 billion	1/7	7	$700 billion
d	$16.67 billion	1/6	6	$100 billion

Chapter 14
Monetary Theory and Policy

Chapter Objectives

After you have read and studied this chapter, you should be able to differentiate between the classical, Keynesian, and modern monetarist approaches to the demand for money; explain how variations in the quantity of money might influence macroeconomic activity, given various states of the economy; and explain why interest rates and bond prices are inversely related.

Chapter Review: Key Points

1. You increase your *spending* when you have "too much" money; your rate of *saving* increases when you have "too little" money.

2. People hold money for predictable spending (*transactions demands*) with a cushion for uncertain outlays or income receipts (*precautionary demands*). People also have *asset demands* for money because: (*a*) money is relatively riskless, (*b*) transaction costs associated with less liquid assets may exceed expected returns, or (*c*) people speculate by holding money when they expect the prices of alternative assets (e.g., stocks, bonds, or real estate) to fall.

3. According to classical monetary theory, the sole rational motive for holding money is *to consummate transactions.*

4. Interest rates and bond prices are *inversely related.* Bond prices fall if interest rates rise, and vice versa.

5. The costs of holding nominal amounts of money are: (*a*) *the reciprocal of the price level (1/P)* if the choice is between saving money or buying consumer goods; or (*b*) *the interest rate*, if money is viewed as an asset substitutable for some highly liquid income-generating asset, say a bond. *Inflation* also imposes costs on holdings of money.

6. The *income velocity (V)* of money equals GDP (or $P \times Q$) divided by the money supply (*M*).

7. The *equation of exchange,* a truism, is written $MV = PQ$. Therefore, the percentage change in the money supply plus the percentage change in velocity roughly equals the percentage change in the price level plus the percentage change in real output:

$$\frac{\Delta M}{M} + \frac{\Delta V}{V} = \frac{\Delta P}{P} + \frac{\Delta Q}{Q}$$

8. Classical economics assumes that *velocity* (*V*) and *output (Q)* are reasonably constant and independent of the money supply (*M*) and the price level (*P*). Classical economists believe that changes in the money supply result in proportional changes in the price level and expressed this belief in early versions of the *quantity theory of money*. The quantity theory of money is more accurately a *monetary theory of the price level*.

9. Keynes's attack on the quantity theory disputes the assumptions that: (*a*) the natural state of the economy is full employment, (*b*) the velocity of money is inherently stable, and (*c*) the only rational motive for holding money is for transactions purposes.

10. Modern monetarists perceive a direct link between the money supply and national income. Since the demand for money is relatively stable, monetary growth puts excess money balances in the hands of consumers and investors who, in turn, spend this surplus money on output. Monetary growth may temporarily expand output, but monetarists conclude that in the long run, higher prices will result.

11. Advocates of eliminating *discretionary policy* and relying on *monetary growth rules* would replace the FED's Open-Market Committee with unimaginative but reliable clerks who would increase the money supply at a fixed small (3 percent?) amount annually, with the federal budget being set to balance at full employment.

Matching Key Terms And Concepts

___ 1. hoarding

___ 2. crude quantity theory of money

___ 3. transaction demand

___ 4. precautionary demand

___ 5. asset demand

___ 6. real money balances

___ 7. liquidity trap

___ 8. income velocity of money

___ 9. opportunity cost of money

___ 10. equation of exchange

a. Causes income velocity of money to decrease.

b. Arises because of transaction costs, risk aversion, and speculation that interest rates might rise soon.

c. Horizontal money demand curve; might occur if people expected currently low interest rates to rise sharply and very soon.

d. Varies directly with income and inversely with the frequency with which people receive income.

e. Positively related both to income and to uncertainty about future purchases.

f. Assumes $\Delta Q/Q = \Delta V/V = 0$, so that the price level is proportional to the nominal money supply.

g. The interest rate if the alternative to holding money is buying bonds; 1/CPI if the next best alternative is consumption.

h. GDP/M.

i. MV = PQ.

j. M/P.

True/False Questions

____ 1. According to classical theory, any changes in the money supply will be reflected in proportional changes in the price level.

____ 2. In classical theory, the interest rate determines the level of saving, while in Keynesian theory, the interest rate determines the composition of an income-determined level of saving.

____ 3. Variations in the money supply affect investment similarly in the classical and Keynesian theoretical models.

____ 4. Keynesian and classical economists agree that equilibrium investment occurs when the rates of return on investment projects are equal to the prevailing market rate of interest.

____ 5. According to John Maynard Keynes, expansionary monetary policy propels an economy out of a depression.

____ 6. Keynesian economists believe investors' expectations about rates of return to be quite stable, and explain wide swings in investment as responses to small changes in interest rates.

____ 7. Classical economic models allow the possibility that a market economy could be in equilibrium at less than full employment.

____ 8. Milton Friedman argues that the demand for money varies inversely with the interest rate on bonds, the rate of return on physical capital, and the expected rate of inflation.

____ 9. Most Keynesian models ignore the institutional mechanisms used to create money.

____10. The Monetarist prescription for a healthy economy is active federal management of Aggregate Demand.

Standard Multiple Choice

There Is One Best Answer To Each Question.

____ 1. The total demand for money does not include:
   a. transactions demands.
   b. stocks and bonds.
   c. asset demands.
   d. precautionary demands.
   e. Any of these.

____ 2. The crude "Quantity Theory of Money" did NOT:
   a. assume full employment.
   b. assume velocity was erratic.
   c. predict money and the price level to be proportional.
   d. blame inflation on too much monetary growth.
   e. rely heavily on the transactions demand for money.

3. Precautionary demands originate in:
   a. people's desires to "cushion" against the unexpected.
   b. fear that interest rates will rise.
   c. fear that prices will rise.
   d. expectations of economic booms.
   e. fears of stock market crashes.

4. People will hold more money if they expect:
   a. the average price level to rise.
   b. interest rates on bonds to fall.
   c. interest rates on bonds to rise.
   d. tremendous economic growth.
   e. to be paid more frequently.

5. The person most responsible for the reemergence of monetarism during the past quarter century is:
   a. Paul Samuelson.
   b. John Maynard Keynes.
   c. John Kenneth Galbraith.
   d. Milton Friedman.
   e. Irving Fisher.

6. We can infer that you have too little money if you:
   a. are a typical college student.
   b. must spend money as quickly as you receive it.
   c. wear rags and eat cheap food.
   d. increase the amount of cash you save from each paycheck.
   e. use credit cards extensively.

7. People's money-holdings tend to grow if there are increases in:
   a. the expected rate of inflation.
   b. interest rates paid on money.
   c. interest rates on bonds.
   d. the average purchasing power of each dollar (1/CPI).
   e. access to easy credit.

8. The asset demand for money will increase if:
   a. for a given expected return, the risk of holding other assets rises.
   b. people desire increased liquidity.
   c. the interest rate is expected to rise.
   d. bond prices are expected to fall.
   e. All of the above.

9. The transaction demand for money is most closely related to its use as a:
   a. medium of exchange.
   b. standard unit of account.
   c. measure of value.
   d. store of value.
   e. standard of deferred payment.

10. Keynesian monetary theory assumes that the cost of holding money is:
    a. 1/CPI.
    b. CPI.
    c. the interest rates on bonds.
    d. the interest banks pay to owners of demand deposits.
    e. the realized rate of inflation.

11. The Equation of Exchange is written:
    a. $MQ = PV$.
    b. $M = QVP$.
    c. $MV = PQ$.
    d. $V = PQ/M$.
    e. $\Delta M/M + \Delta V/V = \Delta P/P + \Delta Q/Q$.

12. In a "liquidity trap," expansionary monetary policies:
    a. rapidly cure inflationary pressures.
    b. primarily affect people's money holdings.
    c. cut interest rates and boost investment and thus, Aggregate Demand.
    d. quickly pull a sluggish economy out of the doldrums.
    e. create new inflationary pressures.

Chapter Review (Fill-In Questions)

1. Why do people want to hold money? Perhaps the most important motive is the
    _____ demand for money, which arises because people expect that they will
    make certain outlays of money in the near future.

2. Uncertainty about future expenditures creates a _____ demand for money.
    Finally, uncertainty about the future values of potential investments generates the
    _____ demand for money.

3. Part of this last source of the demand for money is fear that _____ will rise.
    _____ fall when interest rates rise, so bondholders lose. Keynes identified this
    part of the asset demand for money as the _____ demand for money.

4. Aversion to _____ and _____ costs are other foundations of the
    asset demand for money.

5. Classical economists had focused on the _____ demand for money, which is
    directly related to _____ and negatively related to the frequencies of receipts
    and payments.

6. Irving Fisher helped formalize classical monetary theory by developing the Equation of
    _____, which is written _____.

7. Keynes introduced the _____ motive for holding money, which is reasonably
    compatible with classical theory, and the _____ demand for money, which
    raised the possibility that even huge increases in the money supply might be
    _____ rather than spent if the economy were caught in a _____.

8. Keynes argued that _____ is much influenced by the "animal spirits of
    investors" and relatively insensitive to variations in _____.

9. According to the Keynesian _____, expansion of the
    money supply only influences autonomous spending by reducing interest slightly, which
    stimulates _____ slightly, which then, through the multiplier principle, increases
    Aggregate Expenditures somewhat.

Unlimited Multiple Choice

There Are From Zero To Four Correct Answers For Each Question.

___ 1. Classical economists contend that the:
a. income velocity of money is reasonably constant.
b. quantity of money demanded varies inversely with the interest rate.
c. investment demand is highly sensitive to changes in the expectations of firms.
d. market system is inherently unstable.

___ 2. Modern Monetarists believe that the:
a. demand for money is a positive function of income.
b. demand for money varies inversely with the amount of human capital as a percentage of total wealth.
c. expected rate of inflation does not influence the demand for money.
d. basic cause of instability in a market economy is erratic governmental policy.

___ 3. The crude quantity theory of money:
a. posits that market economies never deviate much from full-employment levels of output.
b. assumes that velocity is reasonably constant.
c. treats velocity as unaffected by the price level, by the level of real output, and by the nominal money supply.
d. posits that people hold money only to consummate transactions.

___ 4. According to the Keynesian monetary transmission mechanism:
a. an increase in the nominal money supply makes people feel wealthier, and they eliminate their excess holdings of money by spending more on goods immediately.
b. an increase in the money supply causes the interest rate to decrease, resulting in an increase in investment and then income.
c. changes in the money supply will affect consumer spending directly.
d. money's effect on interest rates induce changes in aggregate spending.

___ 5. Both Keynesian and classical writers:
a. agree that very high rates of investment lead to somewhat lower rates of return, but disagree about how fast this occurs.
b. believe that investment will occur as long as the expected rate of return to investment at least equals the interest rate.
c. believe that interest rates are determined in the money market.
d. view economic transactors as confronted by much uncertainty.

Problems

Problem 1

Fill in the blanks for interest rates, annual payments, bond prices, etc., so that the following statements are true.

a. An interest rate equaling _____ percent would make perpetual annual payments of $5,000 worth $100,000 today.

b. A perpetual bond would be worth _____ if the interest rate were 12.5 percent annually and the bond paid $2,000 each year.

c. A perpetual bond would need to yield annual payments of roughly _____ to be worth $10,000 if the interest rate were 16.67 percent.

d. If a perpetual bond is priced at $70,000 and pays $10,500 annually, the interest rate yielded is _____ percent.

e. An annual after-tax rental value of a parcel of property equaling $30,000 combined with a current interest rate of 10 percent would make its present value _____.

f. A National Football League franchise costing $12 million is worth buying if the current interest rate is 12 percent and it is forecast to generate _____ million annually after all other expenses.

Problem 2

Use the equation of exchange to answer the following questions.

a. Suppose the money supply grows by 12% and real output grows by 3%, but the income velocity of money is constant. What happens to the price level? _____

b. If potential output grows by 2% while velocity falls by 3%, what rate of monetary growth should keep the price level stable? _____

c. If average prices are rising 20% annually while monetary growth is 12% in a stagnant economy, what is happening to velocity? _____

d. If both velocity and the price level fall by 8% while real output drops 15%, what must be happening to the money supply? _____

Problem 3

Illustrate the Keynesian transmission mechanism in these graphs. Note the steep slope of the investment demand function. Use primes (') to illustrate an expansionary monetary policy.

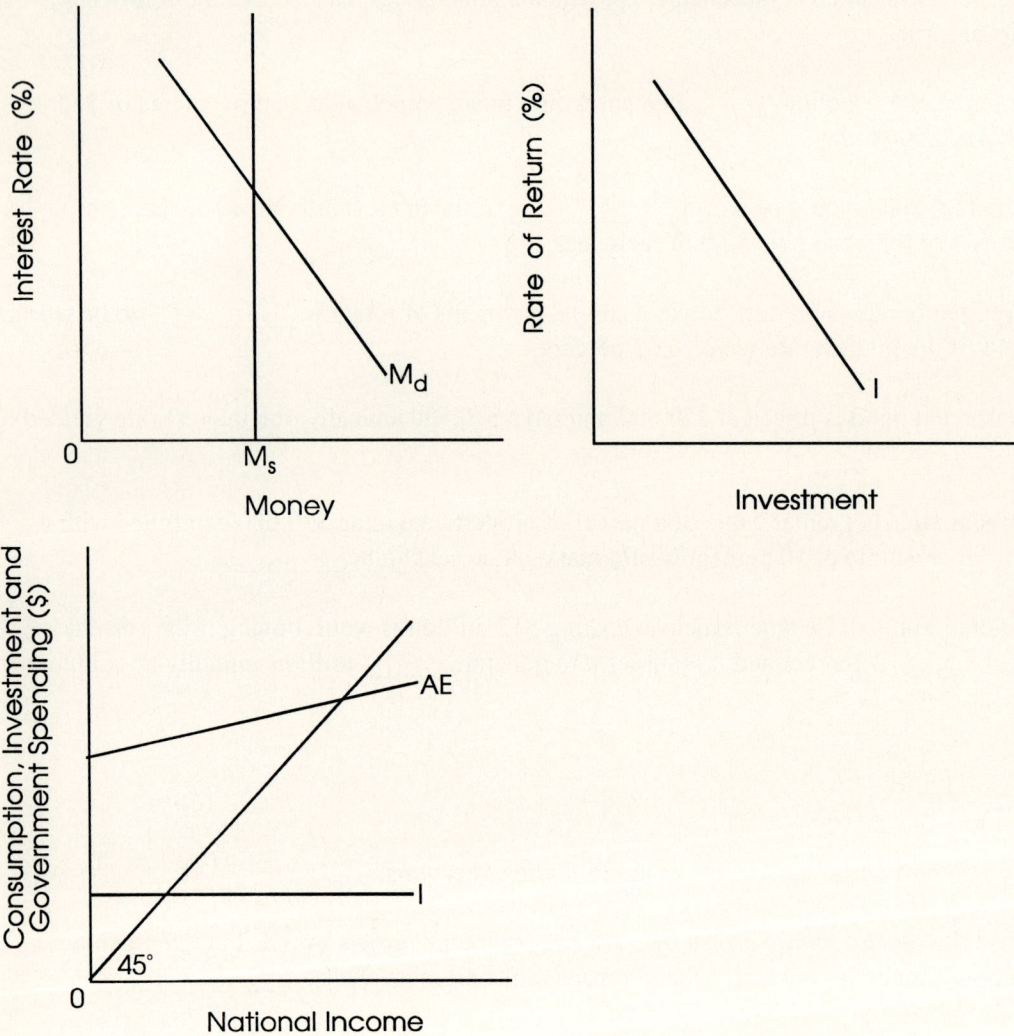

Problem 4

Now that you have developed this Keynesian linkage perhaps a numerical example would be helpful. Suppose that the FED buys $5 million in treasury bonds from the banking system. If the required reserve ratio is 10%, all the banks are fully loaned up, and the non-banking public holds no cash;

a. What is the actual money supply expansion? _____

b. Assume that the money demand curve is linear over the relevant range. If an increase of $20 million in the money supply decreases the interest by 1%, how much will the interest rate decrease? _____

c. Suppose the investment demand curve is linear and that a 1% decrease in the interest rate increases investment by $1 million. How much will investment increase? _____

d. If the MPC = .8, how much will equilibrium income increase? _____

ANSWERS

Matching	True/False	Multiple Choice	Unlimited MC	Fill-In
1. a	1. T	1. b	1. a	1. transactions
2. f	2. T	2. b	2. ad	2. precautionary; asset
3. d	3. F	3. a	3. abcd	3. interest rates; bond prices;
4. e	4. T	4. c	4. bd	speculative
5. b	5. F	5. d	5. ab	4. risk; transactions
6. j	6. F	6. d		5. transactions; income
7. c	7. F	7. b		6. Exchange; $MV = PQ$
8. h	8. T	8. e		7. precautionary; asset;
9. g	9. F	9. a		hoarded; liquidity trap
10. i	10. F	10. c		8. investment; interest rates
		11. c		9. monetary transmission
		12. b		investment

Problem 1

a. 5
b. $16,000
c. $1,667
d. 15
e. $300,000
f. $1.44

Problem 2

a. P increases by 9%.
b. M equals 5% to stabilize the price level.
c. V increases by 8%.
d. M decreases by 15%.

Problem 3

Problem 4

a. $50 million
b. 2.5%
c. $2.5 million
d. $12.5 million

Chapter 15
Budget Deficits and Public Debt

Chapter Objectives

After reading and studying this chapter you should be able to describe problems encountered in balancing the budget; discuss the `crowding out' hypothesis; differentiate between government and private budget constraints; and evaluate the impact of national debt on future generations.

Chapter Review: Key Points

1. The *budget deficit* equals annual government outlays minus receipts. The *public debt* is total federal indebtedness resulting from current and past deficits.

2. *Balancing the budget annually* might result in incorrect fiscal actions to combat either inflation or recession. Some have suggested balancing the budget *over the business cycle*. This would entail running deficits during recessions and surpluses over the boom. Unfortunately, business cycles are not symmetric, and the budget may not be easy to balance over the cycle without hampering prosperity. Advocates of *functional finance* believe that the size of the public debt is unimportant. They suggest that we ignore the problem of balancing the budget and focus on balancing the economy instead.

3. The federal government can finance *public spending* by collecting taxes (T), creating additional monetary base (ΔMB), selling government securities (ΔB), or through confiscation. All of these techniques are drains on *gross private saving* (production minus private consumption) that can crowd out private economic activities. The notion called *Ricardian equivalence* suggests that whether government spending is financed by taxes or borrowing is irrelevant.

4. The *crowding-out hypothesis* states that increases in government purchases inevitably reduces private consumption, investment, or leisure.

5. Federal deficits can be financed by increasing domestic saving, securing the savings of foreigners, or by reducing domestic investment or exports. All else constant, a growing budget deficit will cause growth of a trade deficit.

6. Some government spending is *uncontrollable* (now estimated at 75%). These programs are long-range or are committed by law each and every year. Reducing such outlays may be impossible.

7. A major difference between private and public debt is that *private debt* is owed to persons *external* to the issuing institution, while the bulk of *public debt* is *internal,* being owed to ourselves. Private debt has grown faster than public debt since the 1950s and is currently over twice as large.

8. The *real burden of the national debt* stems from the federal government "crowding out" private investment as it drives interest rates up when competing with the private sector for loanable funds. As a result, future generations may inherit a smaller capital stock and a smaller production-possibilities frontier.

9. Among the major benefits of the public debt are its use as a *stabilization instrument* and as a *risk-free asset* for savers.

Matching Key Terms And Concepts

____ 1. confiscation

____ 2. Ricardian Equivalence

____ 3. uncontrollable spending

____ 4. crowding-out hypothesis

____ 5. government budget constraint

____ 6. external debt

____ 7. roll over

____ 8. internal debt

____ 9. functional finance

____10. national debt

a. IOUs the repayment of which entail no loss of purchasing power.
b. The best way to finance government outlays depends on the least costly policies available.
c. Long term programs like Social Security.
d. Repaying old debts by taking out new loans.
e. The cumulation of all budget deficits through history.
f. Eminent domain and the military draft are examples.
g. The idea that governmental growth entails opportunity costs.
h. $G = T + \Delta B + \Delta MB$.
i. How government debt is financed is irrelevant.
j. Purchasing power is lost when this is repaid.

True/False Questions

____ 1. Selling assets or borrowing to secure resources are methods used by both private and governmental decisionmakers.

____ 2. Consumption by households is financed by sales of assets, by current income, and by borrowing against current assets or expected income.

____ 3. The distribution of the opportunity costs associated with government among the public is not a crucial consideration in determining who really pays for government.

____ 4. Private debt is primarily internally held while public debt is primarily externally held.

____ 5. The 1993 Budget Reduction Act calls for a balanced budget every fiscal year.

____ 6. The military draft covers the opportunity costs of labor resources through taxing, borrowing, and printing new money.

____ 7. Crowding-out does not need to be considered if there are many idle resources during a deep recession.

____ 8. When the government issues bonds to cover a budget deficit, interest rates tend to rise and crowd-out investment.

____ 9. Taxes have been used almost exclusively to finance most of the wars in which the United States has been involved.

____ 10. Government outlays for Medicare are an example of uncontrollable spending.

____ 11. Budget deficits were dramatically reduced during the 1980s.

____ 12. Our government is forbidden by the Constitution from acquiring resources from their owners unless the owners voluntarily agree by contract to surrender their assets.

Multiple Choice

There Is A Single Best Answer For Each Of These Questions.

___ 1. The public debt:
   a. results from cumulative budgetary deficits.
   b. is a stabilization instrument.
   c. provides a relatively riskless investment.
   d. is held primarily by U.S. citizens and institutions.
   e. All of the above.

___ 2. Which has grown fastest since World War II?
   a. National debt.
   b. State and local debt.
   c. Private debt.
   d. Gross Domestic Product.
   e. Unemployment.

___ 3. "Crowding-out" is most significant:
   a. at full employment.
   b. during inflation.
   c. during recession.
   d. during war time.
   e. during stagflation.

___ 4. "Crowding-out" refers to:
   a. cuts in private activities caused when government grows.
   b. TINSTAAFL.
   c. the public burdens of increased private purchases.
   d. the decline in unemployment forced by more rapid inflation.
   e. All of the above.

___ 5. Major differences between private and public debt are:
   a. private debt is a risk free asset.
   b. the private debt is almost entirely owned by external persons.
   c. the public debt is entirely owned by external persons.
   d. all public debt is held by Americans.
   e. None of the above.

___ 6. Government cannot secure extra resources by:
   a. collecting taxes.
   b. backing the dollar with gold.
   c. printing money.
   d. selling government securities.
   e. issuing bonds.

___ 7. If private owners are compelled to sell when the government buys land for public use, it is applying its:
   a. right of eminent domain.
   b. law of economic efficiency.
   c. political right of tax preferences.
   d. rights of economic expansion.
   e. unconstitutional powers that the Supreme Court will overturn.

___ 8. Most of the U.S. federal debt consists of U.S. Treasury bonds owned by:
   a. other federal government agencies.
   b. the Federal Reserve System.
   c. foreign governments.
   d. U.S. citizens and corporations.
   e. individual foreigners.

9. "The mix that works best should be used" best describes:
   a. the growth of public of debt.
   b. Ricardian Equivalence.
   c. government's eminent domain.
   d. the functional finance approach.
   e. a chocolate chip cookie recipe.

10. "Uncontrollable" spending includes:
   a. increasing annual budget deficits.
   b. increased imports of crude oil.
   c. local construction of a new park.
   d. a $50,000 binge at Bloomingdale's.
   e. federal outlays for postal service.

11. Robert Barro's theory that bonds and taxes are equivalent is based upon:
   a. the notion of Functional Finance.
   b. the relationship specified in the government constraint.
   c. Ricardian Equivalence.
   d. international trade theory.
   e. Keynesian analysis.

12. The amount of money "printed" by the FED when it buys Treasury bonds issued to cover a federal budget deficit:
   a. is new monetary base, and consequently causes the money supply to grow even more through the bank "money creation" process.
   b. somewhat replaces crowding-out that would have been accomplished by higher interest rates with crowding-out through inflation.
   c. reduces the amount of national debt in the public's hands.
   d. results in greater growth of Aggregate Spending than would have occurred without such expansionary open market operations.
   e. All of the above.

Chapter Review (Fill-In Questions)

1. Government can obtain resources through sales of existing _____ or current _____, by _____ from citizens, corporations, foreigners or commercial banks, through _____, _____, or by _____.

2. Recognizing that confiscation is a relatively minor source of government revenues, the governmental budget can be summarized by the equation _____. The idea that increases in outlays by government inevitably cause reductions in private consumption or investment is known as the _____ hypothesis.

3. When increased governmental purchases crowds out private individuals, they lose leisure or purchasing power through _____ or higher _____.

4. Issuance of bonds increases the demand for loanable funds which typically drives up _____ imposing an added burden on potential borrowers and investors. If there is efficient and full employment of all resources and government purchases are increased either _____, _____ or _____ must decline.

5. The major difference between private and public debt is that the latter is primarily _____ held. Because private debt is owned by _____ persons their claim on the real assets of the firm or individual can deplete the net worth of private parties.

6. When the government issues new bonds, the purchasing power sacrificed by American bond-buyers just _____ the government's gain in purchasing power. However, increased debt may impose several burdens on the society. If taxes must be raised to pay the interest on the debt, _____ to work and invest may be reduced. Further, if interest rates rise as more public debt is floated, private borrowing may be _____. This could squelch _____ so that the national debt did impose a burden on future generations by reducing growth in the stock of capital.

Unlimited Multiple Choice

Each Question Has From Zero To Four Correct Responses.

____ 1. The federal government can:
   a. finance a deficit by printing money.
   b. finance a deficit by buying bonds from the public.
   c. retire some public debt when tax revenue exceeds expenditure.
   d. finance a deficit by selling bonds to the public.

____ 2. It is unavoidably true that government budgetary:
   a. deficits cause increases in the national debt.
   b. surpluses permit either a reduction in the monetary base or retirement of part of the public debt.
   c. deficits require retirement of part of the public debt or reduction of the money supply.
   d. surpluses cause increases in national debt or in the money supply.

____ 3. Which of the following is a form of taxation if it is defined as the loss in purchasing power that occurs when government outlays increase?
   a. Extra consumption induced via the Keynesian multiplier process when government spending grows to combat a serious depression.
   b. Confiscation, as when a military draft is used to acquire labor resources for the Department of Defense.
   c. Inflation following an increase in the monetary base caused when the FED `monetizes' a huge deficit.
   d. Jumps in the interest rate caused by an enormous budget deficit.

___ 4. According to the crowding-out hypothesis, increased government:
   a. spending has no impact on the private sector.
   b. outlays must reduce private consumption or investment in a full-employment economy.
   c. borrowing pushes up interest rates and reduces profitable private investment opportunities.
   d. tax rates drive up the interest rate.

___ 5. Which of the following represent possible examples of crowding-out by the government:
   a. losses of leisure by previously idle workers.
   b. reduced purchasing power of households caused by inflation.
   c. reduced investments caused by higher interest rates.
   d. reduced borrowing by consumers because of higher interest rates.

Problems

Problem 1

Fill in the blank so that it is compatible with the government budget constraint.

a. G = $1,200 billion, T = $975 billion, ΔMB = $0, ΔB = _____

b. G = $1,250 billion, T = $1,025 billion, ΔMB = _____, ΔB = $150 billion

c. G = $1,300 billion, T = $1,375 billion, ΔMB = -$25 billion, ΔB = _____

d. G = $1,350 billion, T = $1,400 billion, ΔMB = _____, ΔB = $0

e. Which of the scenarios above will result in a budget deficit? _____

f. Which of the scenarios above will result in a budget surplus? _____

g. Which of the scenarios above will result in an increase of public debt? _____

h. Which of the scenarios above will result in a reduction of public debt? _____

i. Which of the scenarios above will result in inflationary pressures if the economy is at full employment? _____

j. Which of the scenarios above will result in deflationary pressures if the economy is at full employment? _____

Problem 2

On the figures provided, illustrate the concept of "crowding out" caused by the government issuing bonds to cover expenditures.

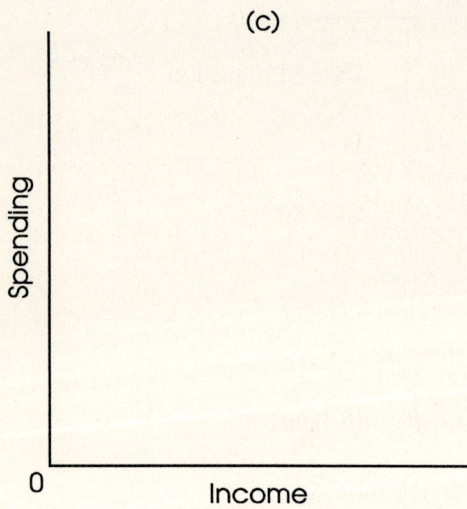

(a)

Price of Bonds

Bonds

(b)

Rate of Return

Investment

(c)

Spending

0

Income

Problem 3

Use this figure to answer the following True/False questions.

____ a. An increase in government spending from G_0 to G_1 will result in crowding out of the private sector equal to C_2-C_1 in an economy with idle resources.

____ b. In an economy with idle resources an increase in government spending from G_0 to G_1 might result in induced consumption equal to *b-d*.

____ c. In a fully employed economy an increase in government spending from G_1 to G_2 will result in a reduction in private spending equal to C_1-C_0.

____ d. If an increase in government spending from G_0 to G_1 results in movement from point *e* to point *b*, the distance between *b* and *d* is equal to the multiplier times the change in government spending.

____ e. An increase in government spending from G_1 to G_2 will result in crowding out equal to *d-c* in an economy with idle resources.

____ f. If the economy is at point *e*, an increase in government spending can enable the economy to move to point *a* through induced consumption.

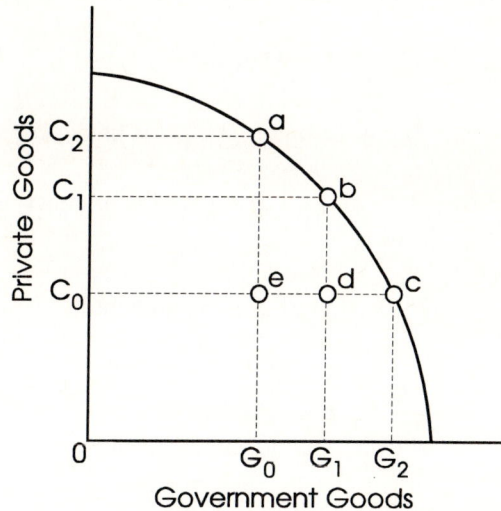

____ g. If the economy is at point *a* an increase in government spending from G_0 to G_1 will result in a decrease in private spending equal to C_2-C_1.

____ h. A movement from point *b* to point *a* illustrates crowding out of private activity by government spending.

____ i. In order to move from point *d* to point *b*, the government will have to increase its outlays and, in the process, crowd out the private sector.

____ j. A decrease in government spending from G_2 to G_1 must result in a movement from point *c* to point *d*.

Problem 4

Use your knowledge about the government budget constraint to answer the following True/False questions, given the following information:

$$G = \$700 \text{ billion} \qquad T = \$500 \text{ billion}$$

___ a. The government budget is balanced.

___ b. If there is no change in the monetary base, the change in national debt is equal to $200 billion.

___ c. If the change in national debt is equal to $75 billion, the change in the monetary base is equal to $125 billion.

___ d. If taxes are increased to a total of $800 billion, the government can retire $100 billion of the national debt and contract the monetary base.

___ e. If taxes are increased to a total of $750 billion, the government can contract the monetary base by $50 billion if there is no change in the national debt.

___ f. In an open economy (international trade takes place) a $100 billion domestic savings surplus will necessitate a $100 billion trade deficit.

___ g. In an open economy a $300 billion domestic savings surplus will necessitate a $100 billion trade deficit.

___ h. In an open economy a $100 billion trade surplus will necessitate a $300 billion domestic savings surplus.

___ i. In an open economy a $200 billion trade surplus will necessitate a domestic savings surplus equal to zero.

___ j. In an open economy a $200 billion trade deficit will necessitate a domestic savings surplus equal to zero.

Problem 5

Fill in the following blanks concerning foreign trade and the government budget constraint.

a. G-T = $200 billion, S-I = $120 billion, M-X = _____

b. G-T = $50 billion, S-I = $90 billion, M-X = _____

c. G-T = $75 billion, S-I = _____, M-X = $60 billion

d. G-T = $20 billion, S-I = _____, M-X = -$50 billion

e. Which of the scenarios above results in a trade deficit? _____

f. Which of the scenarios above results in a trade surplus? _____

g. Which of the scenarios above results in a domestic savings surplus? _____

ANSWERS

Matching	True/False	Multiple Choice	Unlimited MC	Fill-In
1. f	1. T	1. e	1. abcd	1. assets; production; borrowing; taxation; confiscation; printing money
2. i	2. T	2. c	2. b	
3. c	3. T	3. a	3. bcd	
4. g	4. F	4. a	4. bc	2. G=T+ΔB+ΔMB; crowding out
5. h	5. F	5. b	5. abcd	3. inflation; taxes
6. j	6. F	6. b		4. interest rates; consumption; investment; exports
7. d	7. F	7. a		5. internally; external
8. a	8. T	8. d		6. equals; incentives; crowded out; investment
9. b	9. F	9. d		
10. e	10. T	10. e		
	11. F	11. c		
	12. F	12. e		

Problem 1	**Problem 2**	**Problem 3**	**Problem 4**	**Problem 5**
a. $225 billion	a. See figure below	a. F	a. F	a. $80 billion
b. $75 billion		b. T	b. T	b. -$40 billion
c. -$50 billion		c. T	c. T	c. $15 billion
d. -$50 billion		d. T	d. F	d. $70 billion
e. a, b		e. F	e. T	e. a, c
f. c, d		f. F	f. T	f. b, d
g. a, b		g. T	g. F	g. a, b, c, d
h. c		h. F	h. T	
i. b		i. F	i. F	
j. c, d		j. F	j. T	

(a)

(b)

(c)

Chapter 16
Microfoundations of Macroeconomic Policy

Chapter Objectives

After you have read and studied this chapter you should be able to explain the foundations of Aggregate Supply and Demand curves and how changes in their major determinants cause these curves to shift; discuss the processes of supply-side and demand-side inflation; and describe patterns of employment and unemployment across different types of business cycles.

Chapter Review: Key Points

1. Most economists, whether classically-oriented or Keynesians, now agree that, in the long run, Aggregate Supply curves are vertical. However, the new Keynesians contend that *wage and price stickiness* can make the short run Aggregate Supply curve positively-sloped for lengthy periods, and thus short run targets may be most appropriate for macroeconomic policymaking.

2. Long-term *labor contracts* (whether implicit or explicit), *efficiency wages*, and *dual labor markets* all provide microfoundations to help explain wage stickiness and involuntary unemployment in an Aggregate Demand/Aggregate Supply framework.

3. Declines in the Aggregate Supply curve trigger *supply-side inflation* and reduces real income and output. *Demand-side inflation* results from rapid increases in the Aggregate Demand curve, and is usually preceded by higher income and output.

4. If Aggregate Demand grows excessively in a fully employed economy, the first phase of the *demand-side cycle* entails rising prices, outputs, employment, and incomes. In the second phase, supply-side adjustments to the demand-originated disturbances drive up prices further, but total employment, production, and income fall. *Demand-side* inflation induces a path of *counterclockwise adjustment* of real output versus inflation. If the economy starts at less than full employment, only the first phase necessarily occurs when Aggregate Demand is increased.

5. Supply-side inflation generates a *clockwise adjustment* pattern. In the first phase of a *supply-side* (cost-push) *cycle,* prices rise while real output and incomes fall. If the government attempts to correct for the resulting inflationary recession by increasing Aggregate Demand, the second phase occurs--prices continue to rise, but real output and income rise as well.

6. *Stagflation,* a contraction of the terms *stagnation* and *inflation,* is the simultaneous occurrence of high rates of both unemployment and inflation.

7. Mild demand-side inflation accompanied the prosperity of the 1960s. From the mid-1970s into the early 1980s, stagflation took over. Whether this stagflation was the supply-adjustment phase of the earlier demand-pull cycle or originated from supply-related shocks cannot be established conclusively. It seems likely, however, that even if the economy had been stable when the *supply shocks* listed previously emerged, considerable supply-side inflation would have plagued the American economy from 1973 to 1980.

8. *Disinflation* is a significant reduction in the rate of inflation. Most people adjust their behavior if they expect inflation. Their expectations cause disinflation to entail losses in real income before it restores the economy to a relatively stable growth path. Thus, the 1981-83 recession was especially severe.

9. In recent decades, accelerating technological advances and the internationalization of economic activity have increased the speed of structural economic change. A massive wave of corporate mergers in the 1980s and 1990s has lead to significant corporate *down-sizing*, with reduced job security for many workers who had intended to be career employees at large firms.

Matching Key Terms And Concepts

___ 1. wealth effect

___ 2. stagflation

___ 3. demand-side inflation

___ 4. money (inflation) illusion

___ 5. incomes policies

___ 6. supply-side inflation

___ 7. efficiency wages

___ 8. labor contracts

___ 9. interest rate effect

___10. dual labor markets

a. The labor market consists of primary and secondary sectors.

b. Can exist in the short run, but not in the long run.

c. Employment rises in the initial stage.

d. Reduces investment when the price level rises.

e. Purchasing power of assets falls when prices rise.

f. Generates a clockwise adjustment path of the price level versus real output.

g. Intended to raise the cost of dismissal and reduce shirking by employees.

h. Attempts to curb inflation without cutting Aggregate Demand.

i. Explains in part why wages adjust slowly.

j. Inflationary recession.

True/False Questions

___ 1. If no one suffers from money illusion, demand-pull inflation will yield both higher employment and higher prices.

___ 2. Both monetary and fiscal policies can boost the Aggregate Demand.

___ 3. Increasing Aggregate Supply can be done quite quickly.

___ 4. Aggregate Supply curves are shifted by changes in monetary or fiscal policies and changes in consumption or investment expenditures.

___ 5. External shocks that raise resource- or other production costs will shift the economy's demand curve leftward.

___ 6. New regulations that facilitate efficiency cause the Aggregate Supply curve to shift to the right.

___ 7. Labor supplies are partly determined by individual preferences for work versus leisure.

___ 8. Hikes in money wage rates imposed by powerful labor unions tend to shift the Aggregate Supply curve leftward.

___ 9. Labor contracts are easily renegotiated when inflation accelerates slightly.

___10. Money wages can be raised at rates equal to growth rates of labor productivity without causing price inflation.

___11. Efficiency wages are below market-clearing wages, so they encourage moves of less productive workers into their areas of comparative advantage.

___12. Corporate down-sizing has decreased the average length of unemployment.

Standard Multiple Choice

There Is One Best Answer For Each Question.

___ 1. Rightward shifts of the Aggregate
Supply curve cause:
  a. stagflation.
  b. high unemployment.
  c. cost-push inflation.
  d. high interest rates.
  e. deflationary pressure.

___ 2. Aggregate Supply might grow because
of:
  a. reductions in the bargaining
     strength of organized labor.
  b. enhanced unemployment
     compensation programs.
  c. increased inflationary expectations
     by labor.
  d. increased preference for leisure by
     labor.
  e. All of the above.

___ 3. Which of the following actions would
cause a shift to the right in the
Aggregate Demand curve?
  a. Congress decides to terminate all
     highway and water projects.
  b. The President's call for a
     permanent tax decrease is
     approved.
  c. The FED changes the reserve
     requirement from 17% to 20%.
  d. Sales of U.S. bonds to commercial
     banks by the FED are increased.
  e. Welfare spending is slashed.

___ 4. A leftward shift in the Aggregate
Supply curve will initiate _____
inflation, while a shift of the
Aggregate Demand curve to the right
will initiate _____ inflation:
  a. cost-pull; demand-push.
  b. demand-push; cost-pull.
  c. demand-pull; cost-push.
  d. cost-push; demand-pull.
  e. deflationary; recessionary.

___ 5. Rapid technological advances tend to
shift the economy's:
  a. supply of capital leftward.
  b. labor supply curve leftward.
  c. Aggregate Expenditures curve
     rightward.
  d. Aggregate Supply curve rightward.
  e. price level upward.

___ 6. Stagflation is a contraction of _____
and _____:
  a. stagnant; deflation.
  b. stable; defoliation.
  c. stagnation; inflation.
  d. stabilization; repugnant.
  e. staggered; contraction.

___ 7. Stagflation involves simultaneous high
rates of:
  a. unemployment and interest.
  b. interest and inflation.
  c. unemployment and inflation.
  d. economic growth and inflation.
  e. stagnation and degeneracy.

___ 8. Which of the following is NOT a reason why Aggregate Supply curves are positively sloped?
  a. Costs adjust less quickly than prices do to changes in demand.
  b. Price changes trigger wealth effects.
  c. Diminishing returns causes it to become ever more difficult to expand output as the economy approaches its capacity.
  d. Higher prices are needed to cover rising production costs as larger amounts of output are demanded.
  e. Expanding production causes more intense competition for resources when the economy nears full employment.

___ 9. Which of the following would be the LEAST likely to cause demand-pull inflation?
  a. A tax cut.
  b. An increase in government spending.
  c. A hike in the discount rate.
  d. A cut in reserve requirements.
  e. The FED buys bonds from banks.

___10. Stagflation occurs when Aggregate:
  a. Demand and Aggregate Supply shift right.
  b. Demand shifts right.
  c. Demand shifts left.
  d. Supply shifts right.
  e. Supply shifts left.

___11. Cost-push inflation is a likely result if the:
  a. money supply grows faster than our productive capacity.
  b. Aggregate Demand shifts right.
  c. Aggregate Supply curve shifts left.
  d. federal government runs a huge deficit.
  e. Congress repeals all inefficient regulations.

___12. A supply-side inflationary cycle follows a _____ path.
  a. clockwise.
  b. counterclockwise.
  c. cyclical.
  d. countercyclical.
  e. sinusoidal.

___13. Compared to market clearing wages, efficiency wages tend to:
  a. be higher.
  b. increase unemployment.
  c. raise the costs of being fired.
  d. reduce shirking.
  e. All of the above.

___14. The segmentation of the national labor market into primary and secondary sectors is known as the:
  a. foreign sector substitution effect.
  b. interest rate effect.
  c. dual labor market.
  d. wealth effect.
  e. efficiency wages effect.

___15. One reason wages fail to adjust as fast as prices do is the existence of:
  a. efficiency wages.
  b. labor contracts.
  c. dual labor markets.
  d. the wealth effect.
  e. supply-side inflation.

Chapter Review (Fill-In Questions)

1. The short run Aggregate Demand curve is negative sloped in part because the stock of money is assumed constant. This means that _____ will rise when the price level increases, shrinking consumer spending on durable goods, spending by state and local governments, and _____ spending by business firms.

2. In sum, the main determinants of Aggregate Supply are the quantities and costs of _____, production _____, _____ about inflation or deflation, and governmental _____.

3. _____ keep nominal wages from constantly changing, and help to explain the "stickiness" of wages. Increased unemployment over time is explained in part by _____ markets, where workers in the _____ sector are paid better wages and benefits than those in the secondary sector. Unemployment is also exacerbated when firms pay _____ wages in order to reduce the amount of shirking by employees.

4. Price hikes may initially "fool" workers through a process called _____, so that firms' _____ do not rise as fast as prices. During such a period, the _____ rate tends to fall and output grows. Eventually, however, workers adjust their inflationary expectations. Real wages will tend to _____ and output fall because, even though prices continue to rise, nominal _____ will grow even faster. A complete demand-side inflationary cycle follows a _____ path.

5. A supply-side inflationary cycle originates from an initial shift of the Aggregate Supply curve to the left. This drives up both the rates of _____ and _____. Policymakers commonly try to combat the recessionary trend with _____ demand management policies. As a result, the longer-term equilibration path for a supply-side inflationary cycle is _____.

6. The empirical evidence of actual equilibration paths suggests that the inflation of the 1960s was primarily _____, while the inflation of the 1970s was essentially _____. The very high rates of unemployment and inflation that plagued the early 1980s might be interpreted as the latter phases of a _____ inflationary cycle, or as the beginnings of a _____ inflationary cycle.

Unlimited Multiple Choice

Each Question Has From Zero To Four Correct Answers.

____ 1. Workers are said to suffer from money illusion when:
   a. they make their work decisions after adjusting prevailing money wage rates for expected inflation.
   b. they anticipate real wage rates that are not realized.
   c. they work more but realize only decreased real wages because of inflation.
   d. their expected rate of inflation equals realized inflation.

____ 2. Incomes policies:
   a. include various measures intended to dampen inflationary pressures but not Aggregate Demand.
   b. may reduce labor's inflationary expectations.
   c. include such measures as wage and price controls.
   d. may worsen inflationary pressures if their inefficiencies cause the Aggregate Supply curve to shift inward and to the left.

____ 3. During the initial stage of a demand-side inflation:
   a. business firms offer higher money wages for more labor to produce more output at higher prices.
   b. the demand for labor schedule shifts to the left.
   c. the supply schedule of labor will shift leftward, assuming that labor suffers from money illusion.
   d. workers suffering from money illusion offer more labor services at a reduced real wage rate.

____ 4. The Aggregate Supply curve:
   a. would be nearly vertical if workers quickly secured increases in money wage rates offsetting any increases in the price level.
   b. would be nearly vertical if workers' expected rates of inflation were much less than the actual rates of inflation.
   c. shifts rightward as workers revise their inflationary expectations upward.
   d. shifts leftward as business firms lower the prices they charge for goods.

____ 5. Inflationary recession occurs during the:
   a. initial stage of a demand-side inflation.
   b. initial stage of a supply-side inflation.
   c. latter stage of a demand-side inflation as workers adjust their inflationary expectations to agree with actual inflation.
   d. latter stage of a supply-side inflation as government resorts to demand-management policies to restore full-employment.

Problems

Problem 1

Use information drawn from the Aggregate Supply and Demand curves depicted to answer the following True/False questions.

____ a. Full employment occurs at output level Q_2.

____ b. The shift of the Aggregate Demand curve from AD_0 to AD_1 could be accomplished by increased government expenditures.

____ c. The price level is stable as the economy moves from a to b.

____ d. As the economy moves from c to d, the percentage increase in the money wage rate equals the percentage increase in the absolute price level.

____ e. Assuming a constant money wage rate, as the economy moves from b to c, the real wage rate increases, causing firms to hire less labor.

____ f. A technological advance could shift the Aggregate Supply curve outward and to the right.

____ g. The Aggregate Supply curve depicted is composed of both a Keynesian segment and a Classical segment.

____ h. As the economy moves up along the Keynesian segment of its supply curve, the real wage rate remains unchanged.

____ i. The movement from c to d represents pure price inflation.

____ j. An increase in the money wage rate would shift the Keynesian portion of the supply curve upward and to the left.

____ k. An increase in autonomous saving might shift the Aggregate Demand curve from AD_1 to AD_2.

____ l. The demand curve for labor services corresponding to the Keynesian portion of the supply curve is a horizontal line.

Problem 2

Output Q_e is at full employment, with original Aggregate Supply (AS_0) and Demand (AD_0).

____ a. The original equilibrium would be at full employment with price level P_e (point a).

____ b. Increases in federal spending or growth of the money supply could expand Aggregate Demand from AD_0 to AD_1.

____ c. Workers' real wages rise with a move from point a to point d.

____ d. Real wages rise during a move from b to c.

____ e. Realizing that wages have not kept pace with inflation at point d, workers will compensate by reducing their supplies of labor, so that Aggregate Supply shifts from AS_0 to AS_1.

____ f. Movements such as those from point a to point d to point c are often referred to as Supply-side inflation.

____ g. Stagflation occurs when the economy moves from a to b.

____ h. A move from a to b cuts real wages.

____ i. The real wage at c and at a are equal.

____ j. Macroeconomic movements from a to b to c are compatible with a Demand-side inflation.

____ k. Shifts of Aggregate Demand from AD_0 to AD_1 could be induced by a drop in the discount rate.

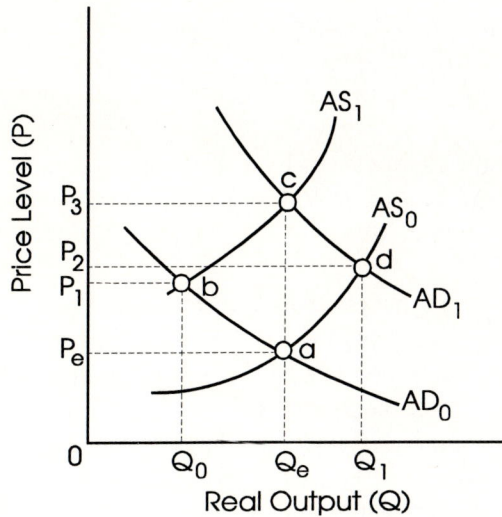

____ l. Unemployment rates are higher at point a than at point b.

____ m. A movement from b to c could follow if policymakers tried to fight a recession originated by supply shocks.

____ n. In the short-run, labor probably suffers from inflationary (money) illusion.

____ o. Labor eventually shrinks its supply curve to offset unexpected inflation.

____ p. A shift from AS_1 to AS_0 could follow an increase in the capital gains tax.

____ q. Policies to reduce monopolistic practices could shift Aggregate Demand from AD_0 to AD_1.

____ r. A movement from a to b could reflect external supply shocks that induced an inflationary recession.

Problem 3

On the space provided, using Aggregate Supply and Aggregate Demand analysis, illustrate an economy at full employment with a normal amount of frictional unemployment. Label the demand curve AD_0, the supply curve AS_0, and the output level Q_f. Label the equilibrium point a.

a. Illustrate a shift caused by a cut in the discount rate. Label the new curve with subscript 1, and the new equilibrium point b.

b. In the long run workers will react to the illusion created by the situation in "a" above. Illustrate by a shift of the appropriate curve to a new equilibrium point c. Label the new curve with a subscript 1. What is the level of real output after the adjustment? _____

c. What kind of cycle have you illustrated? _____

Problem 4

Use Aggregate Demand and Aggregate Supply analysis to illustrate an economy operating at full employment with normal amounts of frictional unemployment. Label the original demand curve AD_0, the original supply curve AS_0, the initial equilibrium point a, and the initial output level Q_f.

a. Lax enforcement of antitrust laws and intense merger activity disturbs the macroeconomic equilibrium. illustrate this shift on your graph by labeling the new curve with a subscript 1. Label the new equilibrium point b, and the new level of output Q_1.

b. The country's leader is alarmed about this situation. She decides to pressure the central bank into lowering the reserve requirement. Illustrate the likely result of this policy on your graph. Label your new curve with a subscript 1. Label the new equilibrium point c. What is the level of real output? _____

c. The situation described above is what kind inflation? _____

Problem 5

Use up arrows (↑), down arrows (↓), zeros (0), or questions marks (?) to indicate how (i) Aggregate Demand and (ii) Aggregate Supply will be shifted by the events described below, and how each will affect (iii) National Income and Output, (iv) employment, (v) unemployment rates, and (vi) the price level. Aggregate Demand and Supply may both be affected in some cases, some reasonable arguments are debatable, and long-run consequences can differ from short-run effects.

a. The FED increases sales of U.S. Treasury bonds to prevent a jump in energy prices from triggering excessive cost-push inflation. i. _____ ii. _____ iii. _____ iv. _____ v. _____ vi. _____

b. Voters blame incumbents for the Depression of 1999-2000. Federal income tax rates are cut by 10% just before the 2000 election. i. _____ ii. _____ iii. _____ iv. _____ v. _____ vi. _____

c. All barriers to free trade between all countries in North and South America are eliminated. i. _____ ii. _____ iii. _____ iv. _____ v. _____ vi. _____

d. An environmental protection law requires all U.S. firms to reduce their pollution per unit of output by 50% before the year 2000. i. _____ ii. _____ iii. _____ iv. _____ v. _____ vi. _____

e. Baby-boomers intent on maintaining standards of living when they retire double the percentages of disposable income they save. i. _____ ii. _____ iii. _____ iv. _____ v. _____ vi. _____

f. The federal budget is balanced by slashing defense spending by $300,000,000,000. i. _____ ii. _____ iii. _____ iv. _____ v. _____ vi. _____

g. The Japanese Parliament eliminates all tariffs and quotas on U.S. agricultural products. i. _____ ii. _____ iii. _____ iv. _____ v. _____ vi. _____

h. Congress relaxes our immigration laws to accommodate a new wave of political refugees. i. _____ ii. _____ iii. _____ iv. _____ v. _____ vi. _____

ANSWERS

Matching	True/False	Multiple Choice	Unlimited MC	Fill-In
1. e	1. F	1. e	1. bc	1. interest rates; investment
2. j	2. T	2. a	2. abcd	2. resources; technology; expectations; regulations
3. c	3. F	3. b	3. ad	3. labor contracts; dual labor; primary; efficiency
4. b	4. F	4. d	4. a	4. money illusion; wage costs; unemployment; rise; wages; counterclockwise
5. h	5. F	5. d	5. bc	5. inflation; unemployment; expansionary; clockwise
6. f	6. T	6. c		6. demand-side; supply-side demand-side; supply-side
7. g	7. T	7. c		
8. i	8. T	8. b		
9. d	9. F	9. c		
10. a	10. T	10. e		
	11. F	11. c		
	12. F	12. a		
		13. e		
		14. c		
		15. b		

Problem 1

a. T
b. T
c. F
d. T
e. F
f. T
g. T
h. F
i. T
j. T
k. F
l. F

Problem 2

a. T
b. T
c. F
d. F
e. T
f. F
g. T
h. F
i. T
j. F
k. T
l. F
m. T
n. T
o. T
p. F
q. F
r. T

Problem 3

a. See Figure A
b. See Figure A; Q_f
c. Demand-side inflation

Problem 4

a. See Figure B
b. See Figure B; Q_f
c. Supply-side inflation

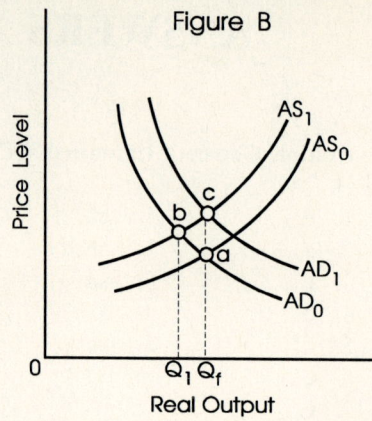

Figure A

Figure B

Problem 5

	i.	ii.	iii.	iv.	v.	vi.
a.	i. ↓	ii. ↓	iii. ↓	iv. ↓	v. ↑	vi. ?
b.	i. ↑	ii. ↑	iii. ↑	iv. ↑	v. ↓	vi. ?
c.	i. ↑	ii. ↑	iii. ↑	iv. ↑	v. ↓	vi. ?
d.	i. 0	ii. ↓	iii. ↓	iv. ↓	v. ↑	vi. ↑
e.	i. ↓	ii. 0	iii. ↓	iv. ↓	v. ↑	vi. ↓
f.	i. ↓	ii. 0	iii. ↓	iv. ↓	v. ↑	vi. ↓
g.	i. ↑	ii. 0	iii. ↑	iv. ↑	v. ↓	vi. ↑
h.	i. ↑	ii. ↑	iii. ↑	iv. ↑	v. ?	vi. ?

Chapter 17
Active vs. Passive Policymaking

Chapter Objectives

After you have read and studied this chapter you should be able to describe alternative interpretations of the Phillips curve hypothesis that inflation and unemployment are inversely related; discuss the theoretical debate concerning the merits of both active verses passive policymaking; evaluate various policies to fight inflation and stagflation, including the theory of the natural rate of unemployment; describe the natural real rate of interest hypothesis, and the Keynes and Fisher effects; and discuss New Classical Macroeconomic theories such as competitive markets, efficient markets, rational expectations, and real business cycles.

Chapter Review: Key Points

1. The *Phillips curve* depicts a trade-off for policymakers between unemployment and inflation. Lower unemployment rates presumably might be purchased through higher inflation, or vice versa; it is up to policymakers to choose the least harmful mix of evils. The Phillips curve appeared to be relatively stable through the 1960s, but it shifted sharply in the 1970s and early 1980s so that much higher rates of unemployment appeared necessary to dampen inflationary pressures. The reasons for the instability of the Phillips curve are the subject of a continuing debate within the economics profession.

2. Modern Keynesian analysis suggests that several factors in addition to inflationary expectations can cause stagflation and instability in the Phillips curve. Wages and prices are assumed "sticky", especially in downward direction. Unexpected shocks to the supply side, rapid structural changes in demand or output, changes in labor institutions that generate disincentives for work, and changes in public regulatory policies can all shift the Phillips curve. The Keynesian *structuralist* approach emphasizes production "bottlenecks" as foundations for the Phillips curve.

3. The *natural rate theory* of the instability in the Phillips trade-off focuses on worker expectations of inflation. As labor begins to anticipate inflation, greater increases in wages are required for a given level of real output. Thus, accelerating inflation is required if policymakers desire to hold unemployment below its "natural rate," but even this policy will not work forever.

4. If interest rate targets or unemployment rate objectives are set below their "natural rates," expansionary policies may ultimately cause *nominal interest rates* to rise, not fall. *Natural-rate* theorists believe that only temporary reductions in interest rates or unemployment can be obtained through expansionary policies, and even in the short run, only by "fooling" lenders or workers.

5. The *Keynes effect* predicts that monetary growth will decrease interest rates, and vice versa. The *Fisher effect* is the upwards adjustment of nominal interest rates when transactors begin expecting inflation.

6. The *new classical macroeconomics* is based on the model of perfect competition, or *efficient markets,* which suggests that even in the short run, macropolicy only works when the economy is operating inefficiently and that this does not occur.

7. The theory of *rational expectations* suggests that people eventually figure out how a given change in policy affects the economy and learn to predict how policymakers react to swings in economic activity. Thereafter, people will focus on what policymakers are doing and make adjustments that prevent the policies from accomplishing their objectives.

8. *Real business cycle theory* views shocks to Aggregate Supply as permanent, and suggests that attempts by macroeconomic policymakers to "fine-tune" the economy are either self defeating or harmful.

Matching Key Terms And Concepts

___ 1. rational expectations theory

___ 2. Keynes effect

___ 3. demand-side stagflation

___ 4. Keynesian `shock' and `structuralist' hypotheses

___ 5. nominal interest rate

___ 6. Fisher effect

___ 7. real interest rate

___ 8. natural rate theory

___ 9. Phillips curves

___10. supply-side stagflation

a. The percentage annual monetary premium paid for borrowing.

b. Trade-offs between inflation and unemployment.

c. People learn to anticipate the results of policies.

d. Deviations from normal frictional unemployment are caused by macropolicy.

e. Monetary interest adjusted for inflation.

f. Expanding the money supply unexpectedly initially causes nominal interest rates to fall.

g. Contracting the money supply unexpectedly ultimately causes the nominal interest rate to fall.

h. Workers adjust to anticipated inflation by reducing labor supplies.

i. Falling Aggregate Supply boosts prices and unemployment.

j. Explains Phillips curves by labor market "bottlenecks" and changing intensities of shocks to our economy.

True/False Questions

___ 1. The nominal rate of interest will be higher than the real rate of interest when the inflation rate is positive.

___ 2. High unemployment generates political pressures for full employment policies that raise Aggregate Supply.

___ 3. The stagflation phase of demand-side inflation resembles the initial phase of supply-side inflation.

___ 4. In the early 1960s, Keynesian policy prescriptions seemed to steer the economy along a prosperous path.

___ 5. External economic shocks may cause the Aggregate Supply to shift to the right, worsening the tradeoff between unemployment and inflation.

___ 6. Natural rate theorists believe that long run Phillips curves are vertical at the natural rate of unemployment.

___ 7. Classical theory suggests that policymakers are faced with a relatively stable Phillips curve tradeoff.

___ 8. Expansionary fiscal policy reduces frictional unemployment because workers are afraid to change jobs.

9. The Phillips curve for the United States shifted to the left during the 1970s.

____10. When Aggregate Demand shifts to the left, the Phillips curve shifts to the left.

____11. Aggregate Supply shifts cause Phillips curve shifts.

____12. As workers anticipate higher inflation the short-run Phillips relation shifts outward (up and to the right).

____13. The particular interest rate paid by a borrower to a lender reflects default risk, length of time to maturity of the note or bond, the anticipated rate of inflation, and legal constraints.

____14. The Fisher effect refers to the change in nominal interest rates as borrowers and lenders compensate for expected inflation.

____15. Advocates of natural rate theory tend to favor the replacement of rules with discretionary policy making.

Standard Multiple Choice

There Is One Best Answer For Each Question.

____ 1. The Phillips curve posits a tradeoff between:
   a. economic stability and growth.
   b. consumption today vs. tomorrow.
   c. unemployment and inflation.
   d. low interest rates and low taxes.
   e. gasoline service stations and screwdrivers.

____ 2. Second phases of demand-pull inflationary cycles entail:
   a. cost-push inflation.
   b. substantial layoffs of workers.
   c. rising unemployment.
   d. accelerating inflation.
   e. All of the above.

____ 3. The Phillips Curve:
   a. shifted inward during the 1970s.
   b. has been very stable.
   c. shows the tradeoff between balanced budgets and inflation.
   d. demonstrates stable economic growth.
   e. None of these.

____ 4. According to "natural rate" theory, macropolicy can't influence long-run rates of:
   a. inflation and unemployment.
   b. real interest and unemployment.
   c. nominal economic growth.
   d. financial capital accumulation.
   e. All of the above.

___ 5. Hikes in nominal interest rates when people expect higher inflation are examples of the:
   a. Keynes effect.
   b. Fisher effect.
   c. real wealth effect.
   d. Friedman effect.
   e. Kuznets effect.

___ 6. In broad terms, natural rate theory assumes:
   a. balanced budgets at full employment.
   b. stable unemployment/inflation tradeoffs.
   c. inflationary biases in healthy economies.
   d. prices rise more easily than they decline.
   e. independence between monetary and "real" variables.

___ 7. The idea of combating inflation by shrinking Aggregate Demand does NOT involve which of the following theories:
   a. recessions moderate labor's inflationary expectations.
   b. recessions foster inflation that improves political incumbents' reelection prospects.
   c. periods of slack demand aid firms in eliminating "deadwood."
   d. fear of job loss stimulates labor productivity.
   e. recessions dampen the inflationary expectations of workers, investors, business firms, and consumers.

___ 8. The "natural rate" theory of the Phillips curve suggests that expansionary macroeconomic policy may temporarily reduce unemployment with only minor inflation because:
   a. workers are temporarily fooled by higher money wage offers.
   b. workers find long-term jobs easier during business booms.
   c. policymakers are fooled by businessmen into expanding Aggregate Demand.
   d. business decisionmakers are fooled by workers who are lazier than they represent themselves to be.
   e. everyone is happier to work when recessions end.

___ 9. Many modern Keynesians suggest that, for the most part, the stagflation of the 1970s was caused by:
   a. workers being fooled by inflation.
   b. policymakers seeing past the inflation illusion of the 1960s.
   c. business expectations being confronted by reality.
   d. such shocks to the economy as OPEC price hikes and the souring of the Russian Wheat Deal.
   e. All of the above.

___10. Overly expansionary monetary and fiscal policies tend to cause:
   a. unemployment to fall temporarily.
   b. rising expectations of inflation.
   c. nominal interest to rise in the long run.
   d. no long-term effect on employment.
   e. All of the above.

___11. The "supply-side" policies adopted in the early 1980s to counter inflation and stimulate economic growth did not include selective:
   a. increasing the money supply.
   b. increasing government spending.
   c. increasing Aggregate Demand.
   d. decreasing Aggregate Supply.
   e. decreasing Aggregate Demand.

___12. The explanation of Phillips curves as consequences of labor and product market "bottlenecks" is at the core of the:
   a. modern monetarist approach.
   b. "natural rate" approach.
   c. Keynesian "composition-shift" approach.
   d. Keynesian "structuralist" approach.
   e. classical approach.

Chapter Review (Fill-In Questions)

1. Between the 1960s and 1970s many economists believed that a reasonably _____ inverse relationship existed between unemployment and inflation. This idea is known as the _____ curve tradeoff.

2. Phillips curves are inverse relationships between unemployment and inflation and the _____ curve indicates a positive relation between the level of output (and thus employment) and the price level; thus, the two curves _____ each other.

3. One Keynesian explanation for the Phillips curve suggests that as _____ is approached, it becomes increasingly costly to produce added output because labor market _____ become increasingly severe.

4. The monetarist explanation for shifts of the Phillips relation focuses on rising _____ expectations of workers and their adjustments that shift Aggregate Supply to the _____.

5. Modern Keynesian explanations for shifts of the Phillips curve emphasize the _____, especially downwards, of wages and prices. Shocks are continually bombarding the economy causing changes in demand for various products. In sectors where demands increase, _____ tend to rise. Where demand declines, workers are reluctant to accept wage _____, so firms commonly cut their production costs through layoffs and _____ in production.

6. Natural rate theory assumes that lenders and borrowers focus on the _____, of interest which is the _____ of interest after adjusting for inflation. In equation form, the real rate of interest equals _____, which implies that the rate of interest lenders will charge equals _____.

7. _____ suggests that economic profits are almost purely the result of luck. A related theory, _____, suggests that people will learn to anticipate any predictable consequence of policy, so that overly expansionary policies will result in high rates of _____ and _____, but nothing else. Instantaneous adjustments eliminate all other effects.

8. _____ theory contend that most fluctuations in real GDP are permanent and the result of _____ shocks. Real business cyclists believe that macropolicy should be _____, since attempts to "fine-tune" the economy will be _____.

Unlimited Multiple Choice

Each Question Has From Zero To Four Right Answers.

___ 1. According to the natural rate hypothesis:
   a. attempts to drive unemployment and real interest rates permanently below their natural rates are futile.
   b. the government can induce a permanent increase in the employment rate by pursuing demand-management policies.
   c. frictional unemployment can only be reduced temporarily.
   d. each Phillips curve exists only for a particular expected rate of inflation.

___ 2. Real interest rates are the annual percentage:
   a. monetary premiums paid to use money.
   b. of real purchasing power paid to a lender by a borrower for the use of money.
   c. of extra goods that can be enjoyed if consumption is deferred.
   d. premiums necessary to induce savers to defer gratification.

___ 3. Markets will operate efficiently if there is:
   a. substantial information about profit making opportunities.
   b. vigorous competition among sellers for profit making opportunities.
   c. federal control of wages and prices.
   d. business collusion to fix prices.

___ 4. According to the rational expectations branch of monetarism:
   a. government can fool the public continually.
   b. policy goals can be predictably achieved in neither the short run nor the long run.
   c. nominal interest rates adjust immediately to expected inflation, if the public knows about past countercyclical policies.
   d. some policy goals might be achievable in the short run only if macroeconomic policies are disguised from the public.

___ 5. According to natural rate theory, if the FED pursues an expansionary monetary policy by buying bonds:
   a. the nominal rate of interest will be reduced permanently.
   b. the initial decline in the interest rate is called the Fisher effect.
   c. the supply of loanable funds initially decreases, causing the nominal interest rate to increase.
   d. despite an initial increase in the real rate of interest, it will return to its natural rate.

Problems

Problem 1

Use your knowledge about interest rates to answer the following questions.

a. If the nominal rate of interest is 8% and the rate of inflation is 8%, then the real rate of interest (r) equals _____.

b. If the nominal rate of interest is 12% and the rate of inflation is 15%, then the real rate of interest (r) equals _____.

c. If the nominal rate of interest is 2% and the rate of inflation is -10%, then the real rate of interest (r) equals _____.

d. If the desired real rate of interest is 8% and inflation is expected to be 8% annually, then the nominal interest rate (i) a lender would charge equals _____.

e. If the desired real rate of interest is 5% and inflation is expected to be -3% annually, then the nominal interest rate (i) a lender would charge equals _____.

f. If the desired real rate of interest is 6% and inflation is expected to be 18% annually, then the nominal interest rate (i) a lender would charge equals _____.

Problem 2

Use this figure to answer the following True/False questions as a "Natural Rate" theorist would.

___ a. The natural rate of unemployment is 6%.

___ b. If workers expect 6% inflation and policymakers expand Aggregate Demand to shrink unemployment to 4%, there would be 12% inflation.

___ c. Eliminating inflation when inflationary expectations are 6% could be accomplished while holding unemployment at 6%.

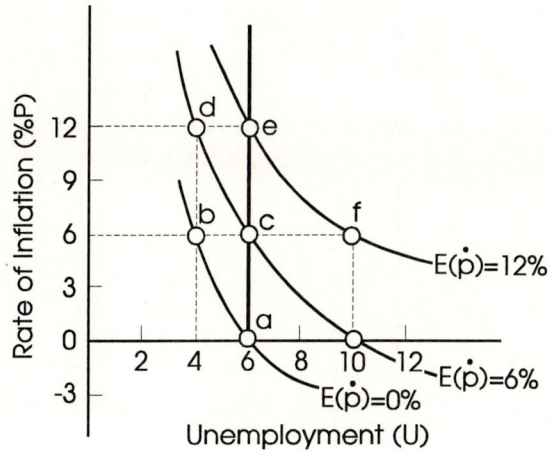

___ d. Reducing inflationary expectations from 12% to 6% worsens the tradeoff between inflation and unemployment.

___ e. If inflationary expectations are originally 12%, maintaining a 10% unemployment rate would eventually (probably rather quickly) bring the economy back to a point where inflation was negligible.

___ f. The expected annual rate of inflation at a is 6%.

___ g. As the economy moves from a to b, the actual real wage rate falls while the expected real wage rate increases.

___ h. Expected inflation at c is 6%.

___ i. Expected inflation at d is 12%.

___ j. At b, the actual rate of inflation equals the expected rate of price change.

___ k. Money wages are higher at c than at b.

___ l. The employment rate decreases as the economy moves from b to c.

___ m. Expected inflation at f is 12%.

___ n. The expected real wage rate is smaller than the actual real wage rate at f.

___ o. Expected inflation at a is zero.

___ p. As the economy moves from a to b, the money wage rate increases at a rate of 6%.

___ q. The expected real wage rate at b is greater than the expected real wage rate at a.

___ r. As the economy moves from b to c, the actual real wage rate increases, since workers' demands for higher money wage rates are partially met.

___ s. An increase in Aggregate Demand could cause the economy to move from a to b in the short run if workers do not suffer from money illusion.

___ t. Workers suffer from money illusion at c.

___ u. Workers do not suffer from money illusion at d.

___ x. According to natural rate theory, there is a permanent trade-off between unemployment and inflation.

___ v. Expected inflation along $E(p) = 12\%$ is 12%.

___ y. Unanticipated higher prices can mean more real production

___ w. A buyers' market exists in the labor market with a movement from e to f.

Problem 3

You are the chief economic advisor to the president. She asks you for your policy prescription for the current economic climate which features high unemployment and high price inflation (stagflation). You believe in the Keynesian structuralist approach.

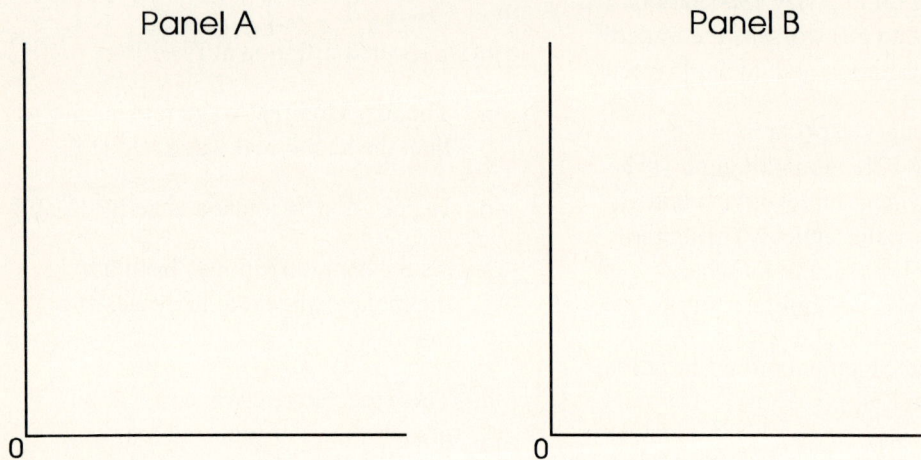

Panel A

Panel B

0   0

a. Illustrate the present situation using Aggregate Demand and Aggregate Supply analysis in Panel A of the Figure. Label your initial curves with a subscript 1.

b. Illustrate, by movements of the curves in Panel A and corresponding shifts of the Phillips curves in Panel B, what the impact of your program(s) would be. Label your original Phillips curve that corresponds to your initial Aggregate Demand-Aggregate Supply equilibrium PC_1. Label each succeeding curve AS_2, AS_3, PC_2, PC_3.

c. What are some of your proposals to attain this goal? _____

_____

ANSWERS

Matching	True/False	Multiple Choice	Unlimited MC	Fill-In
1. c	1. T	1. c	1. acd	1. stable; Phillips
2. f	2. F	2. e	2. bcd	2. Aggregate Supply; mirror
3. h	3. T	3. e	3. ab	3. full employment; bottlenecks
4. j	4. T	4. b	4. bcd	4. inflationary; left
5. a	5. F	5. b	5. none	5. stickiness; prices and wages;
6. g	6. T	6. e		cuts; cutbacks
7. e	7. F	7. b		6. real rate; nominal rate;
8. d	8. F	8. a		$i = rd + E(p)$; $r = i - p$
9. b	9. F	9. d		7. efficient markets;
10. i	10. F	10. e		rational expectations;
	11. T	11. e		interest; inflation
	12. T	12. d		8. Real Business Cycle; supply;
	13. T			passive; self defeating
	14. T			
	15. F			

Problem 1

a. 0%
b. -3%
c. 12%
d. 16%
e. 2%
f. 24%

Problem 2

a.	T	n.	T
b.	T	o.	T
c.	F	p.	F
d.	F	q.	T
e.	T	r.	T
f.	F	s.	F
g.	T	t.	F
h.	T	u.	F
i.	F	v.	T
j.	F	w.	T
k.	T	x.	F
l.	T	y.	T
m.	T		

Problem 3

Panel A — Price Level vs. Real Output, showing AS_1, AS_2, AS_3, and AD_1.

Panel B — Inflation Rate vs. Unemployment Rate, showing PC_1, PC_2, and PC_3.

a. See figure.

b. See figure.

c. Any proposals that reduce rigidity and bottlenecks in the economy, will help solve stagflation problems by shifting the Phillips curve to the left and the Aggregate Supply curve to the right. Most of the policies described in the textbook are mentioned under Supply- side economics, but some programs of the 1970s, particularly job training, were designed to increase Aggregate Supply.

Chapter 18
Limitations of Stabilization Policy

Chapter Objectives

After you have read and studied this chapter you should be able to explain the difficulties for macroeconomic policymaking posed by such factors as missed timing, improper dosages of stimulation or contraction, and how private adjustments may frustrate even well intended discretionary policymaking; discuss the ways that policymaking may be misused to introduce "political" business cycles and a long-term trend for growth in government relative to the private sector; discuss incomes policies and their possible effects on the economy; and discuss national economic planning and national industrial policy, and how they apply to the United States.

Chapter Review: Key Points

1. Macroeconomic policymaking is at least as much art as it is a science. A multitude of problems preclude perfect analysis and policy.

2. A *recognition lag* occurs because it takes time to get even a modestly accurate picture of changes in the state of the economy. An *administrative* (implementation) *lag* exists because it takes a while to get the tax and monetary machinery in gear even when policymakers' plans are made. An *impact lag* confounds the proper timing of policy; the economy budges only stubbornly to the prods of the policymakers' tools. These lags, which may be long and variable, may cause discretionary policy to be more destabilizing than stabilizing.

3. Lack of precise knowledge about recessionary gaps, inflationary gaps, and GNP gaps, as well as uncertainty about multipliers and velocity, mean that estimating the correct doses of monetary and fiscal medicine is extremely difficult.

4. Some modern Keynesians challenge the long-term effectiveness of monetary policy, arguing that adjustments in financial technologies will ultimately *insulate financial institutions* and make monetary tools inoperative.

5. Incumbents' re-election prospects improve as per capita disposable income grows immediately prior to elections. There is some evidence that policymakers try to manipulate Aggregate Demand to enhance their positions in the eyes of voters, which induces *political business cycles*.

6. Critics of Keynesian fiscal policies also suggest that the government grows relative to the private sector when policymakers increase spending and cut taxes during downturns policymakers neither cut spending nor restore taxes, however, during periods of prosperity or inflation.

7. *Intentional recessions* can decompress accumulated inflationary pressures and inflationary expectations. However, recessions tend to be very hard on political incumbents, so many politicians favor incomes policies of various sorts.

8. *Incomes policies* (mandatory wage-price freezes or controls, voluntary guidelines, or "jawboning") muzzle the effectiveness of the price system, creating shortages and widespread misallocations of resources.

9. The more involved a country is in international trade and finance, the less will be the impact of any given monetary or fiscal policy because the effects are diffused by foreign markets.

Matching Key Terms And Concepts

____ 1. Incomes Policies

____ 2. Cost-plus pricing

____ 3. Political business cycles

____ 4. Wage and price freezes

____ 5. Overdosing the economy

____ 6. Underdosing the economy

____ 7. Recognition lag

____ 8. Administration lag

____ 9. Impact lag

____ 10. Financial insulation

a. Caused by underestimation of multipliers or overestimation of the economy's capacity.
b. Financial institutions learn to counteract monetary policies.
c. The period between adoption and effect of a change in policy.
d. Most stringent form of incomes policy.
e. Range from jawboning to freezes.
f. The period between an event and the availability of information about it.
g. The money supply grows rapidly in years divisible by 4.
h. Caused by overestimating multipliers or the economy's capacity.
i. The time required to alter the course of policy.
j. Marking up costs by a fixed percentage to set prices.

True/False Questions

___ 1. The recognition lag occurs because it is generally difficult for monetary and fiscal policymakers to determine quickly how much of which policies to use in steering our sluggish economy along a proper course.

___ 2. Since changes in monetary policy can be implemented quickly through the FED's Open Market Committee, administration lags are not much of a problem for monetary policymaking.

___ 3. Wage and price controls have a long history of considerable success at reducing inflation.

___ 4. The impact lag of monetary policy is comparatively regular and short.

___ 5. Critics contend that wage and price controls may actually increase inflationary expectations.

___ 6. The longer that wage and price controls are in force the more difficult it is for economic transactors to distinguish real from artificial price signals.

___ 7. There is little empirical evidence of political business cycles.

___ 8. The Federal Funds Market provides banks with the opportunity to lend or to borrow millions of dollars for one or two days at comparatively low interest rates.

___ 9. Various studies indicate that voters tend to re-elect incumbents more often the faster disposable income grows during the year immediately preceding elections.

___10. Impact lags make it more difficult to cure the economy than simple Keynesian analysis would suggest.

Standard Multiple Choice

There Is One Best Answer For Each Question.

___ 1. Which of the following is an example of financial insulation?
   a. The FED's discount window.
   b. A wage and price freeze.
   c. A wage and price control.
   d. A bank holding on to excess reserves.
   e. The federal funds market.

___ 2. Which lag is longer for fiscal policy than for monetary policy?
   a. Discretionary lag.
   b. Recognition lag.
   c. Administration lag.
   d. Dosage lag.
   e. Impact lag.

___ 3. Which one of the following
generalizations about economic
theories is not correct?
   a. Keynesians believe that
      macroeconomic policy works.
   b. New classical macroeconomists
      believe that macropolicy does not
      work.
   c. Natural rate theorists believe
      macropolicy works only
      temporarily but is harmful in the
      long run.
   d. Post-Keynesian monetarists believe
      Keynesian analysis is correct for
      the very short run but classical
      assumptions are correct for the
      long run.
   e. Classical economists believed that
      macropolicy was effective in both
      the short and long run.

___ 4. Incomes policies disturb the price
system and cause:
   a. efficient usage of resources.
   b. surpluses.
   c. politicians' jawbones to swell.
   d. inflation upon their
      implementation.
   e. shortages and misallocation of
      resources.

___ 5. Mandatory price controls are an
example of:
   a. monetary policy.
   b. fiscal policy.
   c. automatic stabilizers.
   d. tax policy.
   e. incomes policies.

___ 6. Some new-Keynesians believe that
financial technologies change in
response to changes in:
   a. the size of the workforce.
   b. monetary policy.
   c. the capital stock.
   d. fiscal policy.
   e. All of these.

___ 7. Assume OPEC hikes the price of oil,
and policymakers attempt to offset the
resulting tendency for the economy to
slide into a recession. Which of the
following is NOT a likely
consequence of these events?
   a. The "real" price OPEC gets for oil
      will be less than it expects.
   b. The "real" wages of labor will fall.
   c. "Real" national income will fall
      because of the OPEC hike.
   d. Our "real" national income will fall
      solely because of overly
      expansionary policies.
   e. The price level will rise.

___ 8. Wage and price controls are intended
to:
   a. dampen inflationary expectations.
   b. shift the economy's supply curve to
      the left.
   c. shift the economy's demand curve
      to the right.
   d. reduce corporate profits.
   e. increase corporate profits.

___ 9. Price ceilings are likely to result in:
   a. shortages.
   b. black markets.
   c. queuing.
   d. rationing by favoritism.
   e. All of the above.

___10. Incumbent policymakers that manipulate macroeconomic policies to obtain reelection may cause:
   a. political business cycles.
   b. stagflation.
   c. excessive unemployment.
   d. countercyclical cycles.
   e. tax rates to rise just before election.

___11. During an election year, incumbents are most likely to support:
   a. tax increases.
   b. reduction of subsidies to all special interest groups.
   c. growth of the money supply.
   d. campaign finance reform.
   e. reduction of the money supply.

___12. Critics of discretionary monetary and fiscal policy point to:
   a. political manipulation of the business cycle.
   b. failures to raise taxes and cut spending during inflation.
   c. problems with lags and incorrect doses.
   d. these policies' reliance on "fooling" people.
   e. All of these.

Chapter Review (Fill-In Questions)

1. Even well-intentioned policymakers suffer from a _____ lag because it takes time and resources to acquire sufficient _____ about the state of the economy to make judgments about the proper course of policy.

2. Once a problem is recognized, there is a(n) _____ lag because it takes time for _____ policymakers to tilt open market directions properly, and even more time for _____ policymakers to change _____ laws or alter appropriations for government outlays.

3. Once a policy is changed, the time it takes for policy to affect economic activity results in a(n) _____ lag. The _____ lag is usually longer for fiscal policy than monetary policy, while the _____ lag is longer for monetary policy if changes in _____ policies are the tools used by fiscal policymakers.

4. Tight money policies may teach financial institutions new ways to conserve on their holdings of reserves. Such changes in financial technology are known as _____, and make repeatedly used monetary policies _____ or useless in their effects on macroeconomic activity.

5. Reluctance in using _____ to combat inflation has channeled many political decisionmakers into experiments with _____ policies. Wage-price curbs have ranged from _____ by the president, to mandatory _____.

6. Opponents point to the wage-price controls of _____ to show that incomes policies do not work. They argue that controls can create expectations that prices will _____ when controls are lifted.

Unlimited Multiple Choice

There Are Four To Zero Answers For Each Question.

___ 1. It may be difficult to design and to implement appropriate countercyclical policies:
   a. because of the timing problems inherent in both monetary and fiscal policies.
   b. because adjustments made by private individuals and firms to certain monetary and fiscal policies can eliminate the desired effects of the countercyclical measures.
   c. because policymakers do not possess current or perfect information about the condition of the economy.
   d. because politicians sometimes base policy on the effects that specific countercyclical measures might have on their prospects for re-election.

___ 2. Mandatory wage and price controls:
   a. have typically been associated with wartime efforts.
   b. were imposed by President Nixon in August of 1971.
   c. are imposed to mitigate recessionary pressures which develop automatically in the economy.
   d. seldom distort relative prices.

___ 3. Wage and price guideposts and guidelines:
   a. assume that rates of price increases can parallel increases in labor productivity without causing upward pressure on wage rates.
   b. have traditionally been mandatory.
   c. are typically tied to a socially accepted level of unemployment.
   d. are very effective in relieving inflationary pressures.

___ 4. Proponents of incomes policies argue that controls:
   a. effectively reduce deflationary expectations.
   b. can reduce inflationary expectations.
   c. distort relative price signals and misallocate resources.
   d. can reconcile the goals of monopolistic industries with the goals of society.

___ 5. Decreasing Aggregate Demand in order to reduce inflation:
   a. is generally favored by politicians.
   b. may cause a recession.
   c. might also 'discipline' a 'slack' labor force.
   d. should increase employment.

Problem

Answer the True/False questions below based on the following scenario:

After moderate sales during the Christmas season of 1995 business pessimism leads to a decline in production in the first part of 1996. Consumers' expectations mirror business' hesitation, and outlays on durable goods are delayed or forgotten. First quarter statistics compiled in mid April indicate that a contraction is taking place. Upon receiving the news, the FED undertakes actions to boost the money supply. In Congress rumors begin to circulate about a possible tax cut to deal with the downturn in business activity.

___ a. The time between January 1996 and mid April 1995 is known as a recognition lag.

___ b. If the FED implements an expansion of the money supply by mid May, the administrative lag (of monetary policy) is approximately one month.

___ c. The impact lag will most likely be longer for a tax cut than for open market operations which expand the money supply.

___ d. The administrative lag will most likely be longer for monetary policy as compared to fiscal policy.

___ e. The recognition lag is longer for fiscal policy than for monetary policy.

___ f. Government purchases to combat declining Aggregate Demand will have a shorter administrative lag than lowering the discount rate.

___ g. The impact lag of open market purchases will be of short duration because money expansion is almost instantaneous.

___ h. If a tax cut is finally passed in November of 1996 and implemented in 1997, there is a chance that the tax cut will help to overheat the economy (cause inflation).

___ i. The impact lag of expansionary monetary policy will increase if banks are reluctant to loan out additionally funds acquired through the sale of government securities to the FED.

___ j. The recognition lag could be decreased by compiling business statistics at intervals of 1 month as opposed to each quarter.

ANSWERS

Matching	True/False	Multiple Choice	Unlimited MC	Fill-In
1. e	1. T	1. e	1. abcd	1. recognition; information
2. j	2. T	2. c	2. ab	2. administration; monetary; fiscal; tax
3. g	3. F	3. e	3. none	3. impact; administration; impact; tax
4. d	4. F	4. e	4. bd	4. financial insulation; unpredictable
5. a	5. T	5. e	5. bc	5. recessions; incomes; jawboning; wage/price freezes
6. h	6. T	6. b		6. 1971-73; rise
7. f	7. F	7. d		
8. i	8. T	8. a		
9. c	9. T	9. e		
10. b	10. T	10. a		
		11. c		
		12. e		

Problem

a. T
b. T
c. F
d. F
e. F
f. F
g. F
h. T
i. T
j. T

Chapter 19
Economic Growth and Development

Chapter Objectives

After you have read and studied this chapter, you should be able to describe the processes of economic growth and development; discuss the special hurdles to development faced in poor countries; and discuss the pros and cons of the "trap of underdevelopment" argument.

Chapter Review: Key Points

1. *Economic growth* refers to quantitative changes in the capacity to produce goods and services in a country. It occurs through expanding capital or labor resources, discoveries of new sources of raw materials, or development of more productive technologies. *Economic development* refers to improving the qualitative aspects of economic growth, including changes in the quality of life.

2. The *Rule of 72* is a rule of thumb for estimating how long it takes for a variable to double in value given some percentage growth rate. Simply divide 72 by the growth rate. For example, if growth in GNP is occurring at 6 percent per year, GNP will double in approximately 12 years (72/6 = 12).

3. *Diminishing returns* because of the fixity of land cause output to grow more slowly, even if labor and capital increase in fixed proportions.

4. Reverend Thomas Malthus and other nineteenth-century economists were convinced that population growth is almost uncontrollable, and theorized that equilibrium is attained only when bare subsistence is common to all.

5. *Population growth* tends to slow as a country develops. The least developed countries of the world tend to have the highest rates of population growth.

6. *Capital formation* requires high saving rates. If *voluntary saving* is used to finance development, greater incomes, higher interest rates paid to savers, and (perhaps) less equal income distributions will lead to higher rates of investment. *Involuntary saving* may be used to free investment resources through confiscation, taxation, or inflation.

7. *Capital widening* occurs when the capital stock and labor force grow at the same rates. *Capital deepening* requires the capital stock to grow faster than the labor force.

8. *Technological advances* occur when given amounts of resources acquire greater productive capacity.

9. Rapid development requires a strong *social infrastructure*--education, communications, transportation, and other networks that facilitate production.

Matching Key Terms And Concepts

Set I

____ 1. international credit

____ 2. involuntary saving

____ 3. Rule of "72"

____ 4. economic development

____ 5. economic growth

____ 6. communism

____ 7. capital deepening

____ 8. capital to labor ratio (K/L)

____ 9. high birth rates

____10. voluntary saving

a. According to Karl Marx, follows the "dictatorship of the proletariat" and then the "withering away of the state."

b. Boosts investment beyond domestic capabilities.

c. Expansion of productive capacity.

d. Individual choice between present and future consumption.

e. Investment is proportionally greater than population growth.

f. A quick way of estimating "doubling" times.

g. Qualitative expansion.

h. Associated with underdevelopment.

i. Accomplished by taxes or inflation.

j. A crucial determinant of labor productivity.

Set II

____ 1. technological advance

____ 2. infrastructure

____ 3. "Trap of underdevelopment"

____ 4. high voluntary saving rate

____ 5. Malthusian equilibrium

____ 6. "takeoff"

____ 7. Labor Force Participation Rate

____ 8. surplus value

____ 9. capital widening

____ 10. low birth rates

a. Percentage of a population in the work force.

b. A stage in Rostow's growth theory.

c. Net investment and population growth are proportional.

d. A factor temporarily expanding LFPRs.

e. Difference between wage paid and total value produced by a worker.

f. Inhibits Keynesian Aggregate Spending but facilitates economic growth.

g. The edge of starvation.

h. Producing more from given resources.

i. Low income inhibits capital accumulation.

j. An integral part of economic development.

True/False Questions

____ 1. The labor force as a percentage of the population is known as the capital to labor ratio.

____ 2. An important determinant of the size of the labor force relative to the size of the population is the rate of population growth.

____ 3. Increases in the labor force generally result in an increase in potential real output.

____ 4. Net investment represents net new capital formation during a given time period.

____ 5. Capital widening increases real per capita income.

____ 6. A government can rapidly increase potential Aggregate Supply by pursuing appropriate demand-management policies.

____ 7. An increase in the interest rate received by savers increases the price of present consumption relative to future consumption.

____ 8. Widespread poverty inhibits saving and capital accumulation.

____ 9. Higher interest rates charged investors and lower payments to savers will lead to larger capital stocks over time.

____ 10. Any smoothly functioning economy needs a sophisticated and efficient financial system.

Standard Multiple Choice

There Is One Best Answer For Each Question.

___ 1. The number of years that it takes some variable to double is approximately its annual percentage growth rate divided into:
   a. its current value.
   b. 72.
   c. 76.
   d. 82.
   e. None of the above.

___ 2. Economic development in a primitive society would NOT be fostered by:
   a. an increase in the population growth rate.
   b. expanded investment in capital embodying new technology.
   c. improvements in the education of the work force.
   d. better transportation, communications, and banking networks.
   e. adoption of advanced agricultural technology.

___ 3. Output per capita would probably rise, but output per worker would probably fall if:
   a. capital deepening occurred rapidly.
   b. the labor force participation rate of a given population rose.
   c. technical education of the work force increased.
   d. involuntary saving was increased.
   e. income were distributed equally.

___ 4. In Karl Marx's theory of economic development:
   a. a "takeoff stage" precedes the dictatorship of the proletariat.
   b. feudalism comes just before a "withering away of the state."
   c. communism immediately follows the overthrow of capitalism.
   d. capitalism is succeeded by a dictatorship of the proletariat.
   e. high savings rates launch a takeoff into high mass consumption.

___ 5. Voluntary saving is enhanced by higher:
   a. tax rates and inflation.
   b. surplus values and more central planning.
   c. interest rates and income.
   d. confiscation and inflation.
   e. degrees of equality in the distribution of income.

___ 6. According to Karl Marx, which event immediately precedes pure communism?
   a. The "withering away of the state."
   b. Feudalism.
   c. A "dictatorship of the proletariat."
   d. Distribution "from each according to need, to each according to ability."
   e. A non-sexist, non-racist, non-exploitative Utopia.

___ 7. A problem NOT part of "Trap of Underdevelopment" theory is:
   a. high birth rates.
   b. low per capita income.
   c. a low capital to labor ratio.
   d. low productivity.
   e. high pollution from dirty technology.

___ 8. Voluntary saving will most likely increase if:
   a. tax rates are increased.
   b. income decreases.
   c. interest rates rise.
   d. the distribution of income becomes more unequal.
   e. the rate of inflation increases.

___ 9. An economist who argued that population adjusts to a biological subsistence level given available resources was:
   a. David Ricardo.
   b. Karl Marx.
   c. W. W. Rostow.
   d. Thomas Carlyle.
   e. Rev. Thomas Malthus.

___10. Which of the following would NOT tend to cause economic growth?
   a. Improvement in technology.
   b. Increased labor force participation.
   c. Increased training and education.
   d. Increased marginal propensities to consume
   e. An improved social infrastructure.

Chapter Review (Fill-In Questions)

1. Economic _____ occurs when an economy's capacity expands; economic _____ entails qualitative improvements in economic conditions.

2. The time required for doubling any variable is approximated through calculations using the _____. Dividing the percentage annual change in a variable into _____ yields the number of years required for the variable to double its value.

3. Economic growth is the long-run process of expanding the limits to _____. Increased availability of _____ for production is one source of growth.

4. Per capita income tends to rise when the workforce increases through rising _____ rates, although less than proportionally because of declining _____ ratios, assuming investment does not also rise. Productive capacity may also rise if _____ grows, but _____ income is likely to fall because of growing numbers of mouths to feed.

5. Many early economists, accepting the analyses of the Rev. _____, argued that population would always tend towards the maximum sustainable with given resources, so that people would, on the average, live only at _____ levels. This led critics of the day to term economics "the dismal science." Malthus believed population has a natural tendency to grow, in his terms, _____, while food supplies grow only _____.

6. High levels of investment and research and development expenditures create improvements in _____ and/or physical capital resources in a society. Economy-wide technological changes occur with the development of social overhead capital, also known as the _____. This road to economic development entails a well organized _____, efficient _____, and _____ networks, and an educated and disciplined _____.

Unlimited Multiple Choice

Each Question Has From Zero To Four Correct Responses.

____ 1. Economic growth:
   a. is synonymous with economic development.
   b. refers to qualitative change experienced by an economic system.
   c. occurs when an economic system acquires greater productive capacity.
   d. always results in increased real per capita output or income.

____ 2. An increase in the capital to labor ratio:
   a. increases the productive capacity of an economy.
   b. tends to increase real per capita income.
   c. increases labor productivity more in a less developed country than in a developed country.
   d. generally results in economic growth and development.

____ 3. Saving:
   a. enables production of new capital.
   b. is necessary for the accumulation of capital.
   c. is voluntary when individuals decide on their own to defer consumption to some future date.
   d. is determined by national income, according to the classical model.

____ 4. Potential Aggregate Supply is:
   a. determined partially by the state of technology.
   b. potentially increased if government uses highly inflationary policies and secures large tax revenues.
   c. determined strictly by Aggregate Demand.
   d. determined by the qualities and quantities of available resources.

____ 5. Capital deepening:
   a. is an increase in the ratio of labor to capital.
   b. necessarily increases real per capita output or income.
   c. is less likely to be effective in fostering growth in rich countries than in poor countries.
   d. can occur when saving rates are zero.

Problems

Problem 1

This figure shows production possibility frontiers confronting Urbana and Ruritania. A_0 denotes the original production possibility frontiers for both countries and A_1 denotes the new ones. Each economy begins at point a. Use this information to answer the following True/False questions.

Urbana — Investment Goods vs. Consumption Goods

Ruritania — Investment Goods vs. Consumption Goods

_____ a. Rates of capital accumulation in Urbana exceeds those in Ruritania.

_____ b. Ruritania has experienced economic growth.

_____ c. Urbana must be experiencing economic development.

_____ d. Urbana has experienced economic growth.

_____ e. The PPF for Ruritania has shifted outward the most because of the relatively large amount of net investment that was made at point a.

_____ f. Net additions of real capital in Urbana are probably better suited to produce investment goods than to the production of consumption goods.

_____ g. Ruritanian consumers more greatly prefer present consumption over future consumption relative to those in Urbana.

_____ h. Consumers in Urbana relatively prefer to defer present consumption to some future date.

_____ i. Technological advancement may best explain the relative economic growth that Ruritania has experienced.

_____ j. Households in Urbana save more of their incomes than do Ruritanians.

Problem 2

Use the "Rule of 72" to answer the following True/False questions.

___ a. A country's population will double in 72 years if annual population growth is 1 percent.

___ b. Financial investments will double in value in 18 years if the compounded annual interest rate is 4 percent.

___ c. Financial investments will double in 7.2 years if the annual interest rate is 15 percent.

___ d. A population that grows at an annual rate of 7.2 percent will double in 10 years.

___ e. If the annual rate of inflation in consumer prices is 2 percent, it will take 36 years for the CPI to double.

___ f. If an economy experiences an annual increase of 3.6 percent in real output, it will take 20 years for the economy to double its production of output.

___ g. Financial investments will double in 30 years if the annual interest rate is 2.4 percent.

___ h. Financial investments will double in 7 years if the annual interest rate is 10.28 percent.

___ i. A country's population will double in 60 years if population growth is 1.2 percent annually.

___ j. A country's population will double in 40 years if population growth is 1.8 percent annually.

Problem 3

This figure contains the supply and demand curves for the market for financial capital. Assume that the nominal interest rate is pegged below the equilibrium level by the FED at i_0, that it is then raised to i_1; and that i_e is the unattainable equilibrium interest rate. Assume that the rate of price inflation is 10 percent per annum. Use this information to answer the following True/False questions.

____ a. The supply of saving is a positive function of the rate of interest.

____ b. There is a shortage of financial capital at interest rate i_0 this market.

____ c. The capital stock increases as the nominal interest rate increases from i_0 to i_1.

____ d. The real interest rate remains constant as the nominal interest rate increases from i_0 to i_1.

____ e. The quantity demanded of financial capital increases as the real interest rate rises as the economy moves from a to c.

____ f. In this market, the rate of capital accumulation is positively related to the nominal interest rate but negatively related to the real interest rate.

____ g. The relative price of present consumption would rise if the nominal interest rate declined from i_1 to i_0.

____ h. The relative price of future consumption decreases as the nominal interest rate increases from i_0 to i_1.

____ i. The rate of saving is greater at i_1 than it is at i_0

____ j. The rate of present consumption is greater at i_0 than it is at i_1.

Problem 4

You have retained your job as chief economic advisor based on your fine performance in chapter 17. The president, once again, does not seem convinced that you are competent. You have just told him that fixed land and other resource constraints make it impossible to have continual radial expansions of the PPF without diminishing returns. The initial situation involves 2,000 units of labor and 2,000 units of capital and allows the economy to produce up to 100 tons of wheat or 100 military airplanes.

a. Graph this situation in the figure. Label the curve PPF_1.

b. Illustrate an increase of 2,000 units of labor and 2,000 units of capital if there is no diminishing returns. Label this curve PPF_2.

c. Illustrate a scenario where an additional 2,000 units of labor and capital are added to the production process. This time, however, the additional inputs are constrained by the amount of land in the production process. This constraint is particularly severe in the production of grain where you are only able to get half as much grain output per additional unit of input as before. On the defense side you encounter no resource constraint. Label this curve PPF_3.

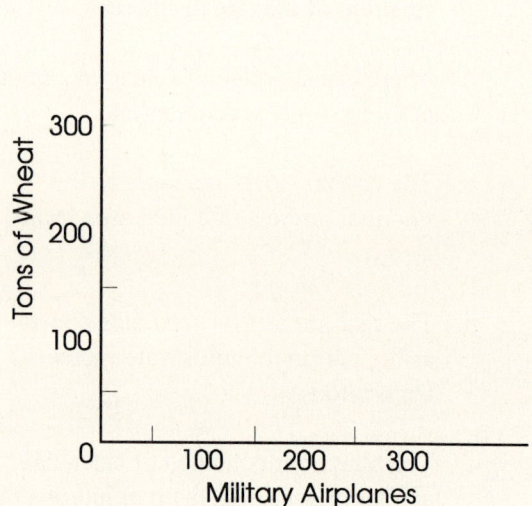

Problem 5

Use the "Rule of 72" to answer the following questions about how long it will take:

a. your savings account to double, if the bank pays annual interest of 4%? _____

b. GDP to double, if economic growth proceeds at 2% annually? _____

c. housing prices to double, if they grow by 6% annually? _____

d. population to double, if the annual population growth rate is 1.5 %? _____

e. for the value of money to fall by one-half if the annual inflation rate is 2%? _____ If it is 12%? _____ If it is 24%? _____

f. for the CPI to move from 100 to 400 if inflation is 1% annually? _____

ANSWERS

	Matching		True/False	Multiple Choice	Unlimited MC
	Set I	Set II			
1.	b	1. h	1. F	1. b	1. c
2.	i	2. j	2. T	2. a	2. abcd
3.	f	3. i	3. T	3. b	3. abc
4.	g	4. f	4. T	4. d	4. abd
5.	c	5. g	5. F	5. c	5. c
6.	a	6. b	6. F	6. c	
7.	e	7. a	7. T	7. e	
8.	j	8. e	8. T	8. c	
9.	h	9. c	9. F	9. e	
10.	d	10. d	10. T	10. d	

Chapter Review (Fill-In Questions)

1. growth; development
2. Rule of 72; 72
3. production; resources
4. labor force participation; capital to labor;
   population; per capita income
5. Thomas Malthus; subsistence; geometrically;
   arithmetically
6. human; infrastructure; financial system;
   communications; transportation; labor force

	Problem 1		Problem 2
a.	T	a.	T
b.	T	b.	T
c.	F	c.	F
d.	T	d.	T
e.	F	e.	T
f.	T	f.	T
g.	T	g.	T
h.	T	h.	T
i.	T	i.	T
j.	T	j.	T

Problem 3

a.   T
b.   T
c.   T
d.   F
e.   F
f.   F
g.   F
h.   T
i.   T
j.   T

Problem 4

See figure.

Problem 5

a.   18 years
b.   36 years
c.   12 years
d.   48 years
e.   36 years; 6 years; 3 years.
f.   144 years.

Chapter 20
Elasticity

Chapter Objectives

After you have read and studied this chapter, you should be able to describe the concept of elasticity and some specific elasticities; indicate the relationships between the incidence of various tax burdens and the price elasticities of supply and demand; compute elasticities from numerical observations; understand why marginal units are important for decision making; and explain the law of equal marginal advantage and its relevance for economic efficiency.

Chapter Review: Key Points

1. The **price-elasticity of demand** is a measure of the responsiveness of the amount demanded to small price changes and is defined as the relative change in quantity demanded divided by the relative change in price:

$$e_d \cong \frac{\%\Delta Q}{\%\Delta P}$$

2. Problems result when calculating elasticity if initial prices and quantities are used as bases, so economists typically use *midpoint bases*. The price-elasticity of demand is negative but, for convenience, we use absolute values to avoid the negative sign.

3. If price elasticity is less than one, then demand is relatively unresponsive to changes in price and is said to be **inelastic**. If elasticity is greater than one, demand is very responsive to price changes and is **elastic**. Demand is **unitarily elastic** if the elasticity coefficient equals one.

4. Elasticity, price changes, and total revenues (expenditures) are related in the following manner: If demand is inelastic (*elastic*) and price increases (*falls*), total revenue will rise. If demand is elastic (*inelastic*) and price rises (*falls*), total revenue (expenditures) will fall. If demand is unitarily elastic ($e_d = 1$), total revenue will be unaffected by price changes.

5. The number and quality of substitutes, the proportion of the total budget spent, and the length of time considered are three important determinants of the elasticity of demand. Demand is more elastic the more substitutes are available, the more of the budget the item consumes, and the longer the time frame considered.

6. Along any negatively sloped linear demand curve, parts of the curve will be elastic, unitarily elastic, and inelastic. The

price-elasticity of demand rises as the price rises.

7. **Income-elasticity of demand** is the proportional change in the amount of a good demanded divided by a given proportionate change in income. Normal goods have income-elasticities above zero, while inferior goods have negative income-elasticities.

8. **Cross-elasticity of demand** measures the responsiveness of the quantity demanded of one good to price changes in a related good. That is, price cross-elasticity is the proportional change in the quantity of good X (Chevrolets) divided by a given proportional change in the price of good Y (Fords). If the cross-elasticity of demand is positive (*negative*), the goods are substitutes (*complements*).

9. The **price-elasticity of supply** measures the responsiveness of suppliers to changes in prices, and is defined to parallel that for the price-elasticity of demand: the proportional change in the amount supplied divided by a given proportional change in price. The price-elasticity of supply is typically positive, reflecting the positive slope of the supply curve.

10. All economic elasticities tend to increase as the time interval considered becomes longer. Thus long run supplies and demands are more price elastic (and flatter) than short run supplies and demands.

11. Individual firms (sellers) often face perfectly elastic demands and individual consumers (buyers) often face perfectly elastic supplies for a product. Market demands and supplies, however, are almost never perfectly elastic.

12. The individual who actually loses purchasing power because of a tax is said to bear the tax's **economic incidence** (*tax burden*). This may be quite different from the individual who is legally responsible for the tax, who bears its *legal incidence*. When these individuals differ, the tax has been shifted. A tax can be *forward-shifted* (to consumers) or *backward-shifted* (to labor or other resource owners).

13. If demand is perfectly inelastic or supply is perfectly elastic, a tax will be completely forward-shifted. If supply is perfectly inelastic or demand is perfectly elastic, the tax will be completely backward-shifted.

Matching Key Terms And Concepts

SET I

___ 1. inelastic demand

___ 2. normal goods

___ 3. complementary goods

___ 4. legal incidence of taxation

___ 5. unitary price elasticity of demand

___ 6. substitute goods

___ 7. determinants of elasticities of demand

___ 8. inferior goods

___ 9. economic incidence of taxation

___ 10. elasticity

a. Income elasticity < 0.

b. Falls on the person who suffers reduced purchasing power because of a tax.

c. Positive cross-elasticity of demand.

d. Income elasticity > 0.

e. Price changes are proportionally greater than resulting quantity changes.

f. Falls on person or firm who pays the tax to the government.

g. The ratio of proportionate changes between two related variables.

h. Time period, availability of substitutes, budget share.

i. Total revenue is immune to price changes.

j. Negative price cross-elasticity of demand.

SET II

___ 1. perfectly inelastic demand

___ 2. relatively inelastic demand

___ 3. unitary demand elasticity

___ 4. relatively elastic demand

___ 5. perfectly elastic demand

___ 6. perfectly inelastic supply

___ 7. relatively inelastic supply

___ 8. unitarily elastic supply

___ 9. relatively elastic supply

___ 10. perfectly elastic supply

a. A straight line through the origin when graphed.

b. A tangent to this curve intersects the horizontal axis.

c. A horizontal curve when perfect substitutes are available.

d. Land is the best single example.

e. When graphed, this is a rectangular hyperbola.

f. Price cuts yield increases in revenue and spending.

g. No one has ever been able to give a satisfactory example.

h. A firm faced by this will profit by raising its prices.

i. When sellers respond vigorously if the price rises slightly.

j. Makes vast amounts of a good available at a constant price.

True/False Questions

____ 1. A point of unitary price elasticity is found at the midpoint of every negatively-sloped linear demand curve.

____ 2. All demand curves possess an elastic range, an inelastic range, and a unitarily elastic range.

____ 3. Total revenue varies directly with price in the inelastic range of a demand curve.

____ 4. Total revenue varies inversely with price in the elastic range of a demand curve.

____ 5. Negative price elasticities of demand are conventionally treated as absolute (positive) coefficients.

____ 6. The price elasticity of supply is a measure of the slope of a supply curve.

____ 7. Substitutes have positive price cross-elasticities of demand.

____ 8. If the price elasticity of demand for good X is greater than one, then a reduction in the price of good X will result in a decrease in consumer spending on the good.

____ 9. Any tax burden is synonymous with its legal incidence.

____ 10. Normal goods have positive income elasticities of demand; inferior goods have negative income elasticity coefficients.

____ 11. If the demand curve for a good is vertical, then an increase in the price of the good results in a reduction in the quantity demanded; demand is perfectly inelastic.

____ 12. If the supply curve for good X is linear and passes through the origin, then the price elasticity of supply for the good changes at every point on the curve.

Standard Multiple Choice

There Is A Uniquely "Best" Answer To Each Of These Questions!

___ 1. Price elasticities of demand tend to be larger:
   a. for necessities than for luxuries.
   b. when producers have good alternatives available.
   c. the higher are the opportunity costs of production.
   d. the larger are the number of uses for a good.
   e. None of these.

___ 2. Cuts in a good's supply tend to cause increases in the:
   a. demand for a complementary good.
   b. industry revenues if its demand is price elastic.
   c. industry revenues if its demand is income inelastic.
   d. demand for the good itself.
   e. demand for a substitute good.

___ 3. As price falls and quantity rises along a negatively-sloped linear demand curve:
   a. total revenue falls up to the point where elasticity equals zero; thereafter, it rises.
   b. the price elasticity of demand decreases.
   c. there is a contradiction to the law of supply.
   d. the incentive for substituting away from the good rises.
   e. a constant negative slope ensures a fixed elasticity.

___ 4. Which of the following lists of taxes or taxed goods is in correct order from most backward-shifted to most forward-shifted?
   a. tobacco, property, payroll, general sales.
   b. land, payroll, property, tobacco.
   c. tobacco, payroll, corporate income, property.
   d. income, inheritance, gift, sales.
   e. gambling, amusement, inheritance, land.

___ 5. Cross-price elasticities of demand are probably most positive for:
   a. shoe repairs and new shoes.
   b. syrup and waffles.
   c. gasoline and limousines.
   d. college tuitions and textbooks.
   e. coal and iron.

___ 6. From which of the following data might you estimate a price elasticity of supply?
   a. A price hike from $7 to $13 causes shirt sales to fall from 16,000 to 8,000 monthly.
   b. Farmers increase soybean plantings 15 percent when the price increases 5 percent.
   c. Ford's production increases because GM raises Chevette prices.
   d. The output of tennis balls slumps 8 percent when the prices of racquets go up 12 percent.
   e. Steel production and sales rise 18 percent when national income grows 13 percent.

7. Which of the following suggest that supply is most price elastic?
   a. A pay hike from $400 to $800 monthly for new recruits raises new army enlistments from 12,000 to 28,000 monthly.
   b. A 20 percent increase in goat milk production follows a 40 percent rise in the price of cow milk.
   c. When wheat prices fall from $8 to $5 per bushel, world output drops from 460 to 340 million tons.
   d. Per capita income rises from $2,500 to $3,500 and auto sales rise from 6 million to 18 million units annually.
   e. New record releases climb from 1,800 to 2,400 annually when album prices rise from $6 to $9 each.

8. Pairs of substitute goods include:
   a. butter and margarine.
   b. polyester fabrics and cotton cloth.
   c. transistor radios and televisions.
   d. jogging shoes and bicycles.
   e. All of these.

9. Sets of complementary goods include:
   a. auto repairs and new cars.
   b. gasoline and gasohol.
   c. diving boards and swimming pools.
   d. saunas and steam baths.
   e. pipes, chewing tobacco, and snuff.

10. Demand for which of the following products is probably the least income elastic for most people?
   a. Rolls Royces.
   b. Big Macs.
   c. pinto beans.
   d. housing.
   e. health care.

11. If each 1-percent price hike causes the amounts sold to fall 2 percent, the price elasticity of demand for bacon is roughly:
   a. 0.5.
   b. 2.0.
   c. .02.
   d. unitary.
   e. .01.

12. If attendance at basketball games falls from 10,000 per game to 8,000 when ticket prices are raised from $6 to $8, the price elasticity of demand is roughly:
   a. 2.00.
   b. 0.78.
   c. 3.33.
   d. 1.29.
   e. 0.50.

13. National income booms from $3.75 trillion to $4.25 trillion and new car sales flourish, rising from 3 million to 5 million annually. The income elasticity of demand for new cars is:
   a. 0.5.
   b. 1.0.
   c. 2.0.
   d. 3.0.
   e. 4.0.

14. Electric heater prices fall from $50 to $30 and the sales of Alaskan igloos melt from 750 to 450 per month. These goods are _____ and the price cross-elasticity of demand equals ___.
   a. inferior; 1.5
   b. necessities; 3.0
   c. substitutes; 1.0
   d. normal; -2.0
   e. complementary; -1.0

___15. The average jail term for being convicted of driving while intoxicated rises from 1 month to 3 months, and traffic fatalities decline from 70,000 to 50,000 per year. The imprisonment elasticity of traffic fatalities is roughly:
   a. -0.333.
   b. 0.667.
   c. 0.333.
   d. 1.000.
   e. -3.000.

___16. New competition causes exercise machines to be slashed from $650 to a rock bottom $350 and sales rise from 70,000 to 210,000 annually. The price elasticity of demand is roughly:
   a. 1.667.
   b. 0.600.
   c. 3.333.
   d. 0.333.
   e. 1.000.

___17. Soaring demand causes the price of sole-sucker beach sandals to rise from $10 to $14 a pair. An influx of new producers raises the total amount available from 3 million to 13 million annually. The price elasticity of supply is:
   a. 0.375.
   b. 0.750.
   c. 3.750.
   d. 1.000.
   e. 7.500.

___18. Suppose that an increase in weekly consumer income from $160 to $170 causes the consumption of good K to fall from 10 to 7 units per week. The income elasticity of demand is roughly:
   a. -10.
   b. -5.
   c. -6.
   d. 8.
   e. 5.

___19. Among the influences of time on supply and demand is that:
   a. longer time intervals make these curves flatter because people can adjust more completely to price changes.
   b. production invariably absorbs more time than consumption.
   c. firms that are in business longer attract more customers.
   d. more experienced buyers are less likely to buy on impulse.
   e. more goods become complements in both production and consumption as time passes.

___20. Government taxes and regulations create wedges that reduce the supply of a good to the extent that they:
   a. artificially stimulate demand.
   b. prevent pollution and industrial blight.
   c. raise the cost of production.
   d. are based on laissez-faire governmental policies.
   e. generate cyclical shortages and then surpluses.

Chapter Review (Fill-In Questions)

1. _____ is a general concept measuring the _____ changes between two related variables.

2. If large changes are involved, we use _____ as bases for computing the relative changes in the variables. Because of problems of scale, etc., _____ is often a misleading indicator of elasticity. If the price elasticity of demand exceeds one, demand is _____ and price hikes will cause total revenues (spending) for a good to _____. Total revenue is unaffected by price when demand curves are _____ hyperbolas; such demand curves are _____ elastic.

3. Elasticity changes along a negatively-sloped, linear demand curve; as the price falls and quantity _____, the price elasticity of demand _____.

4. The _____ elasticity of demand indicates how the consumption of a good varies as a family's purchasing power changes, and is computed as the relative change in the amount of the good demanded divided by the relative change in _____.

5. Cross elasticities of demand measure the relative changes in the amount demanded of one good divided by the relative change in price of some related good. Positive coefficients indicate that the goods are _____, while negative coefficients indicate that the goods are _____ in consumption.

6. The price elasticity of supply is the relative change in quantity supplied divided by the relative change in the price of a good. Unlike its demand counterpart, it is normally a _____ number without adjustments. Both demand and supply elasticities tend to _____ as the time for adjustment is increased, as the closeness of _____ goods increase, or as the ability to shift into other forms of _____ is enhanced.

7. If the price cross elasticity of demand between goods X and Y is -.89, the goods are (complements/inferior/substitutes)_____, while if the price cross elasticity of demand is 1.37, the goods are (complements/inferior/substitutes) _____.

8. Generally speaking, the more time that a consumer has to adjust to a price change in a good, the (more\less) _____ elastic will be the demand for that good.

Unlimited Multiple Choice

Caution: Each Question Has From Zero To Four Correct Answers.

___ 1. The price elasticity of demand is:
   a. generally negative, so we normally consider its absolute value.
   b. a measure of the absolute change in the quantity demanded of a good evoked by an absolute change in its price.
   c. directly related to the time period allowed for consumers to adjust to changes in relative prices.
   d. a measure of the slope of the demand curve.

___ 2. The income elasticity of demand is:
   a. the relative change in the amount of a good demanded divided by the relative change in income.
   b. positively related to price cross elasticities of demand.
   c. positive for normal goods.
   d. negative for inferior goods.

___ 3. Total revenue is:
   a. positively related to the price of an inelastically demanded good.
   b. negatively related to the price of an elastically demanded good.
   c. decreased if the price increases in the elastic range of the demand curve.
   d. decreased if the price decreases in the inelastic range of the demand curve.

___ 4. The price elasticity of supply is:
   a. normally positive.
   b. the relative change in the price of a good caused by a change in the quantity of the good supplied.
   c. positively related to the responsiveness of the quantity of a good demanded to changes in its price.
   d. positive for upward-sloping supply curves.

___ 5. The price-cross elasticity of demand is:
   a. positive for substitute goods.
   b. negative for complementary goods.
   c. the absolute change in the amount of a good demanded caused by an absolute change in the price of another good.
   d. roughly zero for totally unrelated goods.

Problems

Problem 1

Compute the elasticities for the following problems.

a. The Hobbit family buys 72 vegetarian specials annually at a price of $3.00 each but would consume 192 per year if the price dropped to $2.40. Their price elasticity of demand is _____.

b. The Sea Slug Glee Club bought 170 motor scooters when the price was $875 each, but ordered only 30 when the price soared to $2,125. The group's price elasticity of demand for scooters is _____.

c. If weight watchers gulp 205 million milkshakes at $1.15 apiece, but cut back to 155 million weekly when the price rises to $1.85 each, the price elasticity of their demand for shakes equals _____.

d. If a $9.98 sale on regular $19.95 watch fobs raises a store's sales from 30 to 300 per week, the price elasticity of the demand faced by the store is roughly _____.

e. If a strong recovery raises national income from $4.0 trillion to $4.4 trillion and diamond sales jump from 3 to 13 million carats annually, the income elasticity of demand for diamonds is _____.

f. If each 1 percent hike in the price of pencils causes a 2 percent decline in the quantity of erasers sold, the price cross-elasticity of demand for these complementary goods is roughly _____.

g. When Jotux DeHarlabwane can sell totem poles for $1,800 each, he markets 60 annually, but when the price falls to $600 apiece, he is willing to sell only 24 each year. His price elasticity of supply is _____.

h. When the temperature drops from 102° F to 54° F, sales of surf boards slip from 56,000 monthly down to 14,000 for diehard surfers. The temperature elasticity of the demand for surf boards is _____.

i. When 200,000 gallons of water are applied per acre, 4 tons are harvested from each acre of linguini trees annually, but cutting back to 160,000 gallons causes the crop per acre to fall to 2 tons annually. The water elasticity of linguini production is _____.

j. If doubling your viewing of soap operas to 16 hours per week causes your IQ score to fall from a genius level of 140 to a sluggish 70, your TV elasticity of brain power is _____.

Problem 2

This table shows data for four different markets.

	Market A	Market B	Market C	Market D
P_0	$10	$400		$.25 for X
Q_0	16 million	600,000	16	160 tons Z
P_1	$16	$800		$.35 for X
Q_1	10 million	1,800,000	40	240 tons Z
Y_0			$20,000	
Y_1			$40,000	

Complete the blanks in statements a through d, which correspond to markets A through D, respectively.

a. The _____ elasticity of _____ is _____ .

b. The _____ elasticity of _____ is _____ .

c. The _____ elasticity of _____ is _____ and this is a(n) _____ good.

d. The ____ elasticity of ____ is ____ and goods X and Z are ____ goods.

Problem 3

This table shows the demand schedule for books per year for the Scholar family.

Price Elasticity of Demand	Number of Books Demanded	Price per Book	Total Spending (or Revenue)
---	0	$20	_____
_____	10	18	_____
_____	20	16	_____
_____	30	14	_____
_____	40	12	_____
_____	50	10	_____
_____	60	8	_____
_____	70	6	_____
_____	80	4	_____
_____	90	2	_____
_____	100	0	_____

a.   Compute the coefficient of price elasticity for the price ranges given in the schedule and complete the first column of the table.

b.   Why is it conventional to use the absolute values of such numbers when discussing price elasticities of demand? _____

c.   Identify the three ranges of price elasticity of demand in this schedule. (You can only approximate the three ranges.) _____ -
_____

d.   Fill in the total revenue (spending) column.

e.   How does total spending vary with book prices in the elastic range? _____ _____
Why? _____ -
_____

f.   How does total spending vary with book prices in the inelastic range? _____
Why? _____ -
_____

g.   Total spending attains a maximum value approximately in which range of price elasticity?
_____ Why? _____
_____

h.   Graph the demand curve for books in the figure.

i.   Why is the price elasticity of demand different from the slope of a demand curve?

_____

j.   Interpret the coefficient of price elasticity that you computed for the seventh price range: $8 to $6. _____
Do the same for the coefficient corresponding to the second price range. ($18 - $16) _____

Problem 4

This table contains a supply schedule for bouquets of roses. Use these data to answer the following questions.

a. Compute the coefficient of price elasticity of supply for the seven price ranges shown and complete the table.

b. What do you notice about the algebraic signs of the values you just computed? Explain why this is so. _____
_____
_____
_____

Price Elasticity of Supply	Bouquets of Roses Supplied	Price ($)
-----	0	2
_____	2	4
_____	4	6
_____	6	8
_____	8	10
_____	10	12
_____	12	14
_____	14	16

c. Express the price elasticity of supply as the ratio of a marginal concept and an average concept. _____ Explain why all linear supply curves emanating from the origin manifest unitary price elasticity.

_____
_____

Problem 5

This figure shows the supply and demand curves for three different markets. Use this information to answer the following true/false questions, assuming that the legal incidence of taxes is on firms.

_____ a. The tax is shifted forward completely in Market I.

_____ b. The economic incidence of the tax is identical with its legal incidence in Market II.

_____ c. The demand curve in Market III is perfectly price elastic.

_____ d. The supply curve in Market II is perfectly price inelastic.

_____ e. The economic incidence of the tax is identical with its legal incidence of the tax in Market I.

_____ f. The supply curves in Market I have zero price elasticity.

_____ g. The tax is completely shifted backward in Market III.

_____ h. The economic incidence of the tax is different from its legal incidence in Market III.

_____ i. The equilibrium price of the good sold in Market II is a demand determined price.

_____ j. The tax is shifted backward completely in Market II.

Problem 6

This figure shows the markets for four different goods. The numerical subscripts denote the analytic sequence of the demand curves: "0" denotes the original curve, "1" denotes the new curve. Assume that real income has increased by 10 percent. Use income elasticity to determine the kind of good represented in each market.

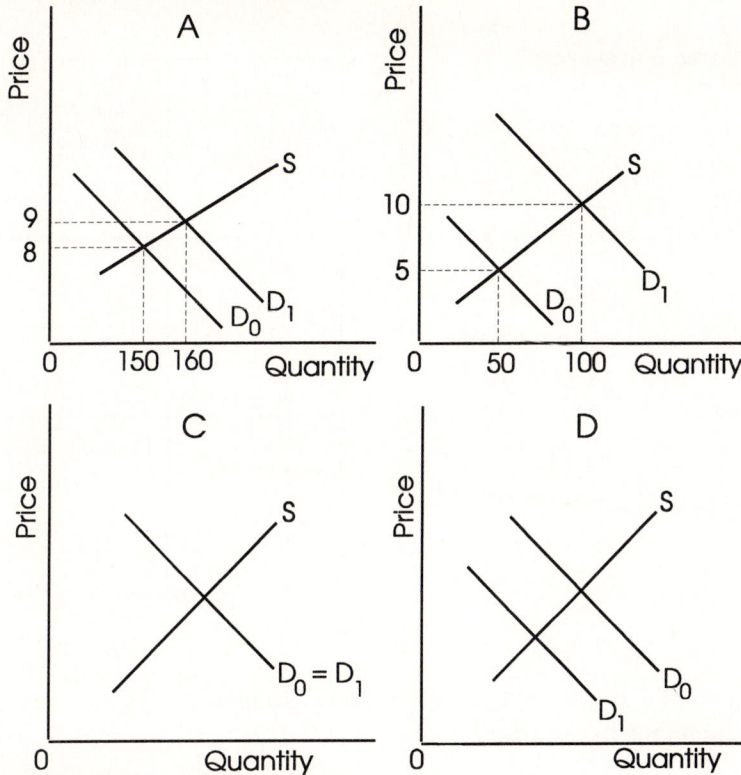

a. What does the income elasticity of demand equal in Graph A? _____ What type of good is this? _____ This good is income _____.

b. What does the income elasticity of demand equal in Graph B? _____ What type of good is this? _____ This good is income _____.

c. What type of good is portrayed in Graph C? _____ Why? _____
_____

d. What type of good is portrayed in Graph D? _____ Why? _____
_____

Problem 7

Suppose that if you work 40 hours a week at a straight-time wage, your income is $240; but if you put in 42 hours, your income rises to $258.

a. Assuming that your hourly overtime wage is constant once you exceed 40 hours of work weekly, draw the relationship between hours worked and income in the figure.

b. What is the overtime wage rate? _____

c. What is your average wage if you work 42 hours? _____

d. What is your average wage if you work 43 hours? _____

e. Once you have worked 42 hours, will whether you are willing to work the 43rd hour or not depend on your average wage or on the marginal (overtime) wage?

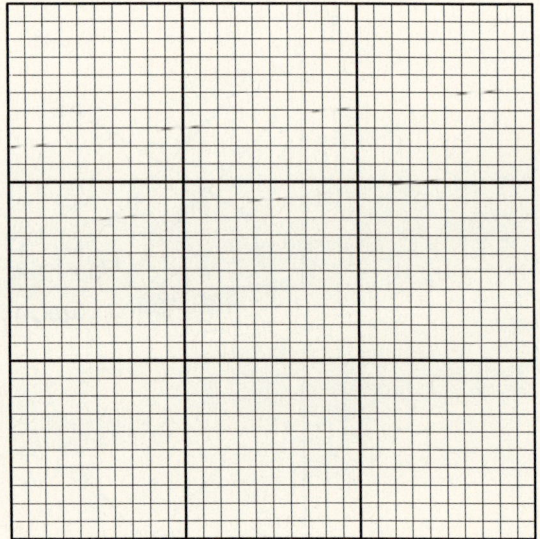

_____

Problem 8

Use the information in this table to answer the following questions about the effects of government policies on the thermal sock market.

Quantity Demanded	Price	Quantity Supplied
0	$10.00	20
2	9.50	18
4	9.00	16
6	8.50	14
8	8.00	12
10	7.50	10
12	7.00	8
14	6.50	6
16	6.00	4
18	5.50	2
20	5.00	0

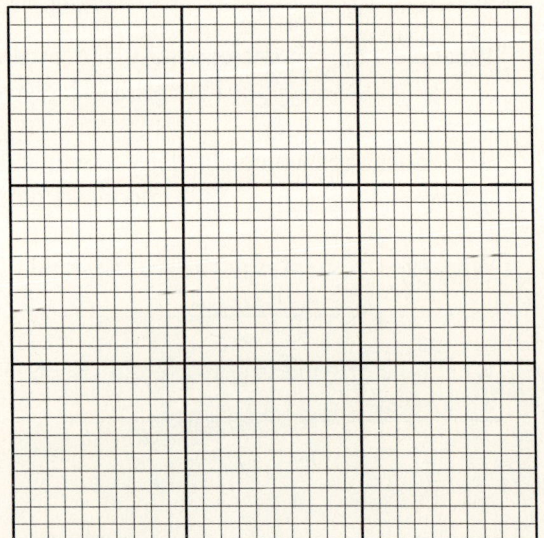

a. Plot the demand and supply curves in the figure above. Label the supply and demand curves S_0 and D_0 respectively.

b. A $2 tax (per pair of socks) is levied on sock manufacturers. Graph the effect of this tax in the figure above, and label the new curve with a subscript 1.

c. The demand price for socks after imposition of the tax is _____.

d. The supply price for socks after imposition of the tax is _____.

e. The $2 tax reduces the quantity demanded and supplied to _____ million pairs of socks.

f. The tax burden on the thermal sock buyer is _____ per pair.

g. The tax burden on sock producers is _____ per pair.

h. Assume that instead of a $2 tax, a $1 subsidy per pair of socks is instituted. Graph the effect of this subsidy and label the new curve with a subscript 2.

i. The buyer's demand price would be _____ in this new equilibrium.

j. The seller's supply price would be _____, including the subsidy.

k. The $1 subsidy increases the equilibrium quantity to _____ million pairs of thermal socks.

l. Sock buyers realize a _____ gain from the subsidy for each pair of socks they buy.

m. Taxes cause the equilibrium quantities demanded and supplied to _____; the opposite is true for subsidies.

n. On scratch paper, draw a demand curve twice as steep as D_0 and a supply curve half as steep as S_0. Now assume that a tax is levied on producers. Relative to original curves, this market imposes more of the tax burden on _____ and less on _____.
Naturally the opposite is true in cases where the demand curves are flatter and the supply curves are steeper.

ANSWERS

Matching		True/False	Multiple Choice		Unlimited Multiple Choice
Set I	Set II				
1. e	1. g	1. T	1. d	11. b	1. ac
2. d	2. h	2. F	2. e	12. b	2. acd
3. j	3. e	3. T	3. b	13. e	3. abcd
4. f	4. f	4. T	4. b	14. c	4. ad
5. i	5. c	5. T	5. a	15. a	5. abd
6. c	6. d	6. F	6. b	16. a	
7. h	7. b	7. T	7. a	17. c	
8. a	8. a	8. F	8. e	18. c	
9. b	9. i	9. F	9. c	19. a	
10. g	10. j	10. T	10. c	20. c	
		11. F			
		12. F			

Chapter Review (Fill-in Questions)

1. Elasticity; proportional or relative
2. mid-points; slope; relatively elastic; fall; rectangular; unitarily
3. increases; falls
4. income; income
5. substitutes; complements
6. positive; rise; substitute; production
7. complements; substitutes
8. more

Problem 1

a.	45/11 or 4.09	f.	-2.0
b.	42/25 or 1.68	g.	6/7 or .857
c.	25/42 or .595	h.	39/20 or 1.95
d.	27/11 or 2.456	i.	3.0
e.	105/8 or 13.125	j.	-1.0

Problem 2

a. price; demand; 1.0 (unitary)
b. price; supply; 1.5
c. income; demand; 1.286 or 9/7; normal
d. cross; demand; 1.2 or 6/5; substitutes

Problem 3

Price Elasticity of Demand	Number of Books Demanded	Price per Book	Total Revenue
----	0	$20	$ 0
19.00	10	18	180
5.67	20	16	320
3.00	30	14	420
1.86	40	12	480
1.22	50	10	500
0.82	60	8	480
0.54	70	6	420
0.33	80	4	320
0.18	90	2	180
0.05	100	0	0

a. See table.
b. Before adjustments the price elasticity of demand is negative because demand curves are negatively sloped.
c. elastic range: $20 to $10; unitary range: roughly $10; inelastic range: $10 to $0.
d. See table.
e. As price is lowered total revenue rises; the percentage change in quantity demanded exceeds the percentage change in price.
f. As price is lowered total revenue falls; the percentage change in quantity demanded is less than the percentage change in price.
g. The unitary range, because on each side of this range, if price is increased, demand is elastic and TR falls, and if price is lowered, demand is inelastic and TR falls.
h. See figure.
i. As can be seen in the table and figure, elasticity varies all along the curve, but the slope is constant.
j. The price elasticity computed for the seventh range is 0.54 and indicates that at a price between $8 and $6 the demand for books is inelastic. The coefficient for the second price change ($18-$16) is 5.67, indicating an elastic demand.

Problem 4

a. See table.
b. The values are positive because the supply curve is positively sloped.
c. $e_s = (\Delta Q/Q)/(\Delta P/P) = (\Delta Q/\Delta P)/(Q/P) = (\Delta Q/\Delta P) \times (P/Q)$. All linear supply curves emanating from the origin have a unitary elasticity since the ratio of change in Q and P is always equal to the ratio of ΔP to ΔQ.

Price Elasticity of Supply	Bouquets of Roses Supplied	Price ($)
-----	0	2
3.00	2	4
1.67	4	6
1.40	6	8
1.29	8	10
1.22	10	12
1.18	12	14
1.15	14	16

Problem 5

a.	T	f.	F
b.	T	g.	T
c.	T	h.	F
d.	T	i.	T
e	F	j.	T

Problem 6

a. 645; normal; inelastic
b. 6.67; normal; elastic
c. neutral; purchases do not change when income increases.
d. inferior; rising income results in less of the good being purchased.

Problem 7

a. See figure.
b. $9.00 an hour.
c. $6.14 an hour.
d. $6.21 an hour.
e. It will depend on the $9 hourly overtime (marginal) wage.

Problem 8

a. See figure.
b. See figure.
c. $8.50.
d. $6.50.
e. 6.
f. $1.
g. $1.
h. See figure.
i. $7.
j. $8.
k. 12.
l. $0.50.
m. shrink
n. buyers; sellers.

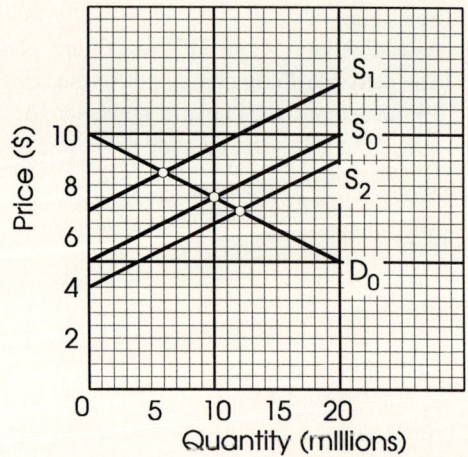

Chapter 21
Consumer Choice

Chapter Objectives

After you have read and studied this chapter, you should be able to define the income effect and the substitution effect of a price change on a particular good; you should also be able to explain why a price change involves both an income and a substitution effect; using marginal utility analysis and the principle of marginal utilities per dollar, explain why the demand curve has a negative slope; show and explain, using a numerical example, the principle of diminishing marginal utility and the effect of a price change on the consumer's attempt to maximize total utility; state the principle of consumer surplus and give an example; explain why a bundle of goods can be considered as a bundle of particular attributes.

Chapter Review: Key Points

1. *Utilitarianism* proposes that the best society is the one that provides the greatest happiness for the greatest number of people.

2. *Marginal utility* is the extra satisfaction gained from consuming a bit more of a good. The *law of diminishing marginal utility* states: The marginal utility of any good eventually declines as the amount consumed increases.

3. Measured in dollars, the declining portion of a marginal utility curve translates into a demand curve.

4. Maximum consumer satisfaction (*consumer equilibrium*) requires that the last cent spent on any good yield the same gain in satisfaction as the last cent spent on any other good: $MU_a/P_a = MU_b/P_b = \ldots = MU_z/P_z$. This application of the *law of equal marginal advantage* is known as the *principle of equal marginal utilities per dollar*.

5. *Substitution effects* are changes in consumer purchasing patterns that emerge if relative prices change, artificially assuming that the purchasing power of income is constant.

6. *Income effects* are changes in buying patterns that occur solely because the purchasing power of one's monetary income changes when the prices of individual goods rise or fall.

7. *Consumer surplus* is the area above the price line and below the demand curve. It is a consumer's gain from buying at a uniform price instead of paying prices equal to the marginal utility of each unit.

8. The *paradox of value* is resolved by recognizing that necessities may yield more total utility than luxuries, but that people adjust their purchases so that prices reflect marginal utility.

9. We are seldom certain about the *attributes* of any unit of a good. Information is costly and its marginal benefits may be trivial. Thus, our decisions are based on less than full information; we are *rationally ignorant* because we pursue information only as long as its expected benefit exceeds its expected cost.

10. Market prices commonly are positively related to quality, but higher prices than necessary often reflect attempts to alter suppliers' behavior so that higher quality is delivered to buyers. These "bribes" are intended to avoid unpleasant surprises arising from decision making in an imperfect world.

11. *Moral hazard* results when some arrangement provides incentives for one party to engage in inefficient behavior that raises costs or reduces benefits to the other party. *Adverse selection* occurs when one party to a bargain has superior information when the bargain is struck, resulting in unexpected losses to the other party.

12. There is an increasing tendency towards government edict as a means of overcoming transaction costs or solving the problems of rational ignorance and uncertainty. This is controversial, as critics ask: Do government experts know better than you do what things are good for you and what things will harm you?

Matching Key Terms And Concepts

SET I

___ 1. consumer surplus

___ 2. marginal utility

___ 3. income effect

___ 4. moral hazard

___ 5. *caveat emptor*

a. "Let the seller beware."

b. Each final bit of money spent must yield equal satisfaction.

c. Occurs when one party to a contract unexpectedly raises the cost or lowers the benefits of the other party who is unable to monitor the first party's actions.

_____ 6. utilitarianism

_____ 7. adverse selection

_____ 8. equal marginal utilities per dollar

_____ 9. *caveat venditor*

_____ 10. law of diminishing marginal utility

d. "The greatest happiness for the greatest number."

e. The change in buying patterns when purchasing power changes because of price changes.

f. Satisfaction gained from additional consumption of a good.

g. As more and more is consumed, after some point less and less extra satisfaction is derived from additional consumption.

h. "Let the buyer beware."

i. Any difference between what you would willingly pay and what you do pay.

j. Occurs when one bargaining party ultimately suffers unexpected disadvantages because the other party conceals information prior to a contract.

SET II
(NOTE: * = optional material from the end of the chapter.)

_____ 1. normal goods

_____ 2. substitution effect

_____ 3. inferior goods

_____ 4. attributes

_____ 5. lemons market

_____ 6. diamond-water paradox

_____ 7. consumer equilibrium

_____ 8. budget lines *

_____ 9. indifference curve *

_____ 10. tangency between #8 and #9 *

a. Maximized satisfaction given income constraints.

b. Constraints determined by income and market prices.

c. Explained by the difference between total and marginal utility.

d. Associated with positive income effects.

e. Associated with negative income effects.

f. All bundles yielding identical satisfaction to a consumer.

g. Arises because of asymmetric information.

h. Qualities of goods that add or detract from satisfaction.

i. Always negative.

j. Graphically portrays consumer equilibrium.

True/False Questions

___ 1. According to the central normative utilitarian principle, superior social organizations are those that fulfill the wishes of an elite group of leaders.

___ 2. Marginal utility equals the satisfaction generated by a given rate of consumption of a particular good.

___ 3. Because of the problem of moral hazard and the presence of so many lemons , the market for used cars is not very large .

___ 4. The law of diminishing marginal utility states that as one consumes equal successive units of a good, a point is inevitably reached where total utility begins to increase at an increasing rate when consumption is extended.

___ 5. Even though marginal utility cannot be measured directly, total satisfaction can be approximated quantitatively by scientific market research.

___ 6. Total utility is maximized when the marginal utilities of all goods consumed are exactly proportional to their prices.

___ 7. For consumers in equilibrium, the ratios of the subjective demand prices of the goods purchased are the same as the relative market prices of the goods.

___ 8. It has been shown empirically that total utility and income are inversely related.

___ 9. Given two entities who are doing business with each other, the problem of moral hazard is more likely to occur if the likelihood of repeat business is great.

___ 10. The substitution effect shows the impact that a change in real income has on the consumption pattern of the consumer.

___ 11. Many goods embody both positive and negative attributes.

___ 12. The substitution effect is positive for luxury goods, roughly zero for most normal goods, and negative for inferior goods.

___ 13. Similar attributes tend to make goods substitutes; complementarity tends to require goods to have dissimilar attributes.

___ 14. Resources and commodities are only valuable to the extent that they embody streams of useful services.

___ 15. Goods may become bads if they are excessively available.

___ 16. Consumers' surplus is often represented by the area under the demand curve that is below the good's market price.

___ 17. *Caveat emptor* has increasingly been replaced by government edict and the doctrine of *caveat venditor*.

___18. Low-priced, standardized goods that are frequently purchased by most consumers are especially appropriate for the doctrine of *caveat emptor*.

___19. Complicated goods that are infrequently purchased and have high prices are good candidates for imposition of the doctrine of *caveat venditor*.

___20. Jeremy Bentham especially admired Adam Smith's idea that an "invisible hand" leads to a natural harmony in human behavior.

Standard Multiple Choice

Each Question Has A Single "Best" Answer.

___ 1. The founder of "utilitarianism" was:
a. Stanley Jevons.
b. John Stuart Mill.
c. Jeremy Bentham.
d. Thorstein Veblen.
e. Adam Smith.

___ 2. The principle of equal marginal utilities per dollar suggests that:
a. the additional satisfaction from consuming a good eventually declines.
b. every good for which you spend identical total amounts are equally useful.
c. $1,000 worth of water and a $1,000 diamond are identically satisfying to consumers.
d. the last cent spent on any item yields the same satisfaction as the last cent spent on any other item.
e. All of these.

___ 3. If your marginal utility from a 25 cent candy bar is 50 utils and the marginal utility of a 30 cent cola is 60 utils, you can:
a. not add to your satisfaction by changing this mix.
b. gain by buying less candy and more cola.
c. gain by devoting less money to both candy and cola.
d. gain by buying less cola and more candy.
e. None of these.

___ 4. Which of the following is the best example of a moral hazard?
a. Purchasing a used computer at a garage sale. .
b. Paying a cabbie in advance to meet you at "this spot" in two hours.
c. Leaving the car keys in the ignition of your uninsured car.
d. Paying a guide a bonus at the end of your jungle trek.
e. Self insuring your small pizza delivery business.

5. Even if your income is adjusted for price changes, your buying patterns respond to changes in relative prices because of the:
   a. substitution effect.
   b. wealth effect.
   c. income effect.
   d. utility-maximizing effect.
   e. marginal utility equality effect.

6. *Caveat emptor* means:
   a. Let the seller beware!
   b. Everything else held constant.
   c. Let things change if they must.
   d. Charge whatever the market will bear.
   e. Let the buyer beware!

7. Substitution away from a good is greater when its price rises:
   a. the more close substitutes there are for the good.
   b. the more different uses to which the good has been put at the previous price.
   c. the longer is the time period allowed for adjustment.
   d. the fewer are the complements for the good.
   e. All of the above.

8. Purchasing a defective VCR because the seller "tricked" you is an example of:
   a. a moral hazard.
   b. adverse selection.
   c. rational ignorance.
   d. the substitution effect.
   e. stupidity.

9. If your income is closely tied to the price of a given product, an increase in its price may cause:
   a. an income effect that, in extreme cases, yields a positively sloped demand curve.
   b. you to go bankrupt.
   c. a powerful positive substitution effect.
   d. elimination of any meaningful budget constraint.
   e. an early heart attack.

10. From which of the following goods do typical Americans derive the greatest consumer surpluses?
    a. soap.
    b. whole wheat bread.
    c. water.
    d. gold jewelry.
    e. alarm clocks.

11. The intrinsic characteristics that create or detract from the satisfaction derived from consuming a good are known as:
    a. factors.
    b. attributes.
    c. utilities.
    d. anomalies.
    e. pedigrees.

12. The idea that, in equilibrium, the more you pay for a good the more it is worth (at the margin) to you is most closely related to the:
    a. law of diminishing returns.
    b. equal satisfaction corollary.
    c. increasing cost hypothesis.
    d. Veblen effect.
    e. principle of equal marginal utilities per dollar.

___13. Wise use of coupons at grocery stores is likely to increase the amount of:
  a. consumer surplus.
  b. deadweight loss.
  c. measured social utility.
  d. entrepreneurial profit.
  e. capitalistic exploitation.

___14. When goods are non standardized and infrequently purchased by an individual, a presumption that sellers will have superior knowledge of product characteristics is an argument for applying the legal doctrine of:
  a. *caveat emptor.*
  b. *nolo contendere.*
  c. no-fault insurance.
  d. *ceteris paribus.*
  e. *caveat venditor.*

___15. NOT a part of the utilitarian philosophy was the assumption that:
  a. "the greatest good for the greatest number" is an appropriate social goal.
  b. individual utilities are summable to a measure of social welfare.
  c. pleasure adds to utility, while pain detracts from utility.
  d. people differ significantly in the ability to enjoy certain goods.
  e. people seek pleasure and try to avoid pain.

___16. Suppose that you consume two goods, A and B, and the marginal utility of the last unit of A consumed is six times as great as the marginal utility of the last unit of B consumed. The price of A, however, is only three times as great as the price of Y. This disequilibrium between the two goods can be resolved by:
  a. consuming more of good A and less of good B.
  b. consuming less of good A and more of good B.
  c. increasing the consumption of both A and B.
  d. decreasing the consumption of both A and B.
  e. refusing to pay three times more for an extra unit of A than you would pay for an extra unit of B.

___17. When consumers reduce their purchases of a good because of a rise in price, the:
  a. total utility enjoyed from other goods declines.
  b. income effect reduces purchases of inferior goods.
  c. marginal utility derived from the good rises.
  d. substitution effect is positive.
  e. law of diminishing returns is violated.

18. Which of the following might contradict the law of diminishing marginal utility?
    a. Dagmar's enthusiasm for the all-you-can-eat buffet diminishes after her fifth plate.
    b. Jethro sells his 1964 Rambler for a 1992 Accord.
    c. Natasha tells Boris that she would like to end their relationship.
    d. Engelbert would rather be promoted than get a big raise.
    e. Melba enjoys her tenth vodka of the night more than her second.

19. A consumer will buy goods until their relative market prices are proportional to the individual's:
    a. cost/benefit ratio.
    b. opportunity costs of production.
    c. subjective demand prices.
    d. comparative advantages.
    e. substitution effect.

20. If, in equilibrium, the marginal utility of a $10 haircut is 25 utils, then the willing purchase of an extra $2 hamburger must generate:
    a. the production of one-fifth of a haircut.
    b. 5 utils.
    c. an extra 20 minutes of work for a short order cook.
    d. 250 utils.
    e. 2 utils.

Chapter Review (Fill-In Questions)

1. If satisfaction could be recorded in _____, a mythical measurement, then social policies could be assessed straightforwardly. Unfortunately, it cannot. However, the law of diminishing _____ suggests that ever greater consumption of any good ultimately yields declining gains in satisfaction and leads to the law of demand. In equilibrium, a consumer must gain the same satisfaction from the last _____ on each good; an idea known as the principle of _____.
For example, if $MU_x/P_x > MU_y/P_y$, the consumer can gain by buying less of _____ and more of _____. As this occurs, the marginal utility of X (MU_x) will _____ and the marginal utility of Y (MU_y) will _____, until $MU_x/P_x = MU_y/P_y$.

2. Price changes alter consumer equilibria. For example, if initially $MU_x/P_x = MU_y/P_y$, increases in P_x cause $MU_x/P_x < MU_y/P_y$; your resultant decrease in purchases of _____ and increased purchases of _____ will, by the law of diminishing marginal utility increase MUx and decrease MU_y until equilibrium is restored.

3. For _____ goods, the income effect is _____ because price cuts increase real income ($\Delta I > 0$) and induce greater consumption ($\Delta Q > 0$); thus, $\Delta Q/\Delta I > 0$.

4. _____ is the difference between the amounts people would willingly pay for various amounts of specific goods and the amounts they do pay at _____ prices. It is roughly the area _____ the _____ curve and above the _____ line. The _____ paradox was a knotty problem for economists because some "necessities" yield huge consumer surpluses but sell at low prices, while some frivolous luxuries are quite expensive. The key to resolving this puzzle is to realize that the subjective demand prices that are brought into equilibrium with market prices reflect marginal, not total, utilities.

5. If you sign a contract and can, at your will, raise your benefits as well as the costs to the other party to the contract, then the agreement is based on _____ information and is known as the _____ problem.

6. Much of our consumer theory assumes that we have good information about the products we buy. The legal doctrine of _____ or "Let the buyer beware," assumes that consumers are the best judges of their individual well-being. Where complex goods that are infrequently purchased by most consumers cause sellers' information to be superior to that possessed by buyers, imposing risks on sellers under the doctrine of _____ may make sense. However, government regulation increasingly restricts the choices available to us when some of the attributes of goods are viewed as so individually or socially harmful that certain goods are forbidden.

Unlimited Multiple Choice

Caution: Each Question Has From Zero To Four Correct Answers.

___ 1. Marginal utility:
   a. is the gain in satisfaction generated by consuming an additional unit of a good.
   b. is computed by dividing the level of consumption of a particular good into the change in total utility.
   c. declines constantly as additional units of a good are consumed.
   d. is given by: ΔTotal utility/ ΔQuantity of good.

___ 2. The substitution effect:
   a. is always positive.
   b. refers to changes in a consumer's buying patterns caused by changes in relative prices, assuming constant real income.
   c. is generally so powerful that it underpins the law of demand.
   d. shows that rational consumers always substitute relatively cheaper goods for relatively more expensive goods.

___ 3. In a world with only two commodities (X and Y) and money (M), total utility is maximized by a consumer when:
   a. $MU_x/P_y = MU_y/P_x = MU_m/P_m$.
   b. $MU_x = MU_y = MU_m$.
   c. $MU_x/MU_y = P_y/P_x$.
   d. $MU_x/P_x = MU_y/P_y = MU_m/P_m$.

___ 4. The income effect:
   a. is negative for inferior goods.
   b. shows the impact on the consumption pattern of the consumer of a change in real income caused by price changes.
   c. makes the demand curve for normal goods more negatively sloped.
   d. is positive for most economic goods.

___ 5. According to the principle of equal marginal utilities per dollar, the consumer maximizes total utility when:
   a. the last cents spent on each good yield equal satisfaction.
   b. there is no reallocation of given money income that could increase total utility.
   c. at the margin, each dollar of money income is allocated in ways that are equally advantageous to the consumer.
   d. the last dollar one spends on any good yields the same satisfaction as the last dollar expended on any other good.

Problems

Problem 1

A consumer's total utilities from consuming various quantities of hats (H) and jelly (J) are provided in this table, along with three sets of price and income data.

Hats (H)	Total Utility	Marginal Utility	Jelly (J)	Total Utility	Marginal Utility
0	0	-----	0	0	-----
1	100	___	1	50	___
2	190	___	2	95	___
3	270	___	3	135	___
4	340	___	4	170	___
5	400	___	5	200	___
6	450	___	6	225	___
7	490	___	7	245	___
8	520	___	8	260	___
9	540	___	9	270	___
10	550	___	10	275	___

DATA SET 1	
Price of Hats	= $2
Price of Jelly	= $1
Income	= $12

DATA SET 2	
Price of Hats	= $1
Price of Jelly	= $1
Income	=$10

DATA SET 3	
Price of Hats	= $2
Price of Jelly	= $1
Income	=$30

a. Complete the marginal utility columns for both goods.

b. What observed tendency or law do the marginal utility columns illustrate? _____
_____ Define this law. _____
_____

c. What do you notice about the rate at which total utility increases as consumption of each
good is increased? _____

d. Using the first data set for money prices and income, real income in terms of hats is
_____, and in terms of jelly is _____. At equilibrium, the consumer purchases
_____ hats and _____ jars of jelly, and the MU_h is _____, while the MU_j
is _____; total utility equals _____. State the marginal condition for utility
maximization _____. The relative price of hats in terms of jelly is
_____, while the relative price of jelly in terms of hats is _____.

e. Based on the second data set for money prices and income, real income in terms of hats is
_____; in terms of jelly, it is _____. At equilibrium, the consumer purchases
_____ hats and _____ jars of jelly, and the MU_h is _____, while that of
jelly is _____; total utility equals _____, and the marginal utility of money is
_____. The relative price of hats in terms of jelly is _____, while the relative
price of jelly in terms of hats is _____.

f. Using the third data set for money prices and income, real income in terms of hats is
_____; in terms of jelly it is _____. At equilibrium, the consumer purchases
_____ hats and _____ jars of jelly, and the MU_h is _____, while the MU_j
is _____; total utility equals _____. In equilibrium, the marginal utility of
money is _____. The relative price of hats in terms of jelly is _____; while the
relative price of jelly in terms of hats is _____.

g. Your answers to questions d through f suggest that total utility varies _____ with
_____; and the marginal utility of money varies _____ with
_____.

Problem 2

This table shows the total utility (TU) that Bubba receives from the consumption of three different goods (A, B, and C). Bubba's weekly income is $42, and the prices of goods A, B, and C are $1, $3, and $8 respectively.

Qua-ntity	GOOD A			GOOD B			GOOD C		
	TU_A	MU_A	MU_A/P_A	TU_B	MU_B	MU_B/P_B	TU_C	MU_C	MU_C/P_C
0	0			0			0		
1	7	___	___	15	___	___	20	___	___
2	13	___	___	27	___	___	38	___	___
3	18	___	___	36	___	___	54	___	___
4	22	___	___	42	___	___	68	___	___
5	25	___	___	45	___	___	80	___	___
6	27	___	___	45	___	___	90	___	___
7	28	___	___	42	___	___	98	___	___
8	28	___	___	36	___	___	104	___	___
9	27	___	___	27	___	___	108	___	___

a. In the table, calculate and enter the marginal utility (MU) for each of the goods consumed.

b. If Bubba only consumed good A, he would consume _____ units because his total utility would be (maximized/minimized) _____, and his marginal utility of an extra unit of the good would be (positive/negative) _____.

c. As Bubba consumes more and more of each good, the marginal utility of each extra unit of the good consumed (increases/decreases) _____, and this reflects the law of _____.

d. Compute the marginal utility per dollar for each unit of each good consumed and enter the results in the columns labeled "MU/P".

e. Bubba does not get any pleasure out of saving money, so he will spend all of his earnings each week. In order to maximize his overall utility, Bubba will consume _____ units of good A, _____ units of good B, and _____ units of good C.

f. When Bubba selects his best consumption bundle, his total spending on each of the three goods is equal to $_____ on good A, $_____ on good B, and $_____ on good C.

g. The maximum total utility Bubba can achieve with his income ($42) is _____, and the marginal utility per dollar derived from the last unit of each of the goods is _____.

Problem 3

a. Suppose that this figure shows your demand curve for widgets, a hypothetical good which sells for $5 each. At a price of $9 per unit, the quantity of widgets that you demand is _____ units. For two units, you would be willing to pay $_____ for the first unit and $_____ for the second unit; however, you have to pay only $_____ per unit, and so you receive a _____ surplus of $_____ for the two units.

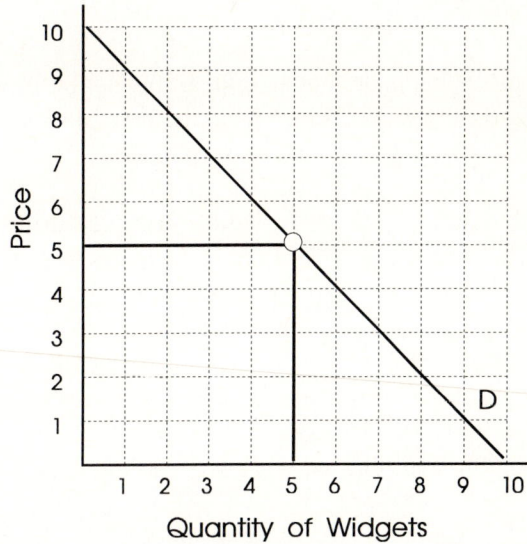

Quantity of Widgets

b. From elementary geometry, you learned that the area of a right triangle is: area = .5(base X height). If the market price of widgets is $5 per unit, the consumer's surplus that you receive is approximately $_____.
Rather than do without any widgets, you would be willing to pay $_____ for the right to purchase them at $5 each.

c. If the price of widgets increases from $5 to $7 each, quantity demanded falls from _____ to _____ units. As a result of this price increase, your consumer's surplus (rises/falls) _____. After the price increase, your consumer's surplus is $_____. You would be willing to pay up to $_____ in order to prevent the price from rising, and so this represents the cost of the price increase to you.

Problem 4

Ruby and Jeter Hapsburg want their daughter, Magda, to become a concert violinist. This figure shows their demand for violin lessons and the supply facing them.

a. What is the dollar value of the total utility they would derive from the first 100 lessons?
_____

b. What is the dollar value of the total utility the Hapsburgs would derive from the first 50 lessons? _____

c. In equilibrium, what is the dollar value of the Hapsburg's consumer surplus? _____

d. Approximately what is the dollar value of the marginal utility from the 100th lesson? _____.
How much would the Hapsburgs willingly spend on the 100th lesson? _____ Why?
_____   _____

e. How much extra consumer surplus do the Hapsburgs derive from the 50th lesson when lessons cost $10? _____

Problem 5

*Optional material. Four of Caleb's indifference curves for avocados and balloons are mapped in this figure, along with budget constraint lines UV (original) and UW (new). Points a and b denote the two points of consumer equilibrium and Caleb's money income is $20. Answer the following true/false questions.

___ a. Budget constraint UV has a slope of -2.

___ b. Caleb originally maximizes total utility at point a because no spending reallocation can raise total utility.

___ c. Balloons are originally $2 each.

___ d. Avocados are originally $4 each.

___ e. Caleb can move to a higher indifference curve because his real income rises when the budget line shifts from UV to UW.

___ f. Growth of money income allows Caleb to move from UV to UW.

___ g. These indifference curves show that the more balloons Caleb has, the fewer avocados he will trade for an additional balloon.

___ h. Indifference curve I_1 has a slope of -1/2 at point b.

___ i. At point a, $MU_a/P_a > MU_b/P_b$.

___ j. Along budget constraint UW, the price of balloons is $2.

___ k. At point a, $MU_b = 2MU_a$.

___ l. At point b, $MU_a = 2MU_b$.

___ m. The slope of budget constraint UV shows the original market rate of substitution between avocados and balloons.

___ n. At point b, the price of balloons is $8 each.

___ o. At point a, the price of avocados is $8 each.

___ p. The substitution effect solely explains why Caleb moves from point a to point b.

___ q. The shift from UV to UW is caused by a decrease in the price of balloons.

ANSWERS

Matching		True/False		Multiple Choice		Unlimited Multiple Choice
Set I	Set II					
1. i	1. d	1. F	11. T	1. c	11. b	1. ad
2. f	2. i	2. F	12. F	2. d	12. e	2. bc
3. e	3. e	3. F	13. T	3. a	13. a	3. d
4. c	4. h	4. F	14. T	4. b	14. e	4. abcd
5. h	5. g	5. F	15. T	5. a	15. d	5. abcd
6. d	6. c	6. T	16. F	6. e	16. a	
7. j	7. a	7. T	17. T	7. e	17. c	
8. b	8. b	8. F	18. T	8. b	18. e	
9. a	9. f	9. F	19. T	9. a	19. c	
10. g	10. j	10. F	20. F	10. c	20. b	

Chapter Review (Fill-in Questions)

1. utils; marginal utility; dollar spent; equal marginal utilities per dollar; Y; X; fall; rise
2. X; Y
3. normal; positive
4. Consumer surplus; market; below; demand; price; diamond-water
5. asymmetric information; moral hazard
6. caveat emptor, caveat venditor

PROBLEM 1

a. See table.
b. Law of diminishing marginal utility; as you consume equal successive units of a commodity, a point is eventually reached where the consumption of an additional unit yields less satisfaction (utility) than that of the preceding unit.
c. It increases at a diminishing rate.
d. 6; 12; 4; 4; 70 utils; 35 utils; 510 utils; $MU_H/P_H = MU_J/P_J$; 2 (1H = 2J); 1/2 (1J = 1/2 H).
e. 10; 10; 7; 3; 40 utils; 40 utils; 625 utils; 40 utils; 1; 1.
f. 15; 30; 10; 10; 10 utils; 5 utils; 825 utils; 5 utils; 2; 1/2.
g. directly; real income; inversely; real income.

Hats (H)	Total Utility	Marginal Utility	Jelly (J)	Total Utility	Marginal Utility
0	0	-----	0	0	-----
1	100	100	1	50	50
2	190	90	2	95	45
3	270	80	3	135	40
4	340	70	4	170	35
5	400	60	5	200	30
6	450	50	6	225	25
7	490	40	7	245	20
8	520	30	8	260	15
9	540	20	9	270	10
10	550	10	10	275	5

PROBLEM 2

a. See table.
b. 8; maximized;
   negative
c. decreases;
   diminishing marginal
   utility
d. See table.
e. 6; 4; 3
f. $6; $12; $24
g. 123 utils; 2

Qua-ntity	TU_A	MU_A	MU_A/P_A	TU_B	MU_B	MU_B/P_B	TU_C	MU_C	MU_C/P_C
0	0			0			0		
1	7	7	7	15	15	5	20	20	2.50
2	13	6	6	27	12	4	38	18	2.25
3	18	5	5	36	9	3	54	16	2.00
4	22	4	4	42	6	2	68	14	1.75
5	25	3	3	45	3	1	80	12	1.50
6	27	2	2	45	0	0	90	10	1.25
7	28	1	1	42	-3	-1	98	8	1.00
8	28	0	0	36	-6	-2	104	6	0.75
9	27	-1	-1	27	-9	-3	108	4	0.50

PROBLEM 3

a. 1; $9; $8; $5; consumer's; $7
b. $12.50; $12.50
c. 5; 3; falls; $4.50; $8

PROBLEM 4

a. $1,000 [the area under the demand curve from P=20 to P=0--(20 x (100/2)].
b. $750 [the area under the demand curve from P=20 to P=10--((10 x 50) + (10 x (50/2))].
c. $250 [the area of the triangle above $10 and below the demand curve--(10 x (50/2))].
d. 0; 0; because the Hapsburg's receive only infinitesimal satisfaction from consuming the 100th unit.
e. An infinitesimal amount (consumer surplus is essentially 0).

PROBLEM 5

a. F   j. T
b. T   k. F
c. F   l. T
d. T   m. T
e. T   n. F
f. F   o. F
g. T   p. F
h. T   q. T
i. F

Chapter 22
Theory Of The Firm

Chapter Objectives

In this chapter you are introduced to the producing side of the economy. After you have completed this chapter, you should be able to describe the general concept of production and state how inputs can be combined to yield outputs; explain how production changes the value of inputs in form, place, possession, or time; state the distinguishing characteristic between the long run and the short run; write, in a sentence or two, a justification of why firms exist; state the role of economies of scale in modern production theory; describe the principal/agent problem; describe the three legal forms of business; list some ways in which business and productive activity can be financed; state the assumed goal of the firm but also state other possible goals; give an example of both an implicit and an explicit cost; and finally state the difference between an accounting profit and an economic profit.

Chapter Review: Key Points

1. Production increases the value of goods in their *form, place, possession,* or *time.*

2. The *short run* is a period in which at least one resource and one cost are fixed. In the *long run* all resources can be varied, but technology is assumed constant. These periods, therefore, are not defined by time, but rather by the nature of the adjustment process. Firms can enter or leave an industry in the long run because all resources are variable.

3. Firms exist primarily to coordinate production teams that will (*a*) reduce transaction costs, and (*b*) exploit economies of scale. *Economies of scale* exist when average production costs decline as the level of output rises. *Economies of scope* occur when firms realize lower costs by producing or distributing multiple products.

4. Four out of five firms are either *sole proprietorships* or *partnerships*, but *corporations* account for more than 90 percent of all goods and services sold and receive roughly two-thirds of all profits in the United States. Compared to corporations, however, sole proprietorships and partnerships are easily formed and less subject to government regulation. The major advantages of corporations are the *limited liabilities* of stockholders and better access to financial capital markets.

5. *Financial intermediaries* channel households' saving into the hands of investors in economic capital, and include such organizations as banks, mutual funds, insurance companies, and stock brokers. Banks are the most important intermediaries, accounting for the vast bulk of the financing of business organizations.

6. Economic costs include both explicit and implicit costs. *Explicit costs* involve outlays of money for goods or resources. *Implicit costs* are the opportunity costs of resources provided by a firm's owner. Payments for rent, electricity, and wages are explicit costs, whereas the values of the owner's labor and capital are implicit costs.

7. Bookkeeping rarely considers implicit costs, while both implicit and explicit costs are included in economic costs. Consequently, *accounting profits* often overstate the economic profitability of an enterprise because the opportunity costs of owner-provided resources are ignored. Normal accounting profits are an economic cost of production.

8. A *principal* is a party with contractual rights for performance of certain tasks by an *agent*. The *principal/agent problem* arises when the principal cannot completely monitor the behavior of the agent and personal motives of the agent conflict with the objectives of the principal.

9. An erratic trend towards increased concentration of economic power in America has continued for more than a century. Corporate goals of making profits are under attack by people who believe that modern corporations are too powerful, both politically and economically. These critics argue that big business should be "socially responsible."

10. Even though control of much of modern economic life is concentrated in the hands of those who control giant corporations, changing market shares and the growth of various imports are evidence that the processes of competition are still reasonably vigorous.

Matching Key Terms And Concepts

Set I

___1. Economies of scale

___2. Principal/agent problem

___3. Sole proprietorship

___4. Partnership

___5. Corporation

a. The legal obligation to pay for debts or damages are not limited to the assets of the business.

b. Occurs only when a firm's revenue exceeds all costs of production; both implicit and explicit.

c. A source of the principal/agent problem; corporate managers may seek maximum power or pay for themselves rather than maximum profits for the stockholders.

_____ 6.   Unlimited liability

_____ 7.   Limited liability

_____ 8.   Accounting profits

_____ 9.   Economic profits

_____ 10. Separation of ownership and control

d.   Occurs when a firm's revenue exceeds only its explicit costs.

e.   A firm owned and operated by a single individual.

f.   Occur when average costs decline in the long run as a firm expands its productive capacity.

g.   Arises when the representatives pursue personal goals that conflict with the principal's contractual rights.

h.   Firms sanctioned by state laws and are considered legal persons separate and distinct from their owners.

i.   Extensions of proprietorships; two or more people combine their resources to form a business.

j.   The legal obligations to pay for debts or damages are limited to the assets of the business; the owners' personal wealth is not in jeopardy.

Set II

_____ 1.   Financial intermediaries

_____ 2.   Economies of Scope

_____ 3.   Long run

_____ 4.   Short run

_____ 5.   Production

_____ 6.   Conglomerates

_____ 7.   Implicit costs

_____ 8.   Explicit costs

_____ 9.   Common stock

_____ 10. Corporate bond

a.   That period of time in which some inputs of production are variable but at least one is fixed.

b.   Shares of ownership in a corporation.

c.   Individuals or firms that channel people's saving to investors in economic capital.

d.   Assets for their holders but liabilities for the corporation that issues them; holders of these are creditors for the corporation.

e.   The opportunity costs of resources the firm's owner makes available with no direct cash outlays.

f.   Those costs that are paid, out of pocket, for the factors of production now owned by the firm.

g.   Occur when lower costs are realized by producing or distributing multiple products.

h.   That period of time in which all inputs are variable; none or fixed.

i.   Occurs when inputs are transformed into outputs which are more valuable in form, place, possession, or time and involves using knowledge to apply energy to transform materials.

j.   Large, multiproduct firms which often operate plants in several different industries.

True/False Questions

___1. One of the results of firms in an industry earning a high economic profit is that more firms will enter the industry and competition will increase.

___2. Transaction costs are increased as a result of firms trying to coordinate team production.

___3. When production takes place, inputs are transformed into outputs, and these outputs may be purchased by consumers, other firms, or government.

___4. One result of production is that goods are transformed so that they are made more valuable in form or place, but not necessarily in possession or time.

___5. During the long run, no inputs are fixed, and firms can enter or leave the market place.

___6. When firms are horizontally integrated, they operate at different levels or stages in the production process.

___7. When a firm experiences economies of scale in production, as it expands its size and capacity, average costs decline in the long run.

___8. The principal/agent problem arises when the agent pursues personal goals that are in conflict with the principal's contractual rights.

___9. One aspect of the principal/agent problem is that the principal gives the agent "free rein" to manage his affairs.

___10. A firm's liability refers to its legal obligations to pay for debts or damages.

___11. When individuals form consumer cooperatives, their basic goal is to achieve savings by purchasing goods in large quantities, so they can be bought at lower per unit prices.

___12. One of the major functions of a financial intermediary is to secure excess funds from firms and households so that the economic system is assured of an adequate pool of savings.

___13. The easiest way for a firm to finance any expansion in its plant or equipment is to use its retained earnings since these funds do not incur any opportunity cost; the firm is using its own money.

___14. Generally speaking, relatively low transaction costs are incurred in identifying which financial investments are likely to be reasonably secure and capable of generating solid returns for savers.

___15. If you own shares of common stock in a corporation, you hope to earn a return on your shares through dividends and, hopefully, capital gains.

___16. It is very rare for an owner of common stock in a corporation to fail to receive a capital gain on the stock when it is sold.

___17. Principal/agent problems are most likely to occur when employees are closely supervised.

___18. Economies of Scope occur when a firm increases its productive capacity.

___19. One way that corporations can finance future growth is by utilizing retained earnings.

___20. Most corporate giants are immune from competitive pressures.

Standard Multiple Choice

There Is One Best Answer For Each Question.

___ 1. Which of the following represent more than three-quarters of the total number of businesses in this country today?
   a. Diversified firms.
   b. Conglomerate firms.
   c. Partnerships and proprietorships.
   d. Corporations.
   e. Financial institutions.

___ 2. Large, highly diversified firms are also known as:
   a. conglomerate firms.
   b. financial intermediaries.
   c. vertically integrated firms.
   d. horizontally integrated firms.
   e. multiplant firms.

___ 3. Sole proprietorships are **NOT** characterized by:
   a. ease of organization.
   b. simplicity of control.
   c. limited availability of capital.
   d. relatively free from regulation.
   e. limited liability.

___ 4. "Double taxation" refers to taxation of:
   a. last year's tax refund as this year's income.
   b. both corporate income and corporate dividends.
   c. dividends earned on shares in a credit union account.
   d. interest accrued on a savings and loan account.
   e. married people at rates that exceed those of "singles".

___ 5. Relative to other business organizations, corporations do not have the advantage of:
   a. little regulation of their activities.
   b. superior access to financial capital.
   c. permanence as long as the business is thriving.
   d. limited legal liabilities for their owners.
   e. better access to specialized professional managers.

___ 6. Which one of the following statements about the corporate form of business in the United States is not correct?
   a. The most dominant form of business in the U.S. in terms of the number of firms is the corporation.
   b. Corporations in the U.S. account for the largest dollar output.
   c. The owners of a corporation are its stockholders, and so the owners may not be the firm's managers.
   d. Legally, the corporation is a separate entity from its owners.
   e. The holder of a corporate bond is a creditor for the corporation.

___ 7. Suppose that you own the Widget Company, a sole proprietorship. We would expect that:
   a. Your firm has limited liability.
   b. You are in business with at least one other person.
   c. Some of your profits will be paid to stockholders.
   d. You will ultimately be responsible for the debts of the Widget Company.
   e. Even though you own the firm, you probably will not control it.

___ 8. Your firm produces widgets and incurs an accounting cost of $2 per unit in production. You produce 2,000 units of output and sell widgets for $4 each. We can conclude that:
   a. your firm has an economic profits of $4,000.
   b. your firm is breaking even.
   c. you only earn a normal profit.
   d. your firm also incurs an implicit cost of $2 per unit produced.
   e. none of the above are necessarily correct.

___ 9. Not among the types of utility created by production is:
   a. form.
   b. substance.
   c. time.
   d. place.
   e. possession.

___ 10. If average costs decline as a firm expands its productive capacity, then it is experiencing:
   a. economies of scope.
   b. vertical integration.
   c. financial intermediation.
   d. economies of scale.
   e. horizontal integration.

___ 11. Short and long runs are different in the:
   a. lengths of time considered.
   b. range of responses available to change profit opportunities.
   c. total amounts of revenues, costs, and profits experienced.
   d. flexibility of government policy makers.
   e. none of the above are correct.

___ 12. The value of an entrepreneur's resources that she uses in production are known as:
   a. explicit costs.
   b. sunk costs.
   c. operating expenses.
   d. technological expenses.
   e. implicit costs.

___13. Typically, the retained earnings of a firm:
   a. are not paid out to its stockholders.
   b. are frequently used to expand the firm's capital stock.
   c. can earn an interest income while they are being held by the firm.
   d. can, other things constant, increase the net worth of the firm.
   e. all of the above are correct.

___14. Suppose that you invest some of your own financial capital in your new business. The:
   a. opportunity cost of the invested funds is zero since no physical capital is used.
   b. opportunity cost of the funds should be included in the proprietor's economic cost of doing business.
   c. financial capital is an explicit cost of production.
   d. firm's accounting costs increase since the financial capital would have to be borrowed otherwise.
   e. firm's accounting profits will be less than its economic profits.

___15. You are considering starting your own business; however, you don't know whether to organize as a partnership (with a friend) or a sole proprietorship. The advantage of a partnership over a proprietorship is that:
   a. partners bear minimal risk if the firm fails.
   b. partners can sell stock.
   c. a partnership will survive even if one of the partners dies.
   d. it is easier to raise the necessary financial capital to get started.
   e. a partnership has limited liability.

___16. In some of today's firms, the owners are not necessarily those who manage or control the firm. This separation of ownership and control is most commonly found in:
   a. corporations but not partnerships or proprietorships.
   b. proprietorships but not partnerships.
   c. proprietorships but not corporations or partnerships.
   d. partnerships but not proprietorships or corporations.
   e. partnerships and some producer cooperatives.

___17. Given the list of firms below, each has limited liability except:
   a. Attorneys Condon, Morgan, and Smith, a general partnership.
   b. General Motors Corporation.
   c. The Green Grass Lawn Care Company, Incorporated.
   d. Drs. Smith and Jones, a professional corporation.
   e. Joe's Auto Repair, Inc.

___18. A primary difference between a share of corporate stock and a corporate bond is that:
   a. secondary markets exist for corporate stock but not for corporate bonds.
   b. the bond represents a share of ownership in the corporation.
   c. the holder of the bond can participate in the decision-making and management of the firm.
   d. the bond, but not stock, can be traded on secondary markets.
   e. the bond represents debt that the corporation owes to the holder of

the bond while a share of stock represents ownership in the firm.

___19. One of the most important differences between a firm's economic profit and its accounting profit is the subtraction of:
   a. costs incurred when hiring labor, capital, and land.
   b. any explicit cost incurred by the entrepreneur for risk taking.
   c. any implicit charges for the use of capital owned by the entrepreneur.
   d. any taxes on the retained earnings of the firm.
   e. the costs of distributing the firm's output.

___20. Which one of the following is **NOT** an argument presented by Galbraith about modern corporations? "The giant corporations of today:
   a. use extensive advertising to avoid meaningful competition."
   b. represent the most efficient form of production that competitive societies have ever experienced."
   c. tend to corrupt government policies to help consolidate managerial power and achieve managers' goals rather than the public interest."
   d. are controlled by corporate managers who seek maximum power and pay for themselves instead of maximum profit for stockholders."
   e. dominate economic activity because small competitive firms cannot afford the modern technologies required for efficient production."

Chapter Review (Fill-In Questions)

1. As you study introductory economics, one of the underlying assumptions when studying the behavior of the firm is that it tries to _____ profits, and this occurs when total revenue minus _____ is (greatest/least) _____.

2. Some of the major advantages of a sole proprietorship are _____, _____, _____, and_____. On the other hand, some major disadvantages of a sole proprietorship are _____, _____, _____, and _____.

3. If a family owns a business, then in order to secure tax advantages and limit liability for the owners, the family might create a _____ corporation or a _____.

4. To the firm's owner, the cost of using self-owned resources in the business as opposed to their best alternative use in other endeavors is a(n)_____, while the cost of securing inputs in the market place is a(n)_____ cost.

5. When a firm earns a normal profit, this profit (is/is not)_____ a cost of production, and the profit (will/will not)_____ be sufficient for the firm to continue in operation.

6. In general, two reasons for the existence of firms is that they _____ costs and coordinate _____ production; as they perform these functions, the goal of the owners is to_____ profits.

7. A _____ is a physical facility in one location involved in manufacturing, processing, or sales; _____ operate one or more. An _____ is comprised of all of the companies competing in the same product market. If one company provides a number of different products it is said to be _____.

8. The three basic forms of business organization are _____, _____, and _____. In addition to superior access to markets for financial capital, a major advantage of the corporate form of business organization is _____.

Unlimited Multiple Choice

Caution: Each Question Has From Zero To Four Correct Answers.

___ 1. Corporations:
   a. are artificial beings sanctioned by state law.
   b. are not subject to extensive government regulations.
   c. are fruitful sources of tax revenue for the government.
   d. enjoy unlimited liability.

___ 2. Common stock:
   a. when issued by the corporation, is one way in which the firm can secure financing for economic capital.
   b. represent shares of ownership in a corporation for its holders.
   c. can provide dividends to its holders if the corporation is profitable.
   d. will provide capital gains for its holders if the holders are able to sell the shares for a price greater than that paid for the shares.

___ 3. If a firm, whether it is a corporation, partnership, or proprietorship, holds some of its profits as retained earnings, then these earnings:
   a. may be used to finance future expansions by the firm.
   b. may be paid to stockholders as dividends after all income taxes have been paid.
   c. do not affect the net worth of the firm because they represent a financial, rather than a physical, asset.
   d. should be included in the cost of production when they are used by the firm for expansion or production.

____ 4. In the long run the typical firm:
   a. has all of its inputs fixed in production.
   b. may change some but not all of its inputs.
   c. has all variable inputs.
   d. incurs only implicit costs in production.

____ 5. If the XYZ Corp. earns an economic profit, then:
   a. its total revenue exceeds its explicit, but not its implicit, costs.
   b. these profits may attract other firms into the industry.
   c. total revenue is greater than all of its out-of-pocket, as well as opportunity, costs.
   d. it cannot, by definition, earn a normal profit.

Problems

Problem 1

In the spaces below, list **two** advantages or disadvantages of each of the legal forms of business.

a. Sole proprietorship--advantages:
   (1)._____.
   (2)._____.

b. Sole proprietorship--disadvantages:
   (1)._____.
   (2)._____.

c. Partnership--advantages:
   (1)._____.
   (2)._____.

d. Partnership--disadvantages:
   (1)._____.
   (2)._____.

e. Corporation--advantages:
   (1)._____.
   (2)._____.

f. Corporation- - disadvantages:
   (1)._____.
   (2)._____.

Problem 2

Presented below are some of the year-end accounts of the ABC Company, a sole proprietorship:

labor expense (10,000 hours @ $9/hr.)	$90,000
cost of office supplies used	$10,000
cost of materials used in production	$300,000
200,000 units of output sold @ $5/unit	$1,000,000
office operating expense	$20,000
advertising expense	$60,000
rental expense on warehouse	$100,000

a. The ABC Company has been in operation for only one year, and you must prepare the income (profit and loss) statement for Mr. Jones, the proprietor. Carefully identify the expenses (costs) and income (revenue) from the information presented above, and complete the table.

ABC Company Income Statement	
Revenues:	
	$
Total Revenue	$
Expenses:	
	$
	$
	$
	$
	$
	$
Total Expense	$
Total Profit	$

b. From your income statement, the expenses represent (accounting/economic)_____ costs, and so Mr. Jones' company had a net (accounting/economic)_____ profit of _____ during the year.

c. Mr. Jones is a highly qualified manager and could be earning a salary of $125,000 plus $50,000 in bonuses if he still worked for the firm which he left in order to start ABC. Mr. Jones also invested $500,000 of his own money to start the ABC Company. This $500,000 had been invested in a certificate of deposit that earned 12% interest per year. Adjust the income statement that you prepared above in the table below. The new income statement should reflect the opportunity (implicit) cost incurred by Mr. Jones in his business.

d   The total value of the
accounting cost plus the
implicit cost is _____,
and as a result, Mr. Jones
earns an economic profit
of _____ as
opposed to an accounting
profit of _____.

Adjusted Income Statement for ABC	
Total Revenue:	$
Expenses:	
Accounting cost from unadjusted statement.	$
Opportunity cost of owner's time	$
Opportunity cost of owner's capital	$
Total Expense (Explicit + Implicit)	$
Total Economic Profit	$

ANSWERS

Matching		True/False		Multiple Choice		Unlimited Multiple Choice
Set I	**Set II**					
1. f	1. c	1. T	11. T	1. c	11. b	1. ac
2. g	2. g	2. F	12. F	2. a	12. e	2. abcd
3. e	3. h	3. T	13. F	3. e	13. e	3. ad
4. i	4. a	4. F	14. F	4. b	14. b	4. c
5. h	5. i	5. T	15. T	5. a	15. d	5. bc
6. a	6. j	6. F	16. F	6. a	16. a	
7. j	7. e	7. T	17. F	7. d	17. a	
8. d	8. f	8. T	18. F	8. e	18. e	
9. b	9. b	9. F	19. T	9. b	19. c	
10. c	10. d	10. T	20. F	10. d	20. b	

Chapter Review (Fill-In Questions)

1. maximize; total cost; greatest
2. easy to form; simple to control; not much government regulation; freedom of operation; difficult to acquire funds; unlimited liability; lacks permanence; owner must perform all functions
3. closely held; limited partnership
4. implicit cost; explicit
5. is; will
6. reduce transaction; team; maximize
7. plant; firms; industry; diversified
8. sole proprietorship; partnership; corporation; limited liability

Problem 1

a. (1). Easy to organize; simple to control.
   (2). Freedom of operation; not much government regulation.
b. (1). Difficult to acquire financial capital; firm lacks permanence.
   (2). Unlimited liability; owner must perform all management functions.
c. (1). Easy to organize; greater specialization in management.
   (2). Access to financial capital is easier; subject to limited govt. regs.
d. (1). Disagreement among partners; death of a partner ends the partnership.
   (2). Unlimited liability; limited access to financial resources.
e. (1). Can raise large sums of capital; stability and permanence.
   (2). Limited liability; specialization of management.
f. (1). Much government regulation; taxes and organization costs are high.
   (2). Double taxation; principal/agent problem.

Problem 2

a. See table.

ABC Company Income Statement	
Revenues:	
200,000 units of output @ $5 per unit	$1,000,000
Total Revenue	$1,000,000
Expenses:	
Labor expense (10,000 hrs. @ $9/hr.)	$90,000
Costs of materials in production of goods	$300,000
Rental expense on warehouse	$100,000
Advertising expense for product	$60,000
Office supplies expense	$10,000
Office operating expense	$20,000
Total Expense	$580,000
Total Profit	$420,000

b. accounting; accounting; $420,000.
c. See table.

Adjusted Income Statement for ABC	
Total Revenue:	$1,000,000
Expenses:	
Accounting cost from unadjusted statement.	$580,00
Opportunity cost of owner's time	$175,000
Opportunity cost of owner's capital	$60,000
Total Expense (Explicit + Implicit)	$815,000
Total Economic Profit	$185,000

d $815,000; $185,000; $420,000.

Chapter 23
Production and Costs

Chapter Objectives

After you have read and studied this chapter, you should be able to define and describe the production relationships between inputs and outputs; draw a short run total product curve along with the associated average and marginal product curves and show where the point where diminishing returns set in; define and calculate from appropriate data the average total, variable, fixed, and marginal cost; show graphically the relationship between the average and marginal product curves and the average and marginal cost curves; state the principle of equal marginal productivities per dollar; draw a long run average cost curve and explain why it might take a "U" shape; using a long run average cost curve, show where a firm experiences its minimum efficient scale.

Note: This relatively technical chapter requires concentrated effort.

Chapter Review: Key Points

1. A *production function* expresses a relationship between inputs and output. Production transforms goods to make them more valuable in form, place, time, or possession. A *total product curve* shows how output is affected as the amount of only one input changes.

2. The *short run* is a period in which at least one resource and one cost are fixed. In the *long run* all resources can be varied, but technology is assumed constant. These periods, therefore, are not defined by time, but rather by the nature of the adjustment process.

3. The *average physical product of labor (APP$_L$)* equals q/L. The *marginal physical product of labor (MPP$_L$)* equals $\Delta q/\Delta L$, and is the output generated by an additional unit of labor.

4. According to the *law of diminishing marginal returns*, when increasing amounts of a variable resource are applied to a fixed resource, although the marginal physical product of the variable factor may initially rise, beyond some point its marginal product inevitably falls.

5. A firm's total costs can be separated into *fixed costs* (or *overhead*) and *variable* (or *operating*) *costs*. Fixed costs do not vary with output and do not alter rational decisions. Leases, utility hookup charges, opportunity costs of an owner's resources, and other overhead expenses are fixed costs in the short run. Wages paid employees, bills for raw materials, and other costs that change when output is changed are variable costs.

6. When total fixed costs and total variable costs are each divided by output, *average fixed costs (AFC)* and *average variable costs (AVC)* are obtained, respectively. Summing the two yields *average total cost (ATC)*. *Marginal cost (MC)* is defined as the additional cost of producing one more unit of a good and equals $\Delta TC/\Delta q$.

7. Firms can enter or leave an industry in the long run because all resources are variable. The *long-run average cost total curve (LRATC)* is an *envelope curve* under all short-run average cost curves (different-sized plants). It shows the minimum long-run average costs for each output level. Long-run average cost curves typically have *economies of scale (LRATC* falling) over some portion of the curve, but eventually exhibit *diseconomies of scale (LRATC* rising).

8. Measuring long-run costs is a complex problem. One method is to examine the size (and cost structure) of firms that have been successful and have "survived" in an industry over a long period of time. Other methods include using both accounting and engineering data to estimate the *LRATC* curve. Economists have estimated *minimum efficient scale (MES)*, the smallest plant that can be operated at minimum LRATC. *MES* is typically reported as a percent of industry output.

9. *Technological progress* increases output from given resources. New technology resides in new knowledge or improved nonhuman resources, and results in new products or lower costs. Technological improvements account for much of our long-term economic growth and rising productivity.

Matching Key Terms And Concepts

SET I

___ 1. marginal cost (MC)

___ 2. sunk costs

___ 3. Average fixed cost (AFC)

___ 4. production function

___ 5. average physical product(APP_L)

___ 6. fixed costs (FC)

a. A type of fixed cost.

b. TFC + TVC

c. Increases at an increasing rate, increases at a decreasing rate, and may even decline.

d. All resources and costs are variable.

e. Costs incurred only when production occurs

___	7.	short run	**f.** The extra cost of an added unit of output.
___	8.	total variable cost (TVC)	**g.** Relationship between inputs and outputs.
___	9.	average variable cost	**h.** At least one factor or cost cannot be altered.
___	10.	long run	**i.** Output per additional worker.
___	11.	marginal physical product (MPP_L)	**j.** Costs incurred regardless of the level of output.
___	12.	average total cost (ATC)	**k.** per unit cost of production.
___	13.	total product curve	**l.** Declines continuously as output rises.
___	14.	total costs	**m.** Per unit costs excluding "overhead".
			n. Output per worker.

SET II

___	1.	law of diminishing marginal returns	**a.** LRAC falls as output grows.
___	2.	minimum efficient scale (MES)	**b.** A synonym for fixed cost.
___	3.	equal marginal productivities per dollar	**c.** An "envelope" curve tangent to the SRAC per dollar for each output level.
___	4.	overhead costs	**d.** LRAC rises as output grows.
___	5.	long run average cost (LRAC) curve	**e.** Occurs when the principle of equal marginal productivities per dollar is met.
___	6.	operating costs	**f.** Increases output with a given set of resources.
___	7.	diseconomies of scale	**g.** Also known as variable cost or direct cost.
___	8.	least cost production	**h.** $\dfrac{MPP_L}{w} = \dfrac{MPP_K}{i} = \ldots$
___	9.	technological change	**i.** Additions of variable inputs to some fixed factor of production ultimately yield less and less additional output.
___	10.	economies of scale.	**j.** Plants that are the smallest that will produce output at minimum average total cost.

True/False Questions

___ 1. When a firm begins to experience diminishing average product of labor, the marginal product of labor is at a maximum.

___ 2. Production functions (how outputs change if one input varies) are synonymous with total product curves.

___ 3. Marginal cost is the change in the total cost of all output produced by an additional unit of labor.

___ 4. The long run average cost (envelope) curve reflects the plant size associated with the minimum average cost of producing each possible level of output.

___ 5. Profitable but inefficient firms inevitably fail.

___ 6. As a firm increases its output in the short run, average fixed costs fall at first, but they will eventually begin to rise as output continues to increase.

___ 7. The law of diminishing marginal returns asserts that if all resources are simultaneously and proportionally increased, a point is inevitably reached where total output diminishes only at an increasing rate.

___ 8. Total product curves allow all resources to vary, while production functions assume that only one input changes.

___ 9. Hiring additional workers results in changes in the marginal and average productivities of workers primarily because of the changing short run amounts of fixed resources per worker.

___10. When the marginal physical product of labor rises, the average physical product of labor falls; and when the marginal physical product of labor is falls, the average physical product of labor rises.

___11. Total variable costs form most bookkeeping costs that are deducted from revenue to compute a firm's taxable income.

___12. The average fixed cost curve, a horizontal line, is a major factor in short run business decisionmaking.

___13. As output is increased, the minimums of the MC, AVC, and ATC curves are encountered in that order.

___14. Overhead, historical cost, sunk cost, and fixed cost are all roughly synonymous; and differ from direct cost, operating cost, and variable cost, which are also roughly synonymous.

___15. The total product curve tends to increase at an increasing rate initially, when the advantages of specialization are being realized, but marginal returns eventually begin to diminish.

___16. The principle of equal marginal productivities per dollar in production theory parallels the principle of equal marginal utilities per dollar from consumer theory.

___17. Technological advances that are responses to profit opportunities in the long run invariably reduce the minimum points of long run average cost curves.

___18. The average variable cost (AVC) and average total cost (ATC) curves are intersected at their minimum points from below by the marginal cost (MC) curve.

___19. Marginal physical productivity curves are direct measures of each worker's contribution to a firm's profits.

___20. Horizontal summation of the AFC and AVC curves yields the ATC curve.

Standard Multiple Choice

There Is Only One Best Answer For Each Question.

___ 1. Suppose that the ABC Corp. shuts down and produces nothing. Which one of the following statements best describes the firm's cost?
   a. Total variable costs are zero but total fixed costs may be positive, so total costs may be positive.
   b. Total fixed costs are zero but total variable costs may be positive, so total costs may be positive.
   c. Total fixed, total variable, and total costs are zero since nothing is being produced
   d. Total fixed and total variable costs may be positive, so total costs may be positive
   e. Marginal costs may be either positive or zero.

___ 2. The relationships between all possible inputs and the level of a firm's output are summarized in a(n):
   a. input/output matrix.
   b. production possibilities frontier.
   c. total product curve.
   d. production function.
   e. envelope curve.

___ 3. Short, and long runs are different in the:
   a. lengths of time considered.
   b. range of responses available to changes in profit opportunities.
   c. total amounts of revenues, costs, and profits experienced.
   d. differences between average and marginal productivity.
   e. flexibility of government policymakers.

4. In the production of corn, all of the following are variable inputs that are used by the farmer except:
   a. the seed used when the crop is planted.
   b. the field that has been cleared of trees and in which the crop is planted.
   c. the fertilizer used by the farmer once the crop is planted.
   d. the tractor used by the farmer in planting and cultivating not only corn but also wheat and barley.
   e. the number of hours that the farmer spends cultivating his field.

5. The total product curve may initially show output increasing at an increasing rate as more labor is hired because of the:
   a. declining quality of the labor force.
   b. principle of comparative advantage.
   c. law of diminishing marginal returns.
   d. increase in marginal physical product.
   e. rapid rate of technological advance.

6. If labor is the only variable resource and its marginal physical product falls as more workers are hired:
   a. the law of diminishing marginal returns is at work.
   b. marginal cost is rising.
   c. average cost may still be declining.
   d. average physical product may still be rising.
   e. All of the above.

7. When both average and total product are greater than zero, and marginal product equals average product, then total product:
   a. is at a maximum.
   b. is positive and rising.
   c. is falling.
   d. is negative but rising.
   e. None of the above.

8. Costs incurred only when production occurs are known as:
   a. explicit costs.
   b. fixed costs.
   c. variable costs.
   d. technological expenses.
   e. implicit costs.

9. The law of diminishing marginal returns is encountered as increasing amounts of labor are hired because:
   a. as production rises, the additional labor hired is less and less skilled.
   b. experienced workers are hired before the less skilled.
   c. each extra worker hired decreases the amounts of land and capital per worker, so the work place becomes more congested and managerial control becomes more difficult.
   d. as more and more is produced, selling it requires cutting prices.
   e. All of the above.

10. Which of the following is irrelevant for rational decisionmaking?
    a. Average variable cost (AVC).
    b. Explicit cost.
    c. Average fixed cost (AFC).
    d. Marginal cost (MC).
    e. Total variable cost (TVC).

___11. Which of the following curves can never be "U" shaped?
a. Average variable cost
b Marginal cost
c. Average fixed cost
d. Average total cost
e. Long run average cost

___12. Diminishing marginal returns are most compatible with:
a. economies of scale.
b. advantages from specialization.
c. positively-sloped marginal cost curves.
d. depreciation of the capital stock.
e. a unionized labor force.

___13. If average variable costs fall as output grows:
a. marginal costs must also be declining.
b. fixed cost must also be declining.
c. total cost must also be declining.
d. average cost must be below average variable cost.
e. marginal costs must be below average variable cost.

___14. The application to production of the law of equal advantage yields the principle of:
a. diminishing marginal returns.
b. equal marginal productivities per dollar.
c. variable compensation.
d. comparable worth.
e. decreasing marginal cost.

___15. Declines in long run average cost when a firm expands its capacity occur under conditions of:
a. economies of scale.
b. increasing cost industries.
c. diminishing marginal returns.
d. diseconomies of scale.
e. accelerated depreciation schedules.

___16. Least cost production in the long run requires firms to adjust their resource mixes until the relative prices of resources are equal to the relative:
a. prices of outputs.
b. total costs for each resource.
c. average productivity per resource.
d. economies of scale of production.
e. marginal productivities of the resources.

___17. When a firm is experiencing diseconomies of scale:
a. larger firms with bigger plants will tend to be more successful.
b. it should increase the amount of labor it hires.
c. it should fire inept executives and get rid of "dead wood."
d. its average cost will decline if it scales down its operations.
e. average cost will be cut by adopting more modern technology.

___18. If long run average cost rises as the output and the size of the plant grows:
a. diseconomies of scale are present.
b. marginal cost is below long run average cost.
c. fixed costs are increasingly important for decision making.
d. this is a decreasing-cost industry.
e. prices and profit expand proportionally.

___19. When a firm achieves its minimum efficient scale of operation:
    a. it can reduce its long run average total costs by increasing its scale of operation.
    b. it will no longer experience any economies of scale if it expands its size.
    c. its long run average total cost curve increases as the level of output rises.
    d. its marginal product curve stops rising and begins to fall.
    e. the long run marginal cost of producing an extra unit of output is zero.

___20. If the wage rate is $5 an hour, and the APP_L for the 5th worker is 10, then AVC when 5 workers are employed is:
    a. $0.50.
    b. $2.00.
    c. $1.00.
    d. $0.10.
    e. impossible to calculate given the information above.

Chapter Review (Fill-In Questions)

1. In the _____, at least one _____ is fixed and the firm's cost of acquiring it are also fixed, but in the _____ all inputs and costs are _____.

2. The total cost of production schedule can be calculated by determining the (maximum/minimum) _____ cost of producing various levels of output; the choice of production technique is determined by both the _____ function along with (input/output)_____ prices.

3. Total costs (TC) include both _____ costs that do not change with output, and _____ costs, which do.

4. Because fixed cost does not change with output, marginal cost can be written as _____ or as _____.

5. The vertical distance between the ATC and AVC curves equals _____ which, when graphed alone, is a _____ because AFC = TFC/Q, so Q x AFC = TFC, which is a constant.

6. When the law of _____ sets in, total product continues to _____ but at a _____ rate; total cost and total variable cost will also rise, but now at _____ rates.

7. By enveloping from below the short run average cost curves associated with various possible levels of the fixed resources, we derive a(n) _____ curve. Where this curve declines as output rises, there are _____ in production.

8. When average total cost is falling, marginal cost will be (above/below/equal to) _____ the average total cost curve; when average total costs are rising, marginal cost is (greater than/less than/equal to)_____ average total cost.

Unlimited Multiple Choice

Caution: Each Question Has From Zero To Four Correct Answers.

___ 1. In the microeconomics of production theory:
   a. all factors of production are fixed in the short run.
   b. at least one resource is fixed in the long run, but firms can freely either enter or leave an industry.
   c. short runs and long runs refer to economic adjustments rather than to time per se.
   d. it is impossible to say what specific temporal time period is sufficient for firms to reach long-run adjustment.

___ 2. The law of diminishing marginal returns suggests that:
   a. declining amounts of a fixed resource per variable resource eventually causes the marginal productivity of the variable resource to fall.
   b. beyond some point, larger enterprises will have higher average costs than smaller production units.
   c. it is impossible to grow the world's food supply in a flower pot.
   d. not all influences on production can be changed proportionally during any finite period.

___ 3. The marginal physical product of labor:
   a. is the change in total cost associated with producing an additional unit of output.
   b. can be computed as w/ATC.
   c. will shift upward if all labor becomes more productive at each possible level of input.
   d. intersects the average product of labor curve from above when the average product of labor attains its maximum value.

___ 4. Average fixed cost:
   a. varies inversely with output.
   b. is the shape of a rectangular hyperbola when graphed.
   c. remains unchanged as output decreases.
   d. varies directly with total fixed cost.

___ 5. Economies and diseconomies of scale, respectively, are:
   a. present when short run average cost falls and then rises.
   b. reflections of diminishing returns and specialization.
   c. the result of fixing labor and then capital.
   d. only realized in the long run.

Problems

Problem 1

This table summarizes a firm's production and cost data.

Labor (L)	Q	APP$_L$	MPP$_L$	w	TFC	TVC	TC	AFC	AVC	ATC	MC
0	0	——	——	$10	$50	——	——	——	——	——	——
1	5	——	——	10	50	——	——	——	——	——	——
2	15	——	——	10	50	——	——	——	——	——	——
3	30	——	——	10	50	——	——	——	——	——	——
4	50	——	——	10	50	——	——	——	——	——	——
5	75	——	——	10	50	——	——	——	——	——	——
6	95	——	——	10	50	——	——	——	——	——	——
7	110	——	——	10	50	——	——	——	——	——	——
8	120	——	——	10	50	——	——	——	——	——	——
9	125	——	——	10	50	——	——	——	——	——	——
10	125	——	——	10	50	——	——	——	——	——	——

a. Which period of production is depicted above? _____ Why? _____
   _____

b. Fill in the blanks in the table.

c. Graph the total product, average, and marginal physical product curves in Figure 1.

d. Use Figure 2 to graph the total cost curve, the total variable cost curve, and the total fixed cost curve.

e. Use Figure 3 to graph the average total cost, average variable cost, average fixed cost, and marginal cost curves.

f. Over what input range do marginal returns increase? _____. Remain constant? _____
   Diminish? _____.

Figure 1

Figure 2

Figure 3

Problem 2

This table summarizes production and cost relationships for a different product and firm.

Labor (L)	Q	APP_L	MPP_L	w	TFC	TVC	TC	AFC	AVC	ATC	MC
0	0	—	—	$20	$100	0	100	—	—	—	—
1	10	10	10	20	100	20	120	10.00	2.00	12.00	2.00
2	22	11	12	20	100	40	140	4.55	1.82	6.36	1.67
3	36	12	14	20	100	60	160	2.78	1.67	4.44	1.43
4	52	13	16	20	100	80	180	1.92	1.54	3.46	1.25
5	70	14	18	20	100	100	200	1.43	1.43	2.86	1.11
6	90	15	20	20	100	120	220	1.11	1.33	2.44	1.00
7	108	15.43	18	20	100	140	240	0.93	1.30	2.22	1.11
8	124	15.50	16	20	100	160	260	0.81	1.29	2.10	1.25
9	138	15.33	14	20	100	180	280	0.72	1.30	2.03	1.43
10	150	15.00	12	20	100	200	300	0.67	1.33	2.00	1.67
11	160	14.55	10	20	100	220	320	0.63	1.38	2.00	2.00
12	168	14.00	8	20	100	240	340	0.60	1.43	2.02	2.50
13	174	13.38	6	20	100	260	360	0.57	1.49	2.07	3.33
14	178	12.71	4	20	100	280	380	0.56	1.57	2.13	5.00
15	180	12.00	2	20	100	300	400	0.56	1.67	2.22	10.00
16	180	11.25	0	20	100	320	420	0.56	1.78	2.33	—

a. Complete the blanks in the table.

b. Which production period is depicted in the table? _____. Why? _____.

c. Over what range of the variable input does this firm encounter increasing marginal returns? _____; Constant marginal returns? _____; Diminishing marginal returns? _____.

Problem 3

Use this figure to answer the following questions.

a. At output Q_2, average variable cost is
_____?

b. At output Q_1, total variable costs are equal
to area _____?

c. At output Q_0, average total costs are
_____?

d. Total cost at output Q_2 is equal to area
_____?

e. Total fixed costs are equal to area
_____?

Problem 4

Use this figure, which illustrates costs per barrel
of crude oil daily at a Nigerian oil field, to answer
the questions below.

a. What do total costs (TC) equal when 40,000
barrels are produced?_____ When
80,000 barrels are produced? _____

b. What do total fixed costs (TFC) equal?

_____

c. What do total variable costs (TVC) equal
when 40,000 barrels are produced?
_____ When 60,000 barrels are
produced? _____

Problem 5

This table 8 illustrates four short-run average cost schedules (curves) for leather purses produced in Guatemala.

Q	SRAC$_A$	SRAC$_B$	SRAC$_C$	SRAC$_D$
1,000	7.50	----	----	----
2,000	5.40	6.00	----	----
3,000	5.00	4.50	5.50	----
4,000	5.30	4.30	4.30	----
5,000	6.00	4.75	3.85	4.50
6,000	----	5.70	3.50	4.10
7,000	----	----	4.00	3.80
8,000	----	----	4.80	4.00
9,000	----	----	6.00	4.75
10,000	----	----	----	6.00

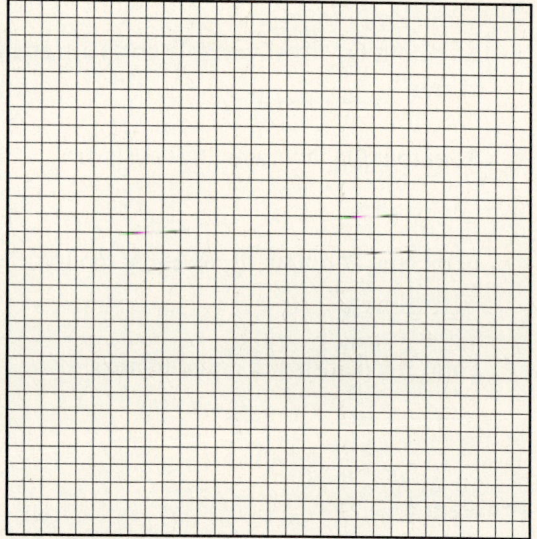

a. Use the figure to graph all four short-run average cost curves, and plot the long-run average cost (envelope) curve.

b. Long-run minimum costs are reached at what level of output?_____

c. If the Guatemalan government limited output to 5,000 purses per month, which plant size would you build? _____

d. Does the envelope curve touch each short-run average cost curve at its minimum point? _____ Why or why not? _____

_____

Problem 6

This problem is based on the optional material at the end of the chapter. The figure shows an isoquant map with original isocost curve AB and new isocost curve AC. The firm is assumed to maximize profits and has $500 available to purchase resources.

a. What is the original price of capital? _____
   How did you compute it? _____

b. What is the original price of labor? _____
   How did you compute it? _____

c. What is the new price of capital? _____
   How did you compute it? _____

d. What is the new price of labor? _____
   How did you compute it? _____

e. The firm is originally in equilibrium at which point? ___ Why? _____
   State the marginal condition for output maximization or cost minimization. _____

f. The new equilibrium point for this firm is at ___. Why? _____

g. The isoquant curves are (convex, concave) to the origin, illustrating the law of (increasing, diminishing, constant) marginal returns. Explain what this physical law means. _____
   _____

h. Write an equation for isocost curve AB. _____ Write an equation for isocost curve AC. _____

i. What are the relative magnitudes of MPP_K and MPP_L at point b? _____ Why? _____

j. What are the relative magnitudes of MPP_K and MPP_L at point a? _____ Why? _____

k. At present, can the firm attain point c? ___ Why or why not? _____
   What must change before point c becomes attainable? _____

l. What is the expression for the slope of AB in terms of the money prices for capital and labor? _____
   _____

m. What is the expression for the slope of AC in terms of the money prices for capital and labor? _____

n. What is the expression for the slope of isoquant I_0 at point a? _____

Answers

Matching		True/False		Multiple Choice		Unlimited Multiple Choice

SET I	SET II					
1. f	1. i	1. F	11. T	1. a	11. c	1. cd
2. a	2. j	2. F	12. F	2. d	12. c	2. abcd
3. l	3. h	3. F	13. T	3. b	13. e	3. cd
4. g	4. b	4. T	14. T	4. b	14. b	4. ab
5. n	5. c	5. F	15. T	5. d	15. a	5. d
6. j	6. g	6. F	16. T	6. e	16. e	
7. h	7. d	7. F	17. T	7. b	17. d	
8. e	8. e	8. F	18. T	8. c	18. a	
9. m	9. f	9. T	19. F	9. c	19. b	
10. d	10. a	10. F	20. F	10. c	20. a	
11. i						
12. k						
13. c						
14. b						

Chapter Review (Fill-in Questions)

1. short-run; resource; long-run; variable
2. minimum; production, input
3. fixed; variable
4. $\Delta TC/\Delta Q$; $\Delta TVC/\Delta Q$
5. average fixed costs (AFC), rectangular hyperbola
6. diminishing marginal returns; grow; decreasing; increasing
7. long run average cost; economies of scale
8. below; greater than

Problem 1

a. Short run; because there are fixed costs.
b. See table below.
c. See Figure 8
d. See Figure 9.
e. See Figure 10.
f. 1-5; 5; 5-10.

Labor (L)	Q	APP_L	MPP_L	w	TFC	TVC	TC	AFC	AVC	ATC	MC
0	0	-----	-----	$10	$50	-----	$50	-----	-----	-----	-----
1	5	5	5	10	50	$10	60	$10	$2	$12	$2
2	15	7.50	10	10	50	20	70	3.33	1.33	4.67	1.00
3	30	10	15	10	50	30	80	1.67	1.00	2.67	0.67
4	50	12.50	20	10	50	40	90	1.00	0.80	1.80	0.50
5	75	15	25	10	50	50	100	0.67	0.67	1.33	0.40
6	95	15.83	20	10	50	60	110	0.53	0.63	1.16	0.50
7	110	15.71	15	10	50	70	120	0.45	0.64	1.09	0.67
8	120	15	10	10	50	80	130	0.42	0.67	1.08	1.00
9	125	13.88	5	10	50	90	140	0.40	0.72	1.12	2.00
10	125	12.50	0	10	50	100	150	0.40	0.80	1.20	∞

Figure 8

Figure 9

Figure 10

Problem 2

a. See Table 4.
b. short run; fixed costs are included in table.
c. 1-6; 6; 6-16.

Problem 3

a. Q_2h
b. $OabQ_1$
c. Q_0g or $0f$
d $OceQ_2$
e. cfgd

Problem 4

a. $140,000; $240,000
b. $60,000.
c. $80,000; $90,000

Problem 5

a. See Figure 11.
b. 6,000 units.
c. $SRAC_C$
d. No;. It touches the short-run curves before their minimum point when the envelope curve (long-run average cost curve) is downward sloping, and touches the short-run curve past their minimum point when the envelope curve is upward sloping.

Table 4

Labor (L)	Q	APP_L	MPP_L	w	TFC	TVC	TC	AFC	AVC	ATC	MC
0	0	-----	-----	$20	$100	$0	$100	-----	----	-----	-----
1	10	10	10	20	100	20	120	$10	$2	$12	$2
2	22	11	12	20	100	40	140	4.55	1.82	6.36	1.67
3	36	12	14	20	100	60	160	2.78	1.67	4.44	1.43
4	52	13	16	20	100	80	180	1.92	1.54	3.46	1.25
5	70	14	18	20	100	100	200	1.43	1.43	2.86	1.11
6	90	15	20	20	100	120	220	1.11	1.33	2.44	1.00
7	108	15.43	18	20	100	140	240	0.93	1.30	2.22	1.11
8	124	15.50	16	20	100	160	260	0.81	1.29	2.10	1.25
9	138	15.33	14	20	100	180	280	0.72	1.30	2.03	1.43
10	150	15	12	20	100	200	300	0.67	1.33	2.00	1.67
11	160	14.55	10	20	100	220	320	0.63	1.38	2.00	2.00
12	168	14	8	20	100	240	340	0.60	1.42	2.02	2.50
13	174	13.38	6	20	100	260	360	0.57	1.49	2.07	3.33
14	178	12.71	4	20	100	280	380	0.56	1.57	2.13	5.00
15	180	12	2	20	100	300	400	0.55	1.67	2.22	10.00
16	180	11.25	0	20	100	320	420	0.55	1.78	2.33	∞

Figure 11

Problem 6

a. $10, $500/50

b. $5, $500/100

c. $5, $500/100

d. $5, $500/100

e. a; output is maximized given the budget constraint; $MPP_L/P_L = MPP_K/P_K$ or $MPP_L/MPP_K = P_L/P_K$

f. b; output is maximized given the budget constraint

g. convex; diminishing; as additional equal units of a variable input are applied to fixed inputs, a point is reached where total output increases at a diminishing rate.

h. $K = 50 - 1/2L$; $K = 100 - L$

i. Same; $P_K = P_L$

j. $MPP_K = 2MPP_L$, $P_K = 2P_L$

k. No; real dollar outlay too small; a decrease in input prices or more outlay on inputs.

l. $-P_L/P_K = -$5/$10 = -1/2$

m. $-P_L/P_K = -$10/$10 = -1$

n. $-MPP_L/MPP_K$

Chapter 24
The Competitive Ideal

Chapter Objectives

After you have read and studied this chapter, you should be able to state the differences between price-taking and price-making as well as the differences between competing and competition. You should be able to state and describe the output decisions of competitive firms and indicate how competitive firms adjust to profit signals in both the short and long run. You should be able to list some features of competitive markets and state why these features make them attractive from the vantage points of efficiency, equity, and prediction. Finally, you should be able to write a short paragraph in which you describe the differences between constant cost, increasing costs, and decreasing cost industries.

Chapter Review: Key Points

1. Freedom of *entry and exit* is the hallmark of competition. A *competitive* market is comprised of numerous potential buyers and sellers of a homogeneous product, none of whom controls its price. All buyers and sellers are sufficiently small relative to the market so that none is a *price maker*.

2. A competitive buyer faces a perfectly elastic supply curve, while competitive sellers face perfectly elastic demand curves. In competition, all are *price-takers* or *quantity adjusters*.

3. A competitive firm maximizes profits by producing output up to the point where *total revenues minus total costs (TR - TC)*, is maximized, which also occurs when *marginal revenue equals marginal cost (MR = MC)*. Price must be greater than the minimum of the average variable cost curve, however, which is the *shutdown point*. Because competitive firms face perfectly elastic demands, price and marginal revenue are identical.

4. A competitive *firm's short-run supply curve* is its marginal cost curve above the minimum of its average variable costs. Horizontally summing the marginal costs from existing firms yields the *short-run industry supply curve*.

5. Firms cannot adjust output in the *market period,* so total supply is perfectly inelastic. In the *short run (SR)*, existing firms in an industry can vary output, but at least one productive factor is fixed and entry and exit cannot occur. Total supply is at least somewhat elastic. Supply is much more elastic in the *long run (LR)*, because all factors of production are variable and firms may enter or leave the industry.

6. Competition erases *economic profits* through entry of new firms in the long run, and economic losses are eradicated by exit from the industry. Thus, competitive firms receive exactly enough revenue over the long run to pay the opportunity costs of resources used and realize only *zero economic profit.*

7. Short-run economic profits are ultimately eliminated because output will be expanded by new firms in a competitive industry or increased competition for profitable inputs will drive up resource costs. The long run adjustments that eliminate short-run losses follow precisely reversed patterns.

8. In the long run, firms are forced by competitive pressures to adopt the most efficient (least costly) plant size and technologies. They operate at output levels where P = MR = SRATC = SRMC = LRATC = LRMC.

9. For *constant-cost industries*, the minimum *LRATC* for firms is the same no matter how many firms are in the industry. Costs increase for each firm as firms enter increasing cost industries and decrease for decreasing-cost industries. Thus, the *long-run industry supply curve* is positively sloped for *increasing-cost industries,* horizontal for *constant-cost industries,* and negatively sloped for *decreasing-cost industries.*

10. A competitive market is efficient in the sense that goods desired by consumers (society) are produced at the lowest possible opportunity cost. Every feasible bit of net gain is squeezed from the resources available; *marginal social benefits* and *marginal social costs* are equated by competitive forces of supply and demand *(MSB = MSC)*, assuming the absence of externalities. This will be socially optimal and maximize social welfare if the distribution of income is deemed appropriate. A market system does not require that decision making power be vested in a central authority. This permits substantial personal freedom and the absence of coercion.

Matching Key Terms And Concepts

Set I

___ 1. MR = P

___ 2. market period

___ 3. MC above AVC

___ 4. freedom of entry and exit

___ 5. Long run

___ 6. MSC = MSB

___ 7. MR = MC

___ 8. Increasing cost industry

___ 9. Short run

___ 10. P = minimum (LRATC)

a. Profit maximizing condition for all firms, regardless of market structure.

b. All aspects of production can be changed, given the technology.

c. Long-run equilibrium for competitive industry.

d. A competitive firm's short-run supply curve.

e. Higher industry outputs cause greater resource costs.

f. True only of price-taking sellers.

g. At least one resource is fixed.

h. A condition assuring economic efficiency.

i. When production cannot be altered.

j. Assures the absence of long-run economic profits in competitive markets.

Set II

___ 1. Price maker

___ 2. Competitive markets

___ 3. Price taker

___ 4. Break-even point

___ 5. Constant cost industry

___ 6. Shut-down point

___ 7. Economic efficiency condition

___ 8. Zero economic profits

___ 9. Normal accounting profits

___ 10. Decreasing cost industry

a. Pure quantity adjuster.

b. When price equals the minimum of AVC.

c. As output expands, input costs decline.

d. Where price equals ATC.

e. P = MC.

f. Realized even when economic profit is zero.

g. Characterized by a large number of potential buyers and sellers of a homogeneous product.

h. Any firm with any monopoly power.

i. Long-run equilibrium condition for a competitive industry.

j. Minimum AC is not influenced by the number of firms in an industry or by industry output.

True/False Questions

___ 1. A profit seeking firm will shut down if it cannot cover all short run costs of production.

___ 2. A firm receives zero economic profits when total revenue equals total cost at the current output level.

___ 3. The demand curve confronting a competitive firm is downward sloping.

___ 4. The demand curve confronting a competitive industry is perfectly price inelastic.

___ 5. The short run supply curve of a competitive firm is the upward-sloping portion of its average variable cost curve.

___ 6. Firms in a competitive industry compete principally by differentiating the goods they produce.

___ 7. Competitive markets tend to be efficient and seem more equitable than solutions yielded by alternative market forms.

___ 8. The results of competitive markets are yardsticks by which all other market structures can be judged.

___ 9. Freedom of entry and exit are unimportant in maintaining the competitive market over time.

___10. In computing economic profits, the opportunity cost of capital must be considered part of long run average total cost.

___11. In competition, all desired entry and exit will have occurred only when profits have returned to normal (zero).

___12. Any industry's response to changes in its demand depends in part on the length of the adjustment period considered.

___13. In a competitive market, the dynamics of entry and exit will drive economic profits to zero in the long run.

___14. Competitive firms in long run equilibria produce where P equals minimum LRATC.

___15. In a competitive market, rational producers employ productive inputs up to the point where the marginal cost of production just equals the price of the good.

___16. In the long run, quantity changes will always be greater and price changes will be smaller for a given change in demand than market or short run periods of production.

___17. Most U.S. industries are characterized by increasing per unit costs of production in the long run period of production.

___18. The domestic petroleum industry is an excellent example of a constant cost industry.

___19. In a constant cost industry, as entry occurs, costs of production are the same for new entrants as for established firms.

___20. The market forces that cause costs to increase in an industry in which most firms reap economic profits also cause decreases in costs when most of the firms incur economic losses.

Standard Multiple Choice

There Is Only One "Best" Answer For Each Question.

___ 1. In the long run for a competitive firm:
   a. P = FC = TC = MC = MR = AC.
   b. P = AR = MR = SRMC = SRATC = LRMC = LRATC.
   c. economic profits are possible for especially effective managers.
   d. pure economic losses may be imposed on inefficient firms.
   e. All of the above.

___ 2. The competitive firm's short run supply curve is:
   a. the amount it produced previously, adjusted for growth.
   b. its marginal cost curve over the entire range of possible prices.
   c. the amount of output that assures zero economic profits.
   d. the upward sloping portion of its average total cost curve.
   e. the positively sloped MC curve above the AVC curve.

___ 3. According to the Austrian school of thought, the major driving force of competition is:
   a. freedom of entry and exit.
   b. many buyers and sellers.
   c. homogenous products.
   d. entrepreneurial innovation.
   e. zero transactions costs.

___ 4. Which of the following markets is most compatible with the requirements for a competitive industry?
   a. Steel.
   b. Comic books.
   c. Sugar-coated cereal.
   d. Stocks and bonds, once issued.
   e. Gasoline.

___ 5. If average costs rise as an industry grows, it is a(n):
   a. economies of scale industry.
   b. diseconomies of scale industry.
   c. increasing cost industry.
   d. decreasing cost industry.
   e. constant cost industry.

___ 6. The most widely accepted description of economic efficiency was first specified by:
   a. Alfred Marshall.
   b. Adam Smith.
   c. Leon Walras.
   d. Louis Pasteur.
   e. Vilfredo Pareto.

___ 7. Modern general equilibrium analysis was founded by:
   a. Leon Walras.
   b. Adam Smith.
   c. Alfred Marshall.
   d. John Maynard Keynes.
   e. Thorstein Veblen.

___ 8. Competition for the resources that generate economic profits may lead to:
   a. increased output prices for complementary goods.
   b. losses of economic efficiency.
   c. higher production costs.
   d. a lack of competition.
   e. price-making behavior.

___ 9. Which of the following does NOT characterize a competitive market?
   a. Substantial barriers to entry and exit.
   b. Many small buyers.
   c. Many small sellers.
   d. A homogeneous product.
   e. An absence of nonprice competition.

___ 10. Rising economic profits in a competitive market do NOT precipitate:
   a. expansions of existing firms.
   b. entry by new firms.
   c. pressures for price hikes.
   d. pressures for increases in the costs of specialized resources.
   e. forces that ultimately will eliminate such profits.

___ 11. If the competitive price is insufficient to cover average total costs, firms should:
   a. definitely shut down as soon as possible.
   b. continue to operate where $P = MC$ if $P > AVC$.
   c. adopt new technologies.
   d. cut back and eliminate their overhead.
   e. operate as long as price covers all fixed costs.

___ 12. The demand curve facing a competitive seller is:
   a. negatively sloped.
   b. horizontal at the market price.
   c. vertical at the market quantity.
   d. $1/n$, where n is the number of firms in the industry.
   e. upward sloping.

___ 13. Economic profits:
   a. cannot exist in the long run in a competitive market structure.
   b. are the same as normal accounting profits.
   c. do not include the opportunity cost of the entrepreneur.
   d. exist whenever total cost exceeds total revenue.
   e. are always present when marginal revenue exceeds marginal cost.

___ 14. The most critical feature of a competitive market over time is that:
   a. firms produce homogenous goods.
   b. there are many buyers of the good at the current price.
   c. all transactors have perfect information and free mobility.
   d. many potential buyers and sellers are free to enter or exit.
   e. All of the above.

___15. Moving towards greater efficiency would require:
   a. expanding output and lowering price if MC > MSB.
   b. lowering both price and output when positive externalities exist.
   c. more efficient firms to enter industries where losses prevail.
   d. lower industry output and higher prices if existing firms experience losses.
   e. All of the above.

Chapter Review (Fill-In Questions)

1. In the short run, all firms maximize profits by maximizing the difference between _____ and _____ or, equivalently, by producing that level of output at which _____ equals _____.

2. If MR > MC, the firm increases _____ if it increases production slightly; if MR < MC, the firm will _____ profits if it reduces output slightly.

3. _____ points occur where P = ATC. No firm will operate if P < AVC, because its revenues will not cover its variable costs. Where P = minimum AVC is known as the _____ point.

4. In the long run, economic profits are eliminated either because _____ rise or _____ fall, while losses have opposite effects.

5. When the level of output or the number of firms in an industry have no influence on costs, the long run industry supply curve is _____ and the industry produces under conditions of _____. If the average cost of output rises as industry output grows, we have a(n) _____ industry. A(n) _____ industry experiences falling costs of production as it grows.

6. Social welfare is maximized if the _____ is deemed proper, and the marginal social benefit (P = MSB) equals the marginal social cost (MC = MSC). In addition to the efficiency and equity of the competitive marketplace, its advocates point to the _____ decision making which minimizes the coercion associated with other forms of decision making.

7. The market may fail, however, because of _____ power, inequity in the distribution of _____, _____, or _____ in the absence of governmental macroeconomic policies.

Unlimited Multiple Choice
Each Question Has From Zero To Four Correct Answers.

___ 1. The demand curve for a competitive firm:
   a. is a horizontal line.
   b. is downward sloping.
   c. is perfectly price elastic.
   d. reflects the firm's inability to influence market price.

___ 2. Marginal revenue:
   a. is the extra revenue generated by additional units of output.
   b. equals a change in total revenue divided by a change in input.
   c. is synonymous with marginal cost for a perfectly competitive firm.
   d. equals price for a purely competitive firm.

___ 3. The short run supply curves of competitive firms are:
   a. horizontal lines.
   b. the portions of the firms' marginal cost curves that lie above their average fixed cost curves.
   c. the full ranges of the firms' marginal cost curves.
   d. summed horizontally to derive the industry supply curve.

___ 4. Competitive firms:
   a. are price makers.
   b. are quantity adjusters, but not price adjusters.
   c. are free to enter or to leave an industry in the long run.
   d. attempt to minimize economic losses by locating the rate of output at which marginal revenue exceeds marginal cost by the greatest amount.

___ 5. Economy-wide economic efficiency requires that:
   a. consumer desires be satisfied at the lowest possible opportunity cost.
   b. the value of output is maximized, given input constraints.
   c. input expenditures or opportunity costs are minimized for each form of output.
   d. when firms produce a given quantity of output, its value relative to the other outputs foregone will be at the lowest possible value.

___ 6. The competitive market system:
   a. allocates inputs and outputs in an optimal manner if the income distribution is judged fair and if there are no externalities.
   b. is unanimously regarded as rather cold-hearted process.
   c. maximizes society's net welfare regardless of the prevailing income distribution.
   d. assuming no externalities, results in the production of output at the point where MSB = MSC.

___ 7. Long run equilibrium for the competitive firm:
   a. occurs where the firm's demand curve is tangent to its long run average total cost curve.
   b. means that the firm reaps only normal accounting profits.
   c. requires revenue to just equal the value of resources used.
   d. occurs where the firm's marginal revenue curve is tangent to the long run average total cost curve.

___ 8. The long run supply curve for a(n):
  a. increasing cost industry is vertical.
  b. constant cost industry is downward sloping.
  c. decreasing cost industry is a horizontal line.
  d. constant cost industry is a vertical line.

___ 9. Efficiency in a competitive economy requires that:
  a. only positive externalities exist in consumption and production.
  b. production or consumption activities have no effects on anyone except through the market prices of goods or productive inputs.
  c. anything that benefits a consumer benefits society by a similar amount.
  d. the prevailing distribution of income is judged fair by society.

___ 10. The competitive industry's supply curve:
  a. has a price elasticity of roughly zero in the market period.
  b. is fairly price inelastic in the long run period of production.
  c. in the long run, graphically represents the relationship that exists between price and the maximum amount of output that an industry is willing to offer after all entry and exit has occurred.
  d. in the short run, is derived by horizontally summing the short run supply curves of the firms comprising the industry.

Problems

Problem 1

This table summarizes revenue and cost data for a profit maximizing competitive firm. Use this information to answer the following questions.

Q_I	Q_O	P_N	P_O	TR	AR	MR	TC	TFC	TVC	ATC	AVC	AFC	MC
0	0	$20	$2					$150					
1	5												
2	15												
3	30												
4	50												
5	75												
6	95												
7	110												
8	120												
9	125												
10	125												

Q_I = Units of Variable Input Q_O = Units of Output P_N = Variable Input Price
P_O = Output Price   TR = Total Revenue   AR = Average Revenue
MR = Marginal Revenue   TC = Total Cost   TFC = Total Fixed Cost
TVC = Total Variable Cost   ATC = Average Total Cost   AFC = Average Fixed Cost
MC = Marginal Cost

a. Complete the table.

b. At what output does the firm maximize profit or minimize losses? _____

c. Use the figure to graph the average revenue, the marginal revenue, the average total cost, the average variable cost, the average fixed cost, and the marginal cost curves. At which rate of output is the firm either maximizing economic profits or minimizing economic losses? _____ Explain _____

_____

_____

_____

_____

Problem 2

This figure contains revenue and cost curves for two different firms producing in the same competitive industry. Use this information to answer the following true/false questions.

a. At output Q_0, Firm I fails to minimize its losses.

b. At output Q_0, Firm II earns only normal profits.

c. Both firms are perfectly competitive in nature.

d. Both firms are operating in the short run.

e. Firm I incurs economic losses equal to area PZab.

f. Firm II earns economic profits equal to area ZPab.

g. Total revenue received by Firm I equals area $0ZaQ_0$.

h. Firm II incurs fixed cost equal to rectangle WZbc.

i. Firm I incurs total variable cost equal to area $0WcQ_0$.

j. Firm I incurs fixed cost equal to area $0VdQ_0$.

k. Firm I faces a demand curve with infinite price elasticity.

l. The demand curve confronting Firm II is perfectly price elastic.

m. Firm I incurs total cost equal to area $0PbQ_0$.

n. Firm II incurs total cost equal to area $0ZbQ_0$.

Problem 3

This figure shows revenue and cost curves for two firms. Use this information to answer the following true/false questions.

Firm A — Price and Cost (vertical axis), Rate of Output (Q) (horizontal axis). Curves: MC, ATC, AVC, AR=MR. Points a, b, c. Price levels P, W, Z. Output Q_e.

Firm B — Price and Cost (vertical axis), Rate of Output (Q) (horizontal axis). Curves: MC, ATC, AR=MR. Point a. Price level P. Output Q_e.

___ a. Firm B is a price taker.

___ b. Firm A is a price maker.

___ c. Both firms are operating in the long run.

___ d. Only short run data are shown for both firms.

___ e. Firm B is earning economic profits.

___ f. Firm A incurs economic losses equal to area WPab.

___ g. At output q_e, firm A maximizes profits, which equal area WPab.

___ h. Firm B is not profit-maximizing.

___ i. Firm A is not producing output efficiently.

___ j. Firm B is not producing output efficiently.

___ k. Firm A will be able to earn long run economic profits.

___ l. Firm A is incurring only variable costs of production.

___ m. Firm B incurs both fixed and variable costs of production.

___ n. Firm A's total revenue equals area $0PaQ_e$.

___ o. Fixed costs for firm A are equal to area $0ZcQ_e$.

___ p. Total fixed costs for firm B are equal to area $0PaQ_e$.

Problem 4

This figure depicts the market supply and demand curves for a given commodity. Assume the market is competitive and generates no externalities, and that society is indifferent about questions of income distribution. Use this information to answer the following true/false questions.

_____ a. The demand curve is a marginal social benefits curve.

_____ b. The supply curve is not related to the marginal social costs incurred in producing this product.

_____ c. Economic efficiency occurs at point b.

_____ d. Total social benefits equal social costs at point a.

_____ e. The dollar value that society places on the Q_0th unit of the good is greater than its opportunity cost.

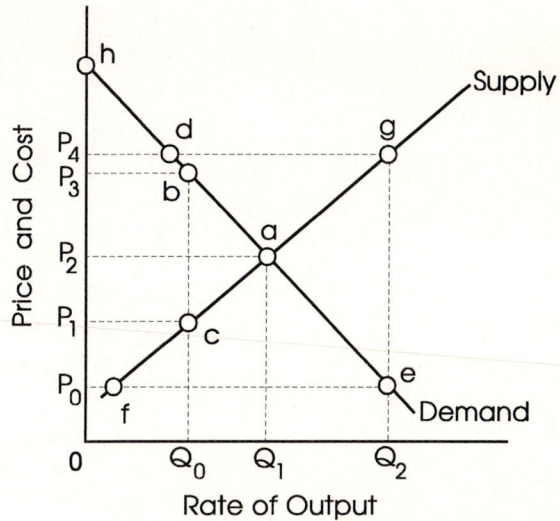

_____ f. The net welfare of the consumers who purchase the good is maximized at point a.

_____ g. The dollar value that society places on the Q_2th unit is greater than its opportunity cost of production.

_____ h. The dollar value that society ascribes to the Q_1th unit is equal to its opportunity cost of production.

_____ i. The marginal social cost of producing the Q_2th unit is equal to the marginal private cost of producing it.

_____ j. The dollar value that society places upon the first Q_1 units of the good is equal to area $OhaQ_1$.

_____ k. The optimal rate of output from society's point of view exceeds Q_0.

_____ l. The optimal rate of output from society's point of view is less than Q_2.

Problem 5

This figure shows two equilibrium situations that confront the same competitive firm. Use this information to answer the following True/False questions.

a. Graph I depicts a short run equilibrium for the firm.

b. Graph II depicts the long run equilibrium situation for the firm.

c. The firm earns economic profits at output Q_0 in Graph I.

d. Costs have remained the same, despite the expansion of the industry, depicted in Graph II.

e. Free entry has caused the price in Graph II to be considerably lower than the price that the firm charged in Graph I.

f. Graph II illustrates a situation where the firm must still worry about the potential threat of further entry by new firms.

g. Graph II shows that the firm is incurring both fixed and variable costs.

h. Graph II suggests that price adjustment was achieved through an increase in the industry's supply curve.

i. Graph I shows that the firm confronts diminishing marginal returns to the variable input.

j. In the long run situation depicted in Graph II all but one factor of production is variable.

Problem 6

This figure includes total cost and total revenue curves for a firm. After studying the figure answer the following questions.

a. What type of market does this show?

_____

Why? _____

_____

b. Is this a short run or long run analysis?

_____

Why? _____

_____

c. What is the firm's fixed cost in this problem?

_____

d. What is the price of the good in this problem?

_____

e. What are this firm's break-even levels of output? _____

f. What is the approximate profit maximizing level of output and what is the level of profit?

_____

Problem 7

In the graph on the left side, illustrate a competitive firm with economic profits. In the graph on the right side, illustrate a competitive market. Use the subscript 0 to label all of the initial positions. Graphically illustrate how competitive processes erode economic profits. Use the subscript 1 to label all the new equilibrium positions.

ANSWERS

Matching		True/False		Multiple Choice		Unlimited Multiple Choice	
Set I	Set II						
1. f	1. h	1. F	11. T	1. b	9. a	1.	acd
2. i	2. g	2. T	12. T	2. e	10. c	2.	ad
3. d	3. a	3. F	13. T	3. d	11. b	3.	d
4. j	4. d	4. F	14. T	4. d	12. b	4.	bc
5. b	5. j	5. F	15. T	5. c	13. a	5.	abc
6. h	6. b	6. F	16. T	6. e	14. d	6.	ad
7. a	7. e	7. T	17. T	7. a	15. d	7.	abcd
8. e	8. i	8. T	18. F	8. c		8.	none
9. g	9. f	9. F	19. T			9.	bc
10. c	10. c	10. T	20. T			10.	acd

Chapter Review (Fill-In Questions)

1. total revenue; total costs; marginal revenue; marginal costs
2. profits; increase
3. Break-even; shut down
4. costs; prices
5. horizontal; constant cost; increasing cost; decreasing cost
6. income distribution; decentralized
7. monopoly; income; externalities; instability

Problem 1

Q_I	Q_O	P_N	P_O	TR	AR	MR	TC	TFC	TVC	ATC	AVC	AFC	MC
0	0	$20	$2	$0	$2	$2	$150	$150	$0	---	---	---	---
1	5	20	2	10	2	2	170	150	20	$34.00	$4.00	$30.00	$4.00
2	15	20	2	30	2	2	190	150	40	12.67	2.67	10.00	2.00
3	30	20	2	60	2	2	210	150	60	7.00	2.00	5.00	1.33
4	50	20	2	100	2	2	230	150	80	4.60	1.60	3.00	1.00
5	75	20	2	150	2	2	250	150	100	3.33	1.33	2.00	0.80
6	95	20	2	190	2	2	270	150	120	2.84	1.26	1.58	1.00
7	110	20	2	220	2	2	290	150	140	2.64	1.27	1.36	1.33
8	120	20	2	240	2	2	310	150	160	2.58	1.33	1.25	2.00
9	125	20	2	250	2	2	330	150	180	2.64	1.44	1.20	4.00
10	125	20	2	250	2	2	350	150	200	2.80	1.60	1.20	∞

a. See Table.
b. 120 units.
c. See figure; 120 units; at that output MR = MC.

Problem 2	Problem 3	Problem 4	Problem 5
a. F	a. T	a. T	a. T
b. F	b. F	b. F	b. T
c. T	c. F	c. F	c. T
d. T	d. F	d. F	d. T
e. T	e. F	e. T	e. T
f. T	f. F	f. T	f. F
g. F	g. T	g. F	g. F
h. T	h. F	h. T	h. T
i. T	i. F	i. T	i. T
j. T	j. F	j. T	j. F
k. T	k. F	k. T	
l. T	l. F	l. T	
m. F	m. F		
n. T	n. T		
	o. F		
	p. F		

Problem 6

a. This is a perfectly competitive market because price is constant to the firm (total revenue is a straight line).
b. This is a short run analysis because there are fixed costs (when output = 0, total costs = $20).
c. $20 (when Q = 0, TC = $20).
d. $4 (when Q = 5, TR = $20, thus P = TR/Q = $20/5 = $4).
e. 7, 15 (break-even occurs where TR = TC).
f. The profit maximizing quantity is approximately 11. Total revenue minus total cost = profit; $45 - $35 = $10.

Problem 7

See figure. The firm initially earns economic profits with output Q_0. Since entry is unrestricted in competitive markets, other firms desire to earn a share of the industry's economic profits causing industry supply to increase to S_1. As entry and increased supplies drive price to P_1, economic profits are eliminated.

Single Firm

Price and Costs ($)

MC

LRAC

P_0

P_1

0 Q_1 Q_0 Q

Quantity (Q)

Industry

Price and Costs ($)

S_0

S_1

P_0

P_1

D_0

0 Q_0 Q_1 Q

Quantity (Q)

Chapter 25
Monopoly

Chapter Objectives

After you have read and studied this chapter, you should be able to write a brief paragraph describing the pricing and output decisions faced by firms with some degree of monopoly power; list some barriers to entry that may permit the monopolist to realize long-run economic profits; explain the effects of price discrimination and describe why inefficiency and inequity may be problems if monopoly power is widespread.

Chapter Review: Key Points

1. An unregulated *monopoly* controls the output and price of a good for which there are no close substitutes.

2. Few monopolies are unregulated, but all firms with any ability to control prices have *market power*. Models of pure monopoly provide insights into the behavior of the many firms with this power.

3. *Barriers to entry* help firms maintain market power. *Regulatory barriers* are established by government policies, and include such things as patents or licenses. *Strategic barriers* include excessive model changes or advertising. *Natural barriers* result from extreme economies of scale, where average costs decline over a large range of output relative to market demand. A *natural monopoly* occurs if one firm can achieve the minimum efficient scale (*MES*) only when producing for the entire market.

4. A nondiscriminating monopolist's *marginal revenue* is less than its price. Marginal revenue equals the price the monopolist receives from the sale of the additional unit minus the revenue lost because prices must be reduced on all other units sold. Market power causes the marginal revenue curve to lie below the demand curve.

5. The demand for a good is elastic when output is below the quantity where marginal revenue is zero. Demand is unitarily elastic when marginal revenue is zero. Demand is inelastic for outputs above the point where marginal revenue is zero.

6. A monopolist maximizes profit (or minimizes loss) by selling that output where marginal revenue equals marginal cost. The price charged corresponds to the maximum price from the demand curve at this $MR = MC$ output level.

7. Monopolists' profit-maximizing (or loss-minimizing) levels of output do not normally occur at the minimum points on average total cost curves. Equilibrium output levels can be less or more than that which minimizes average total cost.

8. If a monopolist is able to maintain its monopoly position in the long run, then pricing, output, and economic profit will reflect variations in demand. A monopolist may also choose inefficient, but comfortable, policies, a problem known as *X-inefficiency*.

9. *Price discrimination* entails sales of essentially the same good at different prices when these differences are not justified by variations in costs. Price discrimination occurs in airline fares, theater ticket prices, charges for medical and dental services, and in many other areas.

10. Effective price discrimination requires a firm to have some market power and the ability to separate customers into groups with different price elasticities of demand. It must also prevent *arbitrage*--the selling of the good to high-price customers by low-price customers.

11. Price discrimination boosts a firm's total profit. *Perfect* price discrimination allows a firm to reap as profit all the consumer surplus that could be derived from the product.

12. A nondiscriminating monopoly is less allocatively efficient from society's point of view than are competitive industries. A monopolist typically produces less than if the industry were purely competitive, and sells at a higher price. Price discrimination may reduce this inefficiency but it intensifies issues of inequity in the distribution of income.

Matching Key Terms And Concepts

____ 1.   Price discrimination

____ 2.   Natural monopoly

____ 3.   Licensing

____ 4.   Total revenue maximization

____ 5.   Marginal revenue

____ 6.   P > MC, so MSB > MSC

____ 7.   Consumer surplus

____ 8.   Arbitrage

____ 9.   High fixed costs, low variable costs

____ 10. Necessary for monopolization

a.   Risklessly buying low in one market, selling high in another.
b.   Typical of a natural barrier to entry.
c.   Charging different prices not justified by cost differences.
d.   A lack of close substitutes for the firm's output.
e.   MR = 0; price elasticity = 1.
f.   Less than price for a non-discriminating monopolist.
g.   Proof that non-discriminating monopoly is inefficient.
h.   When economies of scale for a single firm persist across the full range of market demand.
i.   An example of a legal barrier to entry.
j.   Eliminated by perfect price discrimination.

True/False Questions

___ 1. Profit-maximizing monopolists produce and sell extra output if MR > MC.

___ 2. Profit maximizing monopolists will continue to produce in the long run even if they incur economic losses.

___ 3. Monopolists equate the marginal social cost of production with the marginal social benefits to consumers.

___ 4. Natural monopolies are usually government regulated.

___ 5. All price discrimination is illegal.

___ 6. Barriers to entry ensure profits to all monopolists.

___ 7. Restrictions on entry ensure monopolization.

___ 8. Natural barriers to entry are government sanctioned.

___ 9. In long run equilibrium, the profit maximizing monopolist produces output where marginal revenue is maximized.

___10. Monopolists invariably earn supernormal profits in the long run.

Standard Multiple Choice

There Is A Single "Best" Answer To Each Question.

___ 1. Unlike a perfectly competitive firm, a monopolist:
   a. can select a price and sell as much as it desires.
   b. equates marginal revenue and marginal cost to maximize profits.
   c. can produce any desired amount and charge as much as it desires.
   d. can choose a profit maximizing price and output combination from the market demand curve.
   e. faces a perfectly elastic demand curve.

___ 2. A monopoly with huge fixed costs but no variable costs will maximize profits where:
   a. the price elasticity of demand equals zero.
   b. marginal revenue is maximized.
   c. MR = MC = 0.
   d. average revenue is maximized.
   e. total costs are minimized.

___ 3. A monopolist can sell 10 units for $10 each, but selling 11 units forces a reduction in price to $9.95. Marginal revenue for the eleventh unit is:
   a. $10.00.
   b. $9.95.
   c. $9.45.
   d. $9.40.
   e. $109.95

4. Patents are examples of:
   a. legal economies of substitution.
   b. legal barriers to entry.
   c. natural barriers to entry.
   d. natural economies of complementarity.
   e. illegal marginal diseconomies.

5. An example of a natural monopoly is:
   a. OPEC, the international oil cartel.
   b. United States Steel Corporation.
   c. General Electric.
   d. the New York Times.
   e. your local telephone company.

6. The economist who first specified the MR = MC rule for profit maximization was:
   a. Adam Smith.
   b. A. A. Cournot.
   c. Leon Walras.
   d. Alfred Marshall.
   e. Karl Marx.

7. Price discrimination means:
   a. charging different prices for identical goods.
   b. paying wages according to race or sex rather than productivity.
   c. exploiting the working masses by charging the highest single price possible.
   d. eliminating all costs so that only pure profits are realized.
   e. All of the above.

8. Compared to the outcome of a perfectly competitive market, a nondiscriminating monopolist tends to:
   a. produce less and charge more.
   b. maximize total profits wherever possible.
   c. set price in the inelastic range of the demand curve.
   d. confront a demand curve where P = MR.
   e. produce more and charge more.

9. Most markets in the American economy are:
   a. perfectly competitive.
   b. primarily unregulated monopolies.
   c. mixtures of monopolistic and competitive elements.
   d. regulated monopolies.
   e. governed by the decisions of union leaders.

10. A nondiscriminating monopolist chooses an economically inefficient level of output because:
   a. the difference between MR and MC is maximized.
   b. P > ATC, so MSB > MSC when MR = MC.
   c. all consumer surplus is appropriated.
   d. P > MR = MC, so MSB > MSC when MR = MC.
   e. too much is charged for too much production.

Chapter Review (Fill-In Questions)

1. A firm has a _____ in a market if it controls production of a product for which there are no _____.

2. The profit maximizing output occurs where _____, which is always in the _____ range of demand as long as marginal costs are positive.

3. Firms with monopoly power are not certain to be profitable, because _____ may be too high relative to _____.

4. A _____ occurs when demand is sufficiently small relative to _____ so that only one firm can best serve the market.

5. An unregulated monopolist may increase its profits through _____, which means that different prices are charged for identical goods and there are no differences in production costs. Successful price discrimination requires that the market must be _____ into at least two groups, and the group charged the lower price must be prevented from selling to the group charged the higher price, a practice known as _____. Perfect price discrimination occurs when the full value of the _____ is appropriated by a seller.

6. Competitive markets meet the condition that _____, which is necessary for economic efficiency. Nondiscriminating monopolists do not because _____ in equilibrium, which means that the marginal social _____ of a monopolized good exceeds its marginal social _____.

7. Price discrimination may enhance economic efficiency because the price charged for the _____ unit of the good will equal _____.

Unlimited Multiple Choice

Each Question Has From Zero To Four Correct Answers.

___ 1. A monopoly:
   a. may reap economic profits in the long run.
   b. may incur economic losses in the long run.
   c. produces a rate of output at which marginal social benefits exceed marginal social costs, assuming no price discrimination.
   d. may be able to produce output at lower average costs than would its perfectly competitive counterpart.

___ 2. Perfect price discrimination:
   a. involves charging all customers the same prices for units of output.
   b. results in the seller appropriating all consumer surplus.
   c. involves charging different prices that may not reflect different costs of production.
   d. cannot actually be practiced because the information that firms need to determine all the prices willingly paid by each customer is too costly to acquire.

___ 3. Demand curves facing nondiscriminating monopolists:
   a. are identical to the demand curves for their industries.
   b. are downward sloping..
   c. are also their average revenue curves.
   d. fall more slowly than do their marginal revenue curves.

___ 4. If the same cost conditions confront both a non-discriminating monopoly and firms in a perfectly competitive industry:
   a. the monopoly will produce less output than the total of all firms in the competitive industry.
   b. both types of firms may be able to reap economic profits in the short run.
   c. both types of firms will charge prices equal to marginal revenue.
   d. both types of firms will produce where marginal revenue equals marginal cost.

___ 5. Barriers to entry:
   a. are unimportant in preventing entry into an industry.
   b. may make it extremely difficult for new firms to enter an industry.
   c. aid existing firms in realizing economic profits.
   d. may be natural, illegal, or even created by law.

Problems

Problem 1

Use the information in this table, which lists the demand schedule that confronts a particular monopolist, to answer the following questions.

a. Complete the table.

b. Graph the monopolist's demand and marginal revenue curves in the figure. Once the figure is complete, break the demand schedule into three ranges of price elasticity.

c. What is the relationship between MR and the three ranges of elasticity you noted? _____
_____

Price	Units of Output	Total Revenue	Average Revenue	Marginal Revenue
20	0			
18	2			
16	4			
14	6			
12	8			
10	10			
8	12			
6	14			
4	16			
2	18			
0	20			

d. Compare the monopolist's marginal revenue curve with that of a competitive firm. What causes the differences in their slopes?
_____
_____
_____

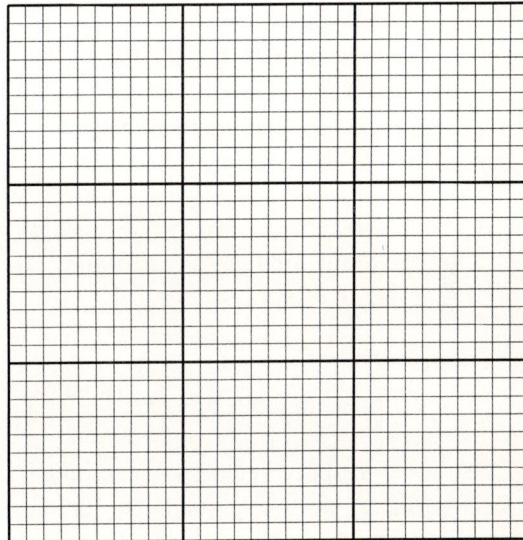

Problem 2

Use the information in this figure, about the revenues and costs for two different monopolists, to answer the following true/false questions.

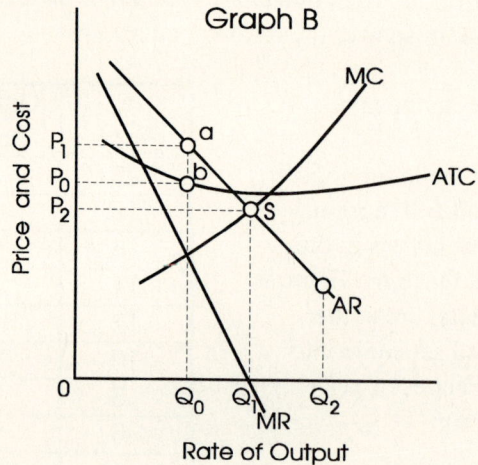

a. Graph A depicts a monopoly that has made all profit maximizing, long run adjustments.

___ b. Graph B shows a monopoly producing in the short run.

___ c. In Graph A, point S lies in the inelastic range of the monopolist's demand curve.

___ d. In Graph B, point a lies in the elastic range of the monopolist's demand curve.

___ e. In Graph B, total revenue is maximized at point S.

___ f. The monopoly in Graph A maximizes profit by producing Q_0 units of output per time period.

___ g. In Graph A, the profit maximizing price is P_0.

___ h. The monopoly in Graph B can maximize its total sales revenue by producing Q_1 units of output, and selling each unit at a price of P_2.

___ i. The monopoly in Graph A can earn maximum profits equal to WP_1ab.

___ j. In Graph B, MR is negative and demand is inelastic at Q_2.

___ k. In Graph B, point S lies in the elastic range of the demand curve.

___ l. In Graph A, the monopolist can maximize total sales (revenues) by producing Q_0 units of output.

___ m. Total fixed costs for the monopolist in Graph A equal area $OWbQ_0$.

___ n. If the monopolist in Graph B attempts to maximize sales revenues it suffers economic losses.

Problem 3

Pictured in Figure 3 are the revenue and cost curves of two different firms. Use this information to answer the following questions.

Firm A

Firm B

_____ a. Firm A has monopoly power.

_____ b. Firm B is a price maker.

_____ c. Firm A is a price taker.

_____ d. Firm B perceives the price of their product as a given.

_____ e. Firm A is operating in the short run period of production.

_____ f. Firm B is operating in the long run period of production.

_____ g. At output Q_0, firm A is profit maximizing.

_____ h. At output q_1, firm B maximizes its potential total revenues.

_____ i. Firm B is a competitive firm.

_____ j. If firm B produces output q_2 it would suffer an economic loss.

_____ k. Total fixed costs for firm B equal area $0P_3cq_1$.

_____ l. Firm B can earn economic profits of up to P_2P_1ab.

_____ m. Output q_1 for firm B represents a point in the inelastic range of the demand curve.

_____ n. To earn economic profits, firm A should produce less than Q_0.

Problem 4

The demand schedules (Q_D) in this table are for two separate markets faced by a monopolist. Assume that ATC = MC = a constant \$4 per unit. Use this information to complete the table and answer the following questions.

Price	Entire Market			Market A			Market B		
	Q_D	TR	MR	Q_D	TR	MR	Q_D	TR	MR
10				10			0		
9				20			2		
8				30			4		
7				40			8		
6				50			16		
5				60			32		
4				70			64		
3				80			100		
2				90			200		
1				100			400		
0				110			1,000		

a. Assume that arbitrage initially prevents price discrimination. Graph the total market demand, marginal revenue and marginal cost curves facing this nondiscriminating monopolist.

b. What will be the profit maximizing output, price, and total profit based on the assumptions in question a? _____

 _____

 _____

c. Now assume the monopolist gains the ability to prevent arbitrage, segments the market, and implements a price discrimination policy. Graph the demand, marginal revenue and marginal cost curves faced by the monopolist in markets A and B in the figures below

d. What will be the profit maximizing output, price, and total profit in each market based on the assumption in question c? _____

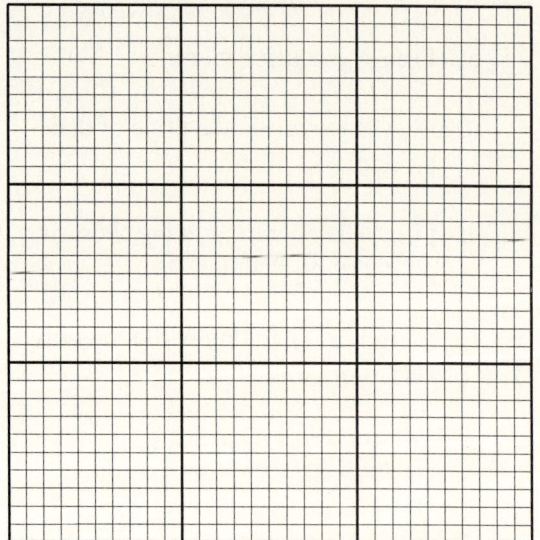

e. How much more profit is realized through price discrimination?_____

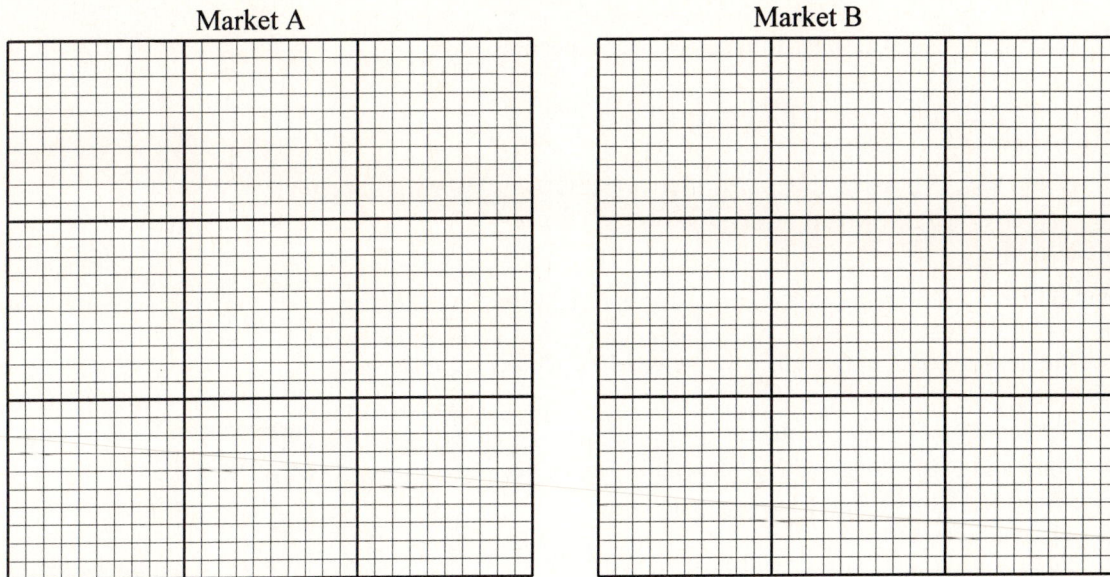

Market A

Market B

Problem 5

The cost and revenue structures for a particular firm are shown in this table.

Q	TVC	TC	ATC	MC	P	TR	MR
0	0	150			200	0	
1	110			110	175		
2		320				300	
3		366			135		
4	250					480	
5		445			105		
6	360				90		

a. Complete the cost and revenue structure in the table.

b. What are the fixed costs of this firm? _____

c. What is the profit maximizing position for this firm? P = _____, Q = _____.

d. Is this a long run equilibrium for an industry with free entry and exit? _____ Why or why not? _____.

e. Is the demand for the firm's product elastic or inelastic over the range of prices described above? _____

f. What is the profit or loss at the equilibrium position? _____

g. Is this firm producing at lowest possible ATC? _____

h. Is this firm in a perfectly competitive market? _____ Why or why not? _____

Problem 6

Use the demand data in this table to answer the following questions.

a. Use the figures to create three separate graphs (A, B, C) illustrating the change in total revenue as price decreases from $7 to $5, $5 to $3, and $3 to $1.

P	Q
7	2
5	6
3	10
1	14

b. What is happening to total revenue as price falls in Graph A? _____ Graph B? _____ Graph C? _____

c. What is the price elasticity of demand in Graph A? _____ In Graph B? _____ In Graph C? _____

Graph A

Graph B

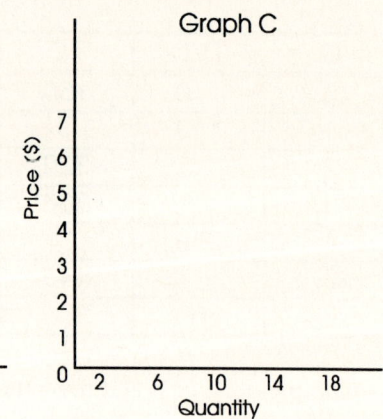
Graph C

Answers

Matching	True/False	Multiple	Unlimited	Chapter Review (Fill-in Questions)
1. c	1. T	1. d	1. acd	1. monopoly; close substitutes
2. h	2. F	2. c	2. bcd	2. MR = MC; elastic
3. i	3. F	3. c	3. abcd	3. production costs; demand
4. e	4. T	4. b	4. abd	4. natural monopoly; economies of scale
5. f	5. F	5. e	5. bcd	5. price discrimination; separable; arbitrage; consumer surplus
6. g	6. F	6. b		6. P = MC; P > MC; benefit; cost
7. j	7. F	7. a		7. last; marginal cost
8. a	8. F	8. a		
9. b	9. F	9. c		
10. d	10. F	10. d		

Problem 1

a. See table.

b. See figure.

c. If MR > 0, ep > 1; if MR = 0, ep = 1; if MR < 0, ep < 1.

d. The monopolist's marginal revenue curve is downward sloping and twice the slope of the respective demand curve, while the competitive firm faces a perfectly elastic (horizontal) demand curve which is also its marginal revenue curve. The difference between the marginal revenue curves of the monopolist and the competitive firm is due to the difference in slope of the demand curve faced by each.

Price	Units of Output	Total Revenue	Average Revenue	Marginal Revenue
20	0	0	xxx	xxx
18	2	36	18	18
16	4	64	16	14
14	6	84	14	10
12	8	96	12	6
10	10	100	10	2
8	12	96	8	-2
6	14	84	6	-6
4	16	64	4	-10
2	18	36	2	-14
0	20	0	0	-18

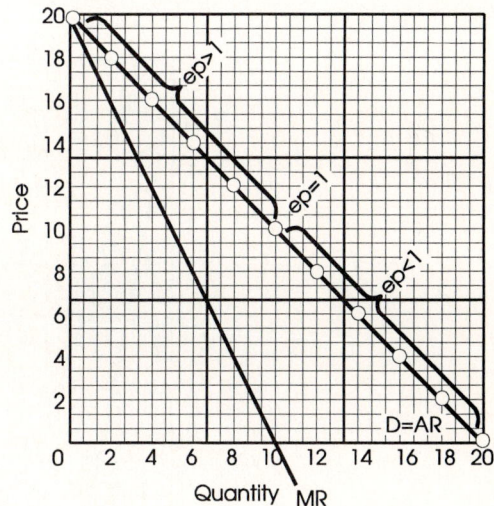

Problem 2

a. F	h. T
b. F	i. T
c. F	j. T
d. T	k. F
e. T	l. F
f. T	m. F
g. F	n. T

Problem 3

a. T	h. F
b. F	i. T
c. F	j. F
d. T	k. F
e. T	l. T
f. F	m. F
g. F	n. T

Problem 4

Price	Entire Market			Market A			Market B		
	Q_D	TR	MR	Q_D	TR	MR	Q_D	TR	MR
10	10	100	10	10	100	10	0	0	0
9	22	198	8.16	20	180	8	2	18	9
8	34	272	6.17	30	240	6	4	32	7
7	48	336	4.57	40	280	4	8	56	6
6	66	396	3.33	50	300	2	16	96	5
5	92	460	2.46	60	300	0	32	160	4
4	134	536	1.81	70	280	-2	64	256	3
3	180	540	.09	80	240	-4	100	300	1.22
2	290	580	.36	90	180	-6	200	400	1
1	500	500	-.38	100	100	-8	400	400	0
0	1,110	0	-.82	110	0	-10	1,000	0	-.67

a. See figure (Entire Market).

b. Q=48, P=$7, profit = TR - TC = $336 - (48 x 4) = 336 - 192 = $144.

c. See figures (Market A & B)

d. Market A: P_A = 7; Q_A = 40; profit = TR_A - TC_A = 280 - 160 = $120.
   Market B: P_B = 5; Q_B = 32; profit = TR_B - TC_B = 160 - 128 = $32.

e. Total profit for a discriminating monopolist = 120 + 32 = $152; for nondiscriminating monopolist = $144; difference = $8.

Entire Market

Market A

Market B

Problem 5

Q	TVC	TC	ATC	MC	P	TR	MR
0	0	150	xxx	0	200	0	xxx
1	110	260	260	110	175	175	175
2	170	320	160	60	150	300	125
3	216	366	122	46	135	405	105
4	250	400	100	34	120	480	75
5	295	445	89	45	105	525	45
6	360	510	85	65	90	540	15

a. See table.
b. $150
c. P = 105, Q = 5
d. No, there are economic profits.
e. elastic (MR > 0)
f. $80 (TR = $525, TC = $445, $525 - $445 = $80)
g. No (A firm with monopoly power will not necessarily produce at lowest possible ATC)
h. No, because the firm faces a downward sloping demand curve.

Problem 6

a. See figure.
b. increasing; constant; decreasing
c. Ep = 3; Ep = 1; Ep = .33

Chapter 26
Imperfect Competition, and Strategic Behavior

Chapter Objectives

After you have read and studied this chapter, you should be able to describe the salient features of monopolistically competitive markets in the short and long run; discuss the features of the kinked demand and cartel models; explain how product differentiation and interdependencies among firms may influence the prices charged and the amounts produced; discuss the long-term prospects for cartels such as OPEC; define and explain the term "strategic behavior"; describe the assumptions, objectives, and different types of game theory; explain how the ability of firms to cooperate with each other will alter the equilibrium price and output from those firms which cannot cooperate with each other; explain the concept of contestable markets; and describe and give an example of both predatory pricing and limit pricing.

Chapter Review: Key Points

1. *Monopolistic competition* occurs when entry into an industry is easy and there are large numbers of suppliers of slightly differentiated products. Demands for a perfect competitor's products are perfectly elastic, but the demands facing monopolistic competitors are negatively-sloped but still highly elastic.

2. *Product differentiation* refers to differences that consumers perceive between close substitutes, which can be real or imagined. They are created by such things as advertising and promotion and/or by differences in the actual goods. Product differentiation is intended to expand the demand for a firm's output and make demand less elastic.

3. Monopolistically competitive firms produce and sell levels of output that equate marginal revenue and marginal cost. The price is then determined by demand. This is similar to pure monopoly, but the level of short run profits derived from market power is generally lower, given that numerous other firms sell close substitutes.

4. Entry is relatively easy in monopolistic competition, so profits fall to normal levels (zero economic profits) in the long run. However, equilibrium output will be less and prices will be higher under monopolistic competition than in perfectly competitive markets.

5. An *oligopoly* is an industry comprised of a few sellers who recognize their mutual interdependence.

6. Economies of scale are among the causes of oligopolies. Some goods require substantial plant and equipment so that efficient production requires servicing a considerable portion of total industry demand. Mergers also facilitate the creation of oligopolies by joining competitors into single firms. Finally, oligopolies may exist because of other types of entry barriers that deter new firms from entering the industry.

7. There are numerous oligopoly models, but they break down into two major categories: *collusive* and *noncollusive*. The noncollusive *kinked demand curve model* assumes that if one firm raises its prices, other firms will ignore the increase, while other firms in the industry will match any price cuts. The result is a demand curve for the firm that is kinked at the current equilibrium price. This irregularity leads to a discontinuity (gap) in the marginal revenue curve. Consequently, changes in costs may not lead to changes in prices. This theory forecasts "sticky" prices in oligopolistic industries, but price stickiness is not confirmed empirically. Kinked demand curve models also fail to explain how the original equilibrium price is established, how prices change, or how entry by new rivals is deterred.

8. A *cartel* is an organization established to facilitate collusion by firms in an industry. It sets price and output ceilings for all its members. Cartels must be concentrated in the hands of a few firms that control significant proportions of an industry's output. The product needs to be reasonably homogeneous, since agreements regarding heterogeneous products would be complex and difficult to enforce.

9. Cartels try to *maximize joint profits* and then allocate territories or industry output quotas. The stability of any cartel is threatened by the profitability associated with undetected price cuts, or "cheating".

10. Industry output will be less and prices will be higher under oligopoly than in perfect or monopolistic competition. .

11. *Strategic behavior* entails ascertaining what other people are likely to do in a specific situation, and then following tactics that maximize your gain or minimize any harm to you.

12. *Game theory* is the study of strategic interactions among interdependent decision makers, including those in oligopoly markets. Pay-off matrices are constructed to examine how transactors minimize their losses or maximize their gains, given the most likely decisions of other players in a game.

13. In a *prisoner's dilemma*, the dominant strategy of each party results in inefficiency. Cooperation would allow both to gain, but lack of cooperation is the dominant strategy.

14. *Dynamic games* involve sequences of choices over time and result in a wide array of possible strategies. A *grim strategy* entails cooperating until your opponent fails to do so, and then clobbering the opponent in every subsequent round. A *tit-for-tat* strategy responds in kind to whatever your opponent did in the previous round.

15. *Predatory behavior* involves activity by firms to drive rivals from the market or to deter entry. Once rivals disappear, predators can set prices consistent with their market power. A problem with this model is that reentry would normally occur when the high price is resumed, unless the predator firm has significant cost advantages so that potential rivals expect reentry to prompt lower prices once again.

16. *Limit pricing* is a strategy intended to inhibit market entry. Limit pricing techniques include low prices that make it unprofitable for new entrants, or to signal that the market is insufficient for a new entrant. Low prices also convey the message that the incumbent firm is a low cost (efficient) firm.

17. Economists have recently begun examining the role that sunk costs as precommitments to capacity have on deterring entry into markets. Game theory has opened up many avenues for future research and has changed our views on the relationship between strategic behavior and industrial structure.

Matching Key Terms And Concepts

Set I

___ 1.	Kinked demand curves	**a.**	Consequence of kinked demand curves.
___ 2.	Oligopoly	**b.**	Conspiratorial price and output setting; usually illegal.
___ 3.	Monopolistic competition	**c.**	A market with only a few, large, interdependent firms.
___ 4.	Product differentiation	**d.**	Example of a successful cartel.
___ 5.	Cartels	**e.**	Attempts to joint-profit maximize.
___ 6.	Incentives to cheat	**f.**	Why cartels tend to be unstable.
___ 7.	Collusion	**g.**	Raise prices, competitors do nothing; lower prices, competitors follow.
___ 8.	OPEC	**h.**	Exists when firms consider their rivals' reactions when making business decisions.
___ 9.	Mutual interdependence	**i.**	Many firms, heterogeneous products.
___10.	Sticky prices	**j.**	Attempts to increase demand and make it less price elastic.

Set II

___ 1.	Game Theory
___ 2.	Dominant Strategy
___ 3.	Nash equilibrium
___ 4.	Grim strategy
___ 5.	Tit for Tat
___ 6.	Contestable Market Theory
___ 7.	Predatory Behavior
___ 8.	Limit Pricing
___ 9.	Sunk cost
___10.	Accommodation

a. Entails refusal to commit to a position until the other player commits to a position.

b. Occurs when firms that possess a relatively large degree of monopoly power set a profitable price that is low enough to discourage new entrants into the market.

c. A player's best response to any strategy that other players might pick.

d. A strategy that begins cooperatively. Thereafter, in any period, this strategy entails echoing what the opponent did in the previous period.

e. Use of an irreversible capital outlay to signal potential rivals to stay away.

f. A strategy combination where no player has a net incentive to change unless other players change.

g. A study of strategic interactions among interdependent decision makers product.

h. Occurs when a firm attempts to drive rivals from the industry and deter entry. After rivals exit, the remaining firm presumably will raise its prices to levels consistent with its market power.

i. Suggests that easy market entry can force even firms that are the sole current sellers of goods to produce the same output levels and set the same prices as would firms in perfect competition.

j. Firms do not fight or attempt to prohibit the entry of new firms in the market; it depends on the estimated payoff of non-opposition.

True/False Questions

___ 1. The costs of product differentiation account for the cost structures of monopolistically competitive firms being higher than for competitive firms.

___ 2. Decision-making by firms in oligopolistic industries depends heavily on the expected reactions of other firms to any changes in prices or outputs.

___ 3. Monopolistically competitive or oligopolistic industries tend to produce lower rates of output and to charge higher prices than purely competitive industries.

___ 4. When economies of scale are such that only a firm of considerable size, relative to the market, is able to produce output efficiently, the market naturally gravitates toward the competitive mold.

___ 5. A monopolistically competitive industry is made up of firms that behave in a consciously interdependent manner.

___ 6. Desires for increased monopoly power probably have been behind the creation of most oligopolies.

___ 7. Cartels tend to be unstable.

___ 8. In a market system, the absence of overt or tacit collusion among firms leads to rivalrous behavior that businesses regard as competition.

___ 9. Cooperative games permit players to make binding agreements, but they cannot form coalitions.

___10. A profit-payoff matrix shows the various equilibria that can result from different strategies adopted by different players.

___11. In the prisoners' dilemma, an individual who sticks to a grim strategy remain silent until the other prisoner confesses, but then he will confess in each subsequent round.

___12. In a tit for tat strategy, the game begins violently; however, it will end with a win-win result.

Standard Multiple Choice

There Is A Single Best Answer For Each Question

___ 1. Monopolistically and perfectly competitive markets have in common:
  a. differentiated products.
  b. many potential buyers and sellers.
  c. that horizontal demand curves face each firm.
  d. homogeneous products.
  e. conscious interdependence in decision-making.

___ 2. Informative advertising:
  a. reduces transactions cost, and hence, is efficient.
  b. decreases supplies because of its cost.
  c. decreases demands for resource inputs.
  d. is less desirable than persuasive advertising.
  e. All of the above.

___ 3. Sticky prices in oligopoly markets are:
  a. predicted by the kinked demand curve model.
  b. confirmed by the evidence.
  c. more common than in other market structures.
  d. explained by limit-pricing models.
  e. All of the above.

___ 4. When monopolistic competition is compared with perfect competition, the monopolistically competitive industry produces:
  a. a smaller variety of products but at a lower per unit cost.
  b. a greater variety of products but at a higher per unit cost.
  c. a greater variety of products but at a lower per unit cost.
  d. a smaller variety of products but at a lower per unit cost.
  e. the same level of output but at a higher per unit cost.

___ 5. If your competitors will follow any of your price cuts, but will ignore any price hikes, your firm:
  a. faces cutthroat competition.
  b. faces a kinked demand curve.
  c. is the price leader of an oligopoly.
  d. must be the most efficient firm in the industry.
  e. must be one of the industry's marginal firms.

___ 6. A member of a cartel would be most likely to increase its profits by:
   a. undercutting the prices of other cartel members, as long as it did not get caught.
   b. setting its price above that of other cartel members.
   c. pursuing an aggressive nonprice promotions policy.
   d. restricting its output below the cartel-set production quota in order to drive the price up.
   e. insisting that the cartel continually raise the price it charges.

___ 7. Defenders of the efficiency of monopolistic competition insist that:
   a. consumers benefit greatly from product differentiation.
   b. the inefficiency of perfect competition exceeds that of pure monopoly.
   c. perfect competition leads to unstable cutthroat competition.
   d. diseconomies of scale are so substantial that differentiation is inevitable.
   e. All of the above.

___ 8. When studying game theory, it is best used to gain an insight into the operation or behavior of:
   a. monopolies.
   b. perfect competitors.
   c. monopolistic competitors.
   d. oligopolies.
   e. producer cooperatives.

___ 9. Basically, the theory of contestable markets suggest that:
   a. in a capitalist system, market entry is difficult in most industries.
   b. ultimately, the price and output level produced in the market will approach that of the pure monopolist.
   c. only a game-theoretic approach to market structure will permit the determination of price, output, and productive efficiency in a capitalist economy.
   d. easy entry into markets can force firms to produce and charge an output and price level that would occur if the market was perfectly competitive.
   e. None of the above are correct.

___ 10. When economists study game theory, they are:
   a. using it to explain and determine pricing and output behavior in a perfectly competitive market.
   b. attempting to study and understand the decision-making process of firms when there is a combination of both conflict and cooperation.
   c. using it to explain the pricing and output decision of a pure monopolist.
   d. examining and attempting to understand the predatory behavior firms in monopolistically competitive markets.
   e. None of the above are correct.

___11. If firms engage in a game in which there is a dominant strategy, then:
   a. each firm will achieve an outcome that is grim.
   b. each firm has some definite, optimal choice.
   c. once a player picks a strategy, no other player can pick the same strategy.
   d. there is no well-defined payoff for any firm.
   e. None of the above are correct.

___12. The source of the prisoners' dilemma is that:
   a. both prisoners obviously have committed a crime.
   b. there is uncertainty among the prisoners.
   c. there is both uncertainty and interdependence among the prisoners.
   d. what one prisoner does will have an effect on the other prisoner.
   e. each prisoner has committed a different crime.

___13. When a firm makes a strategic decision, it is one where:
   a. the objective of the firm is to maximize profits.
   b. the outcomes of all potential actions by rival firms are known.
   c. the firm is unable to estimate the outcomes of any of its competitors with any certainty.
   d. the objective of the firm is to minimize its cost of production.
   e. the decisions and actions of one firm is dependent upon the expected actions of another firm.

___14. Suppose that two firms are engaged in a game of strategy and achieve a Nash equilibrium. This equilibrium is one in which:
   a. both firms earn and divide a monopoly profit.
   b. each firm will most likely often change its strategy.
   c. each firm will consider its decisions optimal, given the decisions of the other firm.
   d. both firms will cooperate in order to maximize joint profits.
   e. None of the above are correct.

___15. If an industry is oligopolistic and the firms in the industry have a strategy of limit pricing, the objective of this strategy is:
   a. set the price so that maximum profits are made.
   b. charge a price just low enough so that new firms do not find it profitable to enter the industry.
   c. establish a price that sets a limit on how much firms can sell.
   d. limit the prices from which firms in the industry can choose to sell their output.
   e. have the firms set marginal cost equal to price.

Chapter Review (Fill-In Questions)

1. Small numbers of firms that base their decisions on what their competitors will do are in
    _____ markets. The theory of _____ markets, however, suggests
    that the number of firms presently in a market is less important than is the threat of entry in
    response to profit opportunities.

2. Oligopolies are caused by substantial _____ or other barriers to entry,
    or are formed through _____.

3. The _____ curve model presumes that each firm fears that its competitors
    will match any price cuts, but will _____ any price increases. This kink in the
    demand curve leaves a gap in the _____ curve, so that changes in
    marginal cost may not change the price charged.

4. A _____ is a collusive oligopoly that usually operates internationally in an
    attempt to maximize the _____ of its members, just as if it were a monopoly.
    Because cheating is potentially so profitable for cartel members, cartels tend to be unstable
    unless controlled, at least in part, by governmental actions.

5. Regardless of their precise form, all non-discriminating market structures that are not
    contestable tend to be economically inefficient because each firm equates marginal revenue
    to marginal cost, and marginal revenue curves lie below the demand (average revenue)
    curves the firms confront. Hence, the marginal social benefit (MSB) of additional production
    will be greater than its _____. The existence of any monopoly power
    causes output to be restricted below the socially optimal level, and the price charged to be
    _____ than would be the case under perfect competition.

6. _____ describes how individual economic units determine what other
    individuals are most likely to do in a certain situation, given specific conditions, and then
    ascertains what tactics are available to _____ any gain or minimize any harm as a
    result of the situation.

7. The "*prisoners' dilemma*" is an example of (cooperative/noncooperative)
    _____ game behavior and confronts each player with the questions: "What
    will my accomplice do; do I _____ to the crime or not?

8. In order for an equilibrium to be achieved in the prisoners' dilemma, each player must pursue
    a (dominant/tit for tat) _____ strategy, and so each prisoner (will
    not/will)_____ confess to the crime.

9. If your are engaged in a _____ strategy, you would wait until your competitors
    committed to a particular action before you commit.

Unlimited Multiple Choice

Each Question Has From Zero To Four Correct Answers.

___ 1. In the long run, monopolistically competitive firms:
    a. produce at the lowest possible per unit cost.
    b. find that entry and exit are relatively easy.
    c. face numerous competitors, all being small relative to the size of the market.
    d. produce a homogeneous commodity.

___ 2. Product differentiation:
    a. only exists in the mind of the consumer.
    b. is frequently used by firms to shift the demand curves for their commodities to the right.
    c. causes the price elasticity of demand to decrease.
    d. is often used as a means by which firms can exert influences over the prices of their outputs.

___ 3. An oligopoly:
    a. is any industry comprised of fewer than ten firms.
    b. produces homogeneous outputs.
    c. is an industry into which entry is relatively easy.
    d. can be created by economies of scale, by mergers, or by substantial barriers to entry.

___ 4. According to the kinked demand curve theory of oligopolistic pricing behavior:
    a. changes in the cost structure of the oligopolist rapidly change the price of output.
    b. marginal cost can change without changes in the price of output.
    c. it is impossible for the price charged by oligopolists to remain rigid in the face of changes in cost.
    d. firms consider the reactions of their competitors whenever a price change is contemplated.

___ 5. Cartels:
    a. are illegal in most instances in the U.S.
    b. normally entail overt collusion on the parts of member firms.
    c. try to joint-profit maximize, meaning that they try to behave as a monopoly would in setting prices and production.
    d. operate primarily in international markets for manufactured goods.

___ 6. Predatory pricing:
    a. cannot occur in highly competitive markets.
    b. is often used as a deterrent to entry into an industry.
    c. may be used to drive existing rivals out of an industry.
    d. is most easy to undertake in oligopolistic markets.

___ 7. In the United States, predatory pricing:
   a. is prohibited by the antitrust laws.
   b. can exist only when there is symmetric information.
   c. is often hard to distinguish from normal competition.
   d. causes the firms in an industry to set price above average total cost for a particular level of output.

___ 8. When economists describe a firm or industry's sunk cost, they mean:
   a. those costs that change as the level of output produced changes.
   b. those costs which determine the shape of the short run average total cost curve.
   c. those costs which are fixed in the short run but variable in the long run.
   d. those implicit costs representing the cost of foregone opportunities.

Problems

Problem 1

Graphed in this figure are the revenue and cost curves for two monopolistically competitive firms. Use this information to answer the following true/false questions.

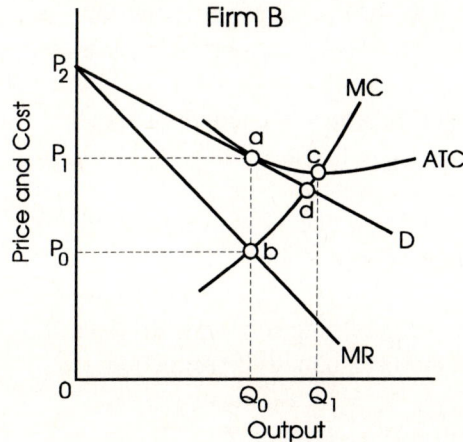

___ a. Firm B is operating in the long run period of production.

___ b. Firm A can maximize total revenue by producing Q1 units of output.

___ c. Firm A is producing in the long run period of production.

___ d. Firm A is incurring an economic loss.

___ e. Point a lies in elastic range of Firm A's demand curve.

___ f. Point d lies in the elastic range of Firm B's demand curve.

___ g. Firm B would maximize society's net benefits by producing Q_1 units of output.

___ h. Firm B is allocating productive inputs efficiently from society's point of view when producing Q_0 units of output.

___ i. Firm A maximizes profit by producing Q_1 units of output.

___ j. Both firms are plagued by excess capacity.

___ k. Firm A will always earn economic profits, regardless of the period of production.

___ l. At output Q_0, Firm B is producing output at the point where total revenue equals total cost.

___ m. Total profits to Firm A are represented by area P_0P_2ac.

___ n. Total profits to Firm B are represented by area P_0P_1ab.

___ o. Total fixed costs for Firm A are represented by area P_0P_1bc.

___ p. Total variable costs for Firm A are equal to area $0P_0cQ_0$.

Problem 2

Illustrated on the following page are the revenue and cost curves for four different profit maximizing firms. Use this information to answer the following true/false questions.

___ a. Firm B is probably a monopolistically competitive firm.

___ b. Firm C is producing in the short run period of production.

___ c. Firm D is earning economic profits in the short run period of production.

___ d. Firm A is a monopolist.

___ e. Firm D is earning normal profits which are equal to the area of rectangle CPab.

___ f. Firm C is pricing at a point along its demand curve that has a price elasticity of one.

___ g. Firm D is a monopolistically competitive firm.

___ h. Firm D will always be compelled to pass forward to the consumer any increases in the costs of production in the form of higher prices.

___ i. Firm A is a sales maximizer.

___ j. Firm B is incurring total variable costs which are equal to the area of rectangle zwbc.

___ k. Firm A incurs total fixed costs equal to zwbc.

___ l. Firm C is a perfectly competitive firm.

Firm A

Firm B

Firm C

Firm D

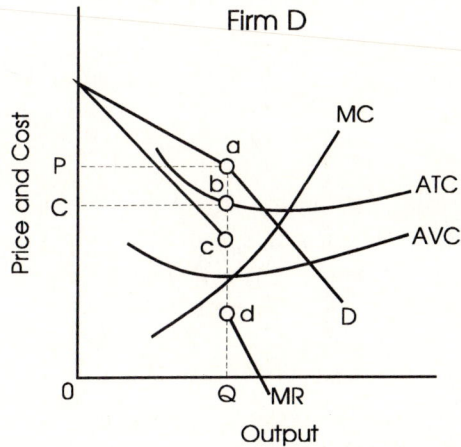

___ m. Firm A is maximizing the net benefits received by society.

___ n. Firm B is producing output at the lowest possible opportunity cost from society's point of view.

___ o. Firm B can earn economic profits in the long run period of production.

___ p. Firm B can reap economic profits in the short run period of production.

Problem 3

Using your knowledge of monopolistically competitive markets and cost curves:

a. In graph "A" illustrate a firm that is suffering economic losses.

b. In graph "B" illustrate the long run solution for a firm in this industry.

c. What has caused the change in the firm's profit picture from A to B? _____

_____

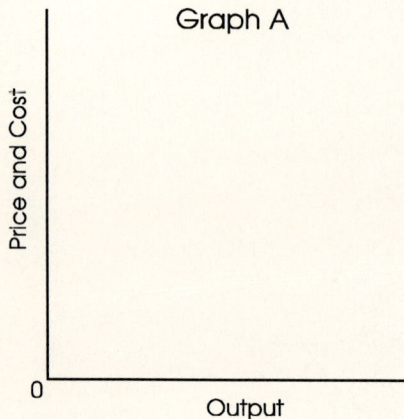

Graph A

Price and Cost

0

Output

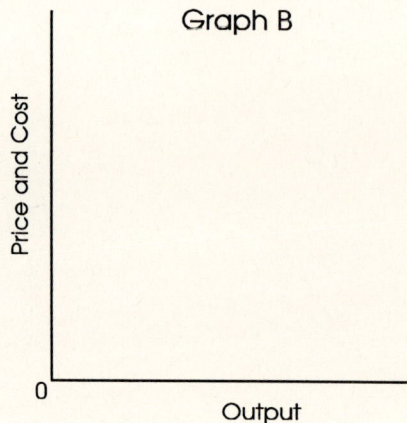

Graph B

Price and Cost

0

Output

Problem 4

Use the figure on the following page, which depicts a firm in a particular oligopoly market model, to answer the following questions.

a. What market model does this graph represent? _____

b. Assume that marginal cost is constant at $3.50. What is the price and quantity of output for this firm. Price? _____ Quantity? _____

c. If the marginal cost increases to $5.00, what are the new equilibrium price and quantity? Price _____, Quantity _____

d. Over what range of quantities will the firm be hesitant to raise price by itself? _____ Over what range of quantities will the firm be hesitant not to match price decreases? _____

e. At what level of output is the firm's price elasticity of demand unitary? _____.

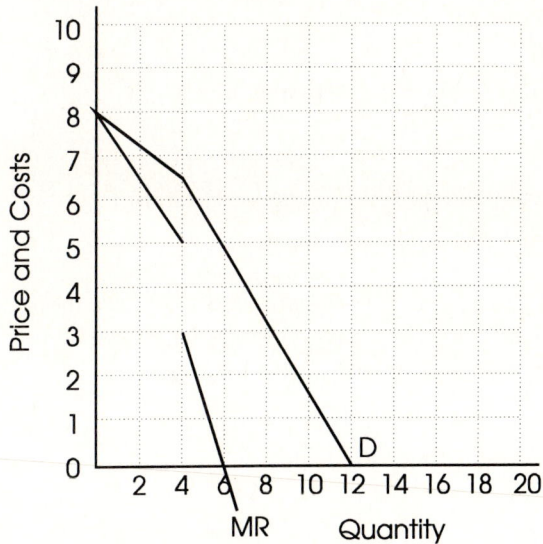

Problem 5

Assume that only two companies manufacture shock absorbers for mountain bikes: Shock! and TBITAD (To brake is to admit defeat). Both firms have the option of adopting a low key (and less expensive) or an aggressive (and more expensive) advertising approach. The payoffs (in thousands of dollars per month) associated with each approach are shown in this payoff matrix. Also assume that both firms cannot cooperate (collude) with each other.

TBITAD

		Aggressive	Low Key
Shock!	Aggressive	0, 0	50, -10
	Low Key	-10, 50	25, 25

a. What is Shock's dominant strategy? _____ What is TBITAD's dominant strategy? _____

b. How much monthly profit can Shock! count on if it follows its dominant strategy? _____ How much monthly profit can TBITAD count on if it follows its dominant strategy?

_____

c. How might both firms increase their monthly profit? _____

Now assume that both firms decide to cooperate with each other.

d. What Strategy will Shock! pursue? _____ What strategy will TBITAD pursue? _____

e. By how much will Shock's monthly profits change? _____ By how much will TBITAD's monthly profits change? _____

f. Would you expect the cooperation between Shock! and TBITAD to be long lasting? _____ Why or Why not? _____

Both Shock! and TBITAD are working on the next generation of shock absorbers. Shock's model uses an internal fluid, while TBITAD's model uses only air. The payoff matrix (in thousands of dollars per month) associated with bringing the new models to the market is shown below.

TBITAD

		Fluid	Air
Shock!	Fluid	50, 30	-10, -10
	Air	-10, -10	30, 50

g. What is the Nash equilibrium if Shock! gets their model on the market first? _____
What is the Nash equilibrium if TBITAD gets their model on the market first? _____

h. Why would either company want to be the first to introduce their model? _____
_____

i. Why would one company abandon their model if their rival gets their model on the market first? _____

ANSWERS

Matching		True/False		Multiple Choice		Unlimited MC
Set I	Set II					
1. g	1. g	1. T	7. T	1. b	9. d	1. bc
2. c	2. c	2. T	8. T	2. a	10. b	2. bd
3. i	3. f	3. T	9. F	3. a	11. b	3. d
4. j	4. a	4. F	10. T	4. b	12. c	4. bd
5. e	5. d	5. F	11. T	5. b	13. e	5. abc
6. f	6. i	6. T	12. F	6. a	14. c	6. abcd
7. b	7. h			7. a	15. b	7. ac
8. d	8. b			8. d		8. none
9. h	9. e					
10. a	10. j					

Chapter 27
Antitrust and Regulation

Chapter Objectives

After you have read and studied this chapter you should be able to differentiate between the various measurements of market power; discuss the different merger "waves" that have occurred in this country's history; know the various antitrust acts and what roll they played in shaping the past merger waves; have an idea of what is presently considered permissible and forbidden under the current antitrust laws; be able to broadly describe the extent and growth of economic regulation; offer some explanations for the growth of regulation, discuss the effects of economic regulation on business efficiency; and discuss the concept of block-pricing and how it affects the efficiency of production

Chapter Review: Key Points

1. *Market power* exists whenever a firm can set the price of its output. (Market power and monopoly are not synonymous.) Market power builds a gap between price and marginal cost. The *Lerner index of monopoly power (LMP)* uses this fact to measure market power as *(P - MC)/P*. However, estimating *MC* with accounting data is almost impossible.

2. Market concentration ratios provide some evidence of monopolization or oligopolistic power. *Concentration ratios* are the percentages of total sales, output, or employment in an industry controlled by a small number of the largest firms in the industry.

3. The *Herfindahl-Hirschman Index (HHI)* is the sum of squared market shares (ΣS_i^2). Squaring places more emphasis on big firms. The Justice Department now uses the *HHI* as a guide to the permissibility of mergers.

4. Major difficulties are encountered in defining an industry. The existence of *close consumption substitutes* is one consideration; the ease with which potential competitors might enter an industry (*contestability*) is another. The Department of Commerce lumps firms into Standard Industrial Classifications (SICs) to try to solve this problem, but with only mixed success.

5. One reason for merger is to increase the scope of a firm's operations so that economies of scale in information, marketing, advertising, production, or financial management may be exploited. Another reason, by far the most important for policy, is that merger eliminates business rivals and facilitates economic concentration and market power. Increases in market power that result from merger may be reflected rapidly in higher prices for the merged companies' stock.

6. *Horizontal mergers* (the absorption of competitors) dominated the first major wave of mergers in the United States from 1890 until 1914. The Clayton Act outlawed most horizontal mergers, so a wave of *vertical mergers* (mergers that unite suppliers of raw materials or intermediate goods with processors or other firms further along the production chain) ensued until the Great Depression increased economic concentration. Merger activity died during the Great Depression, but revived in the mid-1950s where companies that were very dissimilar were merged into *conglomerates*. Merger activities slowed down during the 1970s, but reemerged strongly during the 1980s in a forth wave that some people describe as "the golden age of dealmaking."

7. Big firms might be justified by enormous capital requirements or substantial economies of scale. In such cases, proper public policy may take the form of regulation. The major thrust of public policy where no such justifications for bigness exist has been to encourage competition through *antitrust actions*.

8. Agricultural cooperatives, athletic organizations, labor unions, export trade associations, regulated industries, and insurance companies are largely exempt from antitrust action.

9. In applying the *Sherman Antitrust Act*, the Court has historically taken two different approaches. The rule of reason approach prohibits bad monopolies and permits reasonable restraints on trade, while the *per se doctrine* forbids all monopolies regardless of conduct.

10. The bulk of regulatory agencies in this country were created during three decades. The first great surge occurred during the 1930s, when policymakers attempted to buffer the violent swings in the business cycle on our economic system. Well over half of all regulatory agencies, however, came into existence in the 1960s and 1970s. It is not obvious why regulation increased so dramatically during a period of relative prosperity and high economic growth.

11. The *public interest* theory of regulation focuses on some possible failures of the price system, including poor information, fraud, externalities, and monopoly power.

12. A *natural monopoly* involves substantial economies of scale, rendering direct competition impractical. Society has turned to regulation to prevent natural monopolies from reaping enormous profits and to move them towards socially efficient levels of output.

13. Regulating public utilities is considerably more difficult than simple theory would suggest. Major problems arise in determining the *rate base*, a *"fair" rate of return*, and allowable costs. Regulatory agencies face a difficult task in balancing the interests of consumers and utility investors.

14. The *industry interest* view of regulation expressed by George Stigler suggests that industries can gain from regulation, and therefore "demand" regulation from the government. As Stigler has noted, the state can, and often does, change the profitability of an industry through four main mechanisms: (a) direct taxes or subsidies, (b) restrictions on entry, (c) impacts on an industry's complementary or substitute products, and (d) direct price-fixing policies.

15. *Public choice theory* attributes much of the complexity of modern regulation to empire building by the heads of government agencies.

16. *Direct costs of regulation* arise when a firm incurs costs to comply with laws and regulations. The *indirect costs* of regulation are incurred in attempts to avoid or reshape regulation. The cost of hiring lobbyists to influence regulation is an example. Together, these costs amount to 5-10 percent of U.S. Gross Domestic Product.

Matching Key Terms And Concepts

Set I

____ 1. Sherman Antitrust Act

____ 2. The Clayton Act

____ 3. Market concentration ratio

____ 4. Lerner index

____ 5. Herfindahl-Hirschman index

____ 6. Robinson-Patman Act

____ 7. Federal Trade Commission

____ 8. "Rule of reason" approach

____ 9. Horizontal merger

____ 10. Conglomerate merger

a. Made it illegal to monopolize trade or commerce.

b. "good" trusts were not in violation of the Sherman Act.

c. Investigates and challenges unfair methods of competition used by firms.

d. Amended Section 2 of the Clayton Act to limit price discrimination even further.

e. The percent of total industry sales, employment, assets, value-added, or output accounted for by the largest 4, 8, or 20 firms in an industry.

f. One measure of the monopoly power exercised by a single firm.

g. Acquiring a firm with no intermediate or competitive products.

h. Weights biggest firms disproportionately heavily in estimating concentrations of market power.

i. Made it illegal to price discriminate in many instances.

j. Acquiring a directly competitive firm.

Set II

___ 1.	Trusts	**a.** A schedule of price/quantity combinations set by a regulatory commission.
___ 2.	The per se approach	**b.** Barriers to entry that enhance some workers' incomes.
___ 3.	Vertical merger	**c.** Economic efficiency can be enhanced with this form of price discrimination on utility rates.
___ 4.	Occupational licensing	**d.** Cartel-like combinations of related firms.
___ 5.	Rate structure	**e.** Certain contracts are so restrictive of competition that they are automatically held to be illegal.
___ 6.	Block-pricing	**f.** Regulation is often tailored to the interests of the regulated industries rather than the public interest.
___ 7.	Rate base	**g.** Acquiring a firm that supplies intermediate products.
___ 8.	Public-interest theory of regulation	**h.** Investment that determines the net returns allowed utilities.
___ 9.	Industry-interest theory of regulation	**i.** Regulation can correct for failures of the market system.
___10.	Public choice theory of regulation	**j.** Government bureaucrats increase the complexity of regulations so that their power and budgets will grow.

True/False Questions

___ 1. Economic theory suggests that as monopoly power increases, the difference between price and marginal cost increases.

___ 2. Public policy generally presumes that monopoly power is socially undesirable.

___ 3. Sports organizations have consistently been involved in antitrust actions.

___ 4. In the 1940s, the U.S. Supreme Court replaced its "Rule of Reason" with the "per se" approach to antitrust policy.

___ 5. A pure monopoly generates a Herfindahl index of 10,000.

___ 6. Divestiture is a common result of antitrust prosecution.

___ 7. By forcing a natural monopoly to charge a price for its marginal output which is only equal to marginal cost, the government can structure incentives for the firm to produce the socially optimal rate of output.

___ 8. Rate structures normally permit regulated public utilities to earn a normal return (profit).

___ 9. It is impossible for regulated public utilities to earn economic profits in the short-run period of production.

____10. Uniform (constant) utility rates are socially optimal if they are set equal to average cost.

____11. Occupational licensing improves the economic conditions of those who are licensed.

____12. Externalities exist whenever some production or consumption activity confers either costs or benefits on a party not monetarily involved in the market activity or transaction.

Standard Multiple Choice

There Is A Single "Best" Answer For Each Questions.

____ 1. Which of the following arguments best supports the validity of the Lerner Index of Monopoly Power?
  a. Industries in which four or fewer firms dominate sales are very monopolistic.
  b. Monopoly power is reflected in a relatively great differences between price and marginal cost.
  c. Oligopolies tend to exercise far more monopoly power than do firms in a monopolistically competitive industry.
  d. Conscious parallelism of action is evidence of monopoly power.
  e. Brand proliferation is incompatible with competition; it signifies monopoly power.

____ 2. "Good" trusts were long exempt from antitrust action under the:
  a. per se approach.
  b. Sherman Act.
  c. Clayton Act.
  d. acceptable behavior guideline.
  e. rule of reason approach.

____ 3. Which of the following is largely exempt from antitrust action because of court decisions rather than because of explicit legislation?
  a. Agricultural cooperatives.
  b. Amateur and professional sports organizations.
  c. Labor unions and collective bargaining.
  d. Export associations.
  e. Regulated industries.

____ 4. Defenders of large firms in highly concentrated industries may reasonably argue that:
  a. some industries have huge capital requirements for each firm.
  b. some firms must be large because of substantial diseconomies of scale.
  c. decreasing cost industries are always concentrated.
  d. increasing cost industries are necessarily concentrated.
  e. large firms in all industries are always more efficient than small firms.

5. Recent guidelines to prohibit mergers rely on the:
   a. Lerner index of Monopoly Power (LMP).
   b. Herfindahl-Hirschman index.
   c. occurrence of brand proliferation.
   d. concentration ratios over sales for the four largest firms.
   e. need to have several big firms in industries that historically have had a few dominant firms and many small ones.

6. The public-interest theory of regulation is LEAST compatible with:
   a. limiting consumer access to only top quality merchandise.
   b. limiting natural monopolies to a fair return on investment.
   c. limiting pollutants emitted as manufacturing by-products.
   d. requiring labels describing the characteristics of products.
   e. mandating automobile accessories to improve pedestrian safety.

7. The full costs of a natural monopoly can be covered in an economically efficient manner if the rate structure uses:
   a. uniform average cost pricing.
   b. uniform marginal cost pricing.
   c. uniform average variable cost pricing.
   d. block-pricing.
   e. None of the above.

8. NOT among the major mechanisms by which government can benefit business is:
   a. restriction of entry into an industry.
   b. placing price ceilings on an industry's products.
   c. placing price floors under an industry's output.
   d. direct subsidies or tax breaks.
   e. subsidies for complements or taxes on substitute goods.

9. Deregulation has most obviously enhanced efficiency in:
   a. pharmaceutical research and development.
   b. agriculture.
   c. airlines ticket prices.
   d. the practice of medicine.
   e. education.

10. According to the industry-interest theory, the gains from government regulation favoring an industry:
   a. generally result in increased economic efficiency nationwide.
   b. are secured through expensive lobbying and similar activities.
   c. are offset by consumers' gains from lower utility rates.
   d. increase the risks to a firm of being in the industry.
   e. arise only from special tax advantages or subsidies.

Chapter Review (Fill-In Questions)

1. The degree of monopoly power can be estimated by _____, which measure the percentages of sales, assets, or employees of the top _____ firms in an industry; by the Lerner Index of Monopoly Power, which is computed as _____; or by the _____ index, which is computed as ΣS_i^2.

2. _____ have been a major source of the rapid growth in the _____ of specific industries between 1895 and 1930, and of the slow, but continuing concentration of control of industrial capacity since then.

3. The first wave, _____ mergers, consisted of absorption of direct competitors and lasted from roughly 1895 until 1914, when the _____ Act was passed. The second wave, _____ mergers, began soon after World War I and peaked in 1929, declining until roughly 1935.

4. Under the early _____ approach, good monopolies were held to be legal, but the more recent _____ approach holds certain actions automatically to be violations of antitrust laws, regardless of whether they are the actions of "good" trusts or bad ones.

5. Why is business regulated? One explanation, the _____ theory of regulation, focuses on the idea that consumers need to be protected from business abuses. A challenge to this view is the _____ theory. This theory suggests that regulations are shaped to the interests of regulated firms. A third viewpoint, the _____ theory of regulation, maintains that regulation is a by-product of bureaucrats' attempts to increase their power and prestige.

6. In a world with ideal regulators and regulations, the rate structures of natural monopolies would be set to yield only normal, or _____ rates of return on investment. Because efficiency requires that the price of the marginal good (MSB) would just equal its marginal cost, some form of _____ such as _____ would be required for those industries in which natural monopolies occur.

Unlimited Multiple Choice

Each Question Has From Zero To Four Correct Responses.

____ 1. The Sherman Antitrust Act:
   a. was enacted in 1890.
   b. was originally used to break up unions.
   c. clearly specified illegal activities.
   d. makes the attempt to monopolize illegal.

____ 2. The Lerner index (LMP):
   a. cannot assume a value of zero.
   b. measures a firm's monopoly power.
   c. is a difficult measure to use because of problems in estimating marginal cost.
   d. assumes larger positive values as a firm's monopoly power grows.

____ 3. The Herfindahl-Hirschman index:
   a. was enacted in 1936.
   b. estimates permissible price discrimination, based on differences in production costs.
   c. weights the biggest firms extra heavily in generating a number that summarizes market concentration.
   d. is used by the Justice Department as a guide for challenges of proposed mergers.

____ 4. Industry-interest views of regulation suggest:
   a. externalities generated by production may justify governmental regulations.
   b. natural monopolies should be replaced by perfect competition.
   c. regulation should stimulate production that involves huge positive externalities.
   d. consumers benefit immensely when lower prices are facilitated by economies of scale in production.

____ 5. An efficient rate structure based on block-pricing:
   a. permits a well managed regulated firm to earn normal (zero economic) profits.
   b. enables the continued existence of the regulated firm.
   c. is synonymous with a uniform socially optimal price.
   d. permits a regulated firm to earn long run economic profits.

Problems

Problem 1

Use this table, concerning four different companies, to answer the following questions.

a. Calculate the Lerner index of monopoly power (LMP) for each of the companies and fill in the table.

Company	Price of Product	Marginal Cost	Lerner Index
Alpha Inc.	100	100	
Beta Inc.	0.60	0.20	
Gamma Ltd.	12	10	
Delta Inc.	5	3	

b. Rank the four companies from most to least market power based on your calculations of the LMP. _____

Problem 2

Calculate the Herfindahl-Hirschman Index (HHI) in the following scenarios.

a. Ten firms all share equally in total sales of silver eating utensils. HHI = _____

b. Percentages of total sales of automatic garage door openers are divided as follows: Macron = 40%, Contrails = 30%, Vulcan = 20%, and ten small firms each with 1% of the market. HHI = _____

c. The three largest tobacco companies respectively sell 51%, 29%, and 16% of all tobacco products. There are eight other firms, each accounting for 1/2% of industry sales. HHI = _____

Problem 3

This table shows data for an eight firm industry. Assume that all the firms have identical price/marginal cost relationships at equilibrium. The price of the good produced is $6, and marginal cost equals $5.

a. What is the four firm concentration ratio? _____ The eight firm concentration ratio? _____

b. What is the LMP for a firm in this industry? _____

c. What is the Herfindahl-Hirschman index for this industry? (For simplicity consider "Others" as one firm") _____

Firm	Sales (Millions)	% of Market
A	9	45
B	5	25
C	3	15
D	2	10
Others	1	5

d. If firm B and C merge what happens to the Herfindahl-Hirschman index? _____ The concentration ratios? _____ The Lerner index? _____

Problem 4

Use the information about revenues and costs contained in this graph to answer the following true/false questions.

_____ a. The market structure graphically depicted is a natural monopoly.

_____ b. If this firm was not regulated, it would sell Q_2 units of output at a price of P_1.

_____ c. Proper regulation of this firm would result in production of Q_0 units of output.

_____ d. The firm could break even (earn zero economic profits) by selling Q_1 units of output at a price of P_2 per unit.

_____ e. The socially optimal output is Q_1.

_____ f. This firm can cover its costs and produce a socially optimal level of output through an appropriate "block-pricing" rate structure.

_____ g. If the firm was regulated and forced to produce the socially optimal output

the firm would earn a fair return equal to area P_0gfP_1.

_____ h. If it could not price discriminate but were left to its own devices, this firm would earn economic profits equal to area P_3cbP_4.

____ i.   The natural monopoly policy dilemma
          is illustrated by this figure.

____ j.   The socially optimal output is Q_2.

____ k.   Consumers would be better off if this
          was a competitive industry.

____ l.   Output Q_1 is not the socially optimal
          output because the cost of the
          resources used to produce the last unit
          of output exceeds the benefits to
          society from that last unit.

Problem 5

Use the information in this graph to answer the following questions.

a.   As illustrated this firm exhibits _____
     _____.

b.   If this profit maximizing firm is NOT
     regulated the price would be _____; and
     the quantity _____.

c.   If the firm preferred to maximize total
     revenue as opposed to profits the price
     would be _____; and the quantity
     _____.

d.   If the firm were regulated under the
     efficiency criteria of P = MC, then the firm
     would produce at a uniform price of
     _____; and quantity of _____. This would entail a loss to the firm of _____.

e.   If the firm were regulated and allowed to have price equal to average total cost, then the
     price would be _____; and the quantity _____. The problem with this approach is
     that from an efficiency standpoint
     _____.

f.   If these were the cost curves of a perfectly competitive firm, equilibrium price would be
     _____; and equilibrium quantity would be_____. Is this a fair comparison? _____

g.   What regulatory pricing tool did you learn from the text to deal with situations such as the
     one pictured?_____

Problem 6

A hypothetical supply and demand relationship for Seattle taxis is pictured below. Assume that this is the part of the market that benefited from deregulation. Answer the following questions based on the graph.

a. If this market was not regulated the free market equilibrium price is _____; and quantity is _____. In this situation the industry earns _____ economic profits in the long run.

b. If the market for radio dispatched taxis were regulated and the quantity restricted to Q_1, then the price would rise to _____. If the average cost at Q_1 equals P_2, then there would be economic profits of _____ shared by firms in the industry.

c. As can be seen in your text, industries that are regulated often gain profits from restricted entry into the industry. Our case illustrates just that point. The license to own and operate a taxi earns economic profit. What might you expect to happen to the value of a taxi license after deregulation? _____

d. In a market such as the taxi market, that overtly seems perfectly competitive, why might regulation have occurred in the first place? _____
_____

ANSWERS

Matching		True/False		Multiple Choice	Unlimited MC
Set I	Set II				
1. a	1. d	1. T	7. T	1. b	1. abd
2. i	2. e	2. T	8. T	2. e	2. bcd
3. e	3. g	3. F	9. F	3. b	3. cd
4. f	4. b	4. T	10. F	4. a	4. none
5. h	5. a	5. T	11. T	5. b	5. ab
6. d	6. c	6. F	12. T	6. a	
7. c	7. h			7. d	
8. b	8. i			8. b	
9. j	9. f			9. c	
10. g	10. j			10. b	

Chapter Review (Fill-in Questions)

1. concentration ratios; 4 or 8; (P - MC)/P; Herfindahl-Hirschman
2. Mergers; concentration
3. horizontal; Clayton Antitrust; vertical
4. rule of reason; per se
5. public interest; industry interest; public choice
6. fair; price discrimination; block-pricing

Problem 1

a. See table
b. From most to least market power: Beta Inc., Delta Inc., Gamma Ltd., and Alpha Inc.

Company	Price of Product	Marginal Cost	Lerner Index
Alpha Inc.	100.00	100.00	0.00
Beta Inc.	0.60	0.20	0.67
Gamma Ltd.	12.00	10.00	0.17
Delta Inc.	5.00	3.00	0.40

Problem 2

a. 1,000 (10^2 x 10)
b. 2,910 (1,600 + 900 + 400 + 10)
c. 3,700 (2,601 + 841 + 256 + 2)

Problem 3

a. four firms = 95%, eight firms =100%
b. LMP = .167
c. HHI = 3,000
d. The HHI increases to 3,750 for the industry. The concentration ratios and the LMP index remain unchanged.

Problem 4

a. T
b. F
c. F
d. T
e. F
f. T
g. F
h. T
i. T
j. T
k. F
l. F

Problem 5

a. monopoly power
b. P_6; Q_1.
c. P_5; Q_2.
d. P_1; Q_4. P_1P_3uw.
e. P_4; Q_3. P is greater than MC which violates our efficiency criteria.
f. P_2; Q_5. This is not fair because the whole crux of the problem is that the firm has large economies of scale and therefore is a natural monopoly.
g. block-pricing

Problem 6

a. P_2; Q_2; zero
b. P_3; P_2P_3ab.
c. The license value was largely based on the economic profit. If the economic profit is gone we can assume that most, if not all, of the license value will deteriorate.
d. Quality of service (including safety) might have been poor if competition was cutthroat.

Chapter 28
Competitive Labor Markets

===

Chapter Objectives

After you have read and studied this chapter, you should be able to describe a competitive firm's demand for labor in competitive labor markets; the accumulation of human capital and its effect on the demand for labor; the determinants of labor supplies and the influences on labor force participation rates; equilibrium and efficiency in a competitive labor market; strategic behavior in labor markets; and the reasons for wage differentials between occupations.

Chapter Review: Key Points

1. The demand for any resource is related to the: (a) amounts of other factors employed, (b) production technology used, and (c) demand for the product. Because the demand for labor (or any factor) hinges on the demand for final products, it is a *derived demand.*

2. *Marginal revenue product (MRP)* is the firm's revenues generated by hiring the marginal unit of some input which is equal to MP x MPP_L. In perfect competition, this is the same as the *value of the marginal product (VMP)* which is equal to P x MPP_L.

3. Increases (*decreases*) in the demand for the product, in labor productivity, or in the amounts of other resources used will normally increase (*decrease*) the *VMP* and demand for labor. Technological changes may either increase or decrease labor demands. *Automation* is the replacement of workers by new technologies.

4. The *elasticity of demand for labor* is directly related to the: (a) *elasticity of demand for the final product,* (b) *labor's share of total costs* represented by the wage bill, (c) ease of factor *substitution, and (d) time for adjustment.*

5. The supply of labor depends on: (a) wage rates and structures, (b) labor force participation, (c) the number of hours people are willing to work, and (d) the education, training, and skills of workers.

6. Labor quality improves through investments in *human capital* that include formal education and on-the-job training. Education benefits both the individual and society at large. Training is classified as either general or specific: *General training* enhances a worker's productivity equally for many firms, while *specific training* only increases the worker's productivity for the current employer.

7. Workers experience both *income* and *substitution effects* when wage rates change. Increased wages cause labor to substitute work for leisure because work expands consumption opportunities and leisure is more costly. However, higher wages mean that for a given amount of labor effort, workers will earn more income, and, if leisure is a normal good, they will want to consume more leisure and work less. If the substitution effect is larger than the income effect, supplies are positively sloped. Backward-bending labor supplies result when income effects dominate substitution effects.

8. While the individual's labor supply curve may be backward bending, the supply of labor to any industry will always be positively sloped. Industry supplies and demands for labor establish the *equilibrium wage* as each firm hires additional units of labor until the value of the marginal product equals the market wage rate.

9. Any resource will be employed up to the point where the additional revenue competitive firms receive (*value of the marginal product,* or *VMP*) just equals the cost of an additional unit of the resource (*marginal factor cost*, or *MFC*). In competitive labor markets, the marginal factor cost (*MFC*) equals the *wage rate (w)*, so pure competition in all markets means that $VMP = MRP = MFC = w$

10. Competitive demand curves for labor represent the marginal benefits to society from additional employment, and supply curves reflect the marginal cost to society of using those resources. Employing labor to the point where $D_L = S_L$ is efficient because society's benefits from additional employment equals its costs. More or less employment than where $D_L = S_L$ yields inefficient resource allocations since society gets more (*or less*) than it desires in an opportunity cost sense.

11. Turnover and quit rates are negatively related to the levels of specific training workers have received and to the wage premiums paid them. Firms that invest heavily in their employees have strong incentives to retain them and do so: (a) by paying higher wages than other firms will offer, and (b) through special rules based on seniority or pension provisions that reward longevity with the firm.

12. Wages paid to workers that exceed market clearing wages are called *efficiency wages*. Efficiency wages increase the costs of dismissal and are designed to reduce shirking (the moral hazard problem) by employees. Efficiency wages provide an explanation for involuntary unemployment in labor markets.

13. *Signaling* involve attempts by agents to communicate certain images to potential principals. *Screening* occurs when a principal sets minimum standards before employing an agent.

14. The most important determinants of *wage differentials* are (a) human capital, and (b) working conditions. All else equal, premium wages are paid to compensate workers who endure less pleasant jobs.

Matching Key Terms And Concepts

Set I

___ 1. marginal revenue product (MRP)

___ 2. elasticity of demand for labor

___ 3. backward bending labor supply

___ 4. occupational crowding

___ 5. marginal factor cost (MFC)

___ 6. implicit labor contract

___ 7. marginal productivity theory

___ 8. value of the marginal product (VMP)

___ 9. labor force participation rate

___ 10. labor-leisure trade-off

a. $\Delta wL/\Delta L$.

b. When income effects dominate substitution effects of wage changes.

c. Your income depends on the productivity of your resources.

d. lower wages in return for increased job security.

e. $\Delta TR/\Delta L$, or $\Delta PQ/\Delta L$.

f. $P \times MPP_L$.

g. Occurs when certain groups are pushed towards low paying jobs.

h. Choices that must be made when wage rates change.

i. $\%\Delta L/\%\Delta w$.

j. The percentage of a population that is in the work force.

Set II

___ 1. automation

___ 2. efficiency wages

___ 3. income effect

___ 4. substitution effect

___ 5. screening

___ 6. specific training

___ 7. signaling

___ 8. general training

___ 9. derived demand

___ 10. human capital

a. Involves behavior by agents to communicate special qualifications that will elicit the offer of a contract from a principal.

b. Job skills that are valuable only to the particular firm.

c. Resource demands depend on demands for final goods.

d. When new forms of capital replace workers on a job.

e. Can cause labor supply curves to "bend backward."

f. Occurs when a principal examines the qualifications of a potential agent before offering the agent a contract.

g. Skills valuable to many firms.

h. Skills and experience that enhance MRP.

i. Wages higher than market clearing wages; intended to raise the cost of dismissal and reduce shirking by employees.

j. Accounts for the normal, positive slope of labor supply curves.

True/False Questions

___ 1. In a competitive labor market, the marginal factor cost of labor (MFC) to a firm is the same as the wage rate.

___ 2. Competitive firms will hire workers where MPP = w.

___ 3. Technological advances always raise the demand for labor.

___ 4. Output per worker typically rises when the capital to labor ratio is increased.

___ 5. Firms tend to bear the cost of specific training in hopes of returns, even though such investments are embodied in individual workers.

___ 6. The value of the marginal product (VMP) equals the marginal physical product (MPP) times the wage rate (w).

___ 7. The supply of a specific type of labor skill to a particular firm is normally more elastic than to the entire industry.

___ 8. General training is normally "paid for" by the trainee.

___ 9. If the VMP exceeds the wage rate, the competitive firm gains by hiring more workers.

___ 10. Hikes in wage rates may cause the competitive firm's short- run demand for labor to fall as it substitutes capital for labor.

___ 11. Efficiency wages are often lower than market clearing wages, and so they often encourage the movement of less productive workers to other lines of employment.

___ 12. Signaling behavior by agents is designed to communicate special qualifications that will elicit the offer of a contract from a principal.

___ 13. Adjustments by employers when wages rise increase the productivity of the workers who retain their jobs.

___ 14. Labor productivity tends to rise when workers are provided more land or capital with which to work.

___ 15. The productivity gain that occurs when computer operators learn to apply a particular piece of software to their current employer's business is an example of general training.

___ 16. Advances in technology that allow easier substitution of capital for labor raise the elasticity of demand for labor and encourage automation.

___ 17. Wages can be raised with less loss of employment if the demand for output is highly elastic.

___ 18. A clerk who learns the codes to dial to create particular colors or tints on a Sears Paint Mixer gains productivity in the form of specific training.

___19. If the elasticity of demand for the final output produced by a firm is high, then we would expect the elasticity of demand for the inputs used in production to be high also.

___20. A competitive firm can increase its profits by hiring more workers whenever the MRP of labor exceeds the VMP.

Standard Multiple Choice

Each Question Has A Single Best Answer.

___ 1. Increases in derived demands are best illustrated by rising:
   a. peanut sales during baseball season.
   b. sales of convertibles during hot summers.
   c. new capital orders during economic booms.
   d. beef prices when cowboys unionize.
   e. teenage unemployment when minimum wage laws rise.

___ 2. Marginal productivity theory was primarily developed by:
   a. Thorstein Veblen.
   b. Karl Marx.
   c. Alfred Marshall.
   d. J.B. Clark.
   e. Lorenzo Engels.

___ 3. An increase in the competitively-set wage tends to cause:
   a. firms to reduce the amounts of labor hired.
   b. increases in the MRPs of the workers a firm retains.
   c. higher MFCs of labor to competitive firms.
   d. pressure for greater automation in an industry.
   e. All of the above.

___ 4. A competitive firm will demand more labor if:
   a. technological changes lead to automation.
   b. the price of the firm's output rises.
   c. more firms enter the industry.
   d. the value of the marginal product is below the wage rate.
   e. workers employed by other firms acquire more specific training.

___ 5. If labor is a competitive firm's only variable resource:
   a. labor demand will become less elastic as time goes by.
   b. there will be an elastic demand for labor if the product demand is elastic.
   c. wage hikes are easily accommodated if the demand for the firm's output is highly elastic.
   d. rising capital costs will cause workers to lose their jobs.
   e. the money available to pay workers is only the revenue remaining after all fixed costs are paid.

6. The percentage of a given population who are either employed or unemployed is known as the:
   a. labor force participation rate.
   b. work-force proportion.
   c. labor supply.
   d. substitution effect dominance rate.
   e. income-leisure loss curve.

7. A firm that provides its workers with substantial general training tends to:
   a. pay such individuals premium wages to retain them.
   b. require workers to sign legal contracts of peonage and indenture.
   c. increase worker productivity the most in their current jobs.
   d. pay wages below the market wage during training periods.
   e. hire only workers with MBAs.

8. For most types of labor, the most accurate ranking of labor supplies from most elastic to least elastic is:
   a. firm, industry, occupation.
   b. economy, individual, occupation.
   c. firm, economy, occupation.
   d. individual worker, firm, occupation.
   e. economy, firm, individual worker.

9. As people acquire more formal education, they tend to:
   a. uniformly earn more at every point over their entire lives.
   b. earn more primarily early during their working lives.
   c. earn more, but primarily later during their working lives.
   d. receive ever higher rates of return from their education.
   e. start work at later ages and retire earlier.

10. Workers will eventually be less productive if:
    a. the amount of physical capital is increased.
    b. they acquire more and more human capital.
    c. they receive more specific training and become more specialized.
    d. the wage rate is increased.
    e. more and more people are put on an assembly line.

11. If the income effect of a wage increase is more powerful than the substitution effect, the:
    a. labor supply curve will be "backward bending."
    b. unemployment rate will rise when people become "welfare cheaters."
    c. labor force participation rate will rise.
    d. firm will hire more workers at higher wages.
    e. value of the marginal product will exceed the wage rate.

12. Technological changes that replace workers with machinery are known as:
    a. homeostasis.
    b. periodontalism.
    c. automation.
    d. featherbedding.
    e. solipsism.

13. A government-supported literacy program provided through an employer of unskilled labor is an example of:
    a. human capital depreciation.
    b. business paternalism.
    c. specific training.
    d. laissez-faire economics.
    e. general training.

14. Since World War II, in the United States, the:
    a. amount of human capital per worker has fallen.
    b. labor force participation rate of women has risen.
    c. supply of labor has consistently grown faster than the demand.
    d. rates of return from advanced education have more than tripled.
    e. All of the above.

15. Given the equation $W = MR \times MP_L$, where W is the wage; we would be correct in concluding that:
    a. this firm is maximizing its economic profit.
    b. the firm hires labor up until the point where the marginal product of labor equals the real wage paid to labor.
    c. the firm will earn zero economic profit when the cost of an additional unit of labor equals the value created by an additional unit of capital.
    d. the firm hires labor up until the point where the value created for the firm by the last unit of labor hired is just sufficient to pay for the additional worker.
    e. the price of the labor input is affected by changes in the marginal productivity of labor but not by the price of the output.

16. Competitive equilibria in competitive labor markets require:
    a. $P = MR = AVC$.
    b. $VMP - P$ is maximized.
    c. $VMP = MRP = MFC = w$.
    d. output is at a break-even level.
    e. $MPP = P$.

17. Paying Homer Simpson a salary that exceeds the competitive salary, in order to reduce shirking, is an example of:
    a. stupidity.
    b. occupational crowding.
    c. efficiency wages.
    d. signaling
    e. screening.

18. Workers who retain their jobs will be more productive after firms adjust to increases in:
    a. competition in an industry.
    b. wages.
    c. technological advances.
    d. capital costs.
    e. government regulation.

19. A firm's demand for labor would decrease if the:
    a. price of the output rose.
    b. labor supply curve shifted outward.
    c. price of capital rose.
    d. wage rate rose.
    e. productivity of all workers fell.

20. The elasticity of the demand for labor tends to increase as there are increases in the:
    a. amount of capital used in a production process.
    b. rate of automation in an industry.
    c. difficulty in substituting among different resources.
    d. share of wages in total production costs.
    e. participation rates of women in the labor force.

Chapter Review (Fill-In Questions)

1. The _____ effect occurs because wage changes alter the costs of leisure relative to other goods, but there is an offsetting _____ effect due to the changes in people's purchasing power as wage rates change.

2. The individual's supply curve of labor is _____ sloped if the substitution effect is more powerful than the income effect, and _____ if the income effect is dominant.

3. Even though individual supplies may be negatively sloped, the supplies of labor to firms or individual industries are invariably positively sloped because higher _____ attract more _____.

4. Human capital represents the skills of individuals; training may be either _____, in which case workers become more productive only at their current jobs, or _____, which makes the worker a more productive employee for a number of firms.

5. _____ will pay for specific training, but _____ bear the investment costs for general training in the forms of _____ that are below the workers' _____.

6. In an effort to prevent workers from shirking, and to reduce rates of turnover, firms may pay employees _____ wages. Firms may also require that potential employees have a specific level of education or training. These requirements are often used to _____ potential applicants. Prospective employees attempt to _____ firms that they have the proper credentials by acquiring education and training that the firm views as beneficial or necessary.

Unlimited Multiple Choice

Each Question Has From Zero To Four Correct Responses.

___ 1. The MRP of labor is:
   a. synonymous with the MPP of labor.
   b. the additional total revenue attributable to an additional unit of output.
   c. the additional total revenue associated with an extra worker.
   d. computed by dividing the change in total revenue by the total number of laborers.

___ 2. Marginal factor cost:
   a. equals the wage rate for a firm in a competitive labor market.
   b. is synonymous with the marginal cost of output.
   c. is the addition to total cost attributable to an additional unit of output.
   d. is a measure of total factor cost per unit of input.

___ 3. The supply curve of labor for individuals:
   a. slopes upward when the income effect is less than the substitution effect.
   b. slopes upward whenever the income effect is greater than the substitution effect.
   c. is vertical where the income effect just counterbalances the substitution effect.
   d. is derived from individuals' choices about their labor/leisure trade-offs.

___ 4. Human capital:
   a. consists of improvements to human productive capacity.
   b. explains all differences in the incomes earned by different people.
   c. consists, in part, of increased labor productivity brought about by job training programs.
   d. consists of improvements to raw land brought about by labor.

___ 5. Individual labor force participation is more likely:
   a. the higher are the incomes of other family members.
   b. for female than male family members.
   c. the lower is the education and experience of the individual.
   d. for women 30 to 50 than for women 20 to 30.

Problems

Problem 1

This table displays the cost and revenue data used by a competitive firm to decide how much labor to hire and how much output to produce. Assume that Total Fixed Costs (TFC) are $50. Use this information to answer the following questions:

L	Q	MPP_L	P	MR	TR	w	MFC	TVC	TC	MC	MRP_L
0	0		$3			$15					
1	3		$3			$15					
2	8		$3			$15					
3	15		$3			$15					
4	24		$3			$15					
5	35		$3			$15					
6	48		$3			$15					
7	59		$3			$15					
8	68		$3			$15					
9	75		$3			$15					
10	80		$3			$15					
11	83		$3			$15					
12	84		$3			$15					

L = Units of Labor
Q = Output
MPP_L = Marginal Physical
      Product
P = Price of Output

MR = Marginal Revenue
TR = Total Revenue
w = Wage Rate
MFC = Marginal Factor Cost

TVC = Total Variable Cost
TC = Total Cost
MC = Marginal Cost
MRP_L = Marginal Revenue
      Product

a. Complete the table (remember that Total Fixed Costs are $50).

b. The firm sells its product in what kind of industry? _____
    Explain your answer. _____

c. The firm purchases labor in what type of market? _____
    Explain your answer. _____
    How many units of labor should the firm hire? _____ Why will it hire this much
    labor? _____

e. How much of the good should the firm produce and sell? _____ Why is this the best
    quantity? _____

f. Assume the price of labor (wage rate) falls to $9. How many units of labor should the firm hire? _____ Why? _____

g. Explain why the firm's demand for labor is a derived demand.

    _____

h. Assume the wage rate rises to over $40. How many units of labor should the firm hire? ____ Why? _____

Problem 2

This figure illustrates the short run supply and demand curves for labor for a competitive firm. Use this information to answer the following true/false questions.

____ a. The firm immediately encounters diminishing marginal returns upon hiring the first several units of labor.

____ b. The firm hires labor in a perfectly competitive labor market.

____ c. The firm can influence the price of labor.

____ d. The firm will hire L_0 units of labor per time period.

____ e. The dollar value to the firm of the output produced by L_0 units of labor is given by the area of trapezoid $0W_2bL_0$.

Figure axes: Wage Rate (W) on vertical, Quantity of Labor Hired (L) on horizontal. Points W_2, W_1 (with point a), W_0 (with point b, Supply line). Demand= MRP= VMP. Horizontal points L_1, L_0, L_2.

____ f. The per unit price of labor is $0W_0$.

____ g. The fixed inputs will share total income that equals the area of triangle W_0W_2b.

____ h. Labor receives an amount of income equal to the area of rectangle $0W_0bL_0$.

____ i. The supply curve of labor is also the marginal factor cost curve of labor.

____ j. The MFC of the L_1th unit of labor is W_1.

____ k. The marginal physical product of the L_2th unit of labor is roughly zero.

Problem 3

Use this table, which shows labor productivity for your Zippy Lawn Service, to answer the following questions.

Labor	Output	MPP	VMP (P = $15)	VMP (P = $10)
1	18			
2	34			
3	48			
4	60			
5	70			
6	78			
7	84			
8	88			
9	90			

a. Complete the table by determining the marginal physical product (MPP) of your workers, and the value of their marginal product (VMP) when you charge $15 and $10 per lawn mowed.

b. During the months of April and May you receive $15 per lawn mowed, and labor costs $120 per worker per day. How many workers will you employ during these months? _____

c. Fierce competition from teenagers during June through August drops prices to $10 per lawn. If wages were stuck at $120 per day, how many employees would you lay off each summer? _____ How much of a wage cut would your employees have to take to remain so that everyone remained employed during the summer months? _____

Problem 4

Your sports paraphernalia plant is facing labor cost increases of 20 percent because a new computer plant in your community is attracting workers and tightening the local labor market. You currently employ 50 workers and your wage elasticity of demand for labor is 1.10. How many workers will you continue to employ after the wage increases have taken effect? _____

ANSWERS

	Matching		True/False		Multiple Choice		Unlimited MC

Matching				True/False			Multiple Choice			Unlimited MC	

Matching

Set I		Set II	
1.	e	1.	d
2.	i	2.	i
3.	b	3.	e
4.	g	4.	j
5.	a	5.	f
6.	d	6.	b
7.	c	7.	a
8.	f	8.	g
9.	j	9.	c
10.	h	10.	h

True/False

1.	T	11.	F
2.	F	12.	T
3.	F	13.	T
4.	T	14.	T
5.	T	15.	F
6.	F	16.	T
7.	T	17.	F
8.	T	18.	T
9.	T	19.	T
10.	F	20.	F

Multiple Choice

1.	c	11.	a
2.	d	12.	c
3.	e	13.	e
4.	b	14.	b
5.	b	15.	d
6.	a	16.	c
7.	d	17.	c
8.	a	18.	b
9.	c	19.	e
10.	e	20.	d

Unlimited MC

1.	c
2.	a
3.	acd
4.	ac
5.	none

Chapter Review (Fill-in Questions)

1. substitution; income
2. positively; "backward bending"
3. relative wages; workers
4. specific; general
5. Firms; workers; wages; MRPs
6. efficiency; screen; signal

Problem 1

L	Q	MPP$_L$	P	MR	TR	w	MFC	TVC	TC	MC	MRP$_L$
0	0	--	$3	3	0	$15	15	0	50	--	--
1	3	3	$3	3	9	$15	15	15	65	5	9
2	8	5	$3	3	24	$15	15	30	80	3	15
3	15	7	$3	3	45	$15	15	45	95	2.14	21
4	24	9	$3	3	72	$15	15	60	110	1.67	27
5	35	11	$3	3	105	$15	15	75	125	1.36	33
6	48	13	$3	3	144	$15	15	90	140	1.15	39
7	59	11	$3	3	177	$15	15	105	155	1.36	33
8	68	9	$3	3	204	$15	15	120	170	1.67	27
9	75	7	$3	3	225	$15	15	135	185	2.14	21
10	80	5	$3	3	240	$15	15	150	200	3	15
11	83	3	$3	3	249	$15	15	165	215	5	9
12	84	1	$3	3	252	$15	15	180	230	15	3

a. See Table.
b. Perfectly competitive; product price is the same no matter what level of output.
c. Perfectly competitive; input price (wage rate) is the same no matter how many workers are hired.
d. 10; MRP = MFC = $15 and P = MR = MC = $3.
e. 80; MR = MC = $3.
f. 11; MRP = MFC = $9 and P = MR = MC = $3.
g. The demand for labor is derived from the demand for output.

h.   None; MFC > MRP for all levels of employment; therefore the firm should shut down.

Problem 2

a.   T
b.   T
c.   F
d.   T
e.   T
f.   T
g.   T
h.   T
i.   T
j.   F
k.   T

Problem 3

Labor	Output	MPP	VMP (P = $15)	VMP (P = $10)
1	18	18	270	180
2	34	16	240	160
3	48	14	210	140
4	60	12	180	120
5	70	10	150	100
6	78	8	120	80
7	84	6	90	60
8	88	4	60	40
9	90	2	30	20

a.   See Table.
b.   6
c.   2 (6 - 4); $40 ($120 - $80)

Problem 4

You will employ 39 workers after the wage increases takes effect. (%ΔL/%Δw = 1.10, so X%/20% = 1.10. X = 1.10 x .20 = .22. 50 x .22 = 11. 50 - 11 = 39 workers.)

Chapter 29
Imperfect Competition In Labor Markets

Chapter Objectives

After you have read and studied this chapter you should be able to discuss the effects of a firm's monopoly power and/or monopsony power on wages and hiring; major features of U.S. labor legislation; evolution of the labor union movement; the effects of wage discrimination on the efficiency of the labor market; and the overall effects of unions on economic performance.

Chapter Review: Key Points

1. The *marginal revenue product curve (MRP)* for a firm selling in an imperfectly competitive product market will be below the *value of the marginal product of labor (VMP)* curve. All firms will hire labor until the marginal revenue product equals the *marginal factor cost (MFC)* of labor. Because $MRP < VMP$, employees of firms with market power, are paid less than the values of their marginal products. This difference is called *monopolistic exploitation.*

2. A *monopsonist* is the sole buyer of a particular resource or good. Labor monopsonists face an entire market supply of labor and, if all workers are paid equally, their marginal factor cost curve will lie above the labor supply curve. Relative to pure competitors, labor monopsonists pay lower wages and hire fewer workers. In addition, labor will be paid less than the value of its marginal product, a difference referred to as *monopsonistic exploitation.*

3. When competitive conditions prevail in both resource and product markets, the firm hires labor until $VMP = MRP = MFC = w$. When monopoly prevails in the product market but the monopoly firm hires labor under competitive conditions, labor is hired up to the point where $VMP > MRP = MFC = w$. Given a competitive product market and monopsony power in the labor market, a firm will maximize profits by hiring labor until $VMP = MRP = MFC > w$. Finally, when a firm has both monopoly and monopsony power, labor is hired up to the point where $VMP > MRP = MFC > w$. Any difference between VMP and w represents *exploitation*, a term borrowed from Marxist jargon.

4. A minimum wage legally set above the equilibrium wage in competitive labor markets will raise unemployment. It is possible, but unlikely, that minimum wages might increase employment and wages simultaneously, but only where there is substantial monopsonistic exploitation of unskilled workers and wage discrimination is not practiced, an unlikely combination. A union wage hike might have the same effect. However, the markets where minimum-wage hikes raise existing wages are typically rather competitive. Thus, increased unemployment is the normal result when minimum wages arc increased.

5. Unions have traditionally organized into craft or industrial unions. Craft unions were the bulwark of the *American Federation of Labor (AFL)*; industrial unions comprised the *Congress of Industrial Organizations (CIO)*. Frequent jurisdictional disputes over which organization would represent particular workers caused the two to merge into the AFL-CIO in 1955.

6. Unions and their leaders use several kinds of agreements with organized firms to protect their prerogatives as sole bargaining agents for workers. *Closed shops* require workers to be union members as a precondition for employment. At the other end of the spectrum, *open shops* permit union and nonunion members to work side by side. This arrangement is quite unsatisfactory to unions since nonmembers receive the benefits of collective bargaining but need not pay union dues. *Union shops* are compromises between closed and open shops. The employer can hire union or nonunion workers, but an employee must join the union within some specified period (usually 30 days) to retain the job. The Taft-Hartley Act of 1947 outlawed the closed shop and permitted individual states to pass right-to-work laws forbidding union shops. In many of these states, *agency shops* have been created to protect unions from free riders. Workers may choose not to belong to the union but must pay dues.

7. Unionism developed in a hostile environment. The Great Depression shifted public policy in favor of collective bargaining. As trade unionism grew, many felt that unions became corrupt and too powerful, and tighter organizing and financial reporting constraints were imposed on labor organizations. The union movement was relatively stable from roughly 1950 until 1980, but has declined as a percentage of the total labor force in the 1980s. The labor force increasingly consists of white-collar workers who are reluctant to join unions.

8. *Bilateral monopoly,* a very early model of collective bargaining, describes the limits to the wage bargaining process but provides little predictive power. Sir John Hicks's bargaining model predicts both final wage settlements and the duration of strikes.

9. *Labor unions* have typically employed three methods to increase the wages of their members: (a) reductions of the supply of workers to an industry; (b) establishing higher wages and then parceling the available work to members; and (c) policies designed to increase demands for union labor.

10. *Wage differentials* between union and nonunion workers average roughly 10-15 percent. Some people blame inflation on excessive union wage demands. Large wage hikes in key industries may set the pattern for other industries. Higher wages may raise unemployment and induce public officials to pursue expansionary macroeconomic policies, further intensifying inflationary pressures. Since organized labor represents less than one-sixth of the work force, it is unlikely that unionism explains much inflation.

11. A small percentage of collective bargaining negotiations end in *strikes,* and most are short. Strikes often impose costs on individuals and firms that are not direct parties to labor negotiations. Strikes may cause shortages, shipping delays, or losses of perishable products.

12. Public employee unions frequently mix politics and collective bargaining to win their demands. Public officials negotiating contracts are seldom those who are responsible for developing government budgets; thus, they may have only weak incentives to resist union wage demands.

Matching Key Terms And Concepts

Set I

_____ 1. monopsonist

_____ 2. the Wagner Act

_____ 3. marginal factor cost (MFC)

_____ 4. blacklists

_____ 5. bilateral monopoly

_____ 6. MRP = MFC

_____ 7. the Taft-Hartley Act

_____ 8. public employees

_____ 9. yellow dog contracts

_____ 10. the Clayton Act

a. Guaranteed labor the right to organize unions.
b. Now-outlawed agreements not to join unions.
c. Exempted from the protection of the Wagner Act.
d. Is a price maker as a buyer.
e. Used to prevent union organizers from getting jobs.
f. The equilibrium condition for inputs for all firms.
g. Permits individual states to enact "right-to-work" laws that forbid the closed-shop.
h. Lies above the labor supply curve facing a monopsonist.
i. Exempts most union activity from the Sherman Act.
j. One of the earliest models of collective bargaining.

Set II

___ 1. monopolistic exploitation

___ 2. agency shop

___ 3. "right-to-work" laws

___ 4. open shop

___ 5. perfect wage discrimination

___ 6. closed shop

___ 7. Taft-Hartley Act

___ 8. union shop

___ 9. monopsonistic exploitation

___10. minimum wage laws

a. VMP > MRP = MFC = w.
b. May eliminate inefficiencies of monopsony power.
c. The closed-shop is illegal.
d. VMP = MRP = MFC > w.
e. If monopsony power exists, may cause increases in both wages and employment.
f. All workers eventually must join a union.
g. Only union members may be hired.
h. Employment is not affected by union membership.
i. Dues are paid by nonunion workers.
j. Outlaw the union shop.

True/False Questions

___ 1. A labor monopsonist that does not wage discriminate hires fewer workers and pays lower wages than a perfectly competitive employer.

___ 2. Equilibrium employment falls for all firms when minimum legal wages rise.

___ 3. Firms maximize profits by buying resources until each input's marginal revenue product equals its marginal factor cost.

___ 4. Monopsonists confront perfectly elastic supplies of labor.

___ 5. Values of the marginal product equal the extra revenue that would be generated if a perfectly competitive seller of output hired extra units of a resource.

___ 6. Bilateral monopoly occurs when two powerful oligopolists share an output market, and is also known as duopoly.

___ 7. Firms can exercise either monopolistic exploitation or monopsonistic exploitation, but not both simultaneously.

___ 8. Wage discrimination cannot occur in equilibrium without monopsonistic exploitation of labor.

___ 9. There are incentives for employees not to share wage information if a firm follows a policy of wage discrimination.

___10. Unions existed in the U.S. before the Civil War.

___11. Yellow dog contracts that require employees to agree not to join unions are still a popular union-busting technique.

___12. The Sherman Antitrust Act was originally used to prosecute unions on the grounds that strikes were "restraints of trade."

___13. Union organizers were forbidden by the Taft Hartley Act to place firms that resisted union objectives on "blacklists" that required current union members to boycott these firms.

___14. Cost-push inflation is often blamed on labor unions because of wage increases negotiated through collective bargaining.

___15. In an average year, approximately 12 percent to 14 percent of the total labor force is involved in strikes.

___16. Strikes typically waste 6 to 10 percent of annual GDP.

___17. The typical gap in wages between comparable union and nonunion workers is roughly one third.

___18. Strikes tend to be settled because firms are eventually pressured to meet all union demands.

___19. Federal workers may all now join unions and strike to ensure that the government collectively bargains in good faith.

___20. Union membership has recently declined to less than 20 percent of the U.S. labor force.

Standard Multiple Choice

Each Question Has One Best Answer.

___ 1. If a firm hires to the point where VMP > MRP = MFC = w:
   a. there is a bilateral monopoly situation.
   b. the firm has monopsony power.
   c. there is monopolistic exploitation of workers.
   d. monopolistic economic profits are necessarily being realized.
   e. wage discrimination is being exercised.

___ 2. The employer least likely to have monopsony power would be:
   a. a secretarial service firm in Chicago.
   b. the police force in Macon, Georgia.
   c. the U.S. Army.
   d. a lumber mill in Greer, Arizona.
   e. the community hospital in Pocatello, Idaho.

___ 3. Unlike competitive employers, firms with monopsony power can:
   a. set any wage they want and hire as many workers as they desire.
   b. produce any amount and charge any price they want for output.
   c. be expected to try to maximize their profits.
   d. always wage discriminate to ensure monopolistic exploitation.
   e. pay workers wages less than MRP.

___ 4. When a firm's wage structure reflects the eagerness of individual employees to work, terms that are most applicable include:
   a. monopsonistic exploitation and wage discrimination.
   b. monopolistic exploitation and separation of ownership and control.
   c. surplus values and hedonistic preferences.
   d. wage peonage and capitalistic defoliation.
   e. third degree price discrimination and labor rent controls.

___ 5. An employer can legally follow a policy of:
   a. wage discrimination based on race or gender.
   b. closed shop agreements with unions.
   c. firing workers because they join unions.
   d. price discrimination based on cost differentials.
   e. telling other firms which job applicants are union sympathizers.

___ 6. Minimum wage laws are most likely to raise equilibrium employment if a firm has been exercising:
   a. monopoly power and price discrimination.
   b. employee selection in markets for unskilled workers.
   c. collective bargaining with an aggressive union.
   d. monopsony power without wage discrimination.
   e. racial discrimination in its hiring practices.

___ 7. When a powerful seller confronts a powerful buyer, there is:
   a. reciprocal exploitation.
   b. bilateral monopoly.
   c. dialectical bargaining.
   d. ancillary reciprocity.
   e. strategic bloc management.

___ 8. Agreements not to join unions were once common requirements for employment. Now outlawed, these are known as:
   a. yellow dog contracts.
   b. blacklist contracts.
   c. exclusionary provisions.
   d. employment screens.
   e. union busters.

___ 9. Industrial unions intend to organize all workers within:
   a. a particular company.
   b. the United States.
   c. a particular skill or craft.
   d. a specific occupation.
   e. a broad industry.

10. The idea that unions are more powerful than ever before is:
    a. supported by the effects of unions on inflationary spirals.
    b. reflected in the growing numbers of violent and costly strikes.
    c. contrary to the fact that union membership is declining.
    d. demonstrated by the growing political influence of unions.
    e. especially true in the cases of middle managers.

11. The least likely result if unions succeed in raising their wages is that:
    a. wages in nonunion sectors will fall.
    b. employment will grow in nonunion sectors.
    c. barriers will be constructed to limit entry into unions.
    d. labor's share of national income will grow.
    e. nonunion firms will have competitive advantages over union firms.

12. Prior to the AFL-CIO merger in 1955:
    a. the AFL was an alliance of industrial unions.
    b. the CIO was an alliance of craft unions.
    c. strikes over which unions would represent workers were common.
    d. the union movement was restricted to public employees.
    e. the union movement in the U.S. was declining.

13. Strikes tend to be resolved after workers' savings trickle down into a discomfort zone and there is exhaustion of:
    a. public tolerance, causing government to set a fair settlement.
    b. managers and inventories, causing firms to raise their offers.
    c. diminishing returns to union leaders and business agents.
    d. labor force participation by nonunion "scabs."
    e. legal remedies that might correct managerial misbehavior.

14. The Taft Hartley Act of 1946 made it illegal to have a:
    a. right-to-work law passed by a state legislature.
    b. conviction for a misdemeanor and serve as a union officer.
    c. union for agricultural migrants or government workers.
    d. closed shop agreement that prevents hiring nonunion workers.
    e. yellow dog contract or a blacklist of potential troublemakers.

15. Union membership is most prevalent among:
    a. white collar workers.
    b. supervisors and managers.
    c. pink collar clerical workers.
    d. young, upwardly mobile, urban professionals.
    e. blue collar workers.

___16. The union strategy that probably yields the highest wages for both union members and other workers over the long run is:
a. restricting entry from particular occupations.
b. lobbying for tariffs against imports that compete with union-produced goods.
c. setting rigid rules for firms employing union workers to maximize "feather bedding."
d. facilitating management plans to increase productivity.
e. demanding uniform wage rates with premiums for seniority.

___17. Contracts requiring employment when some workers' jobs have been made obsolete by automation are examples of:
a. blacklisting.
b. featherbedding.
c. check-off provisions.
d. yellow dog contracts.
e. labor-reducing protectionism.

___18. Nonunion members cannot "free-ride" in states with Right-to-Work laws if a company agrees to operate a/an:
a. closed shop.
b. union shop.
c. open shop.
d. agency shop.
e. shoe shop.

___19. If a collective bargaining contract contains a "check-off provision":
a. union workers can be fired if they do not meet production quotas.
b. firms collect union dues by deducting them from paychecks.
c. workers are required to do only tasks in their job descriptions.
d. quality control in a plant is performed by union representatives.
e. seniority creates a first right of refusal for layoffs, so older workers can choose to draw unemployment compensation or work.

___20. Workers who are now allowed to join unions but who still may not legally strike include:
a. civilian federal employees.
b. medical professionals.
c. military personnel.
d. elected state and local officials.
e. television newscasters.

Chapter Review (Fill-In Questions)

1. All firms maximize profits by hiring inputs until their _____ equal their _____.

2. If a firm with monopoly power is a competitive employer, the VMP _____ the MRP, so profit-maximizing equilibrium occurs where _____.

3. _____ is a primitive model of collective bargaining in which a monopsony firm deals with a monopoly union. However, the model only determines the _____ in which wage contracts will fall, not the precise wage rate that will be the outcome of bargaining.

4. _____ unions are organized along occupational lines, while _____ unions include all workers in an industry.

5. When employment is denied to everyone not a union member, there is a(n) _____ agreement, which is a violation of the _____.

6. _____ shops, for which a worker must join a union to maintain employment, are legal unless a state has passed a(n) _____.

7. Union membership is irrelevant for employment in a(n) _____, but non-union members still pay dues if a(n) _____ arrangement exists.

8. Because both union and non-union workers get the same benefits, an agency shop agreement is one means by which non-union workers are prevented from being _____. Firms deduct union dues from workers' paychecks when contracts include _____ provisions.

9. Widespread concern about growth in union power is probably misplaced. It is dubious that union wage demands cause substantial _____. In typical years, only _____ percent of all workers are on strike.

Unlimited Multiple Choice

Each Question Has From Zero To Four Correct Responses.

___ 1. The labor union in a given industry can increase its members' wage rates by implementing policies:
   a. with firms in the industry to increase labor productivity.
   b. that decrease the supply of union workers in the industry.
   c. that increase the demand for union labor.
   d. of featherbedding.

___ 2. A profit maximizing monopsonist in the labor market always hires more workers up to the point where the:
   a. value of labor's marginal product equals its marginal factor cost.
   b. marginal revenue product of labor equals its marginal factor cost.
   c. wage rate is the lowest possible proportion of the marginal factor cost of labor.
   d. wage rate just equals labor's marginal factor cost.

___ 3. The bilateral monopoly model:
   a. is one of the most modern theories of collective bargaining.
   b. specifies equilibrium price when one buyer deals with one seller.
   c. is useful in explaining the limits to bargaining between a monopsonistic buyer and a monopolistic seller of labor services.
   d. describes in general terms the boundaries for wage negotiations.

___ 4. A labor monopsonist that cannot wage discriminate to take advantage of different people's willingness to work confronts a:
   a. perfectly wage elastic supply curve of labor.
   b. marginal factor cost of labor that is upward sloping and above the labor supply curve.
   c. positively sloped labor supply curve.
   d. fixed wage that it must pay, but may then hire as many workers as it chooses.

___ 5. A nondiscriminating firm that is both a monopolist in the output market and a monopsonist in the labor market will employ workers until the:
   a. value of labor's marginal product equals its marginal factor cost.
   b. marginal revenue product of labor equals the value of labor's marginal product.
   c. wage rate most greatly exceeds the marginal factor cost of labor.
   d. marginal revenue product of labor is equal to the wage rate.

Problems

Problem 1

This table contains data on the wage rate (w) structures for two firms that are in perfect competition in different output markets. Use this information to answer the following questions.

	Firm A					Firm B			
L	w	Total Labor Cost	MFC	MRP	L	w	Total Labor Cost	MFC	MRP
0	10			--	0	5.00			--
1	10			12.50	1	5.50			13.00
2	10			12.00	2	6.00			12.50
3	10			11.50	3	6.50			12.00
4	10			11.00	4	7.00			11.50
5	10			10.50	5	7.50			11.00
6	10			10.00	6	8.00			10.50
7	10			9.50	7	8.50			10.00
8	10			9.00	8	9.00			9.50
9	10			8.50	9	9.50			9.00
10	10			8.00	10	10.00			8.50

a. Complete the Table.

b. What type of firm is Firm A in the labor market? _____ Why? _____
   _____

c. What type of firm is Firm B in the labor market? _____ Why? _____
   _____

d. Plot the wage rate (w), the marginal factor cost (MFC), and marginal revenue product (MRP) curves for both firms in the figure below.

e. Firm A will hire _____ workers at an hourly wage rate of _____.

f. Firm B will hire _____ workers at an hourly wage rate of _____.

g. Total monopsonistic exploitation by Firm B is _____.

Firm A

Firm B

Problem 2

This figure shows the revenue and cost curves in different labor markets for two different firms. Use this information to answer the following true/false questions.

Firm A

Firm B

____ a. Firm A is a price maker in the output market.

____ b. Firm A is able to influence the wage rate of the labor service that it purchases.

____ c. Firm B is a competitive seller in the output market.

____ d. Firm B is a price taker in the input market.

____ e. Firm A will hire L_0 workers in equilibrium.

____ f. Firm B will hire L_1 workers in equilibrium.

g. In equilibrium, Firm A will pay a wage of W_0.

h. In equilibrium, Firm B will pay a wage of W_2.

i. The labor supply curve that confronts Firm A is also its marginal factor cost curve.

j. The labor supply curve that confronts Firm B is also its marginal factor cost curve.

k. For Firm B, the line segment ae represents the degree of monopolistic exploitation per unit of labor.

l. For Firm A, the line segment ab represents the degree of monopsonistic exploitation per unit of labor.

Problem 3

This figure depicts the revenue and cost curves of two firms hiring from different labor markets. Use this information to answer the following true/false questions.

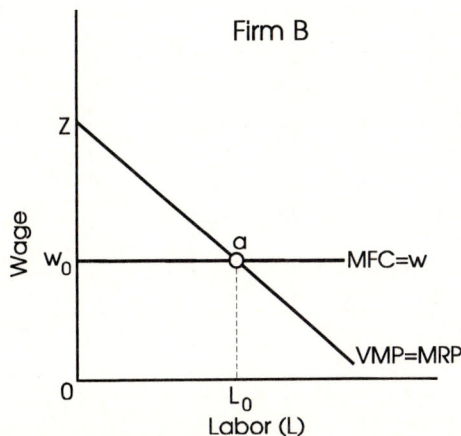

a. Firm A is a price taker in the input market.

b. Firm A is a price taker in the output market.

c. Firm B is a price maker in the output market.

d. Firm B is a price maker in the input market.

e. Firm A will hire L_0 labor to maximize profits.

f. Firm A will pay a wage of $0W_2$ to maximize profits.

___ g. Firm B incurs total labor costs equal to area W_0Z_a.

___ h. Firm A incurs total labor costs equal to area $0W_0eL_0$.

___ i. Firm A's derived demand for labor is actually the value of the marginal product curve.

___ j. Firm A will hire L_0 workers at a wage of $0W_5$.

___ k. If Firm A hires L_0 workers for a wage of W_0, line segment fb is the degree of monopolistic exploitation and line segment be is the degree of monopsonistic exploitation.

___ l. Firm B pays workers the value of their marginal products and no exploitation of labor results.

Problem 4

Use the information contained in this table, concerning the output and demand for your latest product--dehydrated water, to answer the following questions.

L	Q	P	TR	MR	MPP	MRP	VMP	w	TC_L	MFC
0	0	---						---		
1	60	200						200		
2	100	180						300		
3	136	160						400		
4	168	140						800		
5	196	120						1,200		
6	220	100						1,500		
7	240	80						1,800		

a. Fill in the columns for total revenue (TR), marginal revenue (MR), marginal physical product (MPP), marginal revenue product (MRP), and the value of the marginal product (VMP).

b. If labor is purchased from a competitive market and the wage rate is $400 per unit of labor (L), how many units of labor will you hire? _____

c. Given your answer in question b, what is the extent of your monopolistic exploitation?

_____

Suppose that all your competitors for the services of professional water dehydrators go bankrupt, and you become a monopsonist facing the wage rate (w) shown in the table.

d. Fill in the columns for total cost of labor (TC_L) and marginal factor cost (MFC).

e. How many workers will you employ now that you are a monopsonist? _____

f. Given your answer in question f, what is the extent of both your monopolistic and monopsonistic exploitation? _____

ANSWERS

	Matching		True/False				Multiple Choice			Unlimited MC	
Set I		Set II									
1.	d	1.	a	1.	T	11.	F	1.	c	11.	d	1.	abcd
2.	a	2.	i	2.	F	12.	T	2.	a	12.	c	2.	b
3.	h	3.	j	3.	T	13.	F	3.	e	13.	b	3.	cd
4.	e	4.	h	4.	F	14.	T	4.	a	14.	d	4.	bc
5.	j	5.	b	5.	T	15.	F	5.	d	15.	e	5.	none
6.	f	6.	g	6.	F	16.	F	6.	d	16.	d		
7.	g	7.	c	7.	F	17.	F	7.	b	17.	b		
8.	c	8.	f	8.	T	18.	F	8.	a	18.	d		
9.	b	9.	d	9.	T	19.	F	9.	e	19.	b		
10.	i	10.	e	10.	T	20.	T	10.	c	20.	a		

Chapter Review (Fill-in Questions)

1. marginal revenue products (MRP); marginal factor costs (MFC)
2. exceeds; VMP > MRP = MFC = W
3. Bilateral monopoly; range
4. Craft; industrial
5. closed shop; Taft-Hartley Act
6. Union; right-to-work law
7. open shop; agency shop
8. free riders; check-off
9. inflation; 2 to 4

Problem 1

a. See table below.
b. Perfectly competitive; a fixed wage rate faces the firm.
c. The firm has monopsony power; the firm can use its hiring decision to influence the wage rate it pays.
d. See figure below.
e. 6; $10.
f. 6; $8.
g. ($10.50 - 8.00) x 6 = $15.00.

Problem 2

a.	T	g.	T
b.	F	h.	F
c.	T	i.	T
d.	F	j.	F
e.	F	k.	F
f.	T	l.	F

Problem 3

a.	F.	g.	F
b.	F	h.	T
c.	F	i.	F
d.	F	j.	F
e.	T	k.	T
f.	F	l.	T

	Firm A					Firm B			
L	w	Total Labor Cost	MFC	MRP	L	w	Total Labor Cost	MFC	MRP
0	10	0	10	--	0	5.00	0	--	--
1	10	10	10	12.50	1	5.50	5.50	5.50	13.00
2	10	20	10	12.00	2	6.00	12.00	6.50	12.50
3	10	30	10	11.50	3	6.50	19.50	7.50	12.00
4	10	40	10	11.00	4	7.00	28.00	8.50	11.50
5	10	50	10	10.50	5	7.50	37.50	9.50	11.00
6	10	60	10	10.00	6	8.00	48.00	10.50	10.50
7	10	70	10	9.50	7	8.50	59.50	11.50	10.00
8	10	80	10	9.00	8	9.00	72.00	12.50	9.50
9	10	90	10	8.50	9	9.50	85.50	13.50	9.00
10	10	100	10	8.00	10	10.00	100.00	14.50	8.50

Firm A / Firm B

Problem 4

a. See table below.
b. 4 (closest MRP above wage rate)
c. $2,720 ($4,480 - $1,760)
d. See table below.
e. 3 (closest to intersection of MFC and MRP where MFC < MRP)
f. $5,360 ($5,760 - $400)

L	Q	P	TR	MR	MPP	MRP	VMP	w	TC$_L$	MFC
0	0	---	0	--	--	--	--	---	0	--
1	60	200	12,000	200	60	12,000	12,000	200	200	200
2	100	180	18,000	150	40	6,000	7,200	300	600	400
3	136	160	21,760	104.4	36	3,758.4	5,760	400	1,200	600
4	168	140	23,520	55	32	1,760	4,480	800	3,200	2,000
5	196	120	23,520	0	28	0	3,360	1,200	6,000	2,800
6	220	100	22,000	-63.3	24	-1,519.2	2,400	1,500	9,000	3,000
7	240	80	19,200	-140	20	-2,800	1,600	1,800	12,600	3,600

Chapter 30
Rent, Interest, Profits, And Capitalization

Chapter Objectives

After you have completed this chapter you should be able to differentiate between rent, interest, and profits, and describe their determinants; and explain the capitalization process through which income streams are translated into wealth.

Chapter Review: Key Points

1. *Economic rent* exists whenever resource owners receive more than the minimum required for them to supply given amounts of the resource.

2. Land has a unique economic characteristic--is fixed in supply. Thus, its supply curve is perfectly inelastic, and all payments for the use of land are pure rent. Land rents vary by location and particular physical characteristics, such as fertility or stores of minerals.

3. Land is not unique in generating economic rents. Any resource paid more than the minimum required to elicit its availability also generates economic rents.

4. "Single taxers" inspired by Henry George propose a 100 percent tax on land rent as a single tax to finance all government spending. They argue that taxing this unearned surplus would not distort the allocation of land, and thus would not hinder economic efficiency. The *single-tax proposal* suffers from: (a) inability to finance the entire public sector, (b) administrative problems in distinguishing land values arising out of improvements made by owners from rent as an unearned surplus, and (c) reduced incentives for landowners to put their land to the best possible uses if rent is taxed away.

5. Economic rent promotes economic efficiency by providing resource owners with incentives to put their assets to the most valuable uses.

6. *Nominal interest rates* are the percentage annual premiums paid to borrow funds. Interest rates on financial instruments vary according to: (a) risk, (b) maturity, and (c) liquidity. The interest rate normally means the rate on a long-term riskless bond.

7. In the long run, *real* (purchasing power) *interest rates* depend on: (a) premiums required to induce savers to delay consumption, (b) desires for liquidity, and (c) the productivity of capital. These factors determine interest rates through markets for *loanable funds*.

8. *Pure economic profits* are the residual after adjusting accounting profits for the opportunity cost of resources provided by a firm's owners. Profit may arise from *monopoly power*, bearing business *uncertainty*, or *innovation*.

9. Profits are a driving force in a capitalist economy, channeling resources to their most productive uses and stimulating progress as entrepreneurs innovate and endure business uncertainty. Profits induce efficiency; competitive firms that do not produce at the lowest possible cost will suffer economic losses.

10. *Present values* are the sums of the discounted values of future income that may be expected from owning an asset. The present value of an asset and its price will be identical in equilibrium. If the present value exceeds price, then the asset is a profitable investment because the expected rate of return exceeds the interest rate. *Capitalization* is the process whereby prices gravitate toward present values of assets.

Matching Key Terms And Concepts

____ 1. single tax movement

____ 2. economic rents

____ 3. interest rates

____ 4. rate of return

____ 5. location rents

____ 6. capitalization

____ 7. perpetuity

____ 8. economic profit

____ 9. debt capital

____ 10. risk

a. Income per period as a percentage of investment.
b. The prime motivation for innovation.
c. Income generated for landowners because of reduced transaction costs.
d. When probabilities are known of realizing certain outcomes.
e. Corporate bonds.
f. Based on the idea that land rents are unearned surpluses.
g. A promise to pay a specified amount annually, forever.
h. The percentage annual premiums paid to ultimate capital suppliers for the use of money.
i. Transforming income streams into wealth.
j. The area above a resource supply curve but below the market price.

True/False Questions

____ 1. The supply of land is perfectly elastic in the long run.

____ 2. Location rents are more important in explaining the high prices of farm land than the prices of land in urban centers.

____ 3. Reductions of transportation costs for customers and resource suppliers are the major sources of location rents.

____ 4. A single tax of 100 percent of land rents would easily generate sufficient revenues to replace all other taxes.

____ 5. Property taxes would influence resource allocations more than would pure land taxes that generated identical tax revenues.

____ 6. Equilibrium investment occurs when total profits are maximized because rates of return exceed interest rates by the largest possible amounts.

____ 7. A corporation that issues stock instead of bonds to raise money for new investments relies on debt capital.

____ 8. New capital formation is enhanced when people increasingly sacrifice liquidity or delay their consumption.

____ 9. The more liquid a finacial asset, the greater tends to be its expected rate of return.

____ 10. Expanded financial investment in an economic sector tends to promote economic investment in that sector.

____ 11. Capitalists are rewarded with profits, while entrepreneurs earn interest.

____ 12. Widespread industry profits indicate that society would gain by channeling more resources into that industry.

____ 13. Frank Knight argued that riskbearing is a surer way than dealing with uncertainty for individuals to gain economic profits.

____ 14. Inventors are far more important to the dynamic process of capitalism, according to Joseph Schumpeter, than are the entrepreneurs who merely produce and distribute innovations.

____ 15. Monopoly profits stimulate long run economic efficiency.

____ 16. If the rate of return on an asset equals the interest rate, then the price of the asset just equals its present value.

____ 17. Prices of perpetuities rise when interest rates rise.

____ 18. Expected economic profits from an asset cannot be capitalized into wealth in the same way as are rents.

____ 19. The present value of an asset exceeds its current price whenever its rate of return exceeds the market rate of interest.

____ 20. Vigorous competition for profit opportunities cause the expected profits from most investments to be approximately zero.

Standard Multiple Choice

Each Question Has A Single Best Answer.

___ 1. Land values attributable to the ways particular sites reduce transportation costs are known as:
  a. location rents.
  b. transportation rents.
  c. short-term quasi-rents.
  d. parcel posts.
  e. transaction rents.

___ 2. If you lease a building for five years and quickly earn profits because it is convenient for potential customers:
  a. you could still receive all of the pure profits that could be anticipated if you sold your business with a sublease at the end of the second year.
  b. your rent would probably be raised when the lease ran out.
  c. the owner evidently underestimated the building's location rents.
  d. similar firms would likely open businesses near you.
  e. all of the above.

___ 3. Owners of resources other than land receive rents that are equal to the area below the:
  a. consumer surplus rectangle generated by price discrimination.
  b. resource price line but above the resource supply curve.
  c. supply curve and out to the quantity of resource sold.
  d. total cost curve but above the total revenue curve.
  e. marginal cost curve but above the average variable cost curve.

___ 4. The main instigator of the single-tax movement was:
  a. British Prime Minister Lloyd George.
  b. John Stuart Mill.
  c. Henry George.
  d. Henry David Thoreau.
  e. David Ricardo.

___ 5. Taxes on pure economic rents:
  a. pose especially severe problems for economic efficiency.
  b. reduce the incentives to put resources to their best uses.
  c. could easily replace all other forms of taxation.
  d. have much stronger substitution than income effects.
  e. are rapidly shifted forward to users of final products.

___ 6. Economic rents differ most from pure profits in that they are:
  a. received by the owners of productive resources.
  b. costs to the firm using the resources that generate them, but not to society as a whole.
  c. realized only in the short run, but not in the long run.
  d. a major cause of cost-push inflation.
  e. All of the above.

___ 7. Interest rates on given securities will be lower the:
   a. shorter the period to maturity.
   b. greater the risk involved.
   c. less liquid the asset is.
   d. greater the expected rate of inflation.
   e. greater is the face value relative to the market price.

___ 8. Market interest rates are least related to the:
   a. willingness of people to defer consumption (to save) if they are rewarded for doing so.
   b. desires of people for liquidity.
   c. marginal productivity of new capital relative to its price.
   d. par values of stocks relative to their current prices.
   e. current prices of bonds relative to their face values.

___ 9. The monetary premiums paid per period as a percentage of the cost of a financial investment is known as the:
   a. real rate of return.
   b. nominal rate of interest.
   c. rate of capitalization.
   d. financial elasticity coefficient.
   e. real rate of interest.

___ 10. Economic profits are:
   a. signals that society desires more resources in an industry.
   b. rewards to successful innovators.
   c. capitalized as wealth if they can be expected over time.
   d. a residual to a firm's owners for bearing uncertainty.
   e. All of the above.

___ 11. Owners of corporate stock receive pure economic profit only to the extent that the rates of return realized from owning the stock exceed the:
   a. interest rate that would have been generated by other financial investments carrying similar risks.
   b. immediate gratification available by not delaying consumption.
   c. funds saved by taking advantage of tax loopholes.
   d. discount rate offered by exchange rate depreciation.
   e. rate of arbitrage available in real estate investments.

___ 12. According to Frank Knight, unlike uncertainty, risk is:
   a. totally unpredictable.
   b. a major source of pure economic profits.
   c. possible to estimate so that firms can adjust appropriately.
   d. impossible to account for when making rational decisions.
   e. unimportant to entrepreneurs who seek profits through innovation.

___ 13. The rate of return for an asset which costs $1,500 today and pays $1,800 a year from now is:
   a. 5 percent.
   b. 10 percent.
   c. 15 percent.
   d. 17.5 percent.
   e. 20 percent.

14. When the likelihood of a certain event cannot reasonably be predicted, business decisionmakers are confronted by:
    a. random selection.
    b. uncertainty.
    c. stochastic probability.
    d. moral hazards.
    e. risk.

15. That profit functions as an incentive for innovation was among the key contributions to economic thought by:
    a. Karl Marx.
    b. Frank Knight.
    c. Joseph Schumpeter.
    d. Adam Smith.
    e. Alfred Marshall.

16. Securities annually paying specific amounts forever are:
    a. stocks.
    b. perennials.
    c. royalties.
    d. perpetuities.
    e. renewals.

17. Investment is NOT necessarily in equilibrium if:
    a. after adjusting for risk, liquidity, and time to maturity, all assets yield the same returns.
    b. all prices exactly equal their corresponding present values.
    c. the average expected rates of return on all investments equal the market rate of interest.
    d. the risks for all investments are equal, regardless of their rates of return.
    e. the market interest rate on loanable funds and the rates of return on existing capital are all equal.

18. The current worth of an income stream after discounting it by the interest rate is known as the:
    a. present value.
    b. discount rate.
    c. rate of return.
    d. perpetuity.
    e. internal interest rate.

19. If the rate of return on an asset exceeds the interest rate:
    a. its present value exceeds its price.
    b. the market is moving away from equilibrium.
    c. you should sell the asset as quickly as possible.
    d. economic rent is being realized by the resource supplier.
    e. current purchase of the asset would be unprofitable.

20. If the price of each of these assets is $1,000 and the interest rate is 10 percent, investment is most justified for:
    a. a perpetuity paying $90 annually.
    b. a machine with a 3 year life that is leasable for $1 per day.
    c. an income stream paying $500, $400, and $300, respectively, at the ends of each of the next three years.
    d. a bond paying $1,300 two years from today.
    e. an asset with a rate of return calculated at 8.5 percent.

Chapter Review (Fill-In Questions)

1. _____ is any payment greater than the _____ necessary to secure the social use of a resource.

2. Many resources other than land generate economic rent, which is the area _____ the price line for a resource but above its _____.

3. All _____ can also be considered economic rent since it is an unearned surplus. Pure profits are residuals after all opportunity costs to firms are deducted from their _____.

4. Profits are signals that society would like _____ resources devoted to a particular type of production. These desires may be frustrated if _____ power is present, but competition generally causes profitable industries to grow until all profits are eliminated.

5. Joseph _____ emphasized profits as incentives for _____, which is another of the functions of profit.

6. Frank Knight emphasized profit as a pure residual after all costs are deducted from revenue. After concluding that risk involves reasonably certain _____ of certain events, Knight reasoned that entrepreneurs could make such adjustments as buying _____ against undesirable events; hence, risk was a cost of doing business. However, totally unpredictable events create _____ as a source of profit according to Knight.

7. Profit is a reward for bearing _____, or for _____ new products or production techniques; it is also a _____ directing the allocation of resources to their most valuable uses.

8. Using revenues expected over time and the interest rate, the _____ of an asset can be computed as _____.

9. In equilibrium, _____ equals price and the _____ equals the interest rate.

Unlimited Multiple Choice

Each Question Has From Zero To Four Correct Responses.

___ 1. Economic rents are realized whenever resource:
   a. supply curves are perfectly elastic to society as a whole.
   b. payments are the minimums needed to secure current quantities.
   c. coordination by entrepreneurs yields them pure economic profits.
   d. market supplies are less than perfectly elastic.

___ 2. Supplies of loanable funds tend to grow when households:
   a. delay consumption out of current income.
   b. feel more secure and reduce the average liquidity of their assets.
   c. begin to expect higher rates of return on new investments.
   d. seek bigger mortgages because they want to buy bigger houses.

___ 3. The present value of an asset rises when the expected:
   a. interest rate falls.
   b. total fixed income stream is spread over a longer period.
   c. future costs and revenues in each period rise by equal amounts.
   d. number of years rises for which a given annual income is expected.

___ 4. Likely consequences of high rates of economic profit being realized by innovative firms in an industry include:
   a. imitation of successful innovators by other firms.
   b. adoption by other firms of any cost-cutting innovations.
   c. hikes in the incomes of owners of vital resources.
   d. a rise over time in the prices consumers pay.

___ 5. Opportunity costs to the society as a whole include:
   a. pure economic profits.
   b. pure economic rents.
   c. the wages required before people will provide labor services.
   d. interest payments.

Problems

Problem 1

Jane, Lynn, and Tanya are all paid $100,000 annually as doctors in an urban medical clinic. The minimum salaries that each woman would have been willing to accept are, respectively, $35,000, $60,000, and $100,000.

a. What does Jane's economic rent equal? _____

b. What does Lynn's economic rent equal? _____

c. What does Tanya's economic rent equal? _____

Problem 2

Determine the real rate of interest in the following questions.

a. The nominal interest rate is 12% and the inflation rate is 7%. The real rate of interest is? ___

b. The nominal interest rate is 15% and the inflation rate is 4%. The real rate of interest is? ___

c. The nominal interest rate is 6% and the inflation rate is 9%. The real rate of interest is? ___

Problem 3

Determine what interest rate you would charge a borrower in the following questions.

a. The expected rate of inflation is 5%, and you want a 6% real return. You will charge? _____

b. The expected rate of inflation is 8%, and you want a 5% real return. You will charge? _____

c. The expected rate of inflation is -5%, and you want a 7% real return. You will charge? _____

Problem 4

This figure shows a market for raw land. Use this information to answer the following true/false questions.

____ a. If the demand for raw land is D_2, total economic rent is equal to area $0r_2bQs$.

____ b. As the demand for raw land changes, the economic rent on land varies as well.

____ c. If demand for raw land is D_2 and a tax per acre of ab is imposed, economic rent will rise by area r_1r_2ba.

____ d. If demand for raw land rises from D_2 to D_3 and a tax per acre of bc is imposed simultaneously, net economic rent to the owner stays constant.

____ e. A tax on raw land affects the supply because economic rent is reduced.

Problem 5

Determine the rate of return for the following questions.

a. What is the rate of return on a $20,000 investment that yields $25,000 in one year? _____

b. What is the rate of return on a $12,000 investment that yields $16,000 in one year? _____

c. What is the rate of return on a $8,000 investment that yields $8,500 in one year? _____

d. What is the rate of return on a $4,000 investment that yields $4,300 in one year? _____

e. What is the rate of return on a $4,000 investment that yields $4,500 in one year? _____

f. Rank investments a-e from highest to lowest rate of return. _____

g. If you had $20,000 to invest, which investment option(s) would you choose? _____
Why? _____

Problem 6

This figure depicts the supply and demand curves for the loanable funds market. The equilibrium interest rate is i_e, and i_c denotes a ceiling interest rate imposed by the federal government. Use this information to answer the following true/false questions.

___ a. The demand for loanable funds is negatively sloped in part because of diminishing marginal returns to investment.

___ b. At point a, the expected rate of return on the marginal investment project is equal to the interest rate ceiling established by the government.

___ c. The present value of the Q_0th unit of investment is greater than the present value of the Q_1th unit of investment, assuming that both units bear the same price.

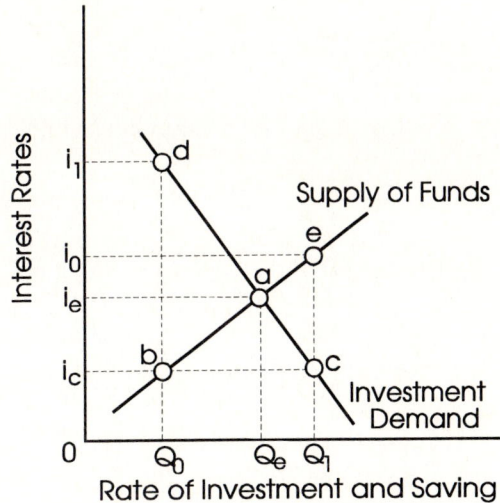

___ d. At interest rate i_c, the quantity demanded is equal to the quantity supplied of loanable funds.

___ e. At point a, the expected rate of return on the Q_eth unit of investment is equal to the interest rate that would be established by the unhindered interaction of supply and demand.

___ f. A shortage of loanable funds exists in the loanable funds market when the interest rate ceiling is i_c.

___ g. Allocative efficiency requires the loanable funds market to be at equilibrium point a.

___ h. Market mechanisms efficiently allocate loanable funds to the investment opportunities yielding the highest rates of return when the interest rate is pegged by the government at i_c.

___ i. The expected rate of return on the Q_0th unit of investment is less than the opportunity cost of the Q_1th unit of investment, expressed in percentage terms.

___ j. Society would realize a net welfare gain if the interest rate were allowed to rise to the equilibrium rate i_e.

Problem 7

Interest rates and asset prices vary inversely. The following examples give you a chance to use discounting to compute present values. The letter R denotes the net revenue in each year; subscripts indicate its time period; and i denotes the market interest rate used to compute discounted present values of the assets.

a. $i = 10\%$, $R_0 = 0$, and $R_1 = 200$. Present discounted value = _____.

b. $i = 5\%$, $R_0 = 0$, and $R_1 = 200$. Present discounted value = _____.

c. $i = 20\%$, $R_0 = 0$, $R_1 = 200$, $R_2 = 400$, and $R_3 = 600$. Present discounted value = _____.

d. $i = 10\%$, $R_0 = 0$, $R_1 = 200$, $R_2 = 400$, and $R_3 = 600$. Present discounted value = _____.

e. $i = 5\%$, $R_0 = 0$, $R_1 = 100$, $R_2 = 200$, $R_3 = 400$, $R_4 = 500$, and R5 = 1,000.
Present discounted value = _____.

f. $i = 10\%$, $R_0 = 0$, $R_1 = 100$, $R_2 = 200$, $R_3 = 400$, $R_4 = 500$, and R5 = 1,000.
Present discounted value = _____.

Problem 8

Winnings from state lotteries are subject to federal, state, and local income taxes, and payments to big winners are typically spread across twenty year periods without interest. Suppose you lived in an area where total income taxes were 40 percent, and you won $5 million in today's lottery.

a. How much would you receive (after taxes) annually from the lottery commission? _____

b. If interest rates were 10 percent annually, how much would someone be willing to pay you today for the rights to next year's check? _____ For the rights to the check you are scheduled to receive two years from now? _____

c. Has winning this lottery made you a millionaire? (A millionaire has a current net worth (present value) of more than $1,000,000.) _____ Why? _____

ANSWERS

Matching	True/False		Multiple Choice		Unlimited MC
1. f	1. F	11. F	1. a	11. a	1. cd
2. j	2. F	12. T	2. e	12. c	2. ab
3. h	3. T	13. F	3. b	13. e	3. ad
4. a	4. F	14. F	4. c	14. b	4. abc
5. c	5. T	15. F	5. b	15. c	5. cd
6. i	6. F	16. T	6. b	16. d	
7. g	7. F	17. F	7. a	17. c	
8. b	8. T	18. F	8. d	18. a	
9. e	9. F	19. T	9. b	19. a	
10. d	10. T	20. T	10. e	20. d	

Chapter Review (Fill-In Questions)

1. Economic rent; minimum
2. below; supply curve
3. economic profit; total revenues
4. more; monopoly
5. Schumpeter; innovation
6. probabilities; insurance; uncertainty
7. uncertainty; innovating; signal
8. present value, $PV = \sum_{t=1}^{n} \dfrac{Y_t}{(1+i)^t}$
9. present value, rate of return

Problem 1

a. $65,000
b. $40,000
c. $0

Problem 2

a. 5%
b. 11%
c. -3%

Problem 3

a. 11%
b. 13%
c. 2%

Problem 4

a. T
b. T
c. F
d. T
e. F

Problem 5

a. 25%
b. 33.3%
c. 6.25%
d. 7.5%
e. 12.5%
f. b, a, e, d, c
g. Option a; this makes the most money for you even though it doesn't give as high of a return as option b.

Problem 6

a. T
b. F
c. T
d. F
e. T
f. T
g. T
h. F
i. F
j. T

Problem 7

a. 181.82
b. 190.48
c. 791.67
d. 963. 15
e   1,817.07
f. 1,519.16

Problem 8

a. $150,000
b. $136,363.63; $123,966.94
c. yes; the present value of
    your after tax winnings is
    greater than $1 million.

Chapter 31
Income Distribution and Poverty

Chapter Objectives

After you have completed this chapter you should be able to discuss alternative criteria for distributing income and wealth; critique our current welfare system, describing the problems posed for economic efficiency and social equity; and evaluate proposals for reform of the current "welfare" mess.

Chapter Review: Key Points

1. *Lorenz curves* are one way to portray inequality. Lorenz curves for income are graphical representations of the cumulative percentages of income received by given cumulative percentages of families. If the Lorenz curve is a straight-line diagonal, the income distribution is perfectly equal. Deviations from this diagonal reflect inequality in distribution.

2. A related statistical measure of income inequality is the *Gini index or coefficient* The Gini index is defined as the ratio of the area between the line of perfect equality and the Lorenz curve to the total area under the line of perfect equality. The Gini index varies form a value of 0 (perfect equality) to 1 (perfect inequality).

3. *Relative income* measures the extent to which income is above or below median income. Today a greater percentage of Americans are making more than twice median income and more are making less than half of median income. The result is a shrinking middle class.

4. Since 1970 income distribution in the United States has become more unequal as shown by pretax and transfer Gini coefficients. Developed nations, in general, tend to have more equal distributions of income that developing nations.

5. The Social Security Administration has developed income indices that define *poverty lines* for various family sizes, ages, and locations.

6. The causes of *poverty* are many and varied. Relative to middle or upper-class families, the poor tend to have less education, fewer earners, and more children. These characteristics of the poor are not necessarily the causes of poverty. *Discrimination* may be an important factor. Persistent discrimination reduces incentives to invest in education and other marketable skills. Discrimination is often cited as the primary reason that a relatively large proportion of black families are in the lower income categories.

7. The major government program to fight poverty is *Aid to Families with Dependent Children (AFDC)*. A floor on family income is established, but as the family earns additional income, reductions of AFDC benefits often pose extreme *disincentives* for work. Given the large number of different programs designed to help the poor, $1 increases in earned income sometimes result in more than $1 of lost benefits.

8. *Negative income tax plans (NITs)* have been suggested as solutions to the "welfare mess." Negative income tax proposals provide a floor on income; as additional income is earned, benefits are reduced but by less than the additional income earned. In general, NIT plans consolidate numerous programs under one administrative roof and might allow either reduced costs or increased benefits. NIT plans have not been widely adopted, but NIT incentives have been adapted to many programs and provide the basic rationale for earned income tax credits aimed at keeping low-income working Americans above the poverty line.

Matching Key Terms and Concepts

Set I

____ 1. equality standard

____ 2. voluntary poverty

____ 3. welfare

____ 4. communist ideal

____ 5. Lorenz curve

____ 6. poverty line

____ 7. diminishing marginal utility of income

____ 8. economic discrimination

____ 9. involuntary poverty

a. Low income caused by circumstances beyond personal control.
b. "To each according to need."
c. Based on the income required to sustain a minimal standard of living.
d. Choosing to be eligible for welfare payments by making a low income.
e. An extra dollar means more to someone poor than to someone rich, according to this hypothesis.
f. Similarly productive workers are paid different wages.
g. Receiving more government benefits, proportionally, than one pays in taxes.
h. "To each, equally."

___10. contribution standard

i. A graph depicting inequality.

j. "To each according to productivity."

Set II

___ 1. negative income taxes

___ 2. family allowance plans (FAPs)

___ 3. relative income

___ 4. needs standard

___ 5. high marginal tax rates on low income

___ 6. Gini index

___ 7. Aid to Families with Dependent Children

___ 8. lowest 20 percent of families by income

___ 9. perfect equality

___10. unemployment compensation

a. Measures a person's divergence from median income.

b. Encourages erratic employment patterns.

c. A statistical measure of income concentration.

d. A welfare program blamed for severely discouraging work effort and breaking up families.

e. A proposal to make income the sole criteria for receiving welfare, which would be cash, not in-kind payments.

f. A definition of poverty making it incurable.

g. An "allowance" is given for minor children, but is absorbed by higher taxes for high income families.

h. A straight-line Lorenz curve.

i. Severe disincentives for work.

j. Income is distributed according to need.

True/False Questions

___ 1. A growing service sector accounts for some of the decline of the middle class in the past decade.

___ 2. It is unarguably equitable when income is distributed to resource suppliers according to their contributions to total output.

___ 3. Distribution of income according to contribution is compatible with a capitalistic system.

___ 4. There has been virtually no change in the pretax distribution of income in the U.S. since 1950.

___ 5. Families in the upper income brackets in the U.S. tend to pay higher taxes and receive fewer transfer payments than those in lower income brackets.

___ 6. Our income tax system has increased the inequality of income distribution over time.

___ 7. Income and wealth are statistically uncorrelated.

___ 8. U.S. welfare programs primarily are intended to aid people who have both few assets and only low incomes.

9. Dramatic growth of welfare payments in the past thirty years has substantially reduced the proportion of the population living below the poverty line.

___10. Human capital discrimination is one form of economic discrimination.

___11. Most Americans have lived below the poverty line for at least one year early in their lives.

___12. People who live below the poverty line have an average life expectancy of less than thirty years.

___13. Numerous studies indicate that price discrimination accounts for over 25 percent of all poverty.

___14. Critics of current welfare programs argue that they stimulate broken homes, illegitimacy, voluntary unemployment, the underground economy, and psychological dependency, and that they also destroy incentives to work.

___15. Subsidized housing, Medicaid, and food stamps are all examples of in-kind payments.

___16. Your $9,000 income would be considered low relative income if the median income in the U.S. is $20,000.

___17. Many European countries are considering adoption of family allowance plans modeled after the one used in the United States.

___18. Critics argue that the view that poor people have been victimized by society actually harms poor people psychologically and makes it more difficult for them to succeed financially.

___19. Several recent studies suggest that involuntary poverty is growing much faster than voluntary poverty.

___20. Negative income tax plans would be more expensive if they have higher implicit marginal tax rates and lower income floors.

Standard Multiple Choice

Each Question Has One Best Answer.

___ 1. The major ethical standard for income distribution that is most compatible with capitalism is the:
   a. traditions standard.
   b. equal distribution standard.
   c. vital necessities standard.
   d. contribution standard.
   e. needs standard.

___ 2. The Marxist ideas are most closely related to a(n):
   a. contribution standard based on average productivity.
   b. equality standard.
   c. needs standard.
   d. optimal distribution of inequality.
   e. system of equal opportunity.

3. Contribution standards are least compatible with the idea that:
   a. income distribution according to marginal productivity is proper.
   b. markets provide fair measures of contribution.
   c. inequality is proof of inequity.
   d. laissez faire economic policies are usually appropriate.
   e. profits stimulate efficient production and economic growth.

4. U.S. income inequality has NOT been intensified by:
   a. major differences among individuals in inherited wealth.
   b. consistently regressive income taxes and progressive transfers.
   c. economic discrimination.
   d. differences in personal attributes.
   e. differences in luck.

5. When comparing income and wealth in the United States:
   a. different distributions reflect economic discrimination precisely.
   b. wealth is a flow variable, while income is a stock variable.
   c. inheritance affects income more than it does wealth differences.
   d. income is much less equally distributed than wealth.
   e. income is more evenly distributed than wealth.

6. Roughly what proportion of pretax income is received by the bottom 40 percent of all families?
   a. Roughly 2%.
   b. Roughly 5%.
   c. Roughly 8%.
   d. Between 10% and 20%.
   e. Between 20% and 30%.

7. A device that illustrates distributional variance is the:
   a. dispersion/diffusion ratio.
   b. Lorenz curve.
   c. wage/price index.
   d. Murray-Sowell graph.
   e. poverty line.

8. Typical age/earnings profiles:
   a. suggest no relationship between age and income.
   b. would cause measured inequality even if all families had identical incomes over their lifetimes.
   c. explain why many families never break out of the trap of poverty.
   d. indicate that, that average income rises continuously with age.
   e. indicate that young people earn more, than middle aged people.

9. The less equal the distribution of income, the greater the:
   a. level of social stability.
   b. disincentives for work effort.
   c. area between a Lorenz curve and a 45-degree reference line.
   d. development of the market system in an economy.
   e. All of the above.

10. Equality in income distribution is most positively related to the:
    a. area between a Lorenz curve and a 45-degree reference line.
    b. extent of wage, price, and employment discrimination.
    c. level of industrial development in a country.
    d. degree to which the government favors socialist policies.
    e. inheritances passed between generations of wealthy families.

___11. In the United States, majorities, or near majorities, of those living below the poverty line have:
   a. televisions, automobiles, major appliances, and other amenities possessed only by the wealthy in other countries.
   b. a razor's edge existence, only a few steps above starvation.
   c. no access to government aid of any kind.
   d. impoverishment throughout their lives.
   e. All of the above.

___12. The proportion of the total U.S. population classified as below the poverty line if only money income is considered:
   a. rises with upturns of the business cycle.
   b. declined from 1960 to 1975, but rose during the 1980s.
   c. has been virtually eliminated by a vigorous "war on poverty".
   d. consistently covers roughly 80 percent of the same people.
   e. is far above that for most of the rest of the world.

___13. Which of the following is false?
   a. Measured wealth is much less equally distributed than income.
   b. Tax and transfer programs redistribute disposable income more evenly.
   c. Even the most efficient of proposed welfare reforms embody some disincentives for work.
   d. Most poor people are poor throughout their lives.
   e. Wealth and income are positively correlated.

___14. Discrimination posing the fewest distributional problems is:
   a. wage discrimination.
   b. human capital discrimination.
   c. price discrimination.
   d. employment discrimination.
   e. occupational discrimination.

___15. In-kind transfer payments include the:
   a. social security retirement system.
   b. unemployment compensation system.
   c. food stamp program.
   d. Aid for Families with Dependent Children (AFDC) program.
   e. negative income tax proposal.

___16. Modern advocates of sharp cuts in transfer payments would disagree with the idea that many welfare programs have:
   a. created disincentives for production.
   b. primarily failed because of underfunding.
   c. fostered unhealthy psychological dependency among poor people.
   d. encouraged illegitimacy and broken families.
   e. caused major increases in voluntary poverty.

___17. A program initiated to help overcome economic discrimination is:
   a. food stamps.
   b. Aid to Families with Dependent Children.
   c. affirmative action.
   d. family allowance plans.
   e. negative income tax.

___18. The welfare program most frequently accused of breaking up families is:
  a. Aid for Families with Dependent Children.
  b. unemployment compensation.
  c. Social Security.
  d. Medicare and Medicaid.
  e. negative income taxes.

___19. A proposed reform that would base welfare payments strictly on family size and income, and which would reduce the inconsistencies and disincentives for work embedded in many current welfare programs, is the:
  a. guaranteed annual income.
  b. strict contribution standard.
  c. consolidated security plan.
  d. negative income tax.
  e. workfare program.

___20. Under a negative income tax system, as the basic income floor is increased and as the marginal income tax rate of low incomes is reduced:
  a. the disincentive to the poor for earning more income is reduced.
  b. the poor have higher minimal standards of living.
  c. government outlays on welfare payments rise.
  d. a growing proportion of the population is on welfare.
  e. All of the above.

Chapter Review (Fill-In Questions)

1. There is evidence that _____ people tend to be happier than _____ people. Less accepted is the proposition that income itself is subject to the law of _____ _____; that is, that additional dollars mean less the _____ of them we have. If true, this might provide a justification for redistributing _____ or _____ from the rich to the poor.

2. Pretax _____ is much more equally distributed than _____, and income appears much more equally distributed, and increasingly so, after adjustments for _____ and _____ payments.

3. _____ discrimination causes high unemployment rates among those who are discriminated against; _____ discrimination denies them access to certain types of work; _____ discrimination denies them training for remunerative jobs; and _____ discrimination occurs when people are paid differently for equivalent labor productivity.

4. People are defined as "on welfare" if the _____ they pay are smaller, proportionally, than the _____ they receive from government programs.

5. Welfare programs other than AFDC include _____ compensation, social security, and such in-kind transfers as food stamps. The welfare "mess" has led to such proposals for reform as the _____, which ensures payments sufficient for minimal standards of living for minor children.

6. The _____ proposal is a suggestion that all welfare programs be replaced with cash transfers based on income alone for families of different sizes. The _____ rate would always be below one to ensure that work effort was always, at least somewhat, encouraged.

Unlimited Multiple Choice

Each Question Has From Zero To Four Correct Answers.

___ 1. The contribution standard of distribution suggests that:
   a. resource owners deserve payment for contributions to output.
   b. paying resources for marginal productivity is efficient.
   c. the marginal productivity theory of income distribution is fair.
   d. markets economize on information needed to distribute income.

___ 2. Lorenz curves can illustrate:
   a. degree of inequality in the income distribution.
   b. distribution of any quantifiable variable across a population.
   c. concentration of wealth.
   d. probabilities that given political parties will win elections.

___ 3. Family allowance plans (FAPs):
   a. are common in Europe.
   b. base payments to all families on the number of minor children.
   c. provide income floors which are then taxed as normal income.
   d. provide payments adequate to clothe and feed each minor child.

___ 4. Aid to Families with Dependent Children (AFDC) payments:
   a. are the major government program designed to alleviate poverty.
   b. are an example of an income maintenance program.
   c. provide welfare recipients with strong incentives to work.
   d. fall by roughly 50 cents for each extra dollar recipients earn.

___ 5. The percentage of families who are poor:
   a. rises during economic downswings.
   b. may be decreased through expansionary macroeconomic policies.
   c. may be decreased by increasing the job opportunities and educational opportunities available to the poor.
   d. is negatively related to the extent to which economic discrimination is practiced.

Problems

Problem 1

Use this table, which gives income distribution data for three hypothetical countries (A, B, and C), to answer the following questions.

Family Group	Percent of Total Income		
	Country A	Country B	Country C
Lowest 20%	10	12	18
Second 20%	15	15	19
Middle 20%	20	20	20
Fourth 20%	25	23	21
Highest 20%	30	30	22

a. Plot a Lorenz curve for each of the three countries in the figure.

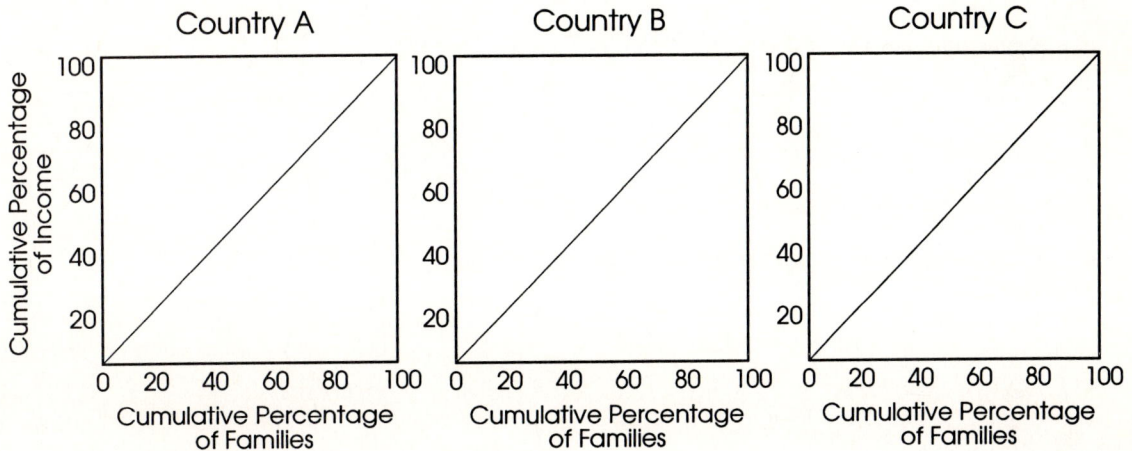

b. Which country has the most unequal distribution of income? _____ Which country has the most equal distribution of income? _____

c. Which country will have the highest Gini index? _____ Which country will the lowest Gini index? _____

d. What would you expect to happen to the Lorenz curve for a country if a more progressive tax system was instituted? _____ If education levels for all citizens became roughly equal? _____ If economic discrimination intensified? _____

Problem 2

Break-even income under a negative income tax (NIT) plan depends on its implicit marginal tax rate and the income floor. Mathematically, break-even income = basic income floor/ marginal tax rate. Use this information to fill in the blanks for the following problems.

a. A marginal tax rate of 40 percent and an income floor of $4,000 yields a break-even income of _____.

b. A marginal tax rate of _____ percent and an income floor of $6,000 yields a break-even income of $15,000.

c. A marginal tax rate of 50 percent and an income floor of _____ yields a break-even income of $18,000.

d. marginal tax rate of 60 percent and an income floor of $8,000 yields a break-even income of _____.

e. A marginal tax rate of 25 percent and an income floor of $6,000 yields a break-even income of _____.

ANSWERS

Matching		True/False		Multiple Choice		Unlimited MC
Set I	Set II					
1. h	1. e	1. T	11. F	1. d	11. a	1. abcd
2. d	2. g	2. F	12. F	2. c	12. b	2. abc
3. g	3. a	3. T	13. F	3. c	13. d	3. abcd
4. b	4. j	4. F	14. T	4. b	14. c	4. abd
5. i	5. i	5. T	15. T	5. e	15. c	5. abc
6. c	6. c	6. F	16. T	6. d	16. b	
7. e	7. d	7. F	17. F	7. b	17. c	
8. f	8. f	8. T	18. T	8. b	18. a	
9. a	9. h	9. F	19. F	9. c	19. d	
10. j	10. b	10. T	20. F	10. c	20. e	

Chapter Review (Fill-in Questions)

1. rich (high income); poor (low income); diminishing marginal returns; more wealth; income
2. income; wealth; taxes; transfer
3. Employment; occupational; human capital; wage
4. taxes; benefits
5. unemployment; family allowance plan (FAP)
6. negative income tax (NIT); marginal income tax

Problem 1

a. See figure.
b. Country A; Country C
c. Country A; Country C
d. shift in; shift in; shift out

Country A   Country B   Country C

Cumulative Percentage of Income (y-axis)

Cumulative Percentage of Families (x-axis)

Problem 2

a. $10,000
b. 40
c. $9,000
d. $13,333.33
e. $24,000

Chapter 32
Market Failure And Public Finance

Chapter Objectives

After you have read and studied this chapter, you should be able to describe the three general categories of market failure: instability, inequity, and allocative inefficiency; explain the circumstances under which each type of failure can occur in the market system; also describe how competitive markets may misallocate resources when markets fail; you should be able to suggest some possible government remedies; and critique the efficiency and equity of our tax system and evaluate proposals for its reform.

Chapter Review: Key Points

1. The economic goals of government are to: (a) provide a stable legal environment, promote competition, and provide efficiently for public wants, (b) stabilize income, employment, and prices, and (c) redistribute income and wealth equitably.

2. When marginal social benefits and marginal social costs diverge *market failure* occurs. In such cases, government may be used to provide the socially optimal quantities of some goods and to limit economic bads.

3. *Externalities* occur when private calculations of benefits or costs differ from the benefits or costs to society because third parties gain or lose from a transaction.

4. *Nonrivalry* means that a good is not used up when any individual enjoys it; a beautiful sunset is an example. *Nonexclusion* means that it is prohibitively expensive to deny access to a good. Note, however, that public provision does not require public production. Private firms often produce goods that government then distributes.

5. A good that is both nonrival and nonexclusive is a *pure public good*. Public goods will be less than optimally provided by the market system, if provided at all, because of attempts to *free ride*. A rival but nonexclusive good embodies *externalities* that often hinders the efficiency of market solutions.

6. The demand for a pure public good is the *vertical summation* of individual demand curves since all can enjoy the good simultaneously, while demands for private goods are summed horizontally. Adequate revenue for optimal quantities of public goods is generated if people pay taxes equal to their marginal benefits multiplied by the amount of public good provided.

7. The *benefit principle of taxation* suggests that people should pay taxes in proportion to the marginal benefits they receive from a governmentally provided good.

8. The *ability-to-pay principle of taxation* requires taxes in proportion to people's income, wealth, or possibly, their consumption. This principle is closely related to the idea that government policies should move the income distribution closer to equality than the market distribution of income.

9. The principle of *horizontal equity* suggests that equals should pay equal taxes; *vertical equity* requires higher taxes on the wealthy than on the poor.

10. If the loss to a taxpayer exceeds the government revenue gained, there is an *excess burden* of taxation. *Neutral taxes* impose only income, not substitution, effects and impose no excess burdens.

11. The *personal income tax* system is nominally progressive, but various loopholes make it somewhat inefficient and inequitable.

12. *Social Security taxes* are the second largest and fastest growing sources of federal revenues. They and other *payroll taxes* may be borne primarily by workers. Moreover, they are regressive, typically declining proportionately as personal income rises.

13. *Sales taxes* are reasonably efficient but, like income taxes, are marred by numerous exemptions. Many *excise taxes* apply to "sin" or "wasteful luxuries." Unless they are based on a benefit principle of taxation (for example, public zoo ticket fees or gasoline taxes), they tend to cause inefficiency and be regressive. (Poor people smoke and drink as much, by volume, as rich people.)

14. The *corporate income tax* discriminates against the corporate form of business and against the goods produced primarily by corporations. In the long run, most of this tax is probably forward-shifted to consumers. Thus, in the minds of most experts, this tax tends to be both inefficient and inequitable.

15. *Property taxes* provide disincentives for improvement and are blamed by some for the deterioration of central cities.

16. *Inheritance* and *gift taxes* have high and progressive rates, but can be avoided because they are riddled with loopholes.

17. A *value-added tax (VAT)* is similar to a sales tax in that it is forward-shifted. VATs only apply to the value added by each firm. VATs, *flat rate taxes,* and progressive *consumption taxes* (not income) have been proposed as replacements for corporate income taxes or Social Security taxes.

Matching Key Terms And Concepts

Set I

___ 1. negative externality

___ 2. free-rider problem

___ 3. positive externality

___ 4. nonrival

___ 5. nonexclusion

___ 6. sales taxes

___ 7. value added taxes (VAT)

___ 8. neutral taxes

___ 9. ability to pay taxation

___ 10. income taxes

a. Taxes that do not cause substitution effects.
b. Arises when people can consume a public good at no charge.
c. Too little of the product is produced.
d. Everyone can enjoy specific goods simultaneously.
e. When barring consumption is prohibitively expensive.
f. Litter is an example.
g. Percentage taxes on the differences between a firm's receipts and its purchases of intermediate goods.
h. Percentage taxes on dollar sales.
i. The 1986 Tax Reform Act attempted to revamp this type of tax.
j. Taxing more as income or wealth rises.

Set II

___ 1. excise taxes

___ 2. payroll taxes

___ 3. corporate income taxes

___ 4. vertical equity

___ 5. excess burden

___ 6. vertical summation

___ 7. flat rate tax

___ 8. pure public good

___ 9. consumption taxes

___ 10. horizontal equity

a. People with equal incomes should pay equal taxes.
b. Taxes applied only to specific goods.
c. Characterized by nonrivalry and nonexclusion.
d. Social security and unemployment compensation taxes are examples.
e. The difference between government receipts and taxpayer costs.
f. Process by which total demands for public goods are derived.
g. An ethical criterion for ability to pay taxation.
h. One tax rate without exemptions or deductions.
i. Either forward shifted to consumers or backward shifted to capital suppliers.
j. Might be like income taxation, but would allow deductions for saving or investment.

True/False Questions

___ 1. Most state and local governments rely on income taxes as their primary sources of revenue.

___ 2. Pure public goods are rival but non-exclusive.

___ 3. Spillovers, or externalities, occur when third-party costs or benefits from an activity are not considered by those directly making decisions.

___ 4. The goals of efficiency, equity, and economic stability are only somewhat resolved in a market system.

___ 5. Government policies have little effect on the allocation of resources in the U.S. economy.

___ 6. Pure private goods are both rival and exclusive.

___ 7. A nonexclusive but rival good is typically never used, assuming that the good is provided.

___ 8. Perfect competition economy-wide would put an end to market failure.

___ 9. Most allocative failures of a market system arise because of monopoly power, externalities, and nonrivalry or nonexclusion.

___ 10. Externalities are only problems with pure private goods.

___ 11. A tax is neutral if its total burden exactly equals the amount of tax revenue collected from the tax.

___ 12. Most taxes directly reduce disposable income and alter the patterns of saving and consumption.

___ 13. A tax is neutral only if its imposition induces absolutely no changes in economic behavior.

___ 14. High marginal income tax rates provide incentives for tax evasion.

___ 15. Tax loopholes tend to be efficient but pose major barriers to equity in the distribution of income.

___ 16. A progressive consumption tax system is a contradiction in terms because the poor spend larger portions of their incomes than rich people do.

___ 17. A proportional income tax would also be a flat tax.

___ 18. U.S. income tax rates are higher on average than income tax rates in Great Britain.

___ 19. Tax avoidance is legal, but tax evasion is not.

___ 20. Social Security taxes provide more federal tax revenues than corporate income taxes do.

Standard Multiple Choice

Each Question Has One Best Answer.

___ 1. The least clear examples of market failures are problems of:
   a. inequities in the distributions of income and wealth.
   b. an unstable price level and high unemployment.
   c. cutthroat competition.
   d. externalities.
   e. nonrivalry and nonexclusion.

___ 2. Nonrivalness and nonexclusiveness characterize:
   a. pure private goods.
   b. goods with negative diseconomies.
   c. natural monopolies.
   d. pure public goods.
   e. goods for which there is persistent excess capacity.

___ 3. If a good is nonexclusive, people tend to:
   a. vote to have the maximum possible amount provided by government.
   b. buy the good according to their demand curve and the good's price.
   c. not care if the good generates negative externalities.
   d. try to be "free riders".
   e. have a high benefit/cost ratio from its purchase.

___ 4. Negative externalities, if uncorrected, cause a good to be:
   a. underproduced and overpriced.
   b. overproduced and overpriced.
   c. underproduced and underpriced.
   d. overproduced and underpriced.
   e. underfinanced because of the "free rider" problem.

___ 5. A major reason why "free riders" pose problems is:
   a. nonexclusion.
   b. exclusion.
   c. rivalry.
   d. nonrivalry.
   e. nonneutrality.

___ 6. When markets fail:
   a. market prices are not equal to the marginal social cost or benefits of the goods traded.
   b. someone can be made better off without making someone else worse off.
   c. government intervention may improve society's overall welfare.
   d. there is not an optimal allocation of society's scarce resources.
   e. all of the above are correct statements.

___ 7. Tax receipts will be exactly adequate to pay for the optimal amount of a public good if:
   a. taxes levied are equal to people's marginal benefits from it times the number of units of the good.
   b. everyone pays taxes equal to their total benefits from the good.
   c. perfect price discrimination is used to pay for all public goods.
   d. individual demands for the public good are summed horizontally.
   e. voluntary taxes are used to pay for nonexclusive but rival goods.

8. Goods such as hamburgers and french fries are examples of:
   a. rival goods.
   b. nonrival goods.
   c. public goods.
   d. nonexclusive goods.
   e. merit goods.

9. Suppose that you live in a steel producing city and you hang out your white shirts to dry in the sunshine. Upon returning from work, you find that your shirts are black from soot. Which one of the following statements is correct?
   a. The steel producers have not paid the full cost of producing their product.
   b. An external cost has been generated that has been spilled over onto you.
   c. Steel is underpriced.
   d. There is an overallocation of resources into the steel industry.
   e. All of the above statements are correct.

10. The ability to pay principle requires:
    a. the "haves" to pay more taxes than the "have nots."
    b. progressive taxes.
    c. proportional taxes.
    d. regressive taxes.
    e. neutral taxes.

11. If we ignore loopholes, good examples of progressive taxes are:
    a. statutory taxes.
    b. sales taxes.
    c. social security taxes.
    d. tobacco and liquor taxes.
    e. income and inheritance taxes.

12. If all taxpayers in equivalent circumstances pay identical taxes, there is:
    a. benefit taxation.
    b. ability to pay taxation.
    c. horizontal equity.
    d. vertical equity.
    e. tax neutrality.

13. If a tax causes substitution effects, it generally is a:
    a. transfer tax.
    b. neutral tax.
    c. source of excess burden.
    d. progressive tax.
    e. pro rata tax.

14. Preferential tax treatment for some forms of income are NOT:
    a. violations of vertical and horizontal equity.
    b. known as loopholes.
    c. as beneficial to the wealthy as the rates alone seem to suggest.
    d. sources of inefficiency that hold down the value of real GNP.
    e. mechanisms that distort production away from consumer preferences.

15. A value-added tax is most closely related to a:
    a. progressive income tax.
    b. retail sales tax.
    c. property tax.
    d. gift or inheritance tax.
    e. corporate income tax.

16. Corporate income taxes are popular with politicians, but are not favored by most economists because:
    a. their incidence is uncertain, and may be inequitable.
    b. they reduce production by corporations in the long run.
    c. they are notably nonneutral.
    d. they are economically inefficient.
    e. All of the above.

17. Taxes that are the most completely borne by workers are:
    a. sales taxes.
    b. social security and other payroll taxes.
    c. property taxes.
    d. income taxes.
    e. excise taxes.

18. Inheritance taxes do not provide wealthy people with incentives to:
    a. lobby for loopholes in the American tax system.
    b. invest in their children's educations.
    c. spend more and save less.
    d. structure their wills so that their heirs avoid these taxes.
    e. work harder to amass huge fortunes.

19. Virtually all taxes are nonneutral in that they induce:
    a. changes in behavior intended to avoid tax burdens.
    b. income effects that more than offset their substitution effects.
    c. growth in government relative to private activities.
    d. substantial reductions of labor productivity.
    e. All of the above.

20. Reforms to plug tax loopholes, flatten income tax progressivity, and lower personal and corporate tax rates were features of major legislation in:
    a. 1890.
    b. 1956.
    c. 1966.
    d. 1976.
    e. 1986.

Chapter Review (Fill-In Questions)

1. Pure public goods are both _____ and _____. Pure public goods pose the problem that voluntary taxes to pay for them will be inadequate because people will attempt to be _____ and will not reveal their true demands for public goods.

2. The total demand for a public good is derived through _____ summation of individual demands. If all taxpayers pay taxes equal to their _____ times the amounts of public goods, there will be adequate revenues to secure the _____ amounts of these goods. This is in accord with the _____ principle of taxation.

3. Major practical problems with the benefit principle cause us to rely heavily on the _____ principle, which suggests that the rich should pay more taxes than the poor, an idea also called _____ equity.

4. When the _____ of a tax exceeds the government revenues generated, there is a(n) _____ on taxpayers.

5. Generally, when the direct effect of a tax is only a(n) _____ effect, there is no such "dead weight" social loss, but if _____ effects are direct results, the tax is inefficient.

6. _____ taxes are perhaps the most loophole ridden, but cannot be avoided by simply giving things away because then _____ taxes apply.

7. A tax on _____ (the difference between a firm's revenues and its outlays for intermediate goods) is one proposed replacement for several of the more seriously flawed taxes (e.g., social security and corporate income tax levies). The complexity of our income tax system has brought about calls for _____ rate taxation, which would eliminate virtually all "loopholes" and make income taxes _____ instead of progressive. Another recent proposal, aimed at stimulating economic growth, would eliminate most loopholes and would replace income taxation with a progressive tax on _____, so that people would be allowed deductions for saving and investing.

Unlimited Multiple Choice

Each Question Has From Zero To Four Correct Responses.

___ 1. Public goods are:
  a. subject to nonrivalry in consumption.
  b. efficiently produced in private markets.
  c. chosen by individuals who vote with money.
  d. subject to the nonexclusion principle.

___ 2. The free rider problem arises:
  a. in consuming all rival economic goods.
  b. because there are few incentives for people to express their true preferences when goods are nonexclusive.
  c. only in the consumption of private goods.
  d. because public goods are viewed as "free."

___ 3. A neutral tax:
   a. is a tax that does not distort relative prices.
   b. generates no excess burdens.
   c. does not induce substitution effects.
   d. will be, on average, more certain, convenient, and economical than a nonneutral tax.

___ 4. A pure private good is a good that is:
   a. nonrival and nonexclusive.
   b. efficiently provided if markets are competitive.
   c. vertically and horizontally equitable.
   d. rival and exclusive in nature.

___ 5. Markets may fail to provide certain goods efficiently because of:
   a. externalities in their consumption or production.
   b. substantial economies of scale relative to market demand.
   c. public goods problems.
   d. rivalry and exclusion.

Problems

Problem 1

Use this table, which shows Matthew's and Rachel's demand for street lights (a public good), to answer the following questions.

Price of Street Lights	Matthew's Demand	Rachel's Demand
9	0	0
8	0	3
7	3	6
6	6	9
5	9	12
4	12	15
3	15	18
2	18	21
1	21	24
0	24	27

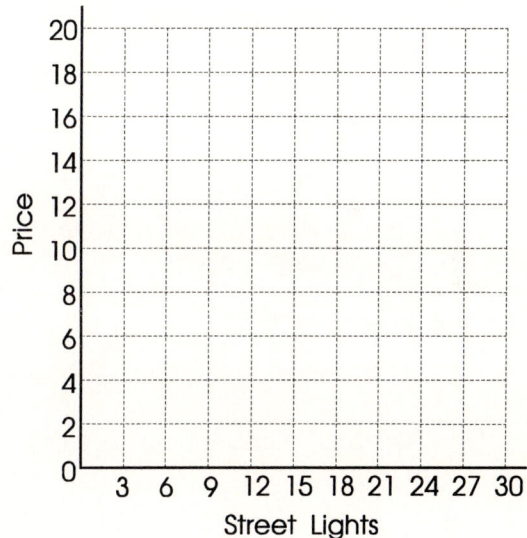

a. Graph Matthew and Rachel's demands, and the social demand for street lights in the figure.

Suppose that maintenance and replacement costs average $7 per street light.

b. What number of street light would be optimal? _____ How did you determine this
    optimal number? _____

c. If Matthew and Rachel are each charged for street lights in proportion to their respective
    marginal benefits, how will the total cost of street lights be shared? Matthew would pay?
    _____ Rachel would pay? _____

Problem 2

Figure 1 depicts supply and demand curves for a particular market. Assume a new per unit tax on
the good shifts the supply from S_0 to S_1. Use this information to answer the following questions.

____ a. The amount of the per unit tax is P_1-P_0.

____ b. The per unit tax is equal to line segment
         bc.

____ c. This per unit tax is neutral.

____ d. The excess burden of this per unit tax is
         zero.

____ e. Prior to the tax, consumer surplus equaled
         trapezoid P_1P_2ba.

____ f. After imposition of the tax, consumer
         surplus equals P_2P_3b.

____ g. The tax causes consumer surplus to
         decrease by area P_1P_2ba.

____ h. The price of the good rises by the
         full amount of the tax.

____ i. The excess burden of this tax equals
         triangle cba.

____ j. The total burden of the tax equals
         P_0P_2bac.

____ k. The total revenue yielded by the tax
         equals area P_0P_2bc.

____ l. The economic incidence of the tax
         falls on both the consumers and
         producers of this good.

Problem 3

Suppose that you have $1,000,000 to invest. Your federal marginal tax rate is fifty percent on normal investment income.

a. How many extra after-tax dollars will you receive annually if you invest in tax free state and local bonds that yield an 8 percent return annually instead of the taxable 12 percent return you could realize if you bought corporate bonds? _____

b. What return would make you indifferent between income from a tax free investment and the taxable 12 percent return on corporate bonds? _____

c. What will happen to rates of return for investments that receive preferential tax treatment? _____ Why? _____
_____

d. What does this example suggest about whether or not high income investors receive the full advantages of such loopholes? _____

e. The adjustments in this exercise are examples of the _____ costs of government.

Problem 4

This figure illustrates the market for candy corn. The market was initially in equilibrium at the intersection of D_0 and S_0. The federal government then levied a tax against candy corn producers, which resulted in supply decreasing to S_1.

a. How much of a tax was levied per pound against candy corn producers? _____

b. How much will the government collect in revenues as a result of the tax? _____

c. By how much did this tax reduce the consumer surplus? _____

d. How much is the excess burden of the tax? _____

e. Who bears the greatest proportion of the burden of the tax? _____

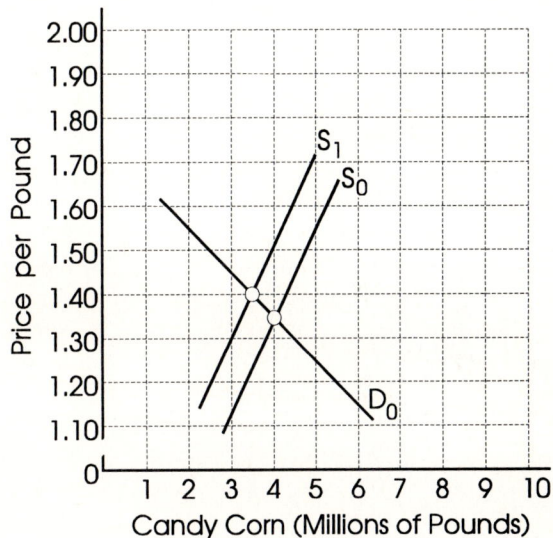

ANSWERS

Matching

Set I		Set II	
1.	f	1.	b
2.	b	2.	d
3.	c	3.	i
4.	d	4.	g
5.	e	5.	e
6.	h	6.	f
7.	g	7.	h
8.	a	8.	c
9.	j	9.	j
10.	i	10.	a

True/False

1.	F	11.	T
2.	F	12.	T
3.	T	13.	F
4.	T	14.	T
5.	F	15.	F
6.	T	16.	F
7.	F	17.	T
8.	F	18.	F
9.	T	19.	T
10.	F	20.	T

Multiple Choice

1.	c	11.	e
2.	d	12.	c
3.	d	13.	c
4.	d	14.	c
5.	a	15.	b
6.	e	16.	e
7.	a	17.	b
8.	a	18.	e
9.	e	19.	a
10.	a	20.	e

Unlimited MC

1.	ad
2.	bd
3.	abcd
4.	bd
5.	abc

Chapter Review (Fill-in Questions)

1. nonrival; nonexclusive; free riders
2. vertical; marginal benefits; optimal; benefit
3. ability to pay; vertical
4. total burden; excess burden
5. income; substitution
6. Inheritance; gift
7. value added; flat; proportional; consumption

Problem 1

a. See Figure
b. 15; intersection of $7 price line with social demand curve
c. $45 ($3 x 15); $60 ($4 x 15)

Problem 2

a.	F	g.	T
b.	T	h.	F
c.	F	i.	T
d.	F	j.	T
e.	F	k.	T
f.	T	l.	T

Problem 3

a. $20,000 [$80,000 - ($120,000/2)]
b. 6% (12% x 50%)
c. They will fall.; Increased supplies of funds into loophole investments will reduce returns.
d. Competition causes the loopholes to yield only small advantages to those who seek to exploit them.
e. indirect

Problem 4

a. 15 cents
b. $525,000 (.15 x 3.5 million)
c. $187,500 ($175,000 + $12,500)
d. $37,500 ($12,500 + $25,000)
e. suppliers

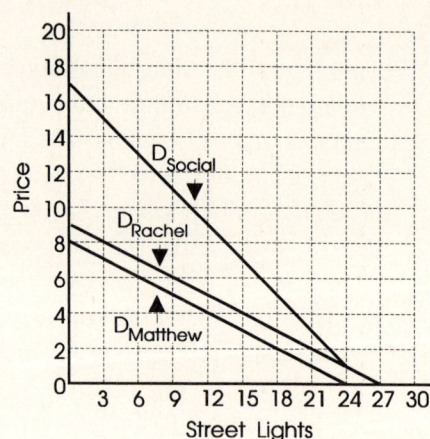

Chapter 33
Public Choice

Chapter Objectives

After you have studied this chapter you should be able to describe the economic effects of various voting systems; the behavior underpinning the public policymaking process; and the extent of public bureaucracies and their consequences.

Chapter Review: Key Points

1. No allocative mechanism works perfectly. Just as markets fail in some cases, forces within all political systems can prevent government from reflecting the preferences of the people governed. *Public choice analysis* entails economic analysis of political behavior.

2. The probability that one vote will swing a major election is close to infinitesimal. Because the personal payoffs from voting are small, many people do not vote, nor do most find it personally worthwhile to inform themselves on a broad range of social issues. This is known as *rational political ignorance,* and tends to be more prevalent than the lack of information confronted when people make market decisions.

3. All voting systems are flawed in that economic efficiency may be lost through political decision making. *Majority rule* voting tends to impose losses on those taking minority positions; this is inefficient if their losses exceed the majority's gains. Majority rule may also lead to inconsistent or unstable political choices.

4. A *unanimity* rule ensures that all changes in laws are efficient because everyone must expect to gain before acquiescing to a change. People who are reasonably indifferent about a policy change, however, might require excessive compensation for agreeing to the change from those who stand to gain much from the change. This would make changes in policies a very cumbersome and time-consuming process. Moreover, a unanimity rule assumes that the initial situation is equitable, which may be untrue.

5. *Point voting* would allow voters to indicate their preferences by allocating votes in proportion to how strongly they felt about some issues relative to others. This system is flawed, however, by the potential for strategic behavior; people might not vote their preferences per se, tending instead to weigh their votes according to how they expected others to vote.

6. Voting is a *lumpy* process; we cannot pick and choose among the political stances taken by the candidates for an office. The market permits us to fine-tune our decisions, but we generally can choose only a single candidate or platform when we vote.

7. Attempts to maximize their chances for election cause candidates and political parties to try to attract the *median voter,* whose vote tends to determine the outcomes of elections. Rational ignorance among voters causes many candidates to avoid taking stands on issues while attempting to project a moderate image. Political competition for the support of the median voter causes candidates and parties to cluster around *middle-of-the-road* positions, and creates pressures for a *two-party system.*

8. *Logrolling* occurs when lawmakers trade votes. This allows legislators to register the intensities of their preferences because they trade votes about which they care little for votes about things which they feel relatively strongly. Logrolling can, however, result in inefficient amounts of *pork barrel legislation,* which occurs when projects that have primarily local benefits are paid for by a broader taxpaying public.

9. *Special interests groups* may be over represented because of low voter turnouts, widespread rational political ignorance, and intense lobbying. However, intensities of preference may be better reflected in political decisions because of this overrepresentation.

10. *Rent-seeking* involves attempts by special interest groups to manipulate government policies for private gain even though the social costs of special laws or regulations would exceed the expected benefits to the interest group that seeks economic rents.

11. The efficiency of most government *bureaucracies* is hard to measure, and the absence of a profit motive reduces incentives for efficiency in the public sector. Managerial salaries and "perks" are often tied to the numbers of employees supervised and the size of the agency budget, which leads to *empire building* and further growth of government.

Matching Key Terms And Concepts

Set I

___ 1. median voter model

___ 2. unanimity requirement

___ 3. government failure

___ 4. lumpy decision

___ 5. point voting

___ 6. majority rule

___ 7. voter "apathy"

___ 8. public choice analysis

___ 9. voting cycle

___ 10. rational ignorance

a. Tries to explain the popularity of middle-of-the-road policies.

b. The study of *homo economicus* in politics.

c. Most protective of existing minority rights; ensures that any policy changes are efficient, but may bar corrections of inequities and promote political "blackmail."

d. Deciding to cast a vote involves trade-offs because you cannot vote for a set of positions other than those taken by one of the candidates.

e. Explained by public choice analysis.

f. Political consequences of rational ignorance.

g. Reasonably efficient if there is no strategic voting.

h. The losses of losers may often exceed the gains to winners.

i. Occurs when marginal costs exceed marginal benefits of obtaining more information.

j. Voting chains that tend to yield erratic policies inconsistent with the will of the majority.

Set II

___ 1. lobbying

___ 2. special interest groups

___ 3. two-party system

___ 4. empire building

___ 5. pork barrel

___ 6. bureaucracy

___ 7. rent-seeking

___ 8. logrolling

a. Their aims are facilitated by intense political action.

b. Exchanges of legislative votes.

c. The employees, rules, and resources of large organizations.

d. Local public projects that are funded nationally.

e. The goal is gains at the expense of the broader society.

f. A consequence of majority rule, according to the median voter model.

g. Attempts by private parties to sway laws and regulations.

h. Campaigns intended to enlarge the budget of a bureaucracy.

True/False Questions

___ 1. The historical rights of minority interest groups are commonly ignored under a unanimity voting rule.

___ 2. Failure to vote is a symptom of irrationality and apathy.

___ 3. Public choice analysis examines private market failure.

___ 4. Political extremists who want to be elected usually gain votes if they moderate their positions.

___ 5. Two major political parties will often jointly support laws that erect barriers against third parties.

___ 6. Voting cycles often yield choices that are very different from those that would be made under a simple majority rule voting system.

___ 7. Inherent in point voting or unanimity rules are incentives for strategic voting that may not reflect voters' true preferences.

___ 8. Fine tuning your choices is easier in the political arena than in the market system.

___ 9. Most economists and political scientists conclude that politicians are inherently wiser than professors, more ethical than used car dealers, and more competent than journalists.

___ 10. Projects that have local benefits but national funding are known as apple dumplings.

___ 11. A policy adopted because of rent-seeking that would double the profits of mustard producers would tend to be favored by most of them even if it decreased the standard of living 2 percent for everyone else in the country.

___ 12. Logrolling enables legislators to register the intensity of their preferences, but often yields inefficient pork barrel legislation.

___ 13. Successful lobbying invariably results in economically inefficient policies.

___ 14. Rent-seeking involves trying to mold laws or regulations to serve the national interest instead of narrow private interests.

___ 15. The general name for relatively small government agencies such as the FBI is "bureau"; such large organizations as the military are known as departments.

___ 16. Rent-seeking is a word used to describe strategies to artificially boost a government agency's budget.

___ 17. Overly precise specifications have driven up the costs of many government contracts.

___ 18. The incomes and "perqs" of bureaucrats tend to be more closely related to their job titles than to the number of people they supervise or the amounts of budget they control.

___19. Most experts in virtually every field favor huge federal spending cuts on programs in their areas of expertise.

___20. In studying the legislative process, economists often question whether the political process results in decisions that reflect society's best interests.

Standard Multiple Choice

There Is One Best Answer For Each Question.

___1. A perception that the personal gains from learning more about politics are less than the expected costs of information leads to:
   a. majority rule voting.
   b. the two-party system.
   c. rational political ignorance.
   d. lumpy "either/or" choices.
   e. political blackmail.

___2. Widespread voter apathy may be a symptom that many people:
   a. fail to realize how frequently one vote swings an election.
   b. dislike politicians and are unaffected by political decisions.
   c. view politics as an extremely enjoyable spectator sport.
   d. realize that single votes are unlikely to change election results.
   e. are unconstitutionally deprived of their voting rights.

___3. A law requiring all adults to vote would tend to reduce the:
   a. ability of voters to register the intensity of their preferences.
   b. apathy of those who vote.
   c. rational political ignorance of most people.
   d. ability of ambitious bureaucrats to build empires.
   e. red tape in government agencies.

___4. The reason why many people do vote is best explained by the:
   a. fact that "every vote counts."
   b. tie-in sales aspects of voting.
   c. slogan, "If you don't vote, you can't complain."
   d. enjoyment some people must receive from voting.
   e. high probability that a single vote will swing a major election.

___5. It is most difficult to "fine tune" your decisions to conform with your preferences when you make choices about:
   a. the accessories to add if you buy a new car.
   b. what to buy at the grocery store.
   c. the candidate for whom you will vote.
   d. your major field of study.
   e. where you will live.

___6. The personal losses resulting from rational ignorance tend to be lowest when you make choices about:
   a. whom to marry.
   b. how much to cheat on your taxes.
   c. voting.
   d. major financial investments.
   e. career paths and occupations.

___ 7. Majority rules voting will be economically inefficient if:
  a. minorities lose more than majorities gain from policies.
  b. rich minorities bribe poor majorities to vote a particular way.
  c. special interest groups donate huge campaign contributions.
  d. people are less rational in politics than in business.
  e. many people choose not to vote.

___ 8. The availability of fine gradations of market choices are not matched in the political arena because of:
  a. overrepresentation of special interests.
  b. voter apathy.
  c. strategic behavior by voters.
  d. the lumpiness of voting.
  e. All of the above.

___ 9. An explanation for the dominance of middle-of-the-road political policies is offered by the:
  a. rational ignorance hypothesis.
  b. theory of structural conformity.
  c. lumpiness of "tie-in sales" voting.
  d. iron law of oligarchy.
  e. median voter model.

___10. Voting cycles tend to result if many voters prefer:
  a. pure capitalism to decentralized planning.
  b. either political extreme to middle-of-the-road positions.
  c. special interest laws to the public interest.
  d. complex bureaucracies to inequitable income distributions.
  e. Republicans to Democrats.

___11. "Pork barrel" tends to result from extensive:
  a. empire building.
  b. boon-doggling.
  c. logrolling.
  d. cut-throat competition.
  e. monopolization.

___12. A law allowing individuals to specify the programs to be funded by their fixed personal tax dollars would tend to stimulate:
  a. strategic voting behavior.
  b. increases in logrolling by legislators.
  c. replacement of cash by in-kind transfers.
  d. everyone trying to be a free rider.

___13. Regulated firms that try to manipulate regulation so that it favors them and harms their competitors provide an example of:
  a. pork barrel.
  b. plutocracy.
  c. survivalism.
  d. rent-seeking.
  e. conflict of interests.

___14. Logrolling may improve economic efficiency to the extent that it enables legislators to:
  a. improve their prospects for reelection.
  b. use federal spending to cover local costs.
  c. focus on morality instead of pure politics.
  d. aid rent-seeking by special interest groups.
  e. register the intensities of their preferences.

___15. Efficiently accommodating the strong preferences of minority interest groups can never involve:
   a. rent-seeking.
   b. lobbying.
   c. logrolling.
   d. a unanimity voting rule.
   e. a point voting rule.

___16. Trying to raise your government agency's budget by overstating the importance and difficulty of its mission is known as:
   a. frosting the cake.
   b. empire building.
   c. gilding the lily.
   d. boosterism.
   e. brown nosing.

___17. Employees of large organizations are known as:
   a. agents.
   b. autocrats.
   c. bureaucrats.
   d. nepotists.
   e. boondogglers.

___18. NOT a reason for the relative growth of government is:
   a. empire building.
   b. logrolling.
   c. rent-seeking.
   d. porkbarrel legislation.
   e. taxpayer revolts.

___19. Higher pay and more "perqs" tend to reward bureaucrats who:
   a. supervise more employees and control larger budgets.
   b. support the party in power.
   c. "blow the whistle" when their supervisors make errors.
   d. develop extremely narrow areas of expertise.
   e. accomplish their tasks at minimal costs.

___20. NOT a reasonable explanation for exorbitant government contract costs are cases where contracts are:
   a. awarded before appropriate technology is developed.
   b. monitored by potential employees of contractors.
   c. overspecified by bureaucrats who want to look busy.
   d. for standard items produced by many cutthroat competitors.
   e. awarded before final specifications are known.

Chapter Review (Fill-In Questions)

1. The economic study of political behavior is known as _____ analysis, which assumes that people are as _____ in the political arena as they are in their private behavior.

2. The _____ model explains why serious candidates often adopt _____ positions and the dominance of the _____ system when a _____ voting system is used.

3. Vote trading by legislators is known as _____ and allows them to express the intensity of their preferences, but it also promotes _____ legislation that uses national _____ for projects that primarily generate local _____.

4. The strong preferences of _____ cause them to _____ intensively and be very active politically. Their aims are often expressed as _____ behavior, which attempts to shape laws and regulations beneficial to themselves even though the _____ costs are substantially higher.

5. People who work in bureaucracies know that their personal power and income are linked to their supervision of large numbers of _____ and to their control over big _____.

6. Managers in private organizations to try to demonstrate above average _____ potential, which facilitates economic _____. Managers of public agencies, however, tend to try _____ by exaggerating the importance and difficulty of their mission, and economic _____ is encouraged.

Unlimited Multiple Choice

Each Question Has From Zero To Four Correct Answers.

___ 1. "Public choice" focuses on such areas as why:
   a. government is so small relative to the business sector.
   b. many people don't vote.
   c. special interest groups devote resources to lobbying.
   d. capitalism is inequitable relative to socialism.

___ 2. Decision making is based on rational ignorance when choices are made about:
   a. voting in political primaries.
   b. laws passed by the congress and signed by the president.
   c. buying goods at your local shopping mall.
   d. how to treat your relatives.

___ 3. The median voter model offers explanations for why:
   a. the median voter is unlikely to vote.
   b. political extremists have so much influence on public policies.
   c. majority rules voting leads to a two party system.
   d. serious political candidates generally adopt moderate positions.

___ 4. Special interests may be overrepresented because their:
   a. members will often vote based on only one issue.
   b. devotion of many hours to lobbying and campaigning is effective.
   c. concerns are issues that matter little to most other people.
   d. members may donate substantially to political campaigns.

___ 5. Public policies only crudely reflect voter preferences because of:
   a. empire building by ambitious bureaucrats.
   b. successful rent-seeking behavior.
   c. lobbying that results in pork barrel legislation.
   d. vote-seeking candidates who advocate moderate positions.

Problems

Problem 1

This table indicates how 300,000 potential voters (110,00 Mugwumps, 100,000 Know Nothings, and 90,000 Goldbugs) rate the other parties' candidates in an election for local dog catcher that must be won by a clear majority. If no one initially receives 50 percent plus 1 vote, a runoff is held between the top two vote getters.

	Mugwumps	Know Nothings	Goldbugs
1st Choice	Mugwump	Know Nothing	Goldbug
2nd Choice	Know Nothing	Goldbug	Mugwump
3rd Choice	Goldbug	Mugwump	Know Nothing

Although everyone votes in the runoff, people differ in their voting patterns on primary election day according to the weather. Instead of voting on snowy days, half of the Mugwumps and one-fifth of Know Nothings stay inside next to a warm fire, but all of the Goldbugs ride their dogsleds to the polls. On sunny primary days, the Mugwumps all vote, but half of the Know Nothings and one-fifth of the Goldbugs go golfing instead. On rainy primary days, the Know Nothings all vote, but half of the Goldbugs and one-fifth of the Mugwumps stay home all day and watch soap operas.

Fill in this table to show how the weather on primary day affects the final results.

Election	Position	Party of Candidate / Votes Received	Weather On Primary Day		
			Sunny	Rainy	Snowy
Primary	First	Party ------------- Votes	----------------	----------------	----------------
	Second	Party ------------- Votes	----------------	----------------	----------------
	Third	Party ------------- Votes	----------------	----------------	----------------
Runoff	Winner	Party ------------- Votes	----------------	----------------	----------------
	Loser	Party ------------- Votes	----------------	----------------	----------------

a. Who will ultimately be elected dog catcher if the weather is sunny on primary day? _____

b. Who will ultimately be elected dog catcher if the weather is rainy on primary day? _____

c. Who will ultimately be elected dog catcher if the weather is snowy on primary day? _____

d. What do the voting results of this mock election illustrate? _____

Problem 2

Use this table, which shows the benefits (Ben) and costs (Cos) to five citizens of various proposals, to answer the following questions.

Proposals	Voters									
	Bruce		Cathy		Debbie		George		Jim	
	Ben	Cos	Ben	Cos	Ben	Cos	Ben	Cos	Ben	Cos
Airport	90	100	25	100	50	100	280	100	300	100
Firehouse	60	100	5	100	10	100	50	100	210	100
Landfill	0	100	50	100	180	100	70	100	180	100
Hospital	130	100	110	100	190	100	0	100	90	100
School	120	100	120	100	120	100	60	100	0	100

a. Fill in the table below to show how these people will cast their ballots (yes or no), and whether proposals will pass or fail when majority rule voting is used.

Majority Rule Voting						
Proposals	Bruce	Cathy	Debbie	George	Jim	Pass/Fail
Airport						
Firehouse						
Landfill						
Hospital						
School						

Efficiency requires proposals to pass if benefits exceed costs, and lose if costs exceed benefits.

b. The airport proposal will _____ (pass/fail); this voting result is _____ (efficient/inefficient).

c. The firehouse proposal will _____; this vote is _____.

d. The landfill proposal will _____; this vote is _____.

e. The hospital proposal will _____ ; this vote is _____ .
f. The school proposal will _____ ; this vote is _____ .

Assume that point voting is instituted, and that each voter has a total of 1,000 points which can then be allocated among the various proposals. You will first need to calculate each voter's points per dollar in order to determine how many points they will allocate to each proposal. To do this, calculate the difference between benefits and costs, and sum the total for all proposals for each individual. You will then divide the 1,000 total points by the number you just calculated to arrive at the points per dollar value. For example, the difference between benefits and costs for the airport proposal for Bruce is $10 ($100 - $90), and the difference between the benefits and costs of the school proposal for Bruce is $20 ($120 - $100). You would then do the same calculation for the three other proposals, and then add up all the values to get a total. Let's say Bruce's total equals $100. Next, divide 1,000 points by your total (1,000/$100 = 10) to get your points per dollar.

Once you have determined each voter's points per dollar, you then need to calculate the number of points they will allocate to each proposal. To do this, once again determine the difference between benefits and costs for a proposal, and then multiply this difference by the points per dollar you already calculated. For example, if the difference between benefits and costs for the airport and school proposals for Bruce is $10 and $20 respectively, and Bruce's points per dollar is 10, then he will allocate -100 ($10 x 10) points against the airport and 200 ($20 x 10) points for the school. (Use a negative sign to indicate points against a proposal.)

g. Fill in the table below, and determine whether proposals will pass or fail when point voting is used.

Point Voting						
	Bruce	Cathy	Debbie	George	Jim	Pass/Fail
Points per $						
Airport						
Firehouse						
Landfill						
Hospital						
School						

h. Are there any inefficient results under point voting? _____

i. Efficient point votes include passage of the _____ and _____ .

j. The _____ , _____ , and _____ proposals will be efficiently defeated.

Assume that strategic point voting occurs because Cathy convinces Debbie (mistakenly) that the hospital and firehouse proposals will pass and fail, respectively, regardless of their votes. As a result of this, these two voters place all of their point votes on the other three issues.

In order to determine how points will be allocated under strategic point voting, recalculate Cathy's and Debbie's points per dollar by focusing only on the three proposals that they will vote on. Once you have calculated the points per dollar, determine how many points each lady will cast for each proposal just as you did in the table above. Strategic voting by Cathy and Debbie will not alter the points per dollar or points allocated to each proposal by the men.

k. Fill in the table below, and determine whether proposals will pass or fail when strategic point voting is used.

		Strategic Point Voting				
	Bruce	Cathy	Debbie	George	Jim	Pass/Fail
Points per $						
Airport						
Firehouse						
Landfill						
Hospital						
School						

l. This strategic voting causes inefficiency because the _____ and _____ proposal fails, while the _____ proposal passes.

m. Losers from this strategic voting are _____

n. Gainers from this strategic voting are _____

o. Would any proposal pass if unanimity were required and bribes were forbidden? _____
   Is this efficient? _____

p. If bribes are permitted under a unanimity rule, what is the structure of feasible bribes that might secure efficiency? _____
   _____
   _____
   _____

ANSWERS

	Matching		True/False			Multiple Choice			Unlimited MC
Set I	Set II								
1. a	1. g	1. F	11. T		1. c	11. c		1. bc
2. c	2. a	2. F	12. T		2. d	12. a		2. abcd
3. e	3. f	3. F	13. F		3. a	13. d		3. cd
4. d	4. h	4. T	14. F		4. d	14. e		4. abcd
5. g	5. d	5. T	15. F		5. c	15. a		5. abcd
6. h	6. c	6. T	16. F		6. c	16. b		
7. f	7. e	7. T	17. T		7. a	17. c		
8. b	8. b	8. F	18. F		8. e	18. e		
9. j		9. F	19. F		9. e	19. a		
10. i		10. F	20. T		10. b	20. d		

Chapter Review (Fill-In Questions)

1. public choice; self interested
2. median voter; middle-of-the-road; two-party; majority rules
3. logrolling; pork barrel; funding; benefits
4. special interest groups; lobby; rent-seeking; social
5. employees; budgets
6. profit; efficiency; empire building; inefficiency

Problem 1

Election	Position	Party of Candidate	Weather On Primary Day		
		Votes Received	Sunny	Rainy	Snowy
Primary	First	Party	Mugwump	Know Nothing	Goldbug
		Votes	110,000	100,000	90,000
	Second	Party	Goldbug	Mugwump	Know Nothing
		Votes	72,000	88,000	80,000
	Third	Party	Know Nothing	Goldbug	Mugwump
		Votes	50,000	45,000	55,000
Runoff	Winner	Party	Goldbug	Mugwump	Know Nothing
		Votes	190,000	200,000	210,000
	Loser	Party	Mugwump	Know Nothing	Goldbug
		Votes	110,000	100,000	90,000

a. Goldbug   c. Know Nothing
b. Mugwump   d. voting cycles

Chapter 33: Public Choice

Problem 2

a. See table.
b. fail; inefficient
c. fail; efficient
d. fail; efficient
e. pass; efficient
f. pass; inefficient

Majority Rule Voting						
Proposals	Bruce	Cathy	Debbie	George	Jim	Pass/Fail
Airport	No	No	No	Yes	Yes	Fail
Firehouse	No	No	No	No	Yes	Fail
Landfill	No	No	Yes	No	Yes	Fail
Hospital	Yes	Yes	Yes	No	No	Pass
School	Yes	Yes	Yes	No	No	Pass

g. See table.
h. no
i. airport; hospital
j. firehouse; landfill; school

Point Voting						
	Bruce	Cathy	Debbie	George	Jim	Pass/Fail
Points per $	5	4	3.03	2.5	2	
Airport	-50	-300	-152	450	400	Pass
Firehouse	-200	-380	-273	-125	220	Fail
Landfill	-500	-200	242	-75	160	Fail
Hospital	150	40	273	-250	-20	Pass
School	100	80	61	-100	-200	Fail

k. See table.
l. airport; hospital; school.
m. Debbie; George; Jim (The benefits from the proposals that were passed under strategic

Strategic Point Voting						
	Bruce	Cathy	Debbie	George	Jim	Pass/Fail
Points per $	5	6.90	6.67	2.5	2	
Airport	-50	-517	-333	450	400	Fail
Firehouse	-200	0	0	-125	220	Fail
Landfill	-500	-345	534	-75	160	Fail
Hospital	150	0	0	-250	-20	Fail
School	100	138	133	-100	-200	Pass

voting are less than the benefits from the proposals that were passed under point voting for these three individuals)
n. Cathy (The benefits from the proposals that were passed under strategic voting are greater than the benefits from the proposals that were passed under point voting for Cathy; Bruce receives the same level of benefits under either voting system)
o. no; no
p. The benefit/cost table suggests that the airport proposal will pass if George and Jim bribe Bruce, Cathy, and Debbie for their votes. Jim would be willing to give up to $200 and George would be willing to give up to $180 to Bruce (who requires at least $10 for his vote), Cathy (who requires at least $75), and Debbie (who must receive at least $50). Bribes in this range improve efficiency if a unanimous vote is required. Similarly, the hospital proposal will pass if Bruce, Cathy, and Debbie (who, respectively, are willing to contribute $30, $10, and $90 for its passage) offer appropriate payoffs to George (who requires at least $100 for his assent), and Jim (who must be paid at least $10). The other proposals each bear total costs that exceed their benefits and so bribery cannot secure unanimity in these cases.

Chapter 34
Environmental Economics

Chapter Objectives

After you have read and studied this chapter you should be able to describe how both positive and negative externalities cause inefficiency; the advantages that cause individuals and firms to pollute; and alternative policies to overcome pollution.

Chapter Review: Key Points

1. Goods that are purely rival and exclusive are *pure private goods*. Such goods (e.g., ice cream or umbrellas) are usually efficiently provided in a private market system. Goods that are nonrival but exclusive entail excess capacity, and are also efficiently provided by markets unless elements of natural monopoly are present. A good that is both nonrival and nonexclusive is a *pure public good*. Public goods will be less than optimally provided by the market system, if provided at all, because of attempts to *free ride*.

2. A rival but nonexclusive good embodies *externalities* that often hinders the efficiency of market solutions. Pollution may be the problem if externalities are negative (costly); underproduction may result if externalities are positive (beneficial).

3. The four stages in the development of property rights are (a) common access/nonscarcity, (b) common access-scarcity, (c) agency restrictions, and (d) fee-simple property rights. The term *fee-simple property rights* means that you can do anything you want with your property so long as you do no physical damage to the property of others.

4. Positive *externalities* occur when an activity confers benefits on external third parties. Too few of such activities are undertaken because private decision makers tend to ignore the external benefits.

5. Pollution situations in which damaged third parties are uncompensated, and hence unconsidered, are examples of negative externalities. Negative externalities impose costs on third parties. Too many activities generating negative externalities are undertaken because private decision makers weigh the costs imposed on others too lightly, if at all.

6. Environmental quality is a public good, and controlling environmental pollution is costly. There are trade-offs between protecting the environment and producing goods that generate pollution, so the *optimal pollution* level is greater than zero.

7. *Pollution abatement* may occur through negotiation, *moral suasion* (jawboning and bad publicity), *effluent charges*, subsidies, lawsuits, the assignment of pollution rights, and government regulation. No single solution applies to all situations of negative externalities; they must generally be resolved on a case by case basis.

8. Pollution rights might be auctioned and then made transferable. The Environmental Protection Agency initially relied heavily on direct regulation through pollution ceilings, but is increasingly using *property rights* solutions to control environmental deterioration.

9. The *bubble concept* sets a pollution performance standard for a plant. A firm can transfer rights to pollute within or between plants inside the "bubble" as long as the standard is met.

10. The *offset policy* allows new firms that wish to produce in a polluted area to operate if they can induce existing firms to reduce air pollutants to "offset" the newcomer's emissions.

Matching Key Terms And Concepts

____ 1. effluent charges

____ 2. internalization

____ 3. fee simple property rights

____ 4. pollution rights

____ 5. regulation

____ 6. moral suasion

____ 7. bubble concept

____ 8. common access

____ 9. abatement subsidies

____ 10. offset policies

a. Social pressure to persuade people or institutions.

b. Payments to a firm for adopting less-polluting technologies.

c. New firms may pollute only if they induce other firms to reduce emissions.

d. Fully considering the effects on others of one's decisions.

e. Limits pollution within an area, but not by specific source.

f. A synonym for nonexclusion.

g. Reduce production and pollution, but lack incentives for cleaner technologies.

h. Rights to use or transfer property as one wishes.

i. Fees per unit of a pollutant.

j. Rights to emit pollution, or to deny emissions.

True/False Questions

_____ 1. A negative externality causes the private supply curve to be to the right of society's optimal supply curve.

_____ 2. Sexually transmitted diseases from promiscuous contacts are examples of negative externalities if people consider their own likelihood of infection but fail to consider possible dangers to their subsequent partners.

_____ 3. Controls over externalities tend to become more formal as increasing numbers of people spread across greater areas are affected.

_____ 4. An example of a positive externality occurs when an erratic golfer whose ball is coming towards you yells "FORE".

_____ 5. Community projects to beautify neighborhood greenbelts and parks are examples of how positive externalities can be internalized.

_____ 6. Developed nations tend to export pollution to less developed countries.

_____ 7. Market exchanges occur between economic transactors whenever they expect personal prospects of gains from the exchange.

_____ 8. The socially optimal rate of pollution is zero.

_____ 9. Moral suasion is among the most effective ways of dealing with the pollution problem.

_____ 10. One politically popular method for reducing environmental damage is direct regulation or prohibition.

_____ 11. Effluent charges to deal with the pollution problem are uniformly relatively easy to administer.

_____ 12. Society's net welfare always attains a maximum value when marginal private benefits are equal to marginal private costs.

_____ 13. Efficiency occurs when competitive firms internalize any external production costs, making consumers of pollution-causing goods pay the marginal social costs of production.

_____ 14. Regulations governing how much firms can pollute are costly to administer and fail to provide firms with incentives to reduce pollution once the firms comply with legal standards.

_____ 15. Market solutions to the pollution problem require sizable government intervention in the marketplace.

_____ 16. Pollution rights are most efficient when bubble charges are bought and sold in a free market.

_____ 17. Increasing automobile emissions standards should increase the amounts of air pollution in most communities.

_____ 18. The evolution from common access to fee simple property rights is the major cause of most current pollution.

___19. Optimal resolution of negative externalities requires reducing the activities that generate them and raising their prices, while positive externalities require increases in the activities that produce them and reductions in their costs to buyers.

___20. Relative to direct regulation, effluent charges create more incentives to adopt cleaner technologies.

Standard Multiple Choice

Each Question Has One Best Answer.

___ 1. Negative (cost) spillovers:
  a. result in too much of a product at too low a price.
  b. are exemplified by air pollution and education.
  c. are exemplified by transportation and immunization.
  d. result in too little of a product at too high a price.
  e. are caused by wastes of taxpayers' dollars.

___ 2. An excise tax newly imposed on a good for which negative externalities are generated in production would tend to cause:
  a. enormous excess burdens relative to tax revenues collected.
  b. unambiguously enhanced economic equity.
  c. greater use of the good to replace its close substitutes.
  d. higher prices and falling production, which may be desirable in such cases.
  e. increased production and consumption.

___ 3. Private decision makers will confront prices that are socially too high and, thus, will pursue too little of an activity relative to a social optimum if the activity generates:
  a. merit goods.
  b. negative externalities.
  c. excess burdens.
  d. cutthroat competition.
  e. positive externalities.

___ 4. Negative externalities are least likely to be created if:
  a. a TV game show host practices smiling in front of a mirror.
  b. your neighbor begins raising pigs in her back yard.
  c. teenagers throw a BYOB party during their parents' vacation.
  d. Ear Throb plays a free high-decibel concert at a local park.
  e. a Soviet nuclear reactor at Chernobyl melts down.

5. Positive externalities are least likely to be created if:
   a. your neighbor cuts her lawn on a regular basis.
   b. rusty, old, pink garbage trucks are repainted a soothing beige.
   c. the driver of a smoky old gas hog has her car engine rebuilt.
   d. the EPA fires half of its inspectors to save tax dollars.
   e. volunteers remove litter from the roadside of a busy highway.

6. In equilibrium, uncontrolled pollution causes the marginal:
   a. social costs to exceed a good's marginal private costs and benefits.
   b. social benefits from the good to exceed marginal private benefits.
   c. private costs to exceed marginal social benefits.
   d. customers to pay prices that exceed production costs.
   e. customers to pay prices exceeding the value of the good to them.

7. Internalizing all costs that were previously external to a polluting industry and its customers causes:
   a. both output and the cost of the product to rise.
   b. output to fall and the private cost of the product to rise.
   c. the standard of living adjacent to polluting factories to fall.
   d. both output and the price of the product to decline.
   e. output to rise and the price of the product to decline.

8. If more stringent emissions controls are placed on new cars:
   a. we will be paying a higher price than currently for clean air.
   b. real national output grows by the value of the control equipment.
   c. average car mileage per gallon of gasoline is likely to rise.
   d. there will be downward pressure on the prices of used cars.
   e. All of the above.

9. Fee simple property rights do not include rights to:
   a. sell property.
   b. make choices reducing the market value of another's property.
   c. destroy your own property.
   d. physically damage another's property.
   e. contract with others to exchange property.

10. If both polluters and pollutees belong to small, easily identified groups:
    a. regulation is the best solution to pollution.
    b. output taxes create proper incentives to adopt cleaner technology.
    c. private bargaining may be the most efficient way to reduce externalities.
    d. it is very difficult for polluters to internalize externalities.
    e. pollution can be eradicated at zero cost.

___11. Unlike pure public goods, environmental quality often involves:
   a. nonrivalry.
   b. nonsatiety.
   c. nonexclusion.
   d. rivalry.
   e. exclusion.

___12. Early government campaigns to cut pollution relied most on:
   a. direct regulation.
   b. effluent charges.
   c. private bargaining.
   d. the bubble concept.
   e. offset policies.

___13. A legal requirement that all pollution be reduced to zero:
   a. is desirable from the vantage point of increasing social welfare.
   b. would efficiently eliminate all forms of production.
   c. is incompatible with the standards of living most Americans enjoy.
   d. could be enforced inexpensively because of its legal simplicity.
   e. would undoubtedly eradicate pollution.

___14. The evolution from common access to fee simple property rights suggests that government policies:
   a. slowly move toward more economically efficient modes of ownership.
   b. yield to pressures for capitalistic environmental exploitation.
   c. are controlled by large, polluting, industrial conglomerates.
   d. headed in the direction of environmental decay.
   e. are backing away from serious commitments to conservation.

___15. Private bargaining of externalities is least feasible when there are:
   a. many polluters and many people damaged by pollutants.
   b. fee-simple property rights to govern environmental use.
   c. easy measurements of emissions.
   d. remote wilderness areas that are being polluted by a few firms.
   e. extremely harmful emissions from long-established firms.

___16. Pollution rights can be sold by existing polluters under:
   a. regulatory standards.
   b. effluent charge policies.
   c. common access doctrines.
   d. offset policies.
   e. the Monroe Doctrine.

___17. Optimal adjustments when externalities are present involve:
   a. forbidding the activities.
   b. internalization of all relevant external costs or benefits.
   c. rigid standards that reduce externalities to tolerable levels.
   d. total benefits from abatement that equal total abatement costs.
   e. maximization of the dollar value of marketable production.

___18. Regulatory standards that limit pollution typically:
   a. are costly to administer.
   b. lack incentives to reduce pollution once the standard is met.
   c. were more important earlier in the history of the EPA.
   d. are applied when pollutants are extremely dangerous and dispersed.
   e. All of the above.

19. Eliminating auto emissions in central cities by requiring that people ride horses instead of cars would:
   a. increase our standard of living.
   b. represent adoption of policies advocated by the auto industry.
   c. give Japan even more of a competitive advantage than it now has.
   d. replace one form of pollution with another.
   e. be one effective way to internalize externalities.

20. If the marginal private costs of pollution abatement exceed its marginal social benefits, efficient moves might entail reducing:
   a. pollution until the external effects were negligible.
   b. abatement programs and allowing more pollution.
   c. the adoption of newer and more efficient capital.
   d. national output to conserve more of our natural resources.
   e. domestic production that generates positive externalities.

Chapter Review (Fill-In Questions)

1. The _____ is normally too high and the level of _____ is too low in the case of positive externalities, while the price is too _____ and the level of production is too _____ when such negative externalities as pollutants are generated.

2. How far to pursue environmental purity and what techniques to use are controversial issues. Environmental use is rival between competing groups, but it is also _____. If, for example, government requires cleaner air, everyone in the vicinity enjoys the benefits-- no one can be _____.

3. Any efficient remedy for problems caused by negative _____ requires _____, and may require correction of problems from either _____ or _____ activities.

4. There are tradeoffs between environmental _____ and high standards of _____. As we approach 100 percent purity the marginal social benefits of abatement _____ while the marginal social costs _____. Optimal pollution abatement requires _____ to equal _____.

5. Common access resources are available to all on a first-come, first-served basis, and when resources become scarce, _____ results. Assigning rights to pollute has been used by the Environmental Protection Agency under what has become known as the _____ concept. Another approach to stabilize pollution in a given area is to require new firms to _____ their anticipated pollution by inducing other firms to _____ their effluents.

Unlimited Multiple Choice

Each Question Has From Zero To Four Correct Responses.

____ 1. Externalities:
   a. are one variety of market failure.
   b. arise whenever some aspect of consumption or production affects people not directly involved in the specific activity.
   c. have no impact on the efficiency of resource allocations.
   d. can be cured through internalization.

____ 2. Economic efficiency occurs whenever:
   a. marginal private benefits are equal to marginal social costs, assuming that no external effects exist.
   b. scarce resources are used to produce the most valuable output.
   c. all outputs are produced at the lowest opportunity costs.
   d. marginal social benefits are equal to marginal social costs.

____ 3. Instances of negative externalities include:
   a. the 1986 nuclear accident at Chernobyl in the U.S.S.R.
   b. commuters that bike instead of drive to work.
   c. someone's bad breath.
   d. your neighbor's brown lawn during the summer months.

____ 4. Whenever all marginal social benefits from production equal the relevant marginal social costs:
   a. the costs incurred in producing given outputs are minimized.
   b. society's total production is at its maximum value.
   c. no resource reallocations would improve society's net welfare.
   d. there is both consumption and production efficiency.

____ 5. Imposing a per unit tax on output to reduce pollution:
   a. is a market approach to dealing with pollution.
   b. is more efficient than the imposition of effluent charges.
   c. shifts the firm's supply curve to the left.
   d. may force the consumers and producers of the output to internalize the external costs it generates.

Problems

Problem 1

Use this figure, which shows the market for steel, to answer the following true/false questions.

____ a. The marginal private cost curve reflects only the private costs of steel production.

____ b. The demand curve reflects the marginal social benefits from consuming extra units of steel.

____ c. Steel production imposes external costs on society that are not captured in the marginal private cost curve.

____ d. External cost per unit of steel equals $P_3 - P_0$

____ e. Steel output generates negative externalities.

____ f. The dollar value that society as a whole places upon the Q_1th unit of steel is less than the dollar value of inputs used in its production.

____ g. The socially optimal rate of production is Q_1.

____ h. The socially optimal per unit price is P_2.

____ i. Allocative efficiency is obtained at point b.

____ j. The net welfare of society would be maximized in this market if the steel industry produced Q2 units per time period.

____ k. A tax per unit of steel equal to $P_1 - P_2$ would result in the socially optimal output of steel if no preferable technologies can be substituted.

____ l. Total tax revenue from such a tax would equal area P_0P_3gb.

Problem 2

This figure illustrates the marginal cost of pollution control for a small pulp mill. Local authorities have just imposed an effluent charge of 80 cents per gallon of effluent in an effort to reduce water pollution.

a. How much effluent will the mill now discharge, if it discharged 20,000 gallons daily prior to the effluent charge?

_____

b. Beyond what quantity of daily effluent will the mill pay the effluent charge? _____ Why? _____

_____

c. If local authorities raise the charge substantially, say to $1.20 per gallon, will the amount of effluent the mill discharges drop substantially? _____ Why?

_____
_____
_____

Quantity of Effluents Controlled
per Day (1,000s of Gallons)

ANSWERS

Matching	True/False		Multiple Choice		Unlimited MC
1. i	1. T	11. F	1. a	11. d	1. abd
2. d	2. T	12. F	2. d	12. a	2. abcd
3. h	3. T	13. T	3. e	13. c	3. acd
4. j	4. F	14. T	4. a	14. a	4. bcd
5. g	5. T	15. F	5. d	15. a	5. cd
6. a	6. T	16. F	6. a	16. d	
7. e	7. T	17. F	7. b	17. b	
8. f	8. F	18. F	8. a	18. e	
9. b	9. F	19. T	9. d	19. d	
10. c	10. T	20. T	10. c	20. b	

Chapter Review (Fill-In Questions)

1. price; output; low; high
2. nonexclusive; excluded
3. externalities; internalization; production; consumption
4. quality; production or consumption; diminish; rise; marginal social benefits; marginal social costs
5. overutilization; bubble; offset; reduce

Problem 1

a. T
b. T
c. T
d. T
e. T
f. T
g. F
h. F
i. F
j. F
k. T
l. F

Problem 2

a. 8,000 (20,000 - 12,000)
b. 12,000; It is less expensive for the firm to incur the effluent charge than to clean up the additional effluent (i.e. MC > effluent charge after 12,000 gallons)
c. No; Increasing the effluent charge to $1.20 a gallon will only decrease daily effluents by less than 2,000 gallons. The large jump in the effluent charge has little impact because of the increasing marginal costs of effluent cleanup.

Chapter 35
The Economics of Health Care

Chapter Objectives

After you have studied this chapter you should be able to explain how health care differs from most other services and what problems this presents, why health care costs have risen rapidly over the past three decades, the role health insurance plays and how it affects peoples' actions, and the strength and weaknesses of centralized and decentralized health care plans.

Chapter Review: Key Points

1. The major issues driving the call for health care reform are high and rapidly rising costs for care and the nearly 35 million people uninsured.

2. The uncertain nature of individuals' needs for medical treatment has resulted in heavy reliance on comprehensive health insurance. Added to this is the massive restructuring taking place in corporate America. Jobs are less secure and more part-time workers have replaced full-time employees, making access to health care more acute.

3. Public health care externalities are widespread. Because people are often concerned with their neighbor's access to care, there is a growing consensus in America that all individuals have a right to quality medical care regardless of their ability to pay.

4. Significant asymmetries of information between patients and medical personnel makes it virtually impossible for patients to evaluate the efficacy of certain types of medical care. This problem is exacerbated by the incentives faced by doctors under the current *fee-for-service* system because doctors have an economic incentive to expand the level of services provided each patient. *Capitation* systems of payment (fixed annual fees per patient) embody incentives to hold health care costs down.

5. The health care industry is rife with market power on the parts of almost all players except individual patients. Licensing enhances the income of MDs.

6. Health care is only one input into the production of health. Health care services, like other inputs is subject to the Law of Diminishing Returns--the benefits from additional health care spending eventually declines.

7. Widespread reliance on medical insurance reduces the elasticity of demand for medical treatment and increases the quantity of medical services consumed. Factors other than medical care enhance a persons overall state of health, but insurance reduces our incentives (creates a moral hazard) to maintain a healthier lifestyle.

8. Because insurance significantly reduces the cost of treatment to the patient, and the medical profession's *Hippocratic oath* mandates provision of all beneficial care, many analysts contend that this industry provides to much *high-cost low-benefit care*.

9. Private (non-group) medical insurance is prohibitively expensive for most individuals because the costs of administering individual plans are huge, and adverse selection problems abound. Adverse selection arises because individuals have better information than insurance companies about their general health. People in poor health gladly purchase insurance at average prices, while those in good health are more likely to self-insure (or, if they won't accept insurance, join managed care). This raises the average risk of the pool, causing prices to rise, further causing more healthy people to self-insure and so on.

10. The demand for medical care began a sharp climb when the government entered the market, with *Medicare* and *Medicaid* insuring the highest risk groups--the elderly and the destitute. Today, nearly half of all medical care spending is accounted for by these two programs. In addition, federal income tax rules heavily subsidize employer provided health insurance. To many observers, this has led to excess insurance coverage and overutilization of the health care system.

11. Widespread comprehensive health care coverage has encouraged the rapid development of high technology treatments. This rapid growth and proliferation of high-tech medical techniques has contributed to rising health care costs.

12. Relative to other industrialized nations, the United States spends 2 to 3 times more in absolute dollars and as a percent of GDP on health care. Unfortunately, our health care outcomes (life expectancies and infant mortality rates) are lower than many other countries. This may be due to data that is not comparable and to differences in social, cultural, economic, and demographic conditions. These data also ignore the fact the United States is a world leader in medical research and development.

Matching Key Terms And Concepts

____ 1. coinsurance

____ 2. cost shifting

____ 3. capitation

____ 4. low-benefit high-cost care

____ 5. insurance principle

____ 6. Medicare

____ 7. Health Maintenance Organizations

____ 8. supplier-induced-demand

____ 9. third party payer problem

____ 10. Medicaid

a. Health care providers use their superior knowledge to influence demand for their self interest.

b. Charging a fixed fee to provide medical services to a patient for one year.

c. Reduces the price paid by the patient while increasing the price received by the health care provider.

d. Patient pays a percentage of the total medical bill.

e. Universal health insurance for persons over 65.

f. Some patients are charged more to makeup for others who cannot pay the full cost of the care they receive.

g. States that most people are willing to pay a fee to reduce the financial consequences of various risks.

h. Federal-state joint ventures to provide health coverage to the poor.

i. Occurs when the marginal social costs of treatment exceed the marginal social benefits.

j. Contract with large firms to provide health care to employees and their families.

True/False

____ 1. From society's point of view, it is impossible to provide too much health care.

____ 2. Administrative fees account for as much as a fifth of the overall cost of health insurance.

____ 3. Health care is very similar to other services that can be purchased.

____ 4. The principal-agent problem is acute in health care because patients rely on doctor's expertise.

____ 5. Health insurance tends to make the demand for health care less elastic.

____ 6. The present federal tax structure discourages health care consumption.

____ 7. Advances in medical technology will always reduce health care costs.

____ 8 Compared to other countries, U.S. citizens are unquestionably the healthiest.

____ 9. Adverse selection is a problem for insurance companies because high risk individuals will gladly purchase insurance at average prices.

____ 10. Rapid growth and proliferation of medical techniques appears to be the main cause of rapidly rising health care costs.

Standard Multiple Choice

There Is One Best Answer For Each Question.

___ 1. Just like other goods and services, health care provision encounters:
    a. increasing marginal social benefits.
    b. declining marginal social costs.
    c. caring externalities.
    d. the Law of Diminishing Returns.
    e. uncertainty about when it will be needed.

___ 2. Comparing health care costs across time fails to take into account:
    a. increases in population size.
    b. improvements in medical care.
    c. the advent of new diseases.
    d. entrepreneurial breakthroughs.
    e. government mandated programs.

___ 3. Increased public support for universal health care coverage that is portable is explained in part by:
    a. the uncertainty of when health care will be needed.
    b. increased awareness of the AMA's monopoly power.
    c. a majority of the population being unable to get health insurance.
    d. the rationing of health care that presently takes place.
    e. structural changes in the labor market.

___ 4. Which of the following is NOT an element of market failure that the health care industry faces?
    a. Uncertainty.
    b. Externalities.
    c. Asymmetric information.
    d. Monopoly power.
    e. Low benefit high-cost ratios.

___ 5. The American Medical Association has effectively:
    a. lowered the costs of health care.
    b. decreased the elasticity of demand for health care.
    c. limited the supply of physicians.
    d. reduced fee for service payments.
    e. decreased the monopsony power of hospitals.

___ 6. If everyone's health insurance came to an end tomorrow, we would expect the demand for health care to:
    a. become more elastic.
    b. become less elastic.
    c. shift to the right.
    d. drop to zero.
    e. be unaffected.

___ 7. Health care tends to be overprovided because:
    a. health insurance reduces the cost to consumers.
    b. some doctors practice defensive medicine.
    c. the Hippocratic oath is not concerned about costs.
    d. doctor's have an incentive to do so.
    e. All of the above.

___ 8. The federal government encourages overconsumption of health care by subsidizing:
    a. doctors.
    b. nurses.
    c. employers who provide health coverage.
    d. the unemployed.
    e. college students.

9. The growth and emphasis on high technology medical treatment has been fueled by:
   a. widespread comprehensive health insurance.
   b. low rates of return to medical research and development.
   c. an emphasis on preventive medicine.
   d. technological breakthroughs.
   e. caring externalities.

____10. Centralized health care systems (such as in Canada):
   a. will always provide the best health care.
   b. can result in long waits with hurried impersonal service.
   c. are quick to adopt the latest technology.
   d. tend to increase the administrative costs of health care.
   e. encourage doctors to reduce the number of patients they see.

Chapter Review (Fill-In Questions)

1. Many products and services are produced and sold in markets where some elements of market failure exist. Health care is no exception, and seems to be affected by all aspects of market failure--_____, _____, _____ information, and _____ power.

2. Because patients rely on doctors' expertise the _____ problem exists. Since doctors are usually paid on a _____ basis, there is an _____ for doctors to steer patients towards more examinations and tests than might be necessary, leading to what some people term as _____.

3. The production/provision of health care faces the Law of _____ just like all other goods and services. This means that the benefits of health care rise at a _____ rate, that the marginal productivity of health care _____ with additional inputs, and that costs rise at an _____ rate.

4. Most health insurance requires the insuree to pay a certain amount of the initial expenses (usually $500), something known as a _____. After this is met, the policy holder typically pays 20% of the next $5,000, something known as _____. Health insurance effectively _____ the cost of health care to the patient and results in the demand for health care become _____ elastic.

5. Buyers of health insurance have a better idea about their general health than insurers do. For insurance companies this leads to the problem of _____. This means that people with _____ health will gladly pay the average price for an insurance policy, while people in _____ health who are not covered by an employer may be tempted to self-insure. Insurance companies therefore have a strong incentive to identify and preclude high-risk people, especially since a _____ portion of the population accounts for the majority of health care spending.

Unlimited Multiple Choice

There Are From Zero To Four Correct Answers For Each Question.

___ 1. Examples of monopoly power in the health care industry include:
  a. Blue Cross/Blue Shield.
  b. the American Medical Association.
  c. the Nursing Institute of America.
  d. Medicaid.

___ 2. Health insurance:
  a. has driven up the cost of health care.
  b. creates a moral hazard problem for many people.
  c. makes demand for health care more elastic.
  d. is a means of dealing with the uncertainty that surrounds health care.

___ 3. Major worldwide health care problems include:
  a. high-benefit low-cost care.
  b. barriers to access.
  c. rapidly rising health care expenditures.
  d. excessive monopoly power.

___ 4. Insurance companies have attempted to limit their payouts and increase their profitability by:
  a. establishing waiting periods before insurance takes effect.
  b. excluding people with preexisting conditions.
  c. designing age and sex profiles to establish risk bands.
  d. covering most high-tech treatments once they become available.

___ 5. Technological advances in health care:
  a. will not always lead to productivity gains.
  b. are stymied by stringent cost containment on the part of insurers.
  c. have significantly reduced health care costs in the past decade.
  d. may ultimately increase total medical spending.

Problem

Use this figure, which shows the marginal social costs and benefits of health care, to answer the following True/False questions.

____ a.   The optimal level of health care from society's point of view is Q_2.

____ b.   The marginal social costs and benefits curves (MSB and MSC) illustrate diminishing returns to increased levels of health care.

____ c.   If health insurance reduces the cost of health care to P_0 for individuals, too little health care will be provided.

____ d.   Between Q_0 and Q_1, the benefits of increasing health care exceed the costs.

____ e.   Output level Q_2 is a likely outcome if doctors are paid on a fee-for-service basis.

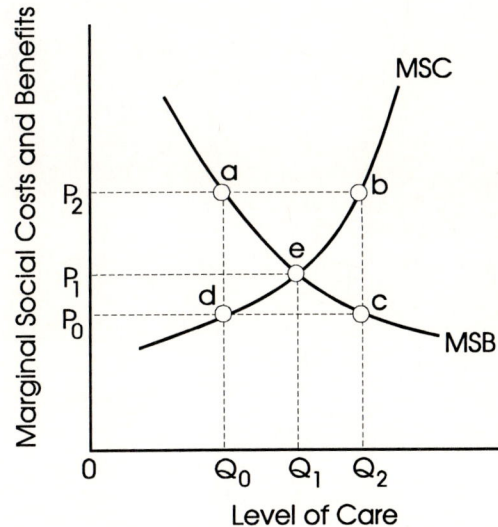

Level of Care

____ f.   The area ceb shows the welfare loss that results if health care output equals Q_2.

____ g.   Output level Q_1 is a likely outcome if doctors practice defensive medicine (e.g. order excessive tests to reduce the possibility of a successful malpractice suit).

____ h.   High-cost low-benefit care would accurately characterize output beyond Q_2.

____ i.   A tax exemption of employer-provided fringe benefits (i.e. health insurance) will result in an output of Q_1 or less health care.

____ j.   If the level of health care is presently Q_2, technological advances will ensure that MSC will eventually be equated with MSB at this level of output.

Answers

Matching	True/False	Multiple	Unlimited	Chapter Review (Fill-in Questions)
1. d	1. F	1. d	1. b	1. uncertainty; externalities; asymmetric; monopoly
2. f	2. T	2. b	2. abd	2. principal-agent; fee-for-service; incentive; supplier-induced-demand
3. b	3. F	3. e	3. bc	3. Diminishing Returns; decreasing; declines; increasing
4. i	4. T	4. e	4. abc	4. deductible; coinsurance; reduces; less
5. g	5. T	5. c	5. ad	5. adverse selection; ill; good; small
6. e	6. F	6. a		
7. j	7. F	7. e		
8. a	8. F	8. c		
9. c	9. T	9. a		
10. h	10. T	10. b		

Problem

a. F
b. T
c. F
d. T
e. T
f. T
g. F
h. T
i. F
j. F

Chapter 36
International Trade

Chapter Objectives

After you have studied this chapter, you should be able to explain why the gains from free trade generally outweigh any losses from free trade; describe the major influences on the composition of a country's imports and exports; and distinguish valid arguments against free trade from arguments that are invalid or abused.

Chapter Review: Key Points

1. *International trade* is important to people throughout the world. The smaller and less diversified an economy is, the greater is the importance of its international trade.

2. The *law of comparative advantage* suggests that there will be net gains to all trading parties whenever their pretrade relative opportunity costs and price structures differ between goods.

3. A country's *consumption possibilities frontier* (*CPF*) expands beyond its production possibilities frontier (*PPF*) with the onset of trade, or with the removal of trade restrictions.

4. The *terms of trade* are the prices of exports relative to the costs of imports. An adverse change in the terms of trade lowers the country's *CPF*, while a favorable change in the terms of trade expands it.

5. Gains from trade arise because international transactions (a) provide *unique* goods that would not otherwise be available, (b) allow highly specialized industries to exploit *economies of scale*, (c) speeds the spread of *technology*, and facilitates *capital accumulation* and *entrepreneurial innovation*, (d) encourages *peaceful international relations*, and (e) facilitates *specialization* according to comparative advantage.

6. Domestic producers of imported goods and domestic consumers of exported goods may suffer short term losses from trade. However, their losses are overshadowed by the specialization gains to consumers of imports and producers of exports. Gainers could always use parts of their gains to compensate the losers so that, on balance, no one loses. Moreover, *uniqueness, scale, dynamic*, and *political gains from trade* make it unlikely that anyone loses from trade in the long run.

7. Even the most valid of the arguments against free trade are substantially overworked. The arguments that are semi-valid include the ideas that: (a) the income redistributions from trade are undesirable; (b) desirable diversity within a narrow economy is hampered by free trade; (c) national defense requires restrictions to avoid dependence on foreign sources, and (more validly) export restrictions to keep certain technologies out of the hands of potential enemies; and (d) major exporters of a commodity can exercise monopolistic power by restricting exports, while important consuming nations can exercise monopsonistic power through import restrictions.

8. Any exercise of international monopoly/monopsony power invites retaliation and causes worldwide economic inefficiency. Those who lose because of trade restrictions will lose far more than is gained by the "winners."

9. If trade is to be restricted, *tariffs* are preferable to *quotas* because of the higher tax revenues and the smaller incentives for bribery and corruption.

10. *Trade adjustment assistance* is one way that gainers from trade might compensate the losers so that all would gain. However, difficulties in identifying losers and the lack of adequate funding have resulted in mounting pressures for trade restrictions.

Matching Key Terms And Concepts

Set I

___ 1. arbitrage

___ 2. law of comparative advantage

___ 3. terms of trade

___ 4. specialization gains from trade

___ 5. political gains from trade

___ 6. principle of absolute advantage

___ 7. tariffs and quotas

___ 8. dumping

___ 9. dynamic gains

___ 10. uniqueness gains

a. Saving and investment fostered by higher real income and transfers of technology.

b. Taxes or fixed limits on imports or exports.

c. Interdependence raises the costs of conflict.

d. (Prices of exports)/(prices of imports).

e. Riskless profit-taking by buying low and selling high.

f. Potential gains from trade among countries exist when relative pretrade costs differ.

g. The expansion of a CPF beyond a PPF that occurs with trade because production costs differ between countries.

h. Arise because some countries lack certain resources.

i. Selling cheaper abroad than domestically.

j. Sell those goods which you produce most, buy those goods which you produce least.

Set II

___ 1. predatory dumping

___ 2. infant industry protection

___ 3. diversification

___ 4. job destruction

___ 5. balance of payments deficits

___ 6. economic power and growth

___ 7. trade adjustment assistance

___ 8. national defense

___ 9. exercising monopoly/ monopsony power

___ 10. exploitation doctrine

a. An overused but legitimate argument against trade that is probably more valid as a restraint on exports than imports.

b. Implicitly assumes that trade is a zero-sum game.

c. Generally reduced by protectionist policies.

d. Problems better dealt with by other policies, not protection.

e. Selling below cost to eradicate foreign competitors.

f. Policies to protect emerging industries from mature foreign competition.

g. This argument against trade may apply in smaller countries but not in large ones.

h. Allows gainers from trade to offset hardships on losers.

i. An argument that ignores employment in export industries and assumes that if foreigners don't produce, we will.

j. Policies that may allow a powerful country to gain, but less than the rest of the world will lose.

True/False Questions

___ 1. Terms of trade are prices of exports relative to the costs of imports.

___ 2. Cheap foreign imports tend to increase the problems caused by concentrated monopoly power in an economy.

___ 3. The Trade Adjustment Assistance in federal laws governing trade were intended to provide retraining and financial assistance for workers displaced because of liberalized trade.

___ 4. When imports threaten the survival of an industry, the marketplace is signaling that the industry is extremely efficient.

___ 5. Import restrictions tend to preserve inefficient industries and to retard the growth of efficient industries.

___ 6. Predatory dumping of an industry's exports is a strategy to drive foreign competitors out of their domestic markets.

___ 7. The specialization gains from trade are positively related to differences in pretrade relative costs of production.

___ 8. Imports add to Aggregate Demand.

___ 9. The gains from trade tend to be smallest for the citizens of small, highly specialized countries.

___ 10. Economic efficiency requires all activities to be accomplished at their lowest possible opportunity costs.

___ 11. Trade only requires one of the trading parties to have an expectation of gain.

___ 12. The dynamic, political, and uniqueness losses common from free trade are normally offset by specialization gains from trade.

___ 13. Standards of living in the United States, more than in most countries, depend heavily on international trade.

___ 14. The infant industry argument for trade barriers applies to protection of the U.S. steel, auto, and textile industries.

___ 15. Dynamic gains from trade are generated by technology transfers and the additional saving and investment made possible by higher real income.

___ 16. Interdependence stimulated by trade raises the cost of international conflict and is an incentive for world peace.

___ 17. Import quotas are less flexible than tariffs in allowing adjustments to changes in demand.

___ 18. Trade barriers that make countries independent of foreign suppliers are more capitalistic than socialistic.

___ 19. Imports tend to cause inflation.

___ 20. In the long run, international trade is almost universally beneficial, although some people may be harmed in the short run by competition from foreign buyers or sellers of certain products.

Standard Multiple Choice

Each Question Has A Single Best Answer.

___ 1. Which of the following countries probably gains the most from international trade:
   a. the United States.
   b. Russia.
   c. Australia.
   d. the United Arab Emirates.
   e. Brazil.

___ 2. The Law of Comparative Advantage was first stated by:
   a. Reverend Thomas Malthus.
   b. David Ricardo.
   c. Adam Smith.
   d. Paul Samuelson.
   e. Alfred Marshall.

___ 3. If, in the absence of trade, an English worker can produce either 4 barrels of wine or 16 shirts weekly, while a Portuguese worker can produce either 10 barrels of wine or 20 shirts weekly:
   a. trade allows wine to exchange for between 2 and 4 shirts.
   b. Portugal has absolute advantages in both wine and shirts.
   c. England will export shirts and import wine when trade commences.
   d. England has a comparative advantage in shirtmaking.
   e. All of the above.

___ 4. When, under normal conditions, trade is expanded, the:
   a. gainers could compensate the losers so that all would gain.
   b. transactions costs of exchange inevitably rise.
   c. owners of capital gain, but workers inevitably lose.
   d. large countries gain far more than the small ones.
   e. PPFs for the trading countries shift inward.

___ 5. Arbitragers ultimately reap only normal profits because of:
   a. comparative advantages disappearing as trade commences.
   b. inevitable governmental regulation limiting profits.
   c. competition that causes prices to differ by transactions costs.
   d. competition for the political rights to receive monopoly profits.
   e. All of the above.

___ 6. When trade between two countries commences, the:
   a. consumption possibilities of both countries expand.
   b. gains from trade are shared by everyone.
   c. value of output must fall in one country if it rises in the other.
   d. gains to one trading party are offset by losses to the other.
   e. country with higher opportunity costs benefits the most from trade.

7. If Japan imports American agricultural products and exports cars to the U.S.:
   a. American farmers gain from trade, while Japanese farmers lose.
   b. U.S. carmakers may lose from trade, but U.S. car buyers gain.
   c. Japanese carmakers and food buyers both gain from trade.
   d. total gains from trade will almost invariably exceed any losses.
   e. All of the above.

8. Dynamic gains from trade include the:
   a. growth fostered by exchanges of technologies and the enhanced saving and investment made possible by higher real incomes.
   b. conquest of foreign markets from a predatory dumping policy.
   c. spread of middle-class values that occurs when primitive cultures absorb more advanced ideas.
   d. pressure for international peace that arises from independence.
   e. expansions of consumption possibilities frontiers realized strictly because pretrade cost structures differ.

9. When a small country and a large country begin trading, the:
   a. costs of imports will fall most in the large country.
   b. prices of exports will fall most in the large country.
   c. prices of exports will rise most in the large country.
   d. gains from trade tend to be greater in the small country.
   e. large country's capitalists exploit the small country's workers.

10. NOT among predictable gains from international trade would be:
    a. political gains.
    b. specialization gains.
    c. uniqueness gains.
    d. dynamic gains.
    e. capital gains.

11. An example of a gain from international trade occurs when:
    a. El Salvador imposes an import tariff on Guatemalan cigars.
    b. Swedish couples drink Brazilian coffee.
    c. French bakers bake cream pastries.
    d. cheap Taiwanese watches cost Swiss watchmakers their jobs.

12. A political gain from trade occurs when:
    a. wars and conflicts are stimulated by rising real incomes.
    b. interdependencies raise the costs of conflicts and so reduce tensions in international relations.
    c. political opponents of free trade impose high tariff barriers.
    d. countries engage in imperialistic wars in the search for markets.
    e. multinational conglomerates exploit cheap foreign labor.

____13. If emerging industries will ultimately be able to produce at lower cost than mature foreign competitors can, the:
   a. infant industry protection argument is a valid reason for tariff barriers.
   b. consumer losses from protection may be offset so that there are net gains from such policies when prices fall later.
   c. producers will gain more from protection than consumers lose.
   d. barriers to foreign trade are both inefficient and unnecessary for the industry to grow.
   e. government should impose export taxes on the emerging industries.

____14. Arguments against free trade that apply more to small homogeneous countries than to large heterogeneous nations focus on:
   a. infant industries.
   b. job destruction.
   c. national defense.
   d. nationalistic or patriotic appeals.
   e. diversification.

____15. Trade barriers imposed in the interest of national security:
   a. are usually valid when used to rationalize import tariffs.
   b. lower the costs of conflict by increasing interdependencies.
   c. probably apply more to restrictions on exports than on imports.
   d. are always inefficient and cause reductions in economic welfare.
   e. raise the costs of conflict by increasing independence.

____16. Some people may lose because of competition from foreign sellers or buyers of certain goods, but it is unlikely that the:
   a. specialization gains from trade ever exceed the dynamic losses.
   b. net effect of all trade in all goods is ever harmful to anyone.
   c. forces of competition will not evolve into monopoly power.
   d. trade deficits that harm them can last more than 2 or 3 years.
   e. country where they live will allow such imports to persist.

____17. Special programs to assist and retrain people who lose their jobs because of liberalized international trade are known as:
   a. Aid to Families Dependent on Trade (AFDT).
   b. tariffs and quotas.
   c. Trade Adjustment Assistance.
   d. the Job Corps.
   e. reindustrialization insurance.

____18. Allowing free competition after imposing tariffs that exactly offset production cost differences would:
   a. erode the potential gains from different comparative advantages.
   b. facilitate efficient diversification.
   c. be incompatible with self-sufficiency policies.
   d. be ideal to protect infant industries.
   e. immensely profit arbitragers.

___19. Corruption of the officials in charge of the program is most likely for a(n):
   a. scientific tariff.
   b. import quota.
   c. import tariff.
   d. tariff on exports.
   e. infant industry protection policy.

___20. A voluntary export restriction on cars from Japan will be most beneficial to:
   a. U.S. consumers.
   b. Japanese consumers.
   c. U.S. taxpayers.
   d. European luxury car makers.
   e. Japanese car manufacturers.

Chapter Review (Fill-In Questions)

1. With no trade, a country's sustainable _____ frontier is limited to its _____ frontier. When trade commences, the uniqueness and specialization gains from trade can be illustrated by a shift in the _____, but not the _____.

2. Gainers from trade include sellers of _____ and buyers of _____; losers include buyers of _____ and sellers of _____.

3. Trade is a _____ sum game, so that the _____ can (at least theoretically) compensate the _____ so that all would _____.

4. _____ gains from trade arise because some countries simply do not have certain resources possessed by others. Rising real incomes stimulate saving and investment, a major source of the _____ gains from trade, which also arise through international transfers of _____. Additionally, _____ gains emerge because trade encourages peace due to the interdependencies associated with the higher incomes from trade. The increases in economic welfare that can be realized through international specialization and exchange are qualitatively the same as those that can be achieved through domestic specialization and exchange.

5. Problems of undesirable income _____ from trade can be offset by _____ to those who lose from freer trade. Generally, import _____ pose more problems than do import _____ as barriers to trade because of the inherent incentives for corruption and the reduced flexibility of response to changes in demand.

Unlimited Multiple Choice

Each Question Has From Zero To Four Correct Answers.

___ 1. The consumption possibility frontier:
   a. depicts sustainable consumption possibilities confronting a country.
   b. is the same as the PPF in the absence of international trade.
   c. shifts inward when a country engages in international trade.
   d. is linear for a pretrade situation of constant opportunity costs.

___ 2. Arbitrage:
   a. moves relative prices toward equality in all markets.
   b. can occur when price differentials exceed transaction costs between two markets for a good.
   c. raises demand in the lower-price market, driving up its price, and raises supply in the higher-price market, driving down its price.
   d. entails buying at a higher price in one market and selling at a lower price in another, where the price differential exceeds transaction costs.

___ 3. When two countries engage in international trade:
   a. the equilibrium international price will exceed the original price of the good in the importing country.
   b. domestic production increases for the good being exported.
   c. domestic production decreases for the good being imported.
   d. consumers of the traded good in the exporting country pay a higher price for the good than they paid prior to trade.

___ 4. When international trade occurs:
   a. the net gains are usually positive.
   b. those who own resources that are relatively scarce worldwide realize gains exceeding any short run losses incurred by those whose resources are relatively abundant worldwide.
   c. gross losses generally exceed any gains to the participants.
   d. the prices of domestic inputs that are abundant worldwide fall, while the prices of inputs that are relatively scarce worldwide rise.

___ 5. According to the infant industry argument for the imposition of tariffs:
   a. domestic industries must be protected from more efficient foreign competitors.
   b. industries in their infancy must charge higher prices because of higher per unit costs of production, so more mature foreign firms have an unfair price advantage over unprotected infant industries.
   c. tariffs generate much needed tax revenue which can be meted out to poor families with many infants.
   d. mature industries need protection from foreign competitors to slow regression into senile infant stages.

Problems

Problem 1

This table indicates the numbers of rollerblades and blue jeans that the United States and Russia can produce in 10 days, given their respective resources. Assume that opportunity costs increase rapidly, and that the final terms of trade fall midway between pretrade costs.

a. Can beneficial trade occur?_____
   Why?_____
   Who would gain? _____
   _____

	U.S.	Russia
Rollerblades	80	60
Blue Jeans	40	10

b. What principle explaining international trade is demonstrated by the table? _____

c. Define this principle. _____

d. What are the pretrade relative prices of rollerblades to jeans in the U.S.? _____ In Russia? _____

e. If international trade commences, the U.S. will export _____, and import _____.

f. If international trade commences, Russia will export _____, and import _____.

g. Assume that the terms of trade are such that the gains from trade are evenly divided between both countries. The terms of trade will be roughly _____ rollerblades for _____ jeans.

h. Draw a production possibility frontier for the U.S. in the figure on the next page. How is it shaped? _____ Why? _____ Draw the post-trade U.S. consumption possibilities frontiers. Now do the same for Russia, emphasizing the relevant differences. What are they? _____

U.S.

Jeans

Rollerblades

Russia

Jeans

Rollerblades

Problem 2

This figure depicts production possibilities curves for Countries Alpha and Beta. The terms of trade are given by the lines TT; points x show consumption and production without trade; points y indicate production combination with trade; points z denote consumption combinations of these goods with trade. Use this information to answer the following true/false questions.

Alpha

Beta

_____ a. Both countries confront constant opportunity costs in the production of both apples and bananas.

_____ b. The slope of both countries' PPFs at points x are consistent with the relative pretrade costs.

_____ c. Once international trade commences, Alpha will produce only apples, while Beta will produce only bananas.

_____ d. In pretrade isolation, each country's PPF also represents its consumption possibility frontier.

_____ e. The pretrade relative costs are the same in both countries.

_____ f. Free trade can enable people in both countries to consume along higher consumption possibility frontiers.

_____ g. Trade cannot yield any net benefits in this example.

_____ h. Once international trade commences, Alpha will produce both commodities.

_____ i. Country Alpha will export bananas and import apples.

_____ j. Country Beta will export apples and import bananas.

_____ k. Before trade, it is cheaper to produce bananas in Alpha than in Beta.

_____ l. The same international terms of trade confront both countries.

Problem 3

Suppose workers in Java can produce 10 tons of sugar or 200 shirts per year, while Cubans can each produce either 15 tons of sugar or 45 shirts annually. There are 10 million workers on each island, and assume that costs are constant.

a. Graph the PPF for Java and Cuba in the figure.

b. In Java, what is the opportunity cost of producing 1 ton of sugar? _____ 1 shirt? _____

c. In Cuba, what is the opportunity cost of producing 1 ton of sugar? _____ 1 shirt? _____

d. If Java and Cuba begin to trade with each other, which island will export sugar? _____ Which will export shirts? _____

e. Draw each country's CPF on the figure after trade commences, assuming that the terms of trade are halfway between the pretrade relative prices.

f. Which parties gain from the commencement of trade? _____
_____

g. Which parties stand to lose in the short run from trade? _____
_____

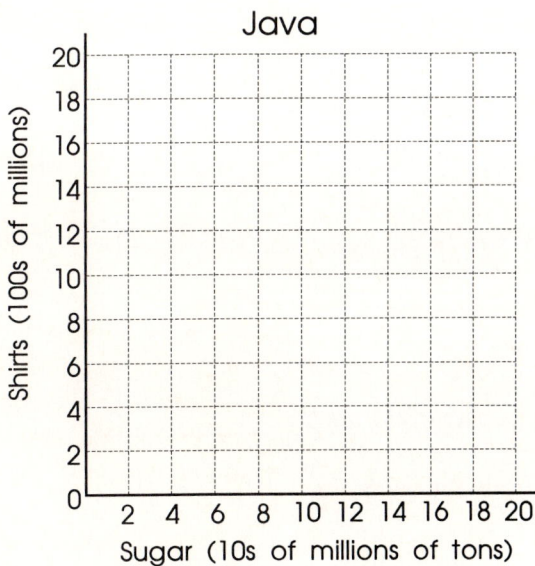

Java

Shirts (100s of millions)

Sugar (10s of millions of tons)

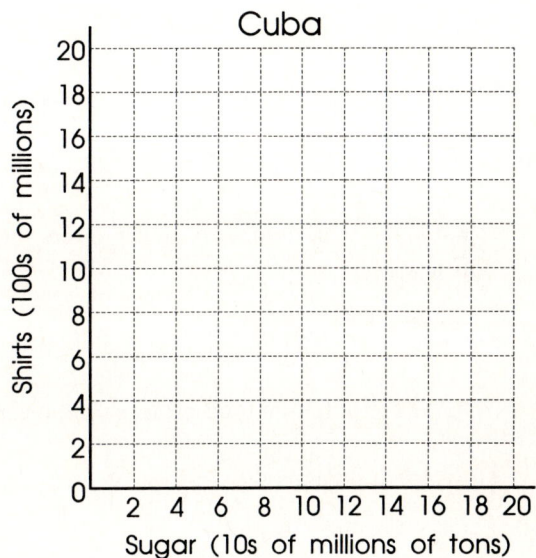

Cuba

Shirts (100s of millions)

Sugar (10s of millions of tons)

Problem 4

Use this figure, which illustrates the U.S. demand and supply of compact disc players, to answer the following questions. Assume that the world price is initially $200 per player.

a. How many disc players will the U.S. import? _____

b. How many disc players will the U.S. manufacture? _____

Assume that the U.S. levies a $50 tariff on each compact disc player

c. What price will U.S. consumers pay for a compact disc player? _____

d. How many disc players will the U.S. now manufacture? _____

e. How many disc players will the U.S. import? _____

f. How much in revenues will the government collect from the tariff? _____

Assume the U.S. is currently importing 6 million CD players a year and that there are no tariffs.

g. What is the world price for a CD player? _____

h. How many disc players are manufactured in the U.S.? _____

Assume that the U.S. institutes an import quota of 4 million CD players annually.

i. What is the total number of disc players that will now be purchased annual by U.S. consumers? _____

j. By how many players will U.S. production increase? _____

k. What is the potential total profit to importers as a result of the quota? _____

l. How much revenue will the government collect from the quota? _____

ANSWERS

Matching		True/False		Multiple Choice		Unlimited MC
Set I	Set II					
1. e	1. e	1. T	11. F	1. d	11. b	1. abd
2. f	2. f	2. F	12. F	2. b	12. b	2. abc
3. d	3. g	3. T	13. F	3. e	13. d	3. bcd
4. g	4. i	4. F	14. F	4. a	14. e	4. abd
5. c	5. d	5. T	15. T	5. c	15. c	5. ab
6. j	6. c	6. T	16. T	6. a	16. b	
7. b	7. h	7. T	17. T	7. e	17. c	
8. i	8. a	8. F	18. F	8. a	18. a	
9. a	9. j	9. F	19. F	9. d	19. b	
10. h	10. b	10. T	20. T	10. a	20. e	

Chapter Review (Fill-In Questions)

1. consumption possibilities; production possibilities; CPF; PPF
2. exports; imports; exports; imports
3. positive; gainers; losers; gain
4. Uniqueness; dynamic; technology; political
5. redistributions; trade adjustment assistance; quotas; tariffs

Problem 1

a. Yes; differences in pretrade costs; Gainers are American jean makers and rollerblade buyers, and Russian jean buyers and rollerblade makers.
b. Comparative advantage
c. Gains from trade exist when pretrade costs differ
d. 1/2; 1/6
e. jeans; rollerblades
f. rollerblades; jeans
g. 4; 1

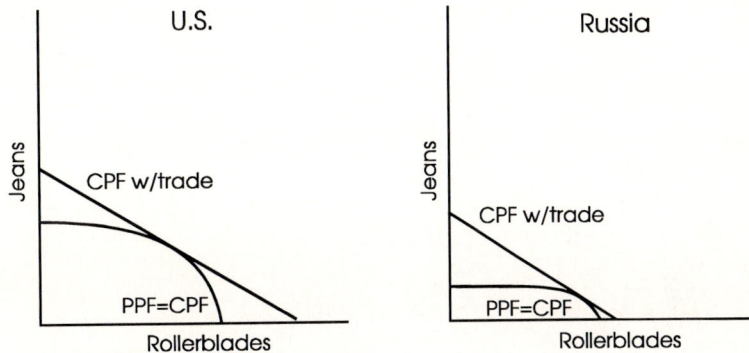

h. See figure; PPF for U.S. is concave to the origin reflecting increasing opportunity costs; PPF of Russia is also concave but skewed towards skates.

Problem 2

a. F
b. T
c. F
d. T
e. F
f. T
g. F
h. T
i. F
j. F
k. F
l. T

Problem 3

a. See figure below.
b. 20 shirts; 1/20 ton of sugar
c. 3 shirts; 1/3 ton of sugar
d. Cuba; Java
e. See figure.
f. Cuban sugar producers, Cuban shirt buyers, Javanese shirt producers, and Javanese sugar buyers.
g. Cuban shirt producers, Cuban sugar buyers, Javanese sugar producers, and Javanese shirt buyers.

Java

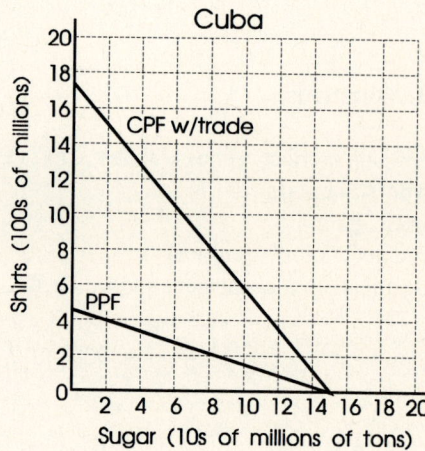

Cuba

Problem 4

a. 4 million
b. 4 million
c. $250
d. 5 million
e. 2 million
f. $100 million
g. $150
h. 3 million
i. 8 million
j. 1 million
k. $200 million
l. $0

Chapter 37
International Finance

Chapter Objectives

After you have studied this chapter, you should be able to discuss the advantages and disadvantages of fixed and flexible systems of international payments; the problems encountered when currency flows or exchange controls are used to maintain exchange rates at nonequilibrium values; explain the persistence of U.S. balance of payments deficits; and describe some possible reasons for the decline of the dollar from a position of undisputed primacy as the world's medium of exchange.

Chapter Review: Key Points

1. Since we have no world currency, we must establish the value of each national currency in terms of all others. The *exchange rate* is the value of one currency in terms of another.

2. *Balance of payments* accounts record the flows of money into and out of a country and provide information about trade relationships among countries.

3. *Flexible*, or *floating*, systems of *exchange rates* permit the values of currencies to be set by market forces. If a country experiences a balance of payments *surplus* (*deficit*) under such a system, it is an indication that the country's citizens or government (*foreigners*) desire foreign (*domestic*) currencies.

4. A *fixed* exchange rate system imposes price ceilings and floors on currencies, often resulting in persistent disequilibria in balances of payments.

5. Explanations for the decline of the dollar in the 1970s range from relative inflation to expectations of continued inflation and payments deficits to federal budget deficits to the emergence of other strong international currencies to the cartelization of oil to too rapid monetary growth. Opposite trends then strengthened the dollar until 1985. Each of these explanations bears the germ of truth, but none alone is adequate to explain the dance of the dollar.

Matching Key Terms And Concepts

Set I

_____ 1. "dirty" float

_____ 2. gold standard

_____ 3. balance of trade

_____ 4. nominal exchange rates

_____ 5. appreciation

_____ 6. fixed exchange rates

_____ 7. depreciation

_____ 8. foreign exchange

_____ 9. balance of payments

_____ 10. flexible exchange rates

a. Most exchange rates are set by international agreement.

b. Exports minus imports.

c. When the value of one currency rises relative to others.

d. Prices of currencies are set by market forces.

e. Foreign exchange inflows minus funds outflows.

f. Foreign currencies, collectively.

g. Fixed amounts of each currency exchange for given amounts of gold.

h. Government intervention in a flexible exchange system.

i. The prices of currencies relative to one another.

j. When a currency's value falls relative to others.

Set II

_____ 1. devaluation

_____ 2. dollar surplus

_____ 3. relative inflation

_____ 4. international portfolio adjustments

_____ 5. oil imports

_____ 6. exchange controls

_____ 7. international supply of dollars

_____ 8. exchange risk

_____ 9. key currency

_____ 10. real exchange rate

a. Decline of the fixed value of one currency versus others.

b. Governments allocate the foreign exchange available to pay for imports.

c. A currency that is widely held internationally for transaction, precautionary, and asset reasons.

d. Potential losses to exporters who agree to accept importers' currency, or to importers who must pay in exporters' currency.

e. Relative price of foreign goods in terms of domestic goods.

f. A classic explanation of currency depreciation.

g. "Mirrors" the U.S. demand for foreign exchange.

h. Replacing the dollar as the asset of a central bank with some other strong currency.

i. Caused substantial increases in the international supplies of dollars in the 1970s.

j. Identical with a shortage of foreign exchange.

True/False Questions

_____ 1. The nominal exchange rate is the value of a currency in terms of itself.

_____ 2. If the dollar value of imports exceeds the dollar value of exports, there is a deficit in our balance of trade.

_____ 3. An international gold standard would be an example of a fixed exchange rate system.

_____ 4. Under a flexible exchange rate system, currencies' relative prices are largely determined by markets.

_____ 5. An international gold standard was established by the United Nations at the end of World War I.

_____ 6. Foreigners demand dollars only to import U.S. goods or invest in the United States.

_____ 7. Unlike other prices, exchange rates seldom change under a system of flexible exchange rates.

_____ 8. As is true of markets for virtually all goods, flexible exchange rate systems tend to drive the prices of all currencies to the equilibrium rates at which supply and demand intersect.

_____ 9. "Dirty floats" tend to hamper flexible exchange rates so that they change less than they otherwise might.

_____ 10. Exchange controls create pressures for government corruption and black markets for foreign currencies.

_____ 11. Governments can more independently conduct macroeconomic policies under a flexible than under a fixed exchange rate system.

_____ 12. From the end of World War II until 1971, the U.S. dollar was the only major world currency consistently backed by gold, at least for purposes of international trade.

_____ 13. The international acceptability of the U.S. dollar has been a major reason why the U.S. has been able to run large and persistent current account deficits from 1981 to the present.

_____ 14. The absorption problem prevents countries from running persistent current account surpluses.

_____ 15. In 1985, almost all of the dollars held by OPEC countries were exchanged for other currencies.

_____ 16. International transactions demands for dollars arise because exporters in many countries view dollars as less prone to exchange risk than the currencies of their customers.

_____ 17. International demands for dollars have enabled the United States to offset persistent payments deficits with trade surpluses.

_____ 18. Other countries have been far more successful than the United States in reaping seignorage from international financial markets.

___19. Foreign loans by U.S. organizations have accounted for most of the recent surpluses in U.S. balances of payments.

___20. A "dirty float" occurs when foreign central banks buy dollars from international money markets and store the dollars in their vaults.

Standard Multiple Choice

Each Question Has A Single Best Answer.

___ 1. A country that exports more than it imports experiences a:
   a. balance of payments surplus.
   b. deficit in its national budget.
   c. balance of trade deficit.
   d. deficit in its balance of payments.
   e. balance of trade surplus.

___ 2. The major reason for Americans to demand foreign money is to:
   a. add to collections of rare stamps and coins.
   b. pay for imports or foreign investments.
   c. profit from seignorage by printing dollars.
   d. finance tourist visits to foreign countries.
   e. avoid U.S. income tax liabilities.

___ 3. Americans demand foreign currencies by:
   a. exporting capital goods.
   b. supplying dollars.
   c. running balance of trade surpluses.
   d. creating shortages of U.S. currency.
   e. following inflationary policies.

___ 4. A gold standard is an example of a:
   a. fixed exchange rate system.
   b. nondiscretionary "pegged" currency.
   c. flexible exchange rate system.
   d. "dirty float."
   e. "crawling peg" automatic stabilizer.

___ 5. Stocks of foreign currencies that have been received to cover international payments are:
   a. gold coins and bullion.
   b. foreign exchange.
   c. international seignorage.
   d. bills of lading.
   e. international transfer payments.

___ 6. A currency's price in terms of a foreign country's currency is known as the:
   a. nominal exchange rate.
   b. terms of trade.
   c. reciprocal value.
   d. counter price.
   e. par value.

___ 7. Currency revaluation under a gold standard would parallel:
   a. depreciation under a silver standard.
   b. appreciation under a flexible exchange rates.
   c. devaluation under fixed exchange rates.
   d. recycling under an ecological system.
   e. repricing costs in an inflationary system.

___ 8. A balance of payments surplus could result from:
   a. international surpluses of the country's currency.
   b. falling imports and rising exports.
   c. contractionary policies by its trading partners.
   d. shifting from a fixed to a floating exchange rate system.
   e. overseas investments by domestic firms.

___ 9. Reversal of a payments deficit if all countries were on a gold standard might entail:
   a. revaluation of the country's currency relative to other currencies.
   b. depreciation of the currency through normal market processes.
   c. contractionary macroeconomic adjustments.
   d. discoveries of new gold supplies in the deficit country.
   e. decreasing Aggregate Demands in surplus countries.

___ 10. If American balance of payments deficits indicate disequilibrium, the markets for currencies of countries experiencing balance of payments surpluses are characterized by:
   a. shortages.
   b. surpluses.
   c. unusual scarcity.
   d. overproduction.
   e. excessive supply.

___ 11. Appreciation will eliminate a balance of payments surplus most rapidly when:
   a. foreign demands for a country's exports and domestic demands for imports are both extremely inelastic.
   b. foreign demands for exports and domestic demands for imports are both elastic.
   c. domestic exchange controls are rigid.
   d. inflows of foreign exchange are used to pay for all foreign purchases.
   e. none of the above.

___ 12. An American balance of payments deficit would be reduced by:
   a. increased U.S. foreign aid programs.
   b. increased imports by consumers.
   c. greater levels of foreign investment by American corporations.
   d. lower prices for imported goods that are elastically demanded by U.S. consumers.
   e. greater foreign purchases of the bonds of American corporations.

13. A substantial increase in the national income of a country will:
    a. cause a balance of payments surplus under a fixed exchange rate system.
    b. generate pressure for the country's currency to be revalued upward.
    c. cause its exports to increase dramatically.
    d. cause devaluation under a flexible exchange rate system.
    e. create pressure for the depreciation of the exchange rate of its currency.

14. Since 1946, relative to the U.S. balance of payments, our balance of trade has:
    a. far more often been in deficit.
    b. balanced or been in surplus quite often.
    c. consistently been in deficit.
    d. consistently experienced larger deficits.
    e. None of the above.

15. The dollar's position as a key international currency has:
    a. allowed Americans to gain through seignorage by issuing international money.
    b. been a major reason for loss of U.S. power and prestige.
    c. stimulated growth of federal deficits.
    d. driven our balance of trade into persistent surpluses.
    e. dampened economic growth internationally.

16. A hike in international oil prices will cause the dollar to fall more under a flexible exchange rate system if:
    a. foreigners believe that the FED will adapt to these hikes with expansionary monetary policies.
    b. our demands for imports and foreign demands for our exports are both quite inelastic.
    c. foreigners quickly lose faith in the dollar when its exchange rate falls even slightly.
    d. other countries with strong currencies are less dependent on imported oil.
    e. All of the above.

17. Which of the following has not been offered seriously as an explanation for the 1970s decline of the dollar?
    a. OPEC petroleum price hikes.
    b. expectations of continued relative inflation in the United States.
    c. rapid increases in prices for gold.
    d. overly expansionary U.S. monetary policy.
    e. the increasing stability and acceptability of other currencies.

18. Until roughly 1970, foreign central bankers could exchange:
    a. $35 to the U.S. Treasury for an ounce of gold.
    b. deficits in their balance of payments for U.S. Treasury bonds.
    c. international loans at a fixed interest rate at the World Bank.
    d. surpluses for silver certificates issued by the International Monetary Fund.
    e. trade surpluses for United Nations payments.

___19. If exporters' currency appreciates, exchange risk losses could be imposed on:
   a. importers who insisted on paying in their own currency.
   b. exporters who insisted on being paid in their own currency.
   c. arbitragers who exploited price differentials between markets.
   d. importers who agreed to pay in the exporters' currency.
   e. speculators who had bought the exporters' currency earlier.

___20. Consistent U.S. balance of payments deficits are partially explained by:
   a. demands in unstable countries for economically stable currencies.
   b. foreign governments bolstering growth by stimulating exports.
   c. habits developed when the dollar was the only currency convertible to gold.
   d. greater foreign demands for dollars than for American goods.
   e. All of the above.

Chapter Review (Fill-In Questions)

1. The price of one currency in terms of another is known as its _____. A country's exports minus its imports is its _____; its inflows of funds minus its outflows is its _____. Currencies received from sales of exports are known as _____.

2. Under a(n) _____ exchange rate system, such as the _____ standard, payments deficits can be met by borrowing or drawing down previously accrued _____, or by _____ controls, under which government allocates the foreign currencies that are available.

3. One problem with _____ exchange rates is that international transactions create exchange risk; if the contract specifies payment in the _____ currency, exchange rate depreciation of that currency will cause the _____ to receive less than expected, while the importer will be forced to pay more than expected if the currency of the _____ is specified and the exchange rate of that currency appreciates. These problems can be finessed, however, if the traders negotiate a contract in either currency and then "buy insurance" against _____ by dealing in the _____ market for foreign exchange.

4. In the past half century, the United States has persistently run _____ in its balance of payments. This has been possible because, internationally, the dollar has been a _____ currency. Foreigners have demanded dollars to facilitate transactions, even when American traders are not involved. Our relative political and economic stability have also caused foreigners to demand dollars for _____ and _____ reasons. The ability of the FED to issue "international money" has allowed Americans to reap _____ because of the huge difference between the _____ of dollars and their value in exchange.

Unlimited Multiple Choice

Each Question Has From Zero To Four Correct Responses.

___ 1. Balance of payments:
   a. deficits occur when a country's receipts of money from foreigners exceed its payments to foreigners.
   b. use double-entry bookkeeping.
   c. accounts record flows of funds among countries that trade.
   d. surpluses occur when receipts of money from foreigners exceed a country's payments to foreigners.

___ 2. In a fixed exchange rate system, if a country's currency experiences:
   a. a surplus, then its balance of payments tends to be in surplus.
   b. a shortage, then its balance of payments tends to be in surplus.
   c. less demand by foreigners than it has demand for foreign exchange, then an international surplus of its currency occurs.
   d. greater demand by foreigners than its demand for foreign exchange, an international shortage of its currency occurs.

___ 3. Fixed exchange rates:
   a. adjust more quickly than flexible exchange rates do to changes in relative supplies and demands for currencies.
   b. pose no special problems as long as exchange rates reflect the true market values of currencies.
   c. warp true values for all currencies.
   d. are not problems as long as they parallel the values that would exist under flexible exchange rates.

___ 4. The United States has been able to run balance of payments deficits fairly consistently for almost four decades because dollars:
   a. are widely used as an international medium of exchange.
   b. have been viewed as "insurance" in politically unstable countries.
   c. have been supported at artificially high exchange rates by West Germany, Japan, etc., to boost U.S. demands for their exports (or, perhaps, to indirectly pay for U.S. provision of national defense).
   d. create volatility in the exchange rates of monkey currencies.

___ 5. An increased American preference for Japanese goods:
   a. will manifest itself in a decreased American demand for the yen.
   b. will manifest itself in an increased American supply of dollars in foreign exchange markets.
   c. means that American importers of Japanese goods may be forced to pay higher dollar prices.
   d. implies a depreciation of the yen in terms of the dollar.

Problems

Problem 1

Use this figure, which depicts markets for the U.S. dollar and the British pound, to answer the following questions.

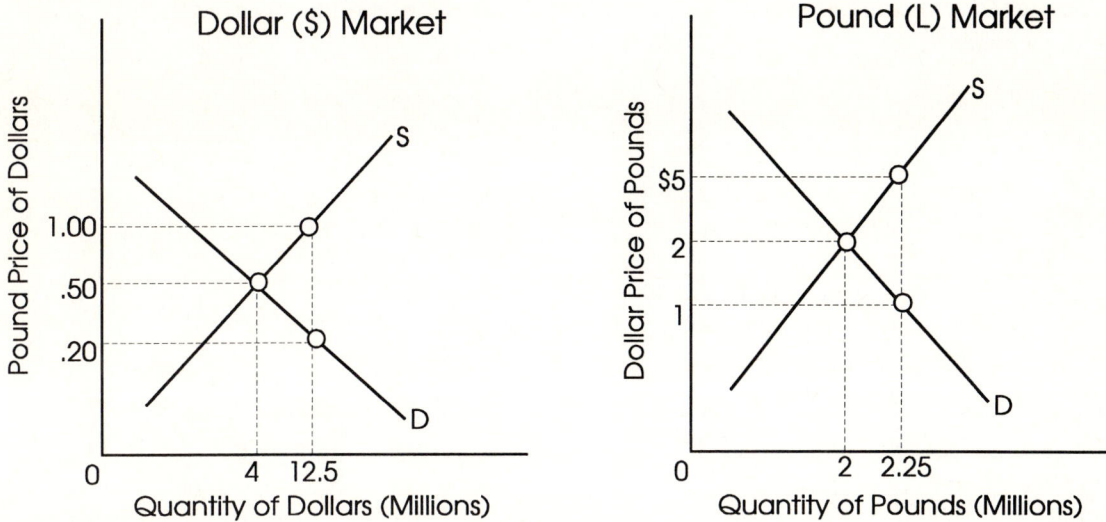

a. What is the equilibrium exchange rate of the dollar? _____

b. What is the equilibrium exchange rate of the pound? _____

c. What is the per unit (pound) price of a dollar? _____

d. What is the per unit price of a U.S. dollar? _____

e. Explain why the U.S. demand for British pounds is downward sloping. _____

f. Explain why the British supply of pounds is upward sloping. _____

g. Suppose Americans purchase British goods valued at $2 million. Americans demand _____ British pounds in equilibrium and supply _____ dollars.

h. Assume the British manifest an increased preference for U.S. goods. Which curves will shift and why? _____ What happens to the British pound? _____ What happens to the dollar? _____ What happens to the pound price of American exports to Britain? _____ What happens to the dollar price of U.S. imports from Britain? _____

i. Assume that the new equilibrium exchange rate is $1 = 1 pound. What is the equilibrium exchange rate of the dollar? _____ Suppose that Britain purchases U.S. goods whose value is $2.5 million. This implies a British demand for dollars of _____ and a British supply of _____.

j. Return to the original equilibrium exchange rate; that is, $.50 = 1 pound. If the exchange rate is pegged artificially high at $1 = 1 pound, what situation would prevail in the U.S. balance of payments? _____ Why? _____

Problem 2

Complete this table to obtain all the possible exchange rates between the six different currencies listed. The first row tells how much foreign currency one U.S. dollar can purchase.

	Dollar	Deutsche Mark	Pound	Franc	Yen
Dollar	1	2	1/2	6	120
Deutsche Mark					
Pound					
Franc					
Yen					

Problem 3

Use this table, which shows the balance of payments for the country of Sata, to answer the following questions

	Receipts	Payments	Balance
Current Account			
Merchandise Exports	+220		
Merchandise Imports		-328	
Trade Balance			
Net Investment Income			
Net Services		-1	
Net Unilateral Transfers		-11	
Current Account Balance			-102
Capital Account			
Capital Outflows			
Capital Inflows	+93		
Statistical Discrepancy	+36		
Official Reserve Transactions Balance			+6
Method of Financing			
Increase in Sata Official Reserve Assets		-9	
Increase in Foreign Official Assets			
Total Financing of Surplus			-6

a. Fill in the missing entries.

b. The trade balance is equal to _____. This indicates a trade (surplus/deficit).

c. The sum of numbers 1 through 10 equals _____. Is this is coincidence? _____

d. The statistical discrepancy accounts for what kinds of transactions? _____

ANSWERS

	Matching		True/False			Multiple Choice			Unlimited MC	
	Set I	Set II								
1.	h	1. a	1. F	11. T		1. e	11. b		1.	bcd
2.	g	2. j	2. T	12. T		2. b	12. e		2.	bcd
3.	b	3. f	3. T	13. T		3. b	13. e		3.	bd
4.	i	4. h	4. T	14. F		4. a	14. b		4.	abc
5.	c	5. i	5. F	15. F		5. b	15. a		5.	bc
6.	a	6. b	6. F	16. T		6. a	16. e			
7.	j	7. g	7. F	17. F		7. b	17. c			
8.	f	8. d	8. T	18. F		8. b	18. a			
9.	e	9. c	9. T	19. F		9. c	19. d			
10.	d	10. e	10. T	20. T		10. a	20. e			

Chapter Review (Fill-In Questions)

1. nominal exchange rate; balance of trade; balance of payments; foreign exchange
2. fixed; gold;   foreign exchange; exchange
3. flexible; importer's; exporter; exporter; exchange risk; forward
4. deficits; key; precautionary; asset; seignorage; production costs

Problem 1

a. .50 pound
b. $2
c. .50 pound
d. $2
e. law of demand
f. law of supply
g. l million; 2 million
h. demand for dollars increases and the supply of pounds increases; depreciates; appreciates; increases; decreases.
i. 1 pound; $2.5 million; 2.5 million pounds
j. deficit; surplus of dollars due to exchange rate imbalance.

Problem 2

	Dollar	Deutsche Mark	Pound	Franc	Yen
Dollar	1	2	1/2	6	120
Deutsche Mark	1/2	1	1/4	3	60
Pound	2	4	1	12	240
Franc	1/6	1/3	1/12	1	20
Yen	1/120	1/60	1/240	1/20	1

Problem 3

	Receipts	Payments	Balance
Current Account			
Merchandise Exports	+220		
Merchandise Imports		-328	
Trade Balance			-108
Net Investment Income	6		
Net Services		-1	
Net Unilateral Transfers		-11	
Current Account Balance			-102
Capital Account			
Capital Outflows		-123	
Capital Inflows	+93		
Statistical Discrepancy	+36		
Official Reserve Transactions Balance			+6
Method of Financing			
Increase in Sata Official Reserve Assets		-9	
Increase in Foreign Official Assets	3		
Total Financing of Surplus			-6